April 2–3, 2016
Atlanta, Georgia, USA

I0041886

**Association for
Computing Machinery**

Advancing Computing as a Science & Profession

VEE'16

Proceedings of the12th ACM SIGPLAN/SIGOPS
International Conference on
Virtual Execution Environments

Sponsored by:

ACM SIGPLAN and ACM SIGOPS

In-cooperation with:

Usenix

Supported by:

**Intel, Facebook, VMWare University Research Fund, IBM,
Microsoft Research, & VMWare**

Association for Computing Machinery

Advancing Computing as a Science & Profession

ISBN: 978-1-4503-3947-6 (Digital)

ISBN: 978-1-4503-4474-6 (Print)

Additional copies may be ordered prepaid from:

ACM Order Department
PO Box 30777
New York, NY 10087-0777, USA

Phone: 1-800-342-6626 (USA and Canada)
+1-212-626-0500 (Global)
Fax: +1-212-944-1318
E-mail: acmhelp@acm.org
Hours of Operation: 8:30 am – 4:30 pm ET

Printed in the USA

VEE 2016 Foreword

Welcome to the 12th ACM SIGPLAN/SIGOPS Conference on Virtual Execution Environments (VEE'16). We are happy to present the community with a strong program covering a wide range of virtualization topics. This year's conference continues its tradition of providing a forum for researchers and practitioners to interact, shared ideas, and discuss the latest work on virtualization. The conference brings together people from different domains of computer science, from the top of the software stack down to the micro-architectural level.

Authors registered 55 papers, of which 39 were finalized as complete submissions. The program committee (PC) consisted of 2 chairs and 16 researchers active in virtualization-related aspects of programming languages and operating systems. Members were allowed to submit papers; the co-chairs chose not to submit anything. Reviewing was double-blind and was done almost entirely by the committee, with a little assistance from external experts. Submissions generally received 4 reviews, and authors were given the opportunity for rebuttal before the PC meeting.

The program committee meeting was held in February at the Intel offices in Santa Clara, California. Most of the committee members were present in person, while the remaining dialed in. In an 8-hour session, we discussed all papers except those that were marked as early rejects for receiving only negative reviews. We followed conventional rules for conflict of interest, with conflicted members (including co-chairs) leaving the room during discussion of the conflicted papers. In the end, we accepted 13 papers for presentation at the conference, of which three were shepherded by PC members.

Submissions	*Reviewed*	*Accepted*	
Full Papers	29	10	38%
Short Papers	10	2	20%
Total	39	13	30%

In addition to the 13 accepted papers, the VEE'16 program includes two keynote presentations by Ada Gavrilovska and Kathryn S. McKinley. This year's program also includes a panel discussion on the state of virtualization. We hope that the resulting proceedings will serve as a valuable reference for researchers and practitioners in the area of virtualization.

Putting together VEE'16 was a team effort. Without the contributions of all the authors, the conference would not continue to be relevant and interesting. The program committee worked hard in reviewing papers and shepherding accepted submissions into their final forms. Our web chair did an outstanding job managing the website. Our colleagues on the organizing committee of ASPLOS 2016 were helpful in coordinating the local arrangements, registration, and logistics for the conference itself. Lastly, we are thankful to our sponsors, ACM SIGPLAN and SIGOPS, for the cooperation with USENIX, and for the corporate support from Intel, Facebook, the VMware University Research Fund, VMware, and Microsoft Research.

We hope that you will find the symposium thought-provoking and that it provides you with opportunity to meet and engage with other researchers and practitioners from institutions from around the world.

Vishakha Gupta-Cledat
Intel Labs
VEE '16 General Chair

Donald E. Porter
Stony Brook University
VEE '16 Program Co-Chair

Vivek Sarkar
Rice University
VEE '16 Program Co-Chair

Table of Contents

Technical Session: Future OS Directions
Session Chair: Dilma Da Silva *(Texas A&M University)*

Panel Session
Session Chair: Carl Waldspurger *(CloudPhysics)*

VEE 2016 Conference Organization

General Chair: Vishakha Gupta-Cledat *(Intel Labs)*

Program Committee Co-Chairs: Donald E. Porter *(Stony Brook University)*
Vivek Sarkar *(Rice University)*

Program Committee: Jonathan Appavoo *(Boston University)*
Tzi-cker Chieuh *(ITRI, Taiwan)*
John Criswell *(University of Rochester)*
Julian Dolby *(IBM Thomas J. Watson Research Center)*
Björn Franke *(University of Edinburgh)*
Soo-Mook Moon *(Seoul National University)*
Guilherme Ottoni *(Facebook)*
Kevin Pedretti *(Sandia National Laboratory)*
Behnam Robatmili *(Qualcomm Research)*
Christopher Rossbach *(VMware Research Group and University of Texas at Austin)*
Mark Silberstein *(Technion – Israel Institute of Technology)*
Mary Lou Soffa *(University of Virginia)*
Malgorzata Steinder *(IBM Research)*
Priyanka Tembey *(VMware)*
Peng Wu *(Huawei America Research Center)*

Steering Committee Chair: Martin Hirzel *(IBM Research)*

Steering Committee: Steve Blackburn *(Australian National University)*
Angela Demke Brown *(University of Toronto)*
Ada Gavrilovska *(Georgia Institute of Technology)*
Gernot Heiser *(NICTA and UNSW)*
Steve Muir *(Comcast)*
Brian Noble *(University of Michigan)*
Erez Petrank *(Technion – Israel Institute of Technology)*
Bjarne Steensgard *(Microsoft Research)*
Dan Tsafrir *(Technion – Israel Institute of Technology)*

Webmaster: Alexander Merritt *(Georgia Institute of Technology)*

Additional reviewers: Chris Rodrigues *(Huawei America Research Center)*
Haichuan Wang *(Huawei America Research Center)*
Jun Wang *(Huawei America Research Center)*
Xuejun Yang *(Huawei America Research Center)*

VEE 2016 Sponsors & Supporters

Sponsors:

SIGPLAN

SIGOPS
ACM SIG on Operating Systems

In cooperation with:

usenix
THE ADVANCED
COMPUTING SYSTEMS
ASSOCIATION

Supporters:

(intel)

f

VMware University
Research Fund

IBM

Microsoft Research

vmware

Virtualizing the Edge of the Cloud—the New Frontier

Ada Gavrilovska

Georgia Tech

Abstract

Over the last two decades, virtualization technologies have turned datacenter infrastructure into multitenant, dynamically provisionable, elastic resource, and formed the basis for the wide adoption of cloud computing. Many of todays cloud applications, however, are based on continuous interactions with end users and their devices, and the trend is only expected to intensify with the expansion of the Internet of Things. The consequent bandwidth and latency requirements of these emerging workloads push the cloud boundary outside of traditional datacenters, giving rise to an edge tier in the end-device-to-cloud-backend infrastructure. Computational resources embedded in anything from standalone microservers to WiFi routers and small cell access points, and their open APIs, present opportunities for deploying application logic and state closer to where it is being used, addressing both latency and backhaul bandwidth problems. This talk will look at the role that existing virtualization technologies can play in providing in this edge tier the required flexibility, dynamic provisioning and isolation, and will outline open problems that require development of new solutions. We will also discuss the opportunities to leverage these technologies to further deal with the diversity in the end-user device and IoT space.

Biography

Dr. Ada Gavrilovska is a Senior Research Scientist at the College of Computing and the Center for Experimental Research in Computer Systems (CERCS) at Georgia Tech. Her research is centered on innovation of the systems software stack, driven by emerging hardware technologies, and focused on supporting data- and communication-intensive applications. Recent projects include systems software innovation in light of large-scale parallelism in multicores, platform-wide compute and memory heterogeneity, novel interconnect capabilities and increases in device-level computational resource density. Gavrilovska's research is supported by the National Science Foundation, the US Department of Energy, and industry grants, including from Cisco, HP, IBM, Intel, Intercontinental Exchange, Lexis-Nexis, VMware, and others. She has published over 80 papers, and edited a book High Performance Communications: A Vertical Approach. In addition to research, she also teaches courses on operating systems and high performance communications. She has a BS degree in Computer Engineering from University Sts. Cyril and Methodius in Macedonia ('98), and a MS ('99) and PhD ('04) degrees in Computer Science from Georgia Tech.

VEE '16   April 02-03, 2016, Atlanta, GA, USA
ACM 978-1-4503-3947-6/16/04
DOI: http://dx.doi.org/10.1145/http://dx.doi.org/10.1145/2892242.2892243

Building a KVM-based Hypervisor for a Heterogeneous System Architecture Compliant System

Yu-Ju Huang

Department of Computer Science, National Chiao Tung University, Taiwan
gic4107@gmail.com

Hsuan-Heng Wu

Department of Computer Science, National Taiwan University, Taiwan
wuxx1279@gmail.com

Yeh-Ching Chung

Department of Computer Science, National Tsing Hua University, Taiwan
ychung@cs.nthu.edu.tw

Wei-Chung Hsu

Department of Computer Science, National Taiwan University, Taiwan
hsuwc@csie.ntu.edu.tw

Abstract

Heterogeneous System Architecture (HSA) is an architecture developed by the HSA foundation aiming at reducing programmability barriers as well as improving communication efficiency for heterogeneous computing. For example, HSA allows heterogeneous computing devices to share the same virtual address space. This feature allows programmers to bypass explicit data copying between devices, as was required in the past. HSA features such as job dispatching through user level queues and memory based signaling help to reduce communication latency between the host and other computing devices.

While the new features in HSA enable more efficient heterogeneous computing, they also introduce new challenges to system virtualization, especially in memory virtualization and I/O virtualization. This work investigates the issues involved in HSA virtualization and implements a KVM-based hypervisor that supports the main features of HSA inside guest operating systems. Furthermore, this work shows that with the newly introduced hypervisor for HSA, system resources in HSA-compliant AMD Kaveri can be effectively shared between multiple guest operating systems.

Keywords Heterogeneous System Architecture; HSA Virtualization; GPU Virtualization; KVM;

VEE '16, April 02-03, 2016, Atlanta, GA, USA.
© 2016 ACM. ISBN 978-1-4503-3947-6/16/04...$15.00.
DOI: http://dx.doi.org/10.1145/2892242.2892246

1. Introduction

Heterogeneous architectures have become popular in recent years. Some computing tasks are more suited for GPGPU while others are a better fit for CPU or FPGA. In a heterogeneous computing system, power efficiency can be vastly improved when each job is dispatched to its most suited computing device.

The GPGPU programming model [1], as one example of heterogeneous computing models, allows programmers to dispatch computational kernels to GPU. The foremost GPGPU programming model, CUDA [2] and the older version OpenCL [3], (i.e. prior to OpenCL 2.0) see GPU as an I/O device so there must be data copying between CPUs and the GPU before a computation job can be launched. Such explicit data copying has caused significant overhead and programming inconvenience. Moreover, since GPU is viewed as an I/O device, every job to be executed has to go through a system driver. Such job dispatching mechanisms have resulted in context switch overheads between user mode and kernel mode.

HSA [4] is an architecture designed to address these inefficiencies and inconveniences. Two major goals of HSA are to (1) Reduce CPU/GPU communication latency such as data copying and jobs dispatching overhead, and (2) Decrease the heterogeneous computing programmability barrier such as the need for programmers to compress complicated data structures into a continuous memory region in order to copy it from CPU to GPU and to decompress it when the data is transferred back from the GPU. To achieve such goals, various features are defined as requirements for a HSA-compliant system. The HSA features and how these features are implemented on AMD Kaveri [5], our target platform, will be described in Section 2.

Table 1. Comparison of GPU programming in Non-HSA and HSA systems.

	Non-HSA systems	HSA systems
GPU job dispatching	Application calls system driver to store commands in GPU channel	Application stores AQL packets in user mode queue and kicks doorbell to signal GPU
GPU job finishing	GPU interrupts CPU	GPU notifies CPU via memory-based signals
GPU memory	Separate virtual address space between CPU and GPU	Shared virtual address space between CPU and GPU

This paper presents HSA virtualization and successfully implements a KVM-based [6] hypervisor. Since HSA is a new heterogeneous computing architecture, there has not been much research investigating system virtualization issues for this architecture. We analysed the features provided by HSA and figured out how to virtualize them so that processes inside guest OSes can also benefit from of it. Table 1 shows a comparison of a GPU programming model between non-HSA and HSA systems. These dissimilar behaviors require non-conventional GPU virtualization. Considering the GPU memory, non-HSA systems have a separate address space for the GPU. To virtualize the GPU so that it may be shared by multiple guest OSes, GPU memory must be virtualized for isolation and protection. In HSA systems, the virtual address is shared between CPU and GPU. All the addresses issued by the GPU are guest virtual addresses, which are the same as what the CPU issues. Thus a table translating guest virtual address to machine physical address is sufficient to virtualize the GPU memory in a HSA system. As for job dispatching, HSA supports user mode queues so that applications can store job attributes inside the queue and the GPU is able to access it as long as the address of the user mode queue is set to the GPU. To virtualize job dispatching in a HSA system, it would only be necessary to set the address of the user mode queue of guest process to the GPU during queue initialization, which is simpler than mapping the guest GPU channel to a physical GPU channel for every job dispatched in conventional GPU virtualization.

Our implementation also achieves GPU sharing, which allows processes of multiple guest OSes to share the same GPU in the HSA-compliant system. To the best of our knowledge, this is the first research pertaining to HSA virtualization and implementation of a hypervisor on a physical HSA-compliant machine. Furthermore, though the implementation is targeted on an AMD Kaveri machine, general analysis and insights about how to virtualize HSA features on other systems are provided. These analyses and insights

can be applied to other architectures with similar features as well.

The rest of this paper is organized as follows. The techniques of how to virtualize various HSA features are presented in Section 3. Our implementation of the HSA-aware hypervisor are described in Section 4. Experiment results and performance evaluation are shown in Section 5. Section 6 discusses related work and Section 7 concludes.

This paper makes the following contributions:

- It investigates the issues involved in virtualizing HSA-compliant systems. It is the first successful implementation of a hypervisor that virtualizes various HSA features to support multiple guest OSes.
- This work achieves GPU sharing among multiple guest OSes and the host OS.
- It looks into issues on AMD IOMMU's two-level address translation mechanism, and provides insights and solutions to work around current hardware limitations.

2. Heterogeneous System Architecture

In this section we introduce more details about the HSA system architecture. We first describe the distinguishing features pertaining to job dispatching and execution in HSA, and we provide analyses on which features benefit from virtualization, given that some features can be simply achieved by hardware or runtime without the hypervisor. Then we explore our target platform, AMD Kaveri, and investigate how these features are implemented on the target machine. Before introducing HSA features, two specific terminologies must be explained.

Architected Queuing Language (AQL): A command interface for dispatching jobs between CPU and HSA devices. When an application wants to execute a job on an HSA device, an AQL packet is created and filled with the information of that job, such as the size of work-group, address of GPU kernel program, arguments and so on. AQL packets are stored inside application queues and the HSA device is able to access these queues to get the job descriptions and carry out the computation.

Doorbell: A signal used to notify the computing devices that there are jobs waiting to be executed. When applications want to perform computation on a HSA device, it first fills out the AQL packet with required information then activates the doorbell signal to notify the computing device. Doorbell is a notification of the existence of a job. The job's scheduled runtime is determined by the device.

2.1 HSA Features

There are many required features for an HSA-compliant system [4], we discuss those features that are related to the virtualization effort.

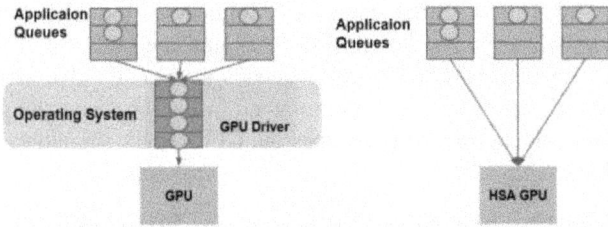

Figure 1. Job enqueuing steps in non-HSA (left) and HSA systems (right).

Shared virtual memory: Heterogeneous computing devices like GPU are integrated on the same bus and share the same virtual memory address space. Each process' virtual address is visible across CPU and other devices. Thus, computing devices can use the virtual address for computation directly without data copying between devices. This feature not only eliminates the data copying overhead but also reduces the programmer's burden to compress and decompress complex data structures as well.

I/O Page faulting: Prior to HSA, device DMA requires memory to be pinned and it could not be swapped out by the OS. This constraint is not practical in HSA since shared virtual memory across devices implies that devices may use all the memory space. If pinned memory is required, all process' address space must be pinned. Therefore, allowing I/O devices to generate page fault is necessary in HSA.

Cache coherence: Cache coherence is an important factor concerning a program's correctness. In HSA, all computing devices see the same memory space so keeping cache coherent is required, even though each computing device might have different cache systems.

User mode queuing: As Figure 1 shows, prior to HSA, every GPU job dispatched by applications must be passed through the GPU driver to be enqueued for execution. With user mode queuing, the GPU is aware of the address of the application queue and applications are allowed to dispatch jobs to the GPU directly without being trapped to a driver which reduces the latency of enqueuing jobs.

Memory-based signaling: This feature also aims at reducing the communication latency. An application assigns a memory address as a job-done listener and writes it into the AQL packet. With that address, a HSA device can directly signal the application or HSA runtime when a job is done rather than going through the traditional interrupt-based signalling.

The features listed above reduce both data communication latency and programing barriers. Moreover, the user mode queuing allows the GPU to access user level queues directly. Doorbell and memory-based signalling allow job dispatching and finishing to communicate without intervening with GPU drivers, which also reduces the CPU/GPU communication overhead as shown in Figure 2.

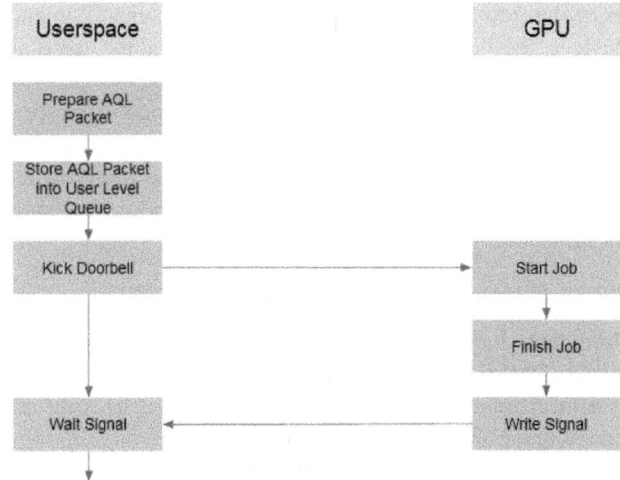

Figure 2. User mode queuing and memory based signaling eliminate GPU driver intervention.

2.2 AMD Kaveri Model

In this section, we describe how the five introduced features are implemented in the AMD Kaveri machine.

Shared virtual memory, I/O page faulting, and user mode queuing are co-implemented by the operating system and hardware. Cache coherence is implemented by hardware only in conventional processor designs. Memory-based signalling is achieved once shared virtual memory is realized. With shared virtual memory, the GPU is able to use the memory address designated for the signal (sent via AQL packet during job dispatching) to notify the user process when the dispatched job is finished (HSA runtime manages the function of waiting signals).

This work focuses on the virtualization of features co-implemented by OS and hardware, including the shared virtual memory, I/O page faulting, and user mode queuing. There are two additional kernel modules in the OS which Kaveri runs on, the IOMMU [7] driver and kernel fusion driver (KFD) [8]. IOMMU is implemented for shared virtual memory and I/O page faulting. And it provides a mechanism called peripheral page request service (PPR) for fixing I/O page faults. KFD, on the other hand, is designed to support user mode queuing. These functions are discussed in more detail.

2.2.1 IOMMU in HSA

IOMMU is a hardware component designed to carry out address translation for I/O devices. On HSA-based systems, computing devices communicate with each other using the shared virtual memory. Since the addresses issued by computing devices are virtual, they must be translated into physical addresses. IOMMU carries out this address translation for computing devices like GPU in Kaveri. Furthermore, since the virtual address space is shared between CPU and devices, the page table walked by IOMMU is the same as what is used by the CPU MMU.

When an application tries to use HSA computing devices, the driver gets the process page table and sets it to IOMMU. After proper configuration of the page table, computing devices are able to access process virtual address, as required by the shared virtual memory feature.

2.2.2 Peripheral Page Service Request (PPR)

Peripheral Page service Request (PPR) is introduced in AMD IOMMU to handle I/O page faulting in Kaveri. PPR is a mechanism that allows peripheral devices to issue requests to CPU for handling I/O page fault.

IOMMU performs a permission check and address translation when I/O devices attempt to access memory. If the page is not in the memory or the device does not have sufficient permission, IOMMU writes the faulting address, the faulting process ID and flags to PPR's log and issues a PPR interrupt to CPU. The PPR handler, which is called by the interrupt handler, reads PPR logs to find the corresponding process' memory control context. With the faulting address and memory control context, Linux API's get_user_pages can be used to grab the faulting page into memory. After the page fault is fixed, the PPR handler sends COM-PLETE_PPR_REQUEST [7] command to IOMMU to finish this I/O page fault.

2.2.3 Kernel Fusion Driver (KFD)

KFD is implemented as a GPU driver for Kaveri to support the user mode queuing feature. The key point of this feature is to allow HSA computing devices, such as GPU, to know where the application queues are. One simple approach, as implemented in KFD, is to send the address of the application queue to GPU, and let the hardware manage the queue binding. Whenever an application wants to perform a computation on a computing device, it creates a user mode queue and sends the address of that queue to KFD. KFD, acting as an agent between application and GPU hardware, then writes the receiving address to GPU's configuration register. This process eventually binds user mode queue to GPU hardware. This queue binding process executes only once for each user mode queue. After queue binding, GPU knows the exact address of the application queue and is therefore able to access the queue without driver's intervention.

One more thing KFD does during queue initializing is re-mapping a doorbell from physical address to virtual address. Since the doorbell is a hardware signal, which is located in a fixed memory-mapped I/O (MMIO) region, a memory remapping has to be done so the user-space application can kick the doorbell directly. With this memory remapping mechanism, application programs would not be constrained by the OS for dispatching GPU jobs.

After these initialization, the application can kick the doorbell to notify the GPU to work and the GPU can get AQL packets from user level queues to execute jobs. The driver's interventions are eliminated in the job dispatching path, which effectively reduces the CPU/GPU communication latency.

3. Design of a HSA-aware Hypervisor

In this section, we discuss how to virtualize the three HSA features mentioned in Section 2.2, the shared virtual memory, I/O page faulting, and user mode queuing,

The focus of this work is on memory and I/O virtualization techniques in the hypervisor design since the shared virtual memory and I/O page faulting features are the main concerns. I/O virtualization helps to realize communication between guest application and the computing device such as the queue binding process.

We adopt the shadow page table approach to carry out memory virtualization and the VirtIO framework [9] to implement I/O virtualization. Modification is required for both KFD and IOMMU drivers. The system architecture and detailed implementation are presented in Section 4. Discussions about why shadow page table is chosen rather than the two-level address translation [10] and why KFD needs to be modified are also explained in Section 4.4 and 4.3 respectively.

3.1 Shared Virtual Memory Virtualization

As described in Section 2.2.1, IOMMU inside Kaveri supports shared virtual memory between the CPUs and the GPU. Kernel programs executing on GPU reside in virtual address space and IOMMU is responsible for translating the virtual addresses issued by GPU into physical addresses.

In a non-virtualized environment, IOMMU shares the same process page table with CPU MMU to conduct the virtual address to physical address translation. In a virtualized environment, however, the addresses issued by GPU are actually in the Guest Virtual Address (GVA) space, hence requiring IOMMU to translate the issued GVA into Machine Physical Address (MPA). Two common techniques used to construct this GVA-to-MPA translation are Shadow Page Table (SPT) and two-level address translation (such as the Extended Page Table approach used in Intel VT-x and Nested Page Table in AMD-V). In this work the shadow page table mechanism is adopted due to some limitations in Kaveri which will be discussed in Section 4.4 that forbids the use of the two-level address translation mechanism, despite its popularity.

Shadow page table has already been implemented in the original KVM code. SPT of each guest OS is constructed by the hypervisor as soon as the guest OS is started. CPU MMU walks the SPT to translate GVA to MPA during the guest OS execution. The key to allow computing devices to support the shared virtual memory feature is to let IOMMU walk the same SPT used by the CPU MMU, where all necessary information for computing devices to perform GVA to MPA translation is provided.

3.2 I/O Page Faulting Virtualization

PPR, as described in Section 2.2.2, is a mechanism that I/O devices use to request page fault handling. PPR logs contain the faulting address and faulty process attributes.

When the GPU executes a guest process' kernel program, IOMMU walks its SPT to carry out the address translation. If a page does not exist in system memory or there is a permission violation, a PPR is issued and the faulty GVA is written into PPR logs. Our hypervisor will first notify the corresponding guest OS to get the faulty GVA as well as the process information, and ask the guest OS to fix the guest level page table. After the guest level page table is fixed, the SPT page fault handler is called to fix the SPT (which IOMMU actually walks). Finally, a finishing command is sent to IOMMU to complete the handling of a guest I/O page fault.

Shadow PPR and VirtIO-IOMMU are implemented in our hypervisor to construct the guest I/O page fault handler. These two modules will be presented in Section 4.2.

3.3 User Mode Queuing Virtualization

As described in Section 2.2.3, KFD sets the address of application queue to GPU device and remaps the doorbell from physical address to the process virtual address. After these initializations, the job dispatching can be conducted by kicking the doorbell.

With the user mode queuing feature, the virtualization of GPU job dispatching is simpler than normal GPU virtualization. Traditionally, GPU virtualization needs to map guest process queues to the hardware queue and is trapped every time a guest process dispatches a job to GPU.

For HSA, there are no hardware queues, only the user mode queues, so the hypervisor does not need to take care of the queue mapping. A hypervisor only needs to set the GVA of a guest application's queue to GPU and remaps the doorbell MPA back to GVA. Since the shadow page table has been set to IOMMU, GPU can therefore access GVA of guest application queues. After this queue binding, guest applications and the GPU can communicate through the application queue, doorbell and job-done signals without being limited to the hypervisor.

In this work a VirtIO-KFD module is implemented, which cooperates with the native KFD to manage guest application queue binding. The implementation details will be presented in Section 4.3.

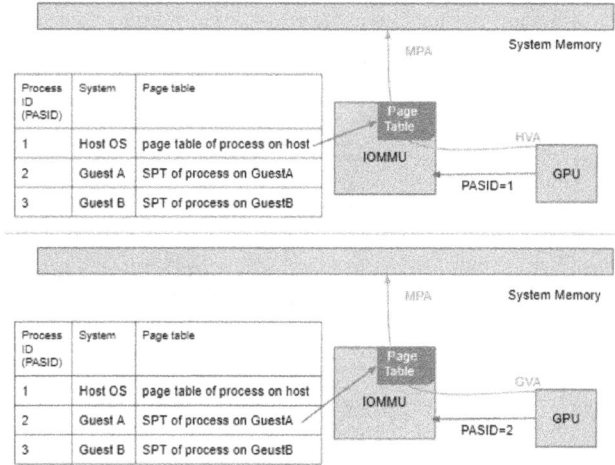

Figure 3. Illustration of GPU executing kernel programs from different systems.

3.4 GPU Sharing

For GPU sharing, two prerequisites have to be met: (1) All processes in multiple guest OSes should be able to dispatch jobs and (2) GPU kernel programs from processes of different guest OSes can be fairly executed, or at least behave like multiple host processes sharing a GPU. We will show how these two requirements are achieved in our design.

To begin, the user mode queuing feature implies the GPU will record information about the user mode queues and which processes they belong to. In a virtualized environment, multiple queues from different guest OSes are simply viewed as different queues on a normal host system. As long as the doorbell addresses are correctly remapped to guest processes' address space, applications from multiple guest OSes can notify the GPU about dispatching jobs.

When the doorbell is kicked, the GPU tries to access the application queue and gets AQL packets from it. An IOMMU page table walk on a properly set page table (the queue address binding to GPU is in virtual address space) allows the GPU to access the application queues. Also, since the SPTs belonging to each guest process are visible to IOMMU, kernel programs from processes of multiple guest OSes can be successfully executed. Figure 3 depicts the illustration of GPU sharing.

As described above, GPU can be shared between processes in different guest OSes and even the host OS, and the job scheduling is managed by the GPU hardware. In Section 5, the experiment shows the performance of multiple jobs dispatched simultaneously by processes from different guest OSes and from the host OS.

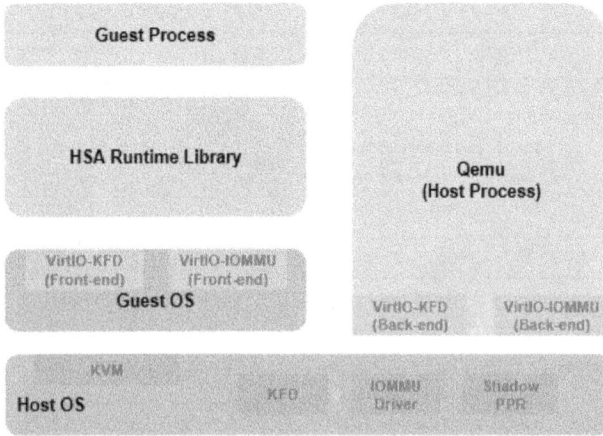

Figure 4. System architecture of our hypervisor implementation.

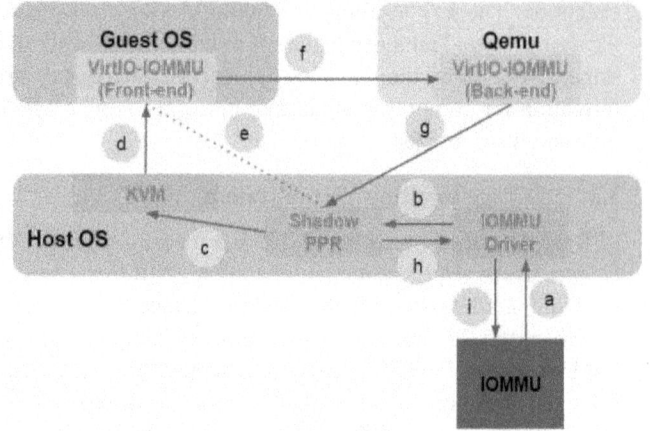

Figure 5. Flow of guest I/O page fault handling.

4. Implementation

Figure 4 shows the system architecture of our implementation. Several modules are modified or created for the hypervisor such that guest OSes can benefit from HSA. In this section, a brief overview of the role of each component is given. The implementations of the three necessary virtualized HSA features are then presented.

KFD acts as an interface between HSA runtime and HSA devices. We implemented a VirtIO-KFD module inside the guest OS. Guest applications and runtime see VirtIO-KFD as how they see KFD in a native environment. The VirtIO-KFD collaborates with native KFD to virtualize the user mode queuing feature.

KVM, the hypervisor that our implementation is based on, manages the SPTs for every processes in guest OSes. The IOMMU driver gets SPTs from KVM and sets it to IOMMU when guest processes are initialized in order to virtualize the shared virtual memory.

Shadow PPR is a newly created module that preserves PPR (peripheral page request) logs pertaining to the I/O page faults caused by guest processes' kernel programs and cooperates with VirtIO-IOMMU as the guest I/O page fault handler. Since PPR logs are stored in a MMIO region, the guest system cannot access it directly. Therefore, the shadow PPR is required for the I/O page faulting feature.

4.1 Shared Virtual Memory Virtualization

Shadow page tables are created and maintained by KVM. Basically, the page table structure is consistent between MMU and IOMMU (the second level page table, translating GPA to MPA, in two-level translation techniques is a little different but does not matter in our implementation since SPT is adopted). Both the page tables of host processes and the SPT use the same page table structure so the only thing that needs to be changed is to get the address of the shadow

page table from KVM and pass it to the driver for setting to IOMMU.

We slightly modify KVM by creating an interface for IOMMU to acquire SPTs of guest processes that attempt to use GPU. Also the IOMMU driver is modified to query SPTs when the guest processes are initialized.

4.2 I/O Page Faulting Virtualization

The VirtIO-IOMMU and Shadow PPR are implemented in order to handle guest I/O page faults. We'll describe how these components are initialized and a detailed flow of guest I/O page fault handling follows.

When a guest OS is ready to boot up, Shadow PPR allocates a region inside the host kernel for storing PPR logs for guest I/O page faults. VirtIO-IOMMU also allocates a region and does memory mapping from this region to the Shadow PPR region inside the host kernel. After this memory mapping, VirtIO-IOMMU can access Shadow PPR region to get logs without any trap.

The guest I/O page fault handling flow is illustrated in Figure 5. (a) When PPR happens, CPU is interrupted by IOMMU and ends up calling the PPR handler. The handler then fetches PPR logs to obtain the faulting process attributes and the faulting address. (b) The process attributes will be used to identify whether this fault is caused by the guest process. If so, the PPR handler stores the logs into the log region of Shadow PPR. (c~d) Sends a virtual interrupt to the guest OS by the IRQFD [11] mechanism, which allows the host kernel module to send an interrupt to the guest OS via KVM. (e) The guest PPR handler implemented inside VirtIO-IOMMU will be called by the guest interrupt handler. It gets PPR logs from Shadow PPR. This part does not cause traps as previous described. Given these logs, Linux API get_user_pages will be used to fix the I/O page fault. (f~i) After fixing the page fault, a finishing command is sent to Shadow PPR via VirtIO-IOMMU back-end driver. Shadow

PPR will first call KVM to synchronize the shadow page table, since only the guest side page tables are fixed in previous steps, and then Shadow PPR calls the IOMMU driver to send the COMPLETE_PPR_REQUEST command to IOMMU to finish this guest I/O page fault.

4.3 User Mode Queuing Virtualization

All HSA related configurations, such as queue creation and destroying, are using Linux IOCTL commands passed to KFD and set to HSA devices. We implemented a VirtIO-KFD front-end driver to replace the original KFD inside a guest OS and receive commands sent from guest user-space. There are front-end and back-end drivers in the VirtIO framework. The front-end driver receives I/O requests from the guest OS and passes them to the back-end driver. Usually the back-end driver calls the host's driver to satisfy the guest's I/O requests.

The implementation of VirtIO-KFD is not complex: the IOCTL commands sent from the user-space will carry arguments, such as the address of application queues for a queue-creation command, are passed to the host KFD via the VirtIO framework. The host KFD, with our modification to accept commands sent from guest processes, will then set these configurations to the GPU hardware. The host KFD will also call the IOMMU driver to get the shadow page table of the related guest process from KVM and set it to IOMMU. Another major concern is the doorbell address mapping. Since the major advantage of user mode queuing is to eliminate the driver's intervention after process initialization, the doorbell address is memory remapped from MPA to GVA. This involves two memory mappings, from MPA to the host virtual address (HVA), which is conducted by the host KFD, and from GPA (can be obtained simply by a linear address translation from HVA) to GVA, which is carried out by VirtIO-KFD. With such efforts, the user mode queuing feature can be successfully virtualized.

Finally, our modification to the host KFD is described. In the original design, the host KFD assigns a unique process address space ID (PASID) to each process that uses it. PASIDs are tied up with page tables in IOMMU to achieve the shared virtual memory feature, as previously illustrated in Figure 3.

In our virtualized environment, it is the VirtIO-KFD back-end driver that calls the host KFD on the behalf of the guest processes, and only one VirtIO-KFD back-end process per guest OS gets an assigned PASID. However, there may be multiple guest processes in a single guest OS that tries to use HSA devices. This causes an asymmetric mapping problem between PASID and the guest processes. To solve this issue, a supplementary VM_CREATE_PROCESS command is appended to create PASIDs for guest processes.

Moreover, the host KFD uses the process memory control context, mm_struct in Linux, to identify the relation between process and PASID. Whenever the host KFD gets an IOCTL command, it gets the mm_struct of the demanding process to figure out the corresponding PAISD. Under this design, the guest application's PASID cannot be recognized since only the VirtIO-KFD back-end process is able to call the host KFD, and the VirtIO-KFD's memory control context will be obtained rather than that of the guest process. To fix this problem, we added a set of new IOCTL commands for the guest-process-related configurations. For instance, VM_CREATE_QUEUE and VM_SET_MEMORY_POLICY are the commands corresponding to CREATE_QUEUE and SET_MEMORY_POLICY commands in the original code. The guest process' memory control context will be carried with these newly created commands so the host KFD can obtain the PASIDs belonging to guest processes and bind it to GPU and IOMMU.

4.4 Issues about Implementing IOMMU Two-level Address Translation

In the early stage of this work, we planned to use two-level address translation instead of shadow page table for virtualizing the shared virtual memory feature. Two-level address translation is supported by hardware, yields lower latency in general, is more advanced in virtualization designs, and is more widely adopted by mainstream hypervisors. As for our target machine, the IOMMU in Kaveri supports two-level address translation as it has been supported in AMD-v, the hardware virtualization extension of AMD processors. So two-level address translation seems feasible and is the first, and may be the best, choice to implement this work.

However, some limitations in the Kaveri machine prevent this approach from working. In Kaveri there are two different paths for translating a GPU virtual address: the IOMMU, and the GPUVM, as illustrated in Figure 6. A basic difference between these two paths is that IOMMU is used to translate the user space address while GPUVM is used to translate kernel space address.

User space address translation can be comprehended easily. The user level queues and GPU kernel programs reside in the user address space. On the other hand, in the kernel space address, the memory queue descriptor (MQD) is allocated and manipulate by KFD inside the host kernel. The MQD is used for user mode queue binding. It contains attributes of user level queues, such as address of queue and size of queue and will be sent to GPU for bind user mode queues. In our implementation, the host KFD is responsible for creating MQDs for both the guest and host user queues since only the host KFD can communicate with GPU. There is also a possible device pass-through [12] like approach discussed later to let guest OS manipulates GPUVM and creates MQD itself.

During user mode queue initializing, the host KFD first fills the attributes of a user queue to MQD and then performs

System Memory

GPUVM

IOMMU

Kernel space address
Eg. Memory queue descriptor (MQD)

User space address
Eg. User queue, GPU kernel program

Kaveri GPU

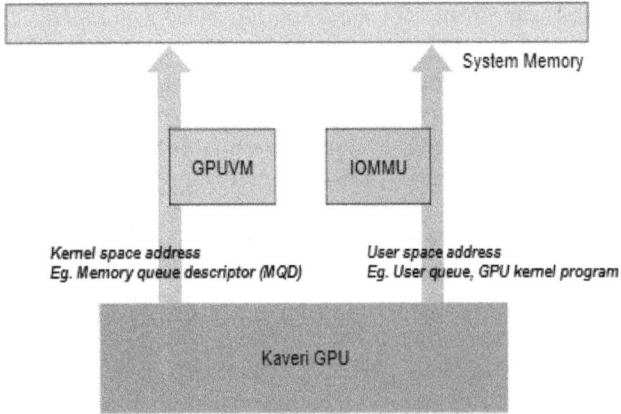

Figure 6. Kaveri GPU address translation components.

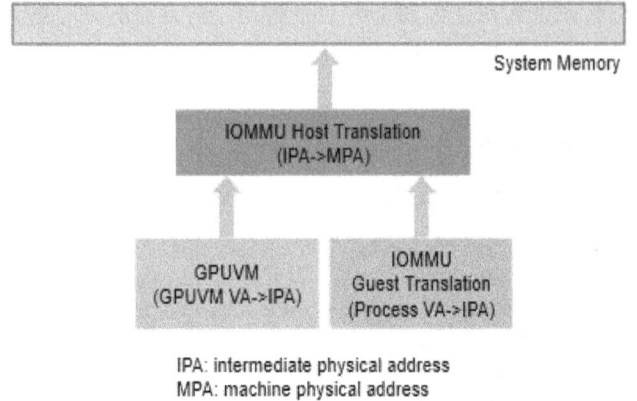

System Memory

IOMMU Host Translation
(IPA->MPA)

GPUVM
(GPUVM VA->IPA)

IOMMU
Guest Translation
(Process VA->IPA)

IPA: intermediate physical address
MPA: machine physical address

Figure 7. Kaveri GPU address translation path.

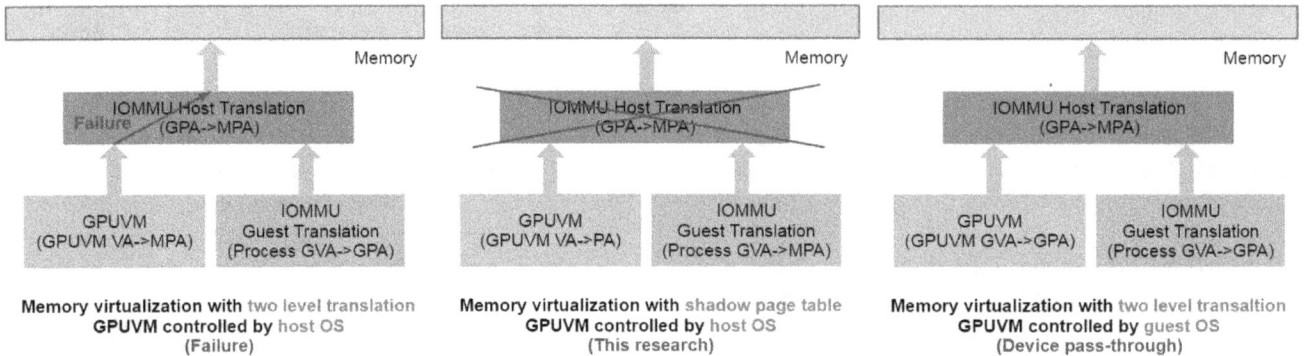

Memory

IOMMU Host Translation
Failure (GPA->MPA)

GPUVM
(GPUVM VA->MPA)

IOMMU
Guest Translation
(Process GVA->GPA)

Memory virtualization with two level translation
GPUVM controlled by host OS
(Failure)

Memory

IOMMU Host Translation
(GPA->MPA)

GPUVM
(GPUVM VA->PA)

IOMMU
Guest Translation
(Process GVA->MPA)

Memory virtualization with shadow page table
GPUVM controlled by host OS
(This research)

Memory

IOMMU Host Translation
(GPA->MPA)

GPUVM
(GPUVM GVA->GPA)

IOMMU
Guest Translation
(Process GVA->GPA)

Memory virtualization with two level transaltion
GPUVM controlled by guest OS
(Device pass-through)

Figure 8. Comparison between different approaches

a memory mapping from the host kernel space address of MQD to GPUVM virtual address space and then sets the GPUVM virtual address (GPUVM VA) to GPU. Once GPU is kicked to execute, it tries to access the MQD corresponding to the process who kicks it and issues the GPUVM VA of that MQD. GPUVM hardware translates the GPUVM VA to a physical address so the GPU can access the MQD and get the address of a user level queue from it. After this, GPU is then able to access the user queue and get AQL packets for execution.

For implementing HSA virtualization with two-level address translation technique, the two-level translation of IOMMU must be enabled. Both of the outputs of GPUVM and IOMMU's first level translation go through the second level translation of IOMMU as shown in Figure 7. This means that if IOMMU two-level translation is enabled, both of the inputs of GPUVM and IOMMU are translated twice. It is reasonable that the input of IOMMU is translated twice, since the guest virtual address needs a GVA-to-GPA-to-MPA translation. For GPUVM, however, the input is GPUVM VA and it should only be translated into MPA with one level translation. If two-level translation is enabled, the GPUVM side translation will cause failures, and this is why

two-level translation does not work in this implementation, as shown in the left-most figure of Figure 8.

The problem described above is caused by setting GPUVM VA of MQDs to GPU. However, if the guest OS is able to control GPUVM and create MQDs as shown in the rightmost figure of Figure 8, then the address of MQDs set to GPU are in the guest GPUVM virtual address space (GPUVM GVA), and it would need two-level address translation. The approach that lets the guest OS control the GPUVM is basically a device pass-through technique, but device pass-through is unsuitable for fair GPU sharing, so the shadow page table approach was adopted in this work. The implementation of device pass-through and the evaluation of its impact on performance are planned for future work.

5. Evaluation

In this section, we present the results of our HSA-aware hypervisor. The evaluation mainly focus on the performance comparison between native and guest's computation on GPU. The results are classified into queue initialization time and GPU kernel execution time. Overheads of VirtIO-KFD are measured by initialization time and the overheads of the shadow page table and guest I/O page fault handling are

Table 2. The set of benchmarks in our experiments.

Benchmark Name	Input Parameters
BinarySearch	array-length=100,000,000
FastWalshTransform	array-length=65536
BitonicSort	array-length=65536
FloydWarshall	nodes=3000
MatrixMultiplication (long)	matrix-a-height=5000
	matrix-a-width=5000
	matrix-b-width=5000
MatrixMultiplication (short) (only use in Section 5.4)	matrix-a-height=2000
	matrix-a-width=2000
	matrix-b-width=2000
MatrixTranspose	matrix-height=8192
	matrix-width=8192
MonteCarloAsian	steps=512

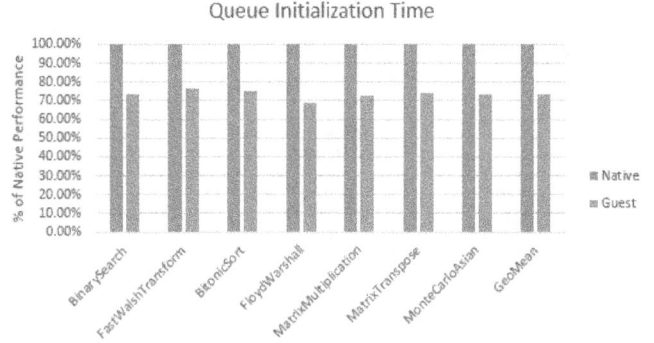

Figure 9. Performance comparison in queue initialization time, normalizing against the native scenario.

measured by GPU kernel execution time. Furthermore, the performance of GPU programs dispatched simultaneously by processes from different guest OSes and the host process are also provided.

5.1 Experiment Configuration

The experiment hardware platform chosen for this experiment is AMD Kaveri A10-7850K APU, the first HSA-compliant machine, including the AMD steamroller processor with 4 CPU cores (running at 3.7Ghz), 8G system memory, and Radeon R7 GPU with 512 cores. Both the host and guest OS ran 64bit Ubuntu 14.04 LTS with a Linux 3.14.11 kernel released by HSA foundation and modified by us. The guest OSes were allocated with 1 VCPU and 4G system memory.

We used the AMD OpenCL SDK [13] as our test suite. The benchmarks and input parameters are listed in Table 2. The POCL-HSA [14] was adopted as an OpenCL runtime implementation that end up calling HSA runtime.

5.2 Queue Initialization Time

Figure 9 shows the time spent on HSA-related initialization and user mode queue creation, from the HSA runtime API hsa_init to hsa_queue_create. In this process, many attributes are sent to KFD and configured to GPU.

The performance drop of the guest system is around 30% in every benchmark. This is due to the propagation delay of KFD IOCTL commands from VirtIO-KFD front-end to back-end and then to the host KFD. This path also incurs overhead of VM world switch from the guest mode to the host mode. Moreover, the guest doorbell memory mapping from MPA to GVA takes more time than only MPA to HVA in the native scenario.

However, this initialization process only performs once for every user mode queue. As long as the queues exist, the application can dispatch jobs without paying such overhead.

In comparison with GPU execution, the performance drop during initialization time would not be a great concern.

5.3 GPU Execution Time

In the shadow page table implementation, both the guest and the native GPU execution go through one level address translation in IOMMU. The factor that may cause performance difference is the I/O page fault handling. The GPU execution time and the I/O page fault handling time of every benchmark are presented in Table 3. Figure 10 shows the GPU virtualization performance normalized against the native run.

To analyze the performance overhead caused by PPR handling, Table 3 shows that native PPR time account for almost 0% of native GPU execute time and guest PPR time accounts for 0~5% for every benchmark. Though the guest PPR handling incurs more overhead than native PPR, the performance influence is still marginal. For Figure 10, it shows that the guest GPU execution achieves nearing 95% of native GPU performance in most benchmarks. The two anomalies, FastWalshTransform and BitonicSort, however, give around 88% of native performance. This is caused by the overhead of multiple job enqueuing and dispatching. Recall the GPU jobs execution flow in Figure 2. There is theoretically neither trap nor VM world switch during job dispatching and finishing because of the user mode queuing and memory-based signalling features. While taking a deeper look inside the job finishing situation, VM world switches may occur due to prolonged signal waiting which may make VM idle or exhaust the time slice allocated. As Figure 11 shows, these world switches do not affect the performance of GPU programs but do slow down the process when the guest application gets signalled and enqueues the next job.

In our test suite, FastWalshTransform, BitonicSort, FloydWarshall, and MonteCarloAsian enqueue and kick GPU many times while BinarySearch, MatrixMultiplication, and MatrixTranspose only activate once. The delay of the application which enqueues the next job is so negligible that

Table 3. GPU execution time and I/O page fault handling time.

Benchmark Name	GPU Execution Time (sec)		Number of I/O Page Fault		I/O Page Fault Handling Time (sec)		I/O Page Fault Handling Time of GPU execution time (%)	
	Native	Guest	Native	Guest	Native	Guest	Native	Guest
BinarySearch	0.011	0.011	0	0	0	0	0.00%	0.00%
FastWalshTransform	0.002	0.002	0	1	0	0.00004	0.00%	1.95%
BitonicSort	0.014	0.016	0	1	0	0.00014	0.00%	0.85%
FloydWarshall	16.094	16.603	75	4730	0.00037	0.30053	0.00%	1.81%
MatrixMultiplication	8.012	8.286	52	167	0.00027	0.00852	0.00%	0.09%
MatrixTranspose	0.502	0.538	114	366	0.00032	0.02485	0.06%	4.62%
MonteCarloAsian	17.458	18.342	6	113	0.00024	0.04454	0.00%	0.24%

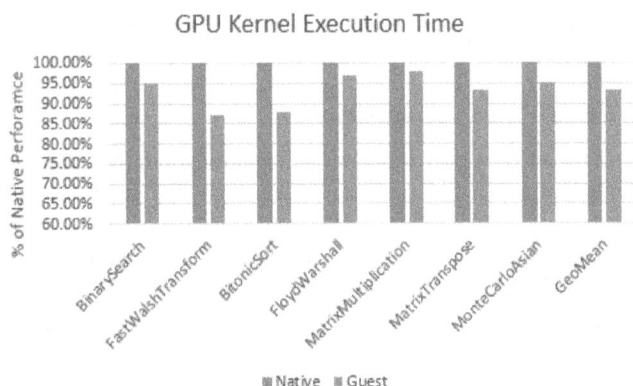

Figure 10. Performance comparison in GPU kernel execution time, normalizing against the native scenario.

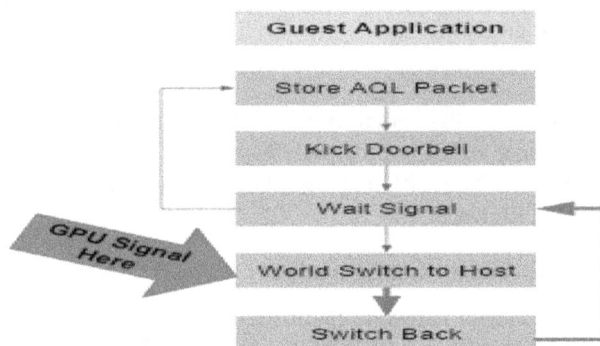

Figure 11. The delay (depicted in red arrow) of enqueuing next job caused by unintentionally world switch.

only the benchmarks with short execution time, FastWalshTransform and BitonicSort, may suffer from it. The overhead of delayed job enqueuing is amortized in the cases for benchmarks with longer execution time.

To sum up, the GPU job dispatched by guest processes on our hypervisor achieve around 95% of native GPU performance in the long-running benchmarks. Though some overhead incurs in short-running benchmarks, it can still achieve near 88% of native performance.

5.4 Multiple GPU Execution

In this subsection, we present multiple GPU execution in the following three scenarios, where the first two scenarios are conducted with process numbers of 1, 2 and 4: (1) All processes execute the MatrixMultiplication with same input parameters. (2) Same benchmark is used but with different input parameters. (3) Two processes execute a long-running and a short-running job respectively. We analyse the virtualization overhead in sharing a GPU in the first scenario and where the degree of sharing of GPU is evaluated in the last two scenarios.

Two process configuration groups are tested: (1) Combination of guest processes from different guest OSes and a host process (2) Mix of all host processes. Through the first configuration group we demonstrate that a GPU can be shared between multiple guest OSes and the host OS. The result of the second configuration group is used as a reference to compare the GPU performance across native and guest execution environments.

In Figure 12, 13 and Table 4, 5 the VM{N} means the process of the Nth guest OS and Host represents process of the host OS. The Native{N} also stands for the process of the host OS but it is in different groups with the Host bar.

The results of the first scenario are shown in Figure 12. It is observed that the GPU execution time scales up as the number of process increases. This corroborates that the GPU in Kaveri is able to compute multiple kernel programs simultaneously and fairly (some limits are discussed in later two experiments). As for the virtualization overhead, the relative performance drop between group 1 and group 2 is within 5%, which remains the same as the result in single kernel program execution scenario described in Section 5.3. This shows that there is almost no additional overhead in sharing GPU between multiple guests OSes based on our implementation.

Table 4. Multiple GPU execution in short MatrixMultiplication (with blue background color) and long MatrixMultiplication.

GPU Execution Time (sec)	Group 1				Group 2			
	VM1	VM2	VM3	Host	Native1	Native2	Native3	Native4
1 Process	0.55				0.53			
2 Processes	3.03	12.63			2.98	12.57		
4 Processes	5.31	5.27	24.81	24.49	5.13	5.06	23.85	23.81

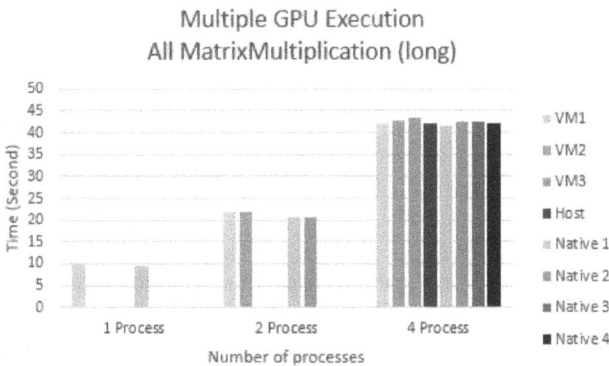

Figure 12. Multiple GPU execution time, all processes execute MatrixMultiplication with large input parameter.

Table 5. Multiple GPU execution time in MatrixTranspose (with blue background color) + MatrixMultiplication.

GPU Execution Time (sec)	Group 1		Group 2	
	VM1	VM2	Native 1	Native 2
1 Process	0.54		0.50	
2 Processes	11.35	10.74	11.29	10.70

In the second scenario, we first launched the MatrixMultiplication with large input parameters, and then launched that with small input parameters (the inputs are listed in Table 2). The result in Table 4 and Figure 13 shows that though a longer job is dispatched and executed beforehand, the shorter job can still be computed and finish earlier, meaning that the GPU computation power is indeed shared by multiple processes.

The last scenario is conducted by the launch of MatrixMultiplication, a longer job, followed by the launch of MatrixTranspose, a shorter job. As Table 5 shows, the GPU execution time of MatrixTranspose is about the time MatrixMultiplication runs plus the time MatrixTranspose runs. This means that the MatrixTranspose job is blocked by the previously launched MatrixMultiplication. From Table 5, we can also observe that the blocking of GPU job not only happens in configuration group 2 but group 1 as well, which means that the GPU hardware does not fully support fair job scheduling.

To conclude these experiments, the results show that the GPU in Kaveri seems able to compute jobs simultaneously

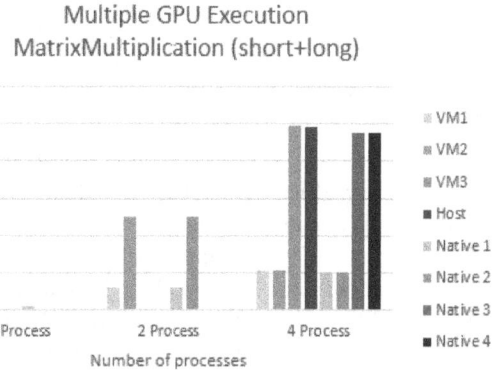

Figure 13. Multiple GPU execution time, left bars in one group are the execution time of short MatrixMultiplication, right bars in another group are that of long MatrixMultiplication.

with fair scheduling if the jobs are in the same kernel program. Otherwise, successive jobs will be blocked by previously dispatched jobs. The scheduling mechanism of the GPU in Kaveri is undocumented so we cannot verify its precise job scheduling policy. But regarding the goal of system virtualization, our implementation allows multiple guest OSes to share the GPU in a way identical to how multiple host processes behave with nearing no additional overhead. Moreover, we believe our work can be applied to other machine that supports full GPU job scheduling mechanism so that guest processes can get more benefits from GPU virtualization.

6. Related Work

Most of the GPU virtualization works are implemented in device pass-through and API forwarding. Device pass-through is a naïve approach that allows a guest system to access one dedicated GPU directly without modifying the guest GPU driver. The I/O virtualization hardware extension such as Intel VT-d [15] or AMD IOMMU [8] are required for the implementation of the pass-through approach. However, device pass-through suffers from an inability to share GPU in a fair manner. To solve this problem, Intel gVirt [16] and NVIDIA VGX [17] were recently proposed to not only allow virtual machines to directly access GPU, but also share it as well. These two approaches, however, require proprietary GPU information and additional hardware design so it is hard to be implemented by non-vendor developers.

API forwarding, on the other hand, modifies the guest runtime library to forward API calls to the hypervisor for further virtualization. The rCUDA [18], vCUDA [19], GViM [20] forward guest level CUDA APIs to the underlying simulation stack. The virtio-CL [21] is another API forwarding implementation for OpenCL. Xen3D [22] and VMGL [23] are implementations for OpenGL. The difficulty of API forwarding is its lack of fidelity, where the description of whether the features supported in virtualized and native environment should be consistent [24]. Since it is difficult to virtualize all APIs inside a guest system, to maintain the consistency is a great challenge.

Our implementation is a para-virtualization that forwards OS level commands only, without modification to the runtime library. Since OS level commands are used only during user mode queue initialization, it is simpler to virtualize GPU at this layer. Furthermore, indebted to user mode queuing, applications can forward their jobs to GPU directly without additional virtualization effort. GPUvm [25] provides full- and para-virtualization design that virtualize the GPU in hypervisor level. It virtualizes the GPU command channel and GART table so that GPU can be shared between multiple guest OSes. The virtualization of GART table requires guest GPU virtual address to be translated to GPU physical address. The main difference between our work and GPUvm is in virtual memory management: how page table and I/O page faults are handled. For page table, since HSA is a shared virtual memory architecture, the shadow page table is updated along with guest process execution. On the other hand, GPUvm's shadow page table is updated when data copy commands are sent. As for I/O page faults, GPUvm needs to scan the entire page tables upon TLB flush since it does not support I/O page faults, where our work does include a framework to support I/O page faults.

7. Conclusion

This work presents the concept, the design and a KVM-based implementation of HSA system virtualization. Though our implementation targets at the AMD Kaveri machine, we believe this work can be applied to other architectures with similar features like the shared virtual memory, the user level queues and the memory-based signals. Moreover, we demonstrate that the sharing of a GPU between multiple guest OSes and the host OS under the HSA compliant system can be accomplished with minor virtualization overhead. The results show that the performance of guest's kernel programs achieves near 95% of native GPU performance in most of the tested benchmarks, especially those with longer execution time.

As for future work, the device pass-through approach and performance comparison are planned. We will also port our work into the latest KFD version and run our hypervisor on the new HSA machine, AMD Carrizo, to measure the effort

of applying our implementation to other HSA machines and conduct more investigation on GPU sharing issues.

References

[1] General-Purpose Computation on Graphic Hardware, http://gpgpu.org/.

[2] Nvidia CUDA, http://www.nvidia.com/object/cuda_home_new.html.

[3] J.E. Stone, D. Gohara, G. Shi, OpenCL: a parallel programming standard for heterogeneous computing systems, Comput. Sci. Eng. 12 (2010) 66–73.

[4] Heterogeneous System Architecture (HSA), http://www.hsafoundation.com/

[5] AMD Kaveri, http://www.amd.com/en-us/products/processors/desktop/a-series-apu.

[6] A. Kivity, Y. Kamay, D. Laor, U. Lublin, and A. Liguori. kvm: the Linux virtual machine monitor. In OLS 2007: Proceedings of the 2007 Ottawa Linux Symposium.

[7] AMD I/O Virtualization Technology (IOMMU) Specification, http://developer.amd.com/wordpress/media/2012/10/488821.pdf, 2012.

[8] Kernel Fusion Driver source code, https://github.com/HSAFoundation/HSA-Drivers-Linux-AMD.

[9] Rusty Russel. virtio: towards a de-facto standard for virtual I/O devices. In Operating Systems Review, 2008.

[10] AMD. AMD64 Virtualization Codenamed "Pacifica" Technology: Secure Virtual Machine Architecture Reference Manual, May 2005.

[11] IRQFD, https://lwn.net/Articles/329837/.

[12] Y. Dong, J. Dai, Z. Huang, H. Guan, K. Tian, Y. Jiang, Towards high-quality I/O virtualization. SYSTOR 2009.

[13] AMD OpcnCL APP SDK, http://developer.amd.com/tools-and-sdks/opencl-zone/.

[14] Portable Computing Language (pocl) for HSA, http://pocl.sourceforge.net/docs/html/hsa.html.

[15] D. Abramson, J. Jackson, S. Muthrasanallur, G. Neiger, G. Regnier, R. Sankaran, I. Schoinas, R. Uhlig, B. Vembu, and J. Wiegert. Intel virtualization technology for directed I/O. Intel Technology Journal, 10, August, 2006.

[16] TIAN, K., DONG, Y., AND COWPERTHWAITE, D. A full gpu virtualization solution with mediated pass-through. In Proc. USENIX ATC (2014).

[17] NVIDIA. NVIDIA GRID VGX SOFTWARE. http://www.nvidia.com/object/grid-vgx-software.html, 2014.

[18] DUATO, J., PENA, A. J., SILLA, F., MAYO, R., AND QUINTANA-ORTI, E. rCUDA: Reducing the number of GPU-based accelerators in high performance clusters. In Proc. of IEEE Int'l Conf. on High Performance Computing Simulation (2010), pp. 224–231.

[19] SHI, L., CHEN, H., SUN, J., AND LI, K. vCUDA: GPU-Accelerated High-Performance Computing in Virtual Machines. IEEE Transactions on Computers 61, 6 (2012), 804–816.

[20] GUPTA, V., GAVRILOVSKA, A., SCHWAN, K., KHARCHE, H., TOLIA, N., TALWAR, V., AND RANGA-NATHAN, P. GViM: GPU-Accelerated Virtual Machines. In Proc. of ACM Workshop on System-level Virtualization for High Performance Computing (2009), pp. 17–24.

[21] Tien, Tsan-Rong, and Yi-Ping You. "Enabling OpenCL support for GPGPU in Kernel-based Virtual Machine." Software: Practice and Experience 44.5 (2014): 483-510.

[22] C. Smowton. Secure 3D graphics for virtual machines. In EuroSEC'09: Proceedings of the Second European Workshop on System Security. ACM, 2009, pp. 36-43.

[23] H. A. Lagar-Cavilla, N. Tolia, M. Satyanarayanan, and E. D. Lara. VMM-independent graphics acceleration. In Proc. VEE (2007), pp. 33-43

[24] M. Dowty and J. Sugerman. GPU Virtualization on VMware's Hosted I/O Architecture. ACM SIGOPS Operating Systems Review, 43:73–82, July 2009.

[25] SUZUKI, Y., KATO, S., YAMADA, H., AND KONO, K. GPUvm: why not virtualizing gpus at the hypervisor? In Proceedings of the 2014 USENIX conference on USENIX Annual Technical Conference (2014), USENIX Association, pp. 109–120.

Shoot4U: Using VMM Assists to Optimize TLB Operations on Preempted vCPUs

Jiannan Ouyang

University of Pittsburgh

ouyang@cs.pitt.edu

John R. Lange

University of Pittsburgh

jacklange@cs.pitt.edu

Haoqiang Zheng

VMware, Inc

hzheng@vmware.com

Abstract

Virtual Machine based approaches to workload consolidation, as seen in IaaS cloud as well as datacenter platforms, have long had to contend with performance degradation caused by synchronization primitives inside the guest environments. These primitives can be affected by virtual CPU preemptions by the host scheduler that can introduce delays that are orders of magnitude longer than those primitives were designed for. While a significant amount of work has focused on the behavior of spinlock primitives as a source of these performance issues, spinlocks do not represent the entirety of synchronization mechanisms that are susceptible to scheduling issues when running in a virtualized environment. In this paper we address the virtualized performance issues introduced by TLB shootdown operations. Our profiling study, based on the PARSEC benchmark suite, has shown that up to 64% of a VM's CPU time can be spent on TLB shootdown operations under certain workloads. In order to address this problem, we present a paravirtual TLB shootdown scheme named Shoot4U. Shoot4U completely eliminates TLB shootdown preemptions by invalidating guest TLB entries from the VMM and allowing guest TLB shootdown operations to complete without waiting for remote virtual CPUs to be scheduled. Our performance evaluation using the PARSEC benchmark suite demonstrates that Shoot4U can reduce benchmark runtime by up to 85% compared an unmodified Linux kernel, and up to 44% over a state-of-the-art paravirtual TLB shootdown scheme.

Categories and Subject Descriptors   D.4.1 [*Process Management*]: Synchronization

Keywords   TLB Shootdown, Virtualization, Preemption

VEE '16,   April 02-03, 2016, Atlanta, GA, USA.
Copyright © 2016 ACM 978-1-4503-3947-6/16/04. . . $15.00.
http://dx.doi.org/10.1145/2892242.2892245

1. Introduction

Several studies have established that the average server utilization in most datacenters is low, ranging from 10% to 50% [2, 9, 12, 14, 18]. While a promising way to improve efficiency is to co-locate multiple virtual machines on the same node in the cloud, the performance overhead introduced by over-commitment inhibits efficient workload co-location. A large body of work has documented the detrimental effects virtual CPU preemption can have on multicore virtual machine performance [10, 11, 13, 15, 16, 20–23]. The majority of this work has focused on the impact of spinlock behaviors, due to the direct effects spinlock delays can have on performance critical code paths. However, relatively little attention has been paid to other sources of local delays caused by preemptions of remote CPU cores. In this paper we focus on the issue of performance overhead caused by TLB operations in the presence of preempted virtual CPU cores (vCPUs).

Cross core TLB operations act as a low level synchronization point in modern Operating Systems in order to maintain consistent application memory mappings. The majority of these operations consist of various cache flushing methods that must be invoked on every CPU in the system. For each TLB flush operation the invoking CPU must wait until the operation has been completed on all other cores before continuing, typically by polling a memory region with kernel preemption disabled. This invocation is achieved by issuing Interprocessor Interrupts (IPIs) to each target CPU, the handlers of which directly invoke a local flush operation. In native environments, these operations have very low latency since at most they only need to wait for a target CPU to exit an atomic region before the IPI is handled. In virtual environments these assumptions no longer hold due to the potential for a target vCPU to be preempted by the underlying host scheduler. This can result in the latencies of TLB flush operations increasing by orders of magnitude depending on the scheduling state of the target vCPUs. We refer to this issue as the *TLB shootdown preemption* problem.

To address this problem we propose Shoot4U, a virtual TLB management mechanism for paravirtualized multicore VMs. Shoot4U eliminates the dependencies on vCPU scheduling states for TLB flush operations and is therefore able to ensure that TLB operations exhibit consistently low latencies. Shoot4U accomplishes this by intercepting cross vCPU TLB flush operations at the VMM layer, and performing the invalidations directly in the VMM instead of requiring that they be handled inside a guest environment. This optimization allows Shoot4U to avoid any delays caused by a preempted vCPU, and to ensure consistent performance of TLB operations. The Shoot4U mechanism provides a better match for the TLB operation semantics, since at the lowest level it shares the same IPI based signalling behavior as the native versions. This not only allows lower latencies in general, but also eliminates preemption based delays that cause a dramatic increase in the latency variance.

In this paper we make the following contributions:

- An analysis of the impact that various low level synchronization operations have on system benchmark performance.

- Shoot4U: A novel virtualized TLB architecture that ensures consistently low latencies for synchronized TLB operations.

- An analysis of the performance benefits achieved by Shoot4U over current state-of-art software and hardware assisted approaches.

2. Related Work

Most previous work that has looked at the problems associated with VM synchronization overheads has focused on spinlocks and the *lock holder preemption* problem, originally identified by V. Uhlig et al. in 2004 [21]. In that work, the authors proposed a paravirtualization based approach in which the guest OS provides scheduling hints to the underlying VMM. These hints demarcated non-preemptable regions of guest execution that corresponded to critical sections in which a spinlock was held. T. Friebel and S. Biemueller [11] proposed a paravirtual spinlock approach, which was later adopted by Xen and KVM [17]. In their scheme a vCPU notifies the VMM via a hypercall if it has been waiting longer than a threshold. The VMM then blocks the spinning vCPU until the requested lock is released. J. Ouyang and J. Lange [16] identified the *lock waiter preemption* problem existing in queue-based FIFO spinlocks and proposed the preemptable ticket spinlock algorithm (pmtlock) to solve this problem. While spinlock optimizations are an important feature to reduce preemption based delays, they do not address other sources of preemption based delays such as TLB operations, which are the topic of this paper.

There are a few examples of previous work that has looked into the *TLB shootdown preemption* problem. In particular, H. Kim et al. [13] studied the performance degradation caused by both spinlock and TLB shootdown preemptions. They proposed the use of TLB shootdown IPIs as a VMM scheduling heuristic in order to reduce the delay introduced by a preempted vCPU. While their approach does help alleviate the delays imposed by TLB shootdowns on preempted vCPUs, it does not address the underlying problem directly. In contrast, our Shoot4U mechanism addresses the source of the problem directly by eliminating the necessity for busy-waiting inside the VM.

Most relevant to our work is the KVM paravirtual remote flush TLB scheme (kvmtlb) developed by the Linux community [4]. This scheme maintains the preemption state of all vCPUs inside the VMM and shares this information with the guest. When initiating TLB operations, if the remote vCPU is running, then the conventional shootdown approach is used. Otherwise, if the remote vCPU is preempted, a *should_flush* flag is set on that remote vCPU and an IPI is not sent. When rescheduling a vCPU, the VMM checks the *should_flush* flag. If set, the VMM invalidates all TLB entries of that vCPU. While this approach does address the underlying problem, it still possesses a number of shortcomings. First it still imposes the overheads of IPI routing between vCPUs which Shoot4U eliminates. Second, in an overcommitted environment it is possible that the preemption state of a vCPU can change after its state has been checked by the invoking CPU but before the IPI is actually delivered. As shown in our evaluation, the worst-case TLB shootdown latency of Shoot4U is an order of magnitude better than kvmtlb.

Other approaches to improving VM performance in the face of cross core synchronizations include improving VMM scheduling policy. H. Kim et al. [13] proposed demand-based coordinated scheduling that controls time-sharing in response to inter-processor interrupts (IPIs) between virtual CPUs. Other work proposed the use of co-scheduling [15]. However, strict co-scheduling is not scalable and may result in CPU fragmentation issues, which has led to more relaxed co-scheduler approaches as seen in VMware ESX [8]. Other co-scheduling variants include adaptive co-scheduling schemes [22, 23] that allow the VMM scheduler to dynamically alternate between co-scheduling and asynchronous scheduling for a particular VM, as well as balanced scheduling [20] which associates a VM's individual vCPUs with dedicated physical CPUs and does not require that the vCPUs be co-scheduled. While each of these approaches alleviate the problems caused by intra-VM synchronizations, they do so by providing workarounds as opposed to addressing the underlying issues.

3. The TLB Shootdown Preemption Problem

Translation Look-aside Buffers (TLBs) are a critical hardware component for virtual memory based systems, however they still require explicit management by the Operating System (OS) in order to maintain cache coherence. This requires the OS itself to directly manage the contents to the TLB caches on each CPU core in the system by ensuring that stale entries are removed before they can be accessed by any hosted applications. This is especially a problem for multi-threaded applications as they leverage shared page tables both as a space saving optimization as well as a way to amortize address space management overheads. Cache coherence is managed by the OS through the use of invalidation and flushing operations that remove one or more entries from a local TLB cache. The operations are propagated to other cores in the system via IPI based signalling that directly invoke a given TLB operation on a remotely targeted CPU, a mechanism that is canonically referred to as a *TLB shootdown.*

Modern operating systems consider TLB shootdown operations to be performance critical and so optimize them to exhibit very low latency. The implementation of these operations is therefore architected to ensure that shootdowns can be completed with very low latencies through the use of IPI based signalling. As such, TLB shootdowns can be implemented using a busy wait based stall of the invoking CPU while the operation is handled on each of the remote CPUs. Unfortunately, the low latency provided by IPI handlers is only ensured when the target CPU is available to handle the resulting interrupt. While this is generally a reasonable assumption in native environments, it does not carry over to virtualized environments as the availability of a given vCPU to handle interrupts is entirely dependent on the behavior of the underlying host scheduler.

The *TLB shootdown preemption problem* is the result of a vCPU invoking a TLB shootdown on a remote vCPU that is currently preempted by the host scheduler and therefore not available to handle the resulting IPI interrupt. In this case the invoking vCPU will block in a polling based loop until the target vCPU is rescheduled and returns to an active state. The scheduling delays, or the time between the preemption and rescheduling of a vCPU, are often orders of magnitude larger than the latency that TLB shootdown operations were designed for. This is especially true when multiple vCPUs are sharing the same underlying physical CPU. These unexpected delays can cause significant impacts on application performance depending on the workload, with particularly dramatic effects seen on multi-threaded workloads that require large amounts of address space modifications.

3.1 Performance Analysis

In order to better understand the effects that vCPU preemption has on TLB operations as well as other low level operations, we measured the performance degradation caused by CPU overcommitment on the PARSEC [5] benchmark suite. Specifically, we used the Linux perf [6] tool set to measure the percentage of time spent in various kernel functions.

We first measured the PARSEC performance using a single KVM based guest without overcommitting resources (1-VM), before adding a second KVM guest on the same machine running a CPU bounded workload using sysbench [7] (2-VMs). Each VM was configured to use the same number of vCPUs (12) evenly distributed on the underlying physical CPUs, so that each physical core was shared by two vCPU

cores from different VMs. Equal time sharing between vCPUs was ensured using Linux cgroups [1] and the Pause-Loop Exiting (PLE) [19] feature was disabled.

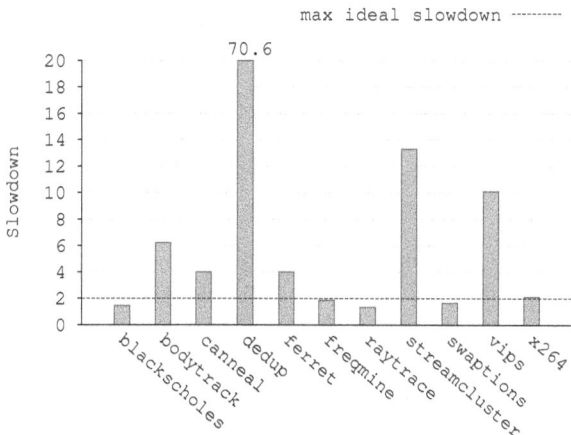

Figure 1: Performance Slowdown of CPU Overcommitment

Figure 1 shows the benchmark results for the 1-VM and 2-VMs configurations. The ideal slowdown would be 2x, due to the equal time sharing configuration of each physical CPU. As the results show 6 out of the 11 benchmarks have performance slowdowns of over 4x; 3 exhibit more than 10x slowdown; and the dedup benchmark has a slowdown of 70.6x.

For each of the applications we separated out the overheads resulting from TLB shootdowns (k:tlb) as well as spinlocks (k:lock), being the two most common causes of preemption based performance problems. The remaining overhead was split between other kernel level functions (k:other) and time spent in userspace (u:*). Figure 2 shows these results. With the exception of dedup, all benchmarks spent the majority of time in userspace for the 1-VM scenario. However, for the 2-VMs case a significant number of benchmarks exhibit noticeable increases in kernel based overheads. For dedup in particular, 64% of the CPU time is spent on TLB shootdown operations. As the results show, overheads resulting from spinlocks and TLB shootdowns account for the majority of the added overhead.

Next, we instrumented the Linux kernel using ktap [3], and measured the latency of TLB shootdown operations directly when running the dedup benchmark. Figure 3 shows the cumulative distribution function (CDF) of TLB shootdown latencies using a logarithmic X axis. As the figure shows, the 2-VMs case exhibits a significant increase in the average operation latency with the 90th percentile increasing by two orders of magnitude over the 1-VM configuration.

4. Shoot4U

To address the TLB shootdown preemption problem we present Shoot4U, a paravirtual TLB management interface. Shoot4U uses a VMM-assist technique to optimize

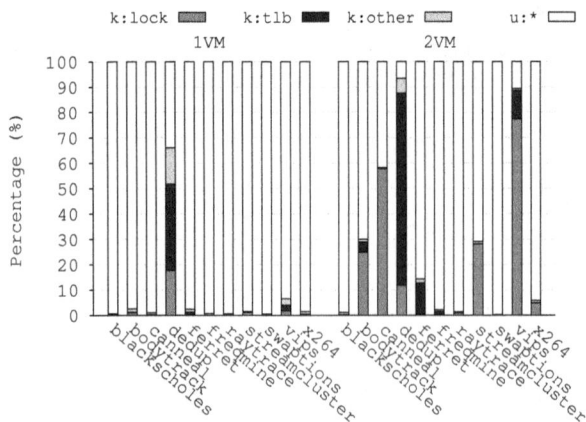

Figure 2: CPU Usage Profiling

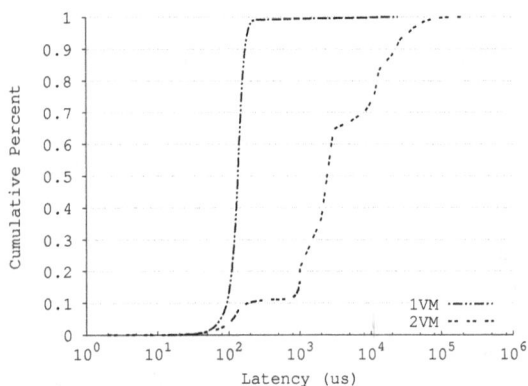

Figure 3: CDF of TLB Shootdown Latency

TLB shootdowns by performing the invalidations inside the VMM itself without the need to invoke or signal the guest OS. Shoot4U relies on hardware instructions available as part of the virtualization extensions on modern x86 based CPU architectures. These instructions allow targeted invalidation of TLB entries that belong to a specific VM environment.

Before explaining how Shoot4U works, it is necessary to understand how a conventional TLB shootdown operation works in a virtual environment. To initiate a TLB shootdown operation, the invoking vCPU sends an IPI with a specific vector number to a set of target vCPUs. The invoker then enters a polling loop until all receiver vCPUs have processed and acknowledged the requests by setting a flag located in shared memory. The transmission of the IPI by the vCPU causes the hardware to trap into the underlying VMM where it can be emulated, ultimately resulting in the VMM generating a new IPI that is actually transmitted to the VMM on the physical CPUs hosting the targeted vCPUs. Typically an IPI delivery by the hardware will indirectly cause any running VM to trap, so that the underlying host system software can handle it. In this case the IPI is handed off to the VMM,

which completes the IPI emulation by delivering an IPI to the targeted vCPU via the injection of a virtual interrupt. After the virtual interrupt has been injected, it will be handled as soon as the target vCPU resumes execution.

Shoot4U is based on the observation that modern hardware allows the underlying VMM to perform the invalidation operation internally, thus removing the need to inject a virtual interrupt into the target vCPU. Current x86 processors from both Intel and AMD support the use of Virtual Processor IDs or VPIDs (Intel) and Address Space IDs or ASIDs (AMD) to tag TLB entries with a given ID assigned to a VM context. Our implementation targets the Intel architecture (using KVM/Linux 3.16), but there is nothing preventing the same approach from being used on an AMD based system. Along with the ability to tag TLB entries with an associated VPID/ASID these CPUs support a new set of invalidation instructions (e.g. *invpid*) that selectively flush TLB entries based on a given ID tag. These instructions can be executed by the VMM itself, without any involvement of the VM's guest OS. Therefore, instead of relying on IPI injection as described above, Shoot4U enables the VMM to process the TLB invalidation request immediately by invalidating guest TLB entries itself.

Our implementation of Shoot4U introduces a paravirtual hypercall interface that replaces the existing IPI based TLB shootdown mechanism. In Shoot4U, the invoking vCPU issues a hypercall down to the underlying VMM with the target vCPUs and address range being invalidated specified as parameters. Upon trapping into the hypercall handler, the VMM determines the set of physical CPUs that are currently hosting the set of vCPUs, and issues a physical IPI to each of them. These IPIs are handled by the VMM itself, which then executes the appropriate set of invalidation operations internally without any interaction with the VM context. While the VMM handles the invalidations for the target vCPUs, the VMM on the invoking CPU polls for completion in a busy wait loop. Once the operations complete the VMM then returns from the hypercall and the VM resumes operation. While superficially it might appear that we have just moved the polling loop from the guest into the VMM, it should be noted that operation completion is no longer dependent on host scheduler behaviors since it does not have to wait for a vCPU to be running in order to complete.

Figure 4 shows the paravirtual hypercall interface provided by a KVM host with Shoot4U support. To utilize this interface, the guest VM needs to specify the hypercall ID, a bitmap of targeted vCPUs, and the address range being invalidated. Our current implementation of Shoot4U supports up to 64 vCPUs due to the size of the bitmap. However, we can easily support more vCPUs by mapping the bitmap into memory.

5. Evaluation

We evaluated Shoot4U on a dual socket Dell R450 server configured with Intel "Ivy-Bridge" Xeon processors (6 cores each) with hyperthreading enabled and 24 GB of RAM split across two NUMA domains. Each server was running CentOS 7 with Linux Kernel 3.16 with a modified version of KVM implementing the Shoot4U interface. We performed the evaluation using 2 separate VMs each with 12 vCPUs both mapped to the same socket. Each vCPU was pinned to a single hyperthreaded CPU core, so that each core was shared by 2 vCPUs. The Linux cgroups [1] interface was used to allocate an equal share of CPU time to each VM. One VM (VM1) was configured to run the PARSEC benchmark suite [5], while the other (VM2) ran a CPU bounded competing workload based on sysbench [7]. We used the Linux default TLB shootdown scheme with as the baseline, and compared it with Shoot4U as well as the current TLB shootdown optimization provided by KVM, denoted kvmtlb [4].

5.1 TLB Shootdown Latency

		baseline	kvmtlb	shoot4u
1VM	Mean	166	122	28
	Max	24,428	9,953	453
2VM	Mean	9,048	5,401	22
	Max	194,108	126,923	15,034

Table 1: TLB Shootdown Latency (usec)

The first experiment used ktap [3] to measure the completion time of TLB shootdown requests in the guest, running the dedup benchmark from PARSEC. The results are shown in Table 1, including the average and maximum completion time both with and without a 2nd VM sharing a physical CPU. It shows that both kvmtlb and Shoot4U significantly improve TLB shootdown performance in both cases. However, Shoot4U outperforms the other schemes: it is 4.3 and 245.5 times faster than kvmtlb on average for the 1-VM and 2-VMs cases respectively. Its worse case performance is also order of magnitude better than others.

Figure 5 shows the cumulative distribution function (CDF) of TLB shootdown latencies from the same experiment. Shoot4U not only provides better overall performance, but also exhibits much less variance than other approaches. In a non-overcommitted configuration Shoot4U provides superior performance by reducing the overheads of a TLB shootdown by reducing the number of world switches

```
kvm_hypercall3(unsigned long KVM_HC_SHOOT4U,
    unsigned long vcpu_bitmap,
    unsigned long start,
    unsigned long end);
```

Figure 4: Shoot4U API

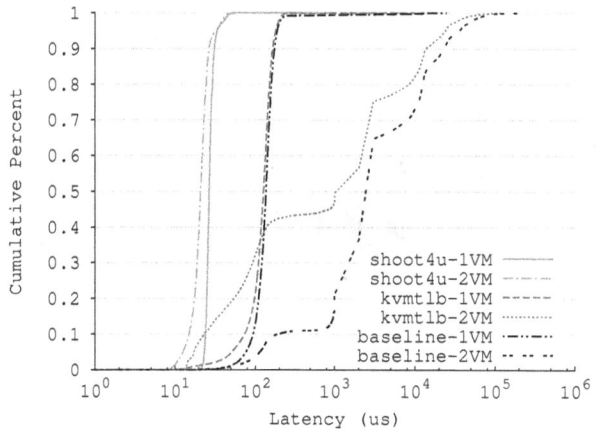

Figure 5: CDF of TLB Shootdown Latencies

needed for IPI propagation. Moreover, Shoot4U is able to maintain consistent performance in an overcommitted configuration, while the other solutions experience slowdowns due to vCPU preemptions, which Shoot4U is immune to.

5.2 Macro-Benchmark Performance

Our next experiment evaluated various TLB shootdown schemes using multi-threaded benchmarks from the PARSEC [5] benchmark suite. Each configuration was evaluated 3 times, and the average is reported. We also incorporated an optimized spinlock mechanism based on the preemptable ticket spinlock (PMT) algorithm [16]. This allowed us to compare the performance impact of spinlock based locking versus TLB operations. We also studied the impact of Pause-Loop Exiting (PLE), a hardware assisted spinning detection and optimization feature supported by KVM and recent Intel processors.

Figure 6 shows the normalized execution time of each benchmark using a sweep of various configurations. In the 2-VMs case on the left, it can be observed that Shoot4U achieves the best performance on almost all benchmarks. It outperforms kvmtlb by more than 10% on 4 benchmarks, and in the best cases, it is 85% faster than the baseline on dedup, and 44% faster than kvmtlb on ferret. It can also be observed that PLE yields pretty good performance improvements on many benchmarks; moreover, further improvements can be achieved when combined with Shoot4U. In the 1-VM case, performance of various schemes are comparable as the preemption rate is low when the system is not over-committed. However, Shoot4U still achieves about 20% performance improvement on dedup, which is the most TLB shootdown intensive workload. It is also notable that enabling PLE introduces about 10% overhead on x264 in this case.

Finally we reran the experiments from Section 3.1 in order to compare the reduction of synchronization overheads possible using Shoot4U and optimized spinlocks based on

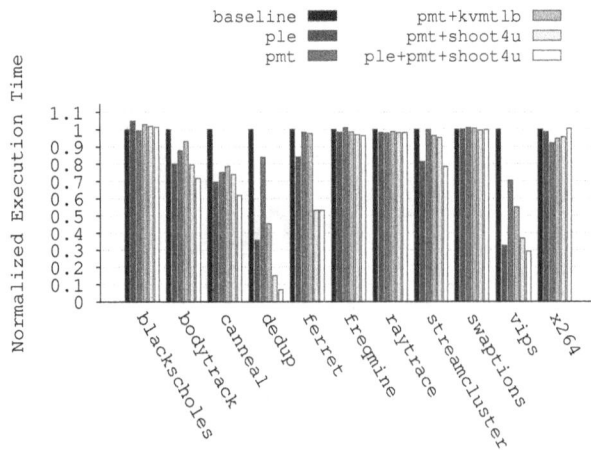

(a) With Competing VM (2-VMs)   (b) Without Competing VM (1-VM)

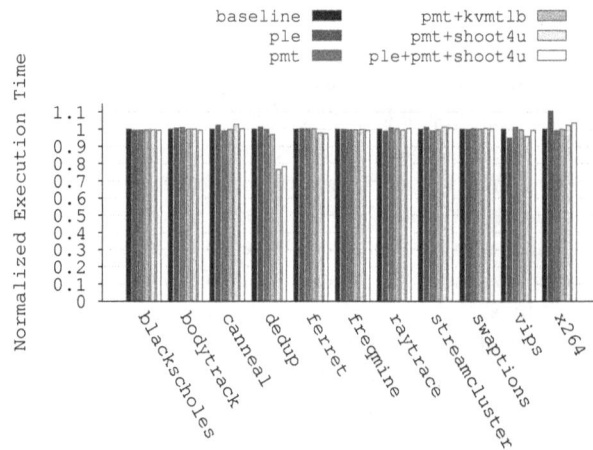

Figure 6: PARSEC Performance Evaluation with Shoot4U

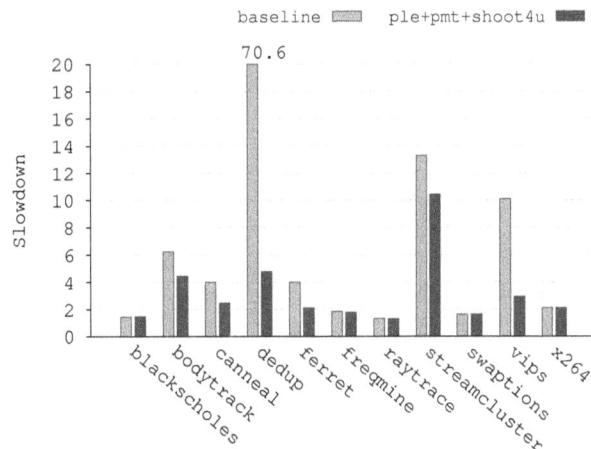

(a) Performance Slowdown of CPU Overcommitment   (b) CPU Usage Profiling

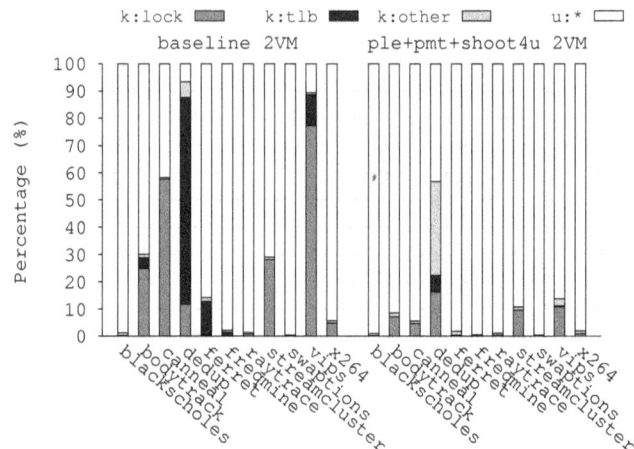

Figure 7: PARSEC Performance Analysis

PMT. Figure 7 (a) compares the slowdown of both the baseline and optimized configurations in the 2-VMs scenario. Significant performance improvement is observed on 6 out of the 11 benchmarks. For dedup and vips in particular, the slowdown decreases from 70.6 to 4.8 and from 10.1 to 2.9 respectively.

Figure 7 (b) provides a profile of the sources of overheads for the two configurations. There are significant reductions of kernel based overhead for all kernel intensive benchmarks, explaining the overall performance improvements for those benchmarks. Furthermore, for nearly every benchmark the time spent in TLB related functions is almost eliminated, with the exception of dedup which is still greatly reduced.

6. Conclusion

This paper presents Shoot4U, an approach to optimizing TLB operations across virtual CPUs allocated to a given virtual machine. We conducted a set of experiments in order to provide a breakdown of overheads caused by preempted virtual CPU cores, showing that TLB operations can have a significant impact on performance with certain workloads. To address that problem we introduced Shoot4U, an optimization for TLB shootdown operations that internalizes the operation in the VMM and so no longer requires the involvement of a guest's vCPUs. Our evaluation of Shoot4U demonstrates the effectiveness of our approach, and illustrates how under certain workloads our approach is dramatically better than current state of the art techniques.

References

[1] Linux Control Groups (cgroups). `https://www.kernel.org/doc/Documentation/cgroups/cgroups.txt`.

[2] Gartner Says Efficient Data Center Design Can Lead to 300 Percent Capacity Growth in 60 Percent Less Space. `http://www.gartner.com/newsroom/id/1472714`.

[3] ktap: A lightweight script-based dynamic tracing tool for Linux. `http://www.ktap.org/`.

[4] KVM Paravirt Remote Flush TLB. `https://lwn.net/Articles/500188/`.

[5] The PARSEC Benchmark Suite. `http://parsec.cs.princeton.edu/`.

[6] perf: Linux Profiling with Performance Counters. `https://perf.wiki.kernel.org/`.

[7] Sysbench. `https://github.com/akopytov/sysbench`.

[8] Vmware(r) vsphere(tm): The cpu scheduler in vmware esx(r) 4.1. Technical report, VMware, Inc, 2010.

[9] L. A. Barroso, J. Clidaras, and U. Hölzle. The Datacenter as a Computer: An Introduction to the Design of Warehouse-Scale Machines. *Synthesis Lectures on Computer Architecture*, 2013.

[10] X. Ding, P. B. Gibbons, M. A. Kozuch, and J. Shan. Gleaner: Mitigating the Blocked-Waiter Wakeup Problem for Virtualized Multicore Applications. In *Proc. 2014 USENIX Conference on USENIX Annual Technical Conference (USENIX ATC)*, Philadelphia, PA, June 2014. USENIX Association. URL `https://www.usenix.org/conference/atc14/technical-sessions/presentation/ding`.

[11] T. Friebel. How to Deal with Lock-Holder Preemption. Presented at the Xen Summit North America, 2008.

[12] J. Kaplan, W. Forrest, and N. Kindler. Revolutionizing Data Center Energy Efficiency. Technical report, McKinsey & Company, 2008.

[13] H. Kim, S. Kim, J. Jeong, J. Lee, and S. Maeng. Demand-based Coordinated Scheduling for SMP VMs. In *Proc. International Conference on Architectural Support for Programming Languages and Operating Systems (ASPLOS)*, 2013.

[14] D. Lo, L. Cheng, R. Govindaraju, P. Ranganathan, and C. Kozyrakis. Heracles: Improving Resource Efficiency at Scale. In *Proc. of the 42nd Annual International Symposium on Computer Architecture (ISCA)*, ISCA '15, 2015. . URL `http://doi.acm.org/10.1145/2749469.2749475`.

[15] J. Ousterhout. Scheduling Techniques for Concurrent Systems. In *Proc. 3rd International Conference on Distributed Computing Systems*, 1982.

[16] J. Ouyang and J. R. Lange. Preemptable Ticket Spinlocks: Improving Consolidated Performance in the Cloud. In *Proc. 9th ACM SIGPLAN/SIGOPS International Conference on Virtual Execution Environments (VEE)*, 2013.

[17] K. Raghavendra and J. Fitzhardinge. Paravirtualized ticket spinlocks, May 2012. URL `http://lwn.net/Articles/495597/`.

[18] C. Reiss, A. Tumanov, G. R. Ganger, R. H. Katz, and M. A. Kozuch. Heterogeneity and Dynamicity of Clouds at Scale: Google Trace Analysis. In *Proc. 3rd ACM Symposium on Cloud Computing (SoCC)*, 2012. ISBN 978-1-4503-1761-0. . URL `http://doi.acm.org/10.1145/2391229.2391236`.

[19] R. v. Riel. Directed yield for pause loop exiting, 2011. URL `http://lwn.net/Articles/424960/`.

[20] O. Sukwong and H. S. Kim. Is Co-scheduling Too Expensive for SMP VMs? In *Proc. 6th European Conference on Computer Systems (EuroSys)*, 2011.

[21] V. Uhlig, J. LeVasseur, E. Skoglund, and U. Dannowski. Towards Scalable Multiprocessor Virtual Machines. In *Proc. 3rd conference on Virtual Machine Research And Technology Symposium*, 2004.

[22] C. Weng, Q. Liu, L. Yu, and M. Li. Dynamic Adaptive Scheduling for Virtual Machines. In *Proc. 20th International Symposium on High Performance Parallel and Distributed Computing (HPDC)*, 2011.

[23] L. Zhang, Y. Chen, Y. Dong, and C. Liu. Lock-Visor: An Efficient Transitory Co-scheduling for MP Guest. In *Proc. 41st International Conference on Parallel Processing (ICPP)*, 2012.

Performance Implications of Extended Page Tables on Virtualized x86 Processors

Timothy Merrifield

University of Illinois at Chicago

tmerri4@uic.edu

H. Reza Taheri

VMware Inc.

rtaheri@vmware.com

Abstract

Managing virtual memory is an expensive operation, and becomes even more expensive on virtualized servers. Processing TLB misses on a virtualized x86 server requires a two-dimensional page walk that can have 6x more page table lookups, hence 6x more memory references, than a native page table walk. Thus much of the recent research on the subject starts from the assumption that TLB miss processing in virtual environments is significantly more expensive than on native servers. However, we will show that with the latest software stack on modern x86 processors, most of these page table lookups are satisfied by internal paging structure caches and the L1/L2 data caches, and the actual virtualization overhead of TLB miss processing is a modest fraction of the overall time spent processing TLB misses.

In this paper, we present a detailed accounting of the TLB miss processing costs on virtualized x86 servers for an exhaustive set of workloads, in particular, two very demanding industry standard workloads. We show that an implementation of the TPC-C workload that actively uses 475 GB of memory on a 72-CPU Haswell-EP server spends 20% of its time processing TLB misses when the application runs in a VM. Although this is a non-trivial amount, it is only 4.2% higher than the TLB miss processing costs on bare metal. The multi-VM VMmark benchmark sees 12.3% in TLB miss processing, but only 4.3% of that can be attributed to virtualization overheads. We show that even for the heaviest workloads, a well-tuned application that uses large pages on a recent OS release with a modern hypervisor running on the latest x86 processors sees only minimal degradation from the additional overhead of the two-dimensional page walks in a virtualized server.

Permission to make digital or hard copies of all or part of this work for personal or classroom use is granted without fee provided that copies are not made or distributed for profit or commercial advantage and that copies bear this notice and the full citation on the first page. Copyrights for components of this work owned by others than the author(s) must be honored. Abstracting with credit is permitted. To copy otherwise, or republish, to post on servers or to redistribute to lists, requires prior specific permission and/or a fee. Request permissions from Permissions@acm.org.

VEE '16, April 02-03, 2016, Atlanta, GA, USA

Copyright is held by the owner/author(s). Publication rights licensed to ACM.

ACM 978-1-4503-3947-6/16/04...$15.00

http://dx.doi.org/10.1145/2892242.2892258

1. Introduction

Much of the recent research in virtual memory management has focused on the increased cost of TLB miss processing in virtual environments, where the amount of work required to translate a (guest) virtual address can increase dramatically over native execution. In fact, in the worst case, the number of memory loads performed by the hardware page walker can increase by six times over native execution. Previous research has shown various benchmarks spend anywhere from 10-40% of cycles in TLB miss processing [2, 4, 7, 9, 15]. Anecdotally, we have observed a well-written commercial Java application on a SandyBridge CPU spend 40% of its cycles in TLB miss processing even after the application of usual optimization techniques to reduce the TLB miss processing costs. This application was an outlier, but shows that such rare cases do exist.

Given this apparent increase in TLB miss processing costs on virtualized systems, several proposals [9, 18, 19] have been made to lower the cost of TLB misses. Although innovative and effective, these proposals have generally been based on data collected on older hardware, SandyBridge or even Westmere class Intel processors [13], sometimes on dated software stacks, at times using 4K pages, and even occasionally with configurations that force the hypervisor to use 4KB pages when 2MB pages would normally be used absent memory overcommitment, etc.

The main contribution of this paper is showing that the additional TLB miss processing overhead of virtualized environments is actually a fraction of the overall TLB miss processing cost if one uses up-to-date hardware and software stacks. Even though TLB miss processing costs can be a significant component of CPI (cycles per instruction), and the costs are higher in a virtual environment, the difference in TLB miss processing costs between native and virtual is dropping with advances in address translation hardware and software. Despite the worst case 6x increase in memory loads [7], we will show a difference of only 3-5% between native and virtual servers for two very demanding, complex benchmarks that stress the TLB and spend 10-20% of the time in TLB miss processing.

We will document the TLB miss processing costs of both native and virtual cases across a large number of benchmarks. We start out with a micro-benchmark with well-understood characteristics. The micro-benchmark allows us to dial in a given TLB miss rate, profile it, and show how an EPT page walk adds to processing time. We then extend that to several CPU-intensive benchmark suites, and demonstrate only modest increases in address translation overhead across 49 programs from the Parsec[6], SPLASH-2[24] and SPEC CPU2006[10] benchmark suites. Finally, we use two demanding, industry-standard, Tier 1 benchmarks to show what real world applications experience. We do not know of previous research that has characterized the TLB miss processing costs for benchmarks such as full-fledged TPC-C [21] and VMmark [23].

Given the large cost of TLB miss processing, yet small contribution of virtualization to this cost, it is imperative for the research community to look for ways to extend the TLB reach and reduce the frequency and the cost of TLB misses across both native and virtual execution environments.

2. Background

Modern systems support virtual memory by providing a page table data structure for each process. The page table provides a mapping from a virtual address to an underlying physical address. To support a large 64-bit (and potentially quite sparse) virtual address space operating systems and x86 processors currently use a four-level hierarchical page table [13].

In this section we describe the process of address translation by way of the page table in detail as well as how x86 processors extend this approach to virtual environments.

2.1 Native address translation

To make use of virtual addresses, an x86 processor must first perform a virtual to physical address translation, referred to as a page table walk [5]. The page table has four levels, or five if we count the read of the CR3 register. In Intel parlance these levels (starting at L4) are referred to as PML4, PDPT, PD and PT.[1] Figure 1 details such an endeavor as well as the caching structures that reduce the latency of this operation. Putting these caches aside for now, the walk begins with the CR3 register (L5), which points to the root of the process' page table. The walk proceeds from there through the primary four levels, terminating early if the page table entry points to a 2MB page, or continuing through L1 in the case of a 4KB page (1GB size pages are omitted from the figure for simplicity). The page table itself is located in main memory and thus requires four memory loads (L4-L1).

To avoid frequent page table walks, the resulting translation (virtual address to physical address) is cached in the TLB for future use. TLB entries are typically flushed when the page table entry is modified or the entire TLB may

---

[1] We use both L1-L4 and the Intel names interchangeably throughout.

be flushed as the result of a context switch. When a TLB lookup misses, the subsequent page table walk can be short-circuited by the use of additional page structure caches. As shown in Figure 1 such caches are indexed by a smaller portion of the virtual address, thus caching a partial translation for a larger range of memory than the single page translation stored in the TLB. Providing separate caches for each level of the table is referred to as a Split Translation Cache architecture [2] and is used by Intel processors [13], though other designs are possible.

For example, an L3 page structure cache entry for a 4KB page handles a range of 1GB and reduces a page walk to two memory loads instead of four.

2.2 "Virtualizing" virtual memory

With respect to main memory, the hypervisor's goal of guest isolation and resource allocation is analogous to the operating system's goals vis à vis processes. In service to this objective, the hypervisor must provide an additional layer of virtualization between the guest operating system and the physical memory. Historically this problem has been solved either by using shadow page tables or through direct hardware support for virtualized address translation [22].

2.2.1 Software-Managed Shadow Page Tables

When using the shadow page table approach, the guest page tables are never accessed directly by the hardware. Instead, the hypervisor maintains separate page tables that provide the actual guest virtual address to host physical address mappings. In order to maintain the shadow page table, any modifications made by the guest kernel to a process's page table (a copy-on-write page fault for example) require a trap in to the hypervisor [8] - sometimes referred to as a VM exit. The high cost of frequent VM exits as well as the extra memory needed to maintain the shadow page tables led to a search for alternative designs [1].

2.2.2 Hardware Supported Virtual MMU

In this scheme the guest operating system kernel will provide a process with page tables that map guest virtual addresses (gVA) to guest physical addresses (gPA). In turn, these gPA's are mapped to host physical addresses (hPA) by the hypervisor's own page table. This two page table design leads to the so-called "two-dimensional" (2-D) page walk.

Through Intel's Extended Page Tables (EPT) [13] and AMD's Nested Page Tables (NPT) [5], x86 processors provide direct support for the virtualized approach described previously. Figure 2 summarizes the EPT mechanism (the design of NPT has many similarities). With EPT enabled (and once again ignoring the translation caches for now), the guest virtual address (gVA) to host physical address (hPA) translation begins at the gCR3, however, now the address stored in the register is a guest physical address (gPA) and needs to be translated to a hPA to be used by the hardware. This begins the first host-level walk, which begins at the

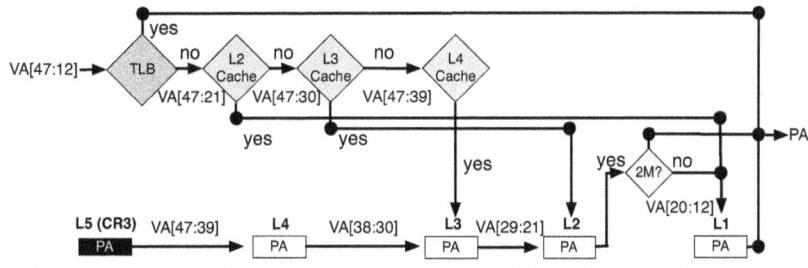

Figure 1. The x86 native page walk.

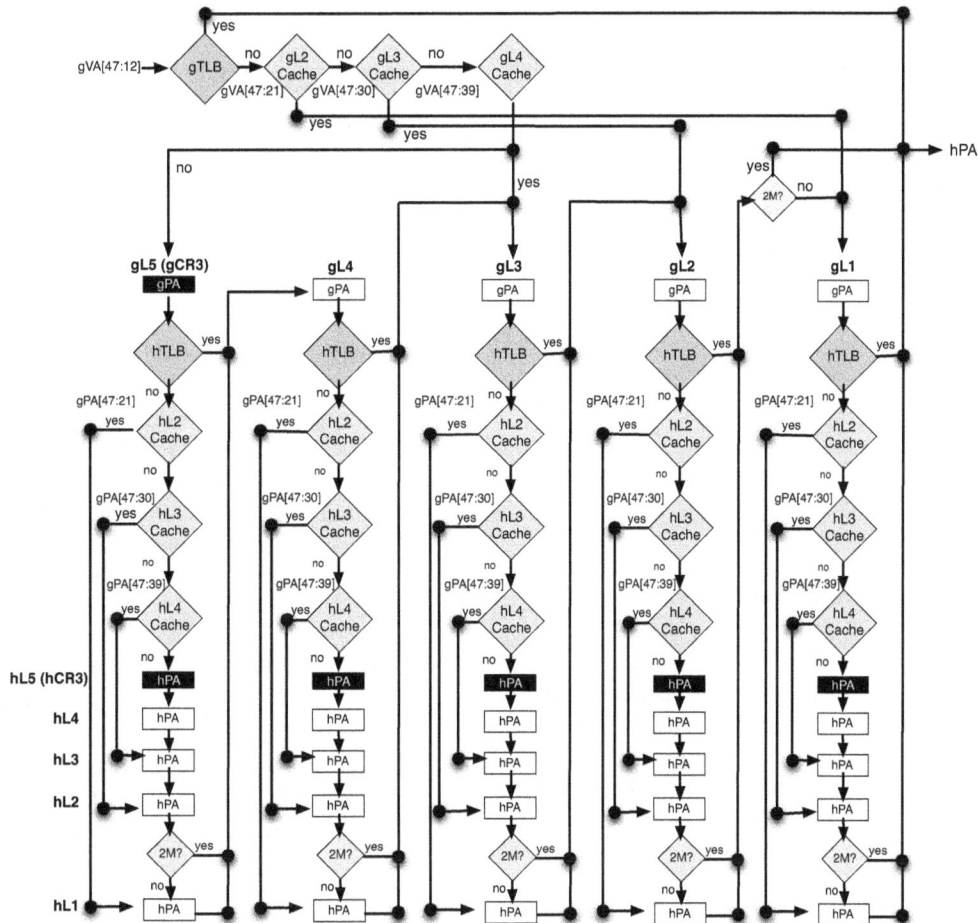

Figure 2. The x86 2-D (virtual) page walk.

hCR3; the register that points to the hypervisor's page table for the currently executing guest. The host-level walk is a maximum four level walk conceptually identical to the original native walk described in §2.1. The extra walk occurs for each gPA encountered in the guest-level walk and results in a maximum total of 24 memory loads when both guest and host are mapping at a 4KB granularity.

2.3 Reducing the length of the 2-D walk

The exorbitant length of the walk described above would render the two-dimensional design completely unusable if not for the help of the page structure caches and TLB [2, 13]. First, the guest-level TLB provides the full gVA to hPA address translation and thus avoids the need for any additional work. Second, the guest-level paging structure caches also store the gVA to hPA translation and can reduce the length of the guest-level walk, also eliminating the need to perform some host-level walks. And finally, the host-level walk itself also provides a set of paging structure caches to reduce the length of that walk. While it is also possible for the host-level to cache a full gPA to hPA translation

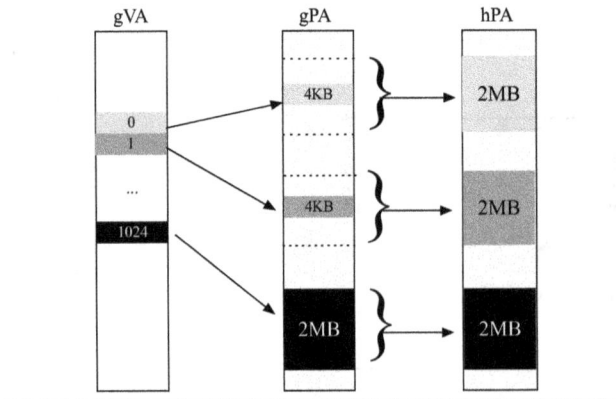

Figure 3. Guest and Host Page Mappings

via an hTLB, this cache is currently not employed by Intel processors supporting EPT.

Beyond the use of caches, mapping larger page granularities at both the guest and host level can further shorten the two-dimensional walk. For example, when translating an address mapped by 2MB pages at both the guest and host level, the worst-case page walk goes from 24 memory loads to 15. We will see in §4 that with page structure caches and larger granularity mappings, the length of the 2-D page walk is surprisingly short.

2.4 TLB Caching and Page Size

While using large page mappings can reduce TLB misses, in a virtualized environment both the guest and the host must map the page at 2MB to allow the processor to use a 2MB TLB entry. Figure 3 demonstrates this effect; with 4KB gVA regions backed at the guest-level by either 4KB pages (page 0 and 1) or 2MB pages (page 1024) and all pages backed at the host-level by 2MB pages. Clearly a 2MB TLB entry starting at page 0 is not possible as the physical memory backing pages 0 and 1 are non-contiguous. However, a 2MB TLB entry could be used for page 1024.

3. Experimental Setup

We survey the cost of 2-D TLB-miss processing using a mixture of microbenchmarks, well-known benchmark suites and more intensive "real world" programs. Our goal is an in-depth examination of virtualized address translation across a large swath of workloads.

Our primary testbed machine is a Dell PowerEdge R730 with two 2.30GHz 18-core Intel Processors Xeon E5-2699 v3 (Haswell-EP) and 512GB of memory. The system is running VMware ESXi vSphere Release 6.0, with a single guest (RHEL 7.1) using 64 virtual CPUs and 475GB of memory.

We didn't have access to a server with 18-core Haswell processors for the VMmark benchmark experiments. We used a secondary testbed machine with two E5-2687W v3 (Haswell-EP) processors with 10 cores per processor. All ex-

periments were executed with hyperthreading enabled. The E5-2687W v3 processor has fewer cores, a smaller L3 cache, and a higher clock rate than the E5-2699 v3 processor, but is otherwise identical to it.

3.1 Address Translation Hardware

	Page Size	*Haswell* Entries	*SandyBridge* Entries
L1 ITLB	4KB	128	128
L1 ITLB	2MB	8/thread	8/thread
L1 DTLB	4KB	64	64
L1 DTLB	2MB	32	32
L1 DTLB	1GB	4	4
L2 Unified	4KB	None	512
L2 Unified	4KB or 2MB	1024	None

Table 1. TLB characteristics

The SandyBridge processor is the *Tock* generation immediately preceding the Haswell microarchitecure, and is commonly used in studying TLB miss processing costs. Both Intel processors provide the EPT mechanism for virtualized address translation used by the hypervisor. Regarding TLB caches, Table 1 outlines the configurations for the Haswell and Sandybridge processors [12]. One notable difference between the two is that the unified second-level TLB on the Haswell supports both 4KB and 2MB page sizes. Beyond an increase in the size of the second-level TLB, the ability to cache both 4KB and 2MB translations makes a big difference in the effectiveness of the Haswell TLB for large page mappings.

3.2 Hardware Event Counters

For most of our analysis we relied on the Performance Monitoring Events provided by the processor [16]. The Linux perf(1) command with the stat option [20] was used to extract the hardware event counts. In the virtual case, we used two methods to access the hardware counters. The ESXi hypervisor has a feature that exposes the performance monitoring MSRs to the guest OS. This allowed us to use the same perf stat commands that were used in native. This method was especially useful in the single-VM experiments. For the multi-VM experiments and for some of the single-VM experiments, we also used the ESXi command vmkperf, which collects data for the entire server.

3.3 Virtual MMU Simulation

There are a number of EPT events we would like to measure that are not currently made available by the hardware. For example, the number of EPT walks or memory loads that occur per TLB-miss. In order to estimate these counts, we use a custom simulator built as a Pin [16] tool. The simulator models the address translation hardware, and uses its own gVA to gPA page tables for the guest portion of the walk. We base the page size in our simulation page tables on the actual

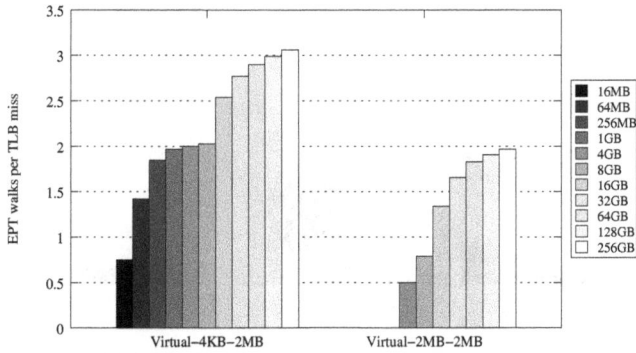

Figure 5. The average number of EPT walks that occur per TLB-miss *(from simulation)*.

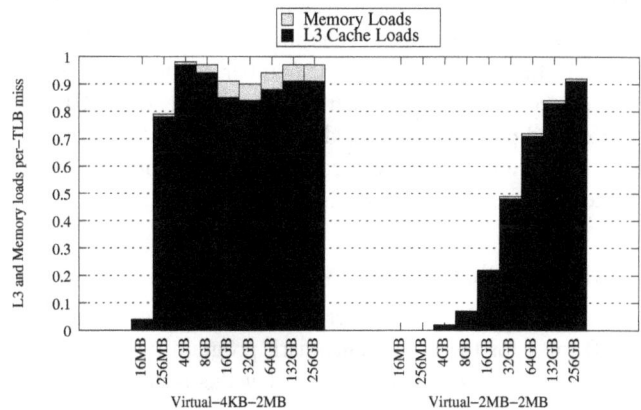

Figure 6. The average number of EPT loads that occur per TLB-miss for all EPT walks *(from simulation)*.

page size used in the program, detected by using a kernel module to walk the guest page table to determine page size. Our simulation tool is used to produce the results in §4.1.1 and §4.1.2.

4. Microbenchmark

We begin our analysis by looking at EPT performance on a simple microbenchmark program with straightforward semantics. Our program maps a variable sized memory segment as an array and performs a load and store to a random array index in a loop. As the segment grows larger, the working set will overwhelm the TLB and each operation will trigger a page walk. For this experiment we examine both native and virtual execution environments, as well as page mapping granularity at the guest and host level. We describe each configuration using the format: *(execution environment)-(page size)-(hypervisor page size)*. For example, Virtual-4KB-2MB indicates the experiment was done in a virtual environment with 4KB guest-level page mappings and 2MB host-level page mappings. All results are gathered from hardware performance counters unless specified as from simulation.

Figure 4 shows the TLB-miss processing cycles (lower is better) spent per operation (a memory load and store). The best performing variants here are those that use 2MB pages exclusively, whether executing in a native or virtual environment. For the virtual runs with 2MB mappings in the hypervisor, the percentage of cycles spent on the EPT portion of the walk is dependent on the mapping size in the guest. For example with a 64GB segment and 4KB pages in the guest, only 30% of TLB-miss cycles are spent on the EPT side.

Going forward we focus on the configuration where the hypervisor uses 2MB mappings, as this is the typical case in a virtual environment (see §5.2.1 for more discussion).

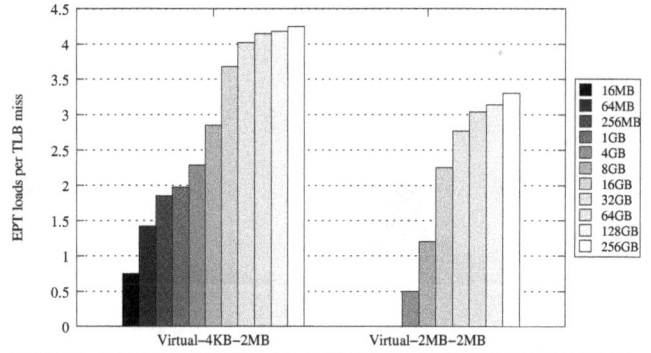

Figure 7. The average guest-level memory loads that hit the L3 cache or main memory per operation.

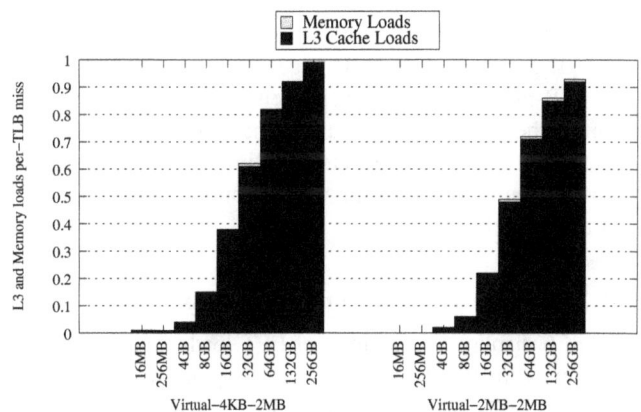

Figure 8. The average EPT-level memory loads that hit the L3 cache or main memory per operation.

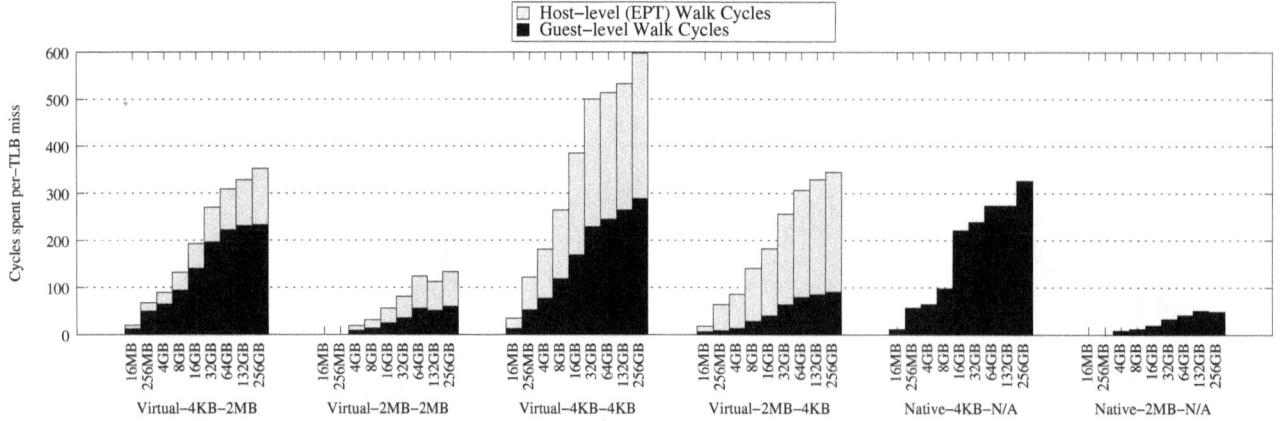

Figure 4. Cycles spent per TLB miss. The configuration names are in the format: *(execution environment)-(page size)-(hypervisor page size).*

4.1 Characterizing the EPT Walk

The amount of cycles spent in address translation for a given TLB miss depends on: (1) the number of EPT walks performed (this is equivalent to the number of guest-level loads performed by the page walker), (2) the number of EPT loads performed per EPT walk, and (3) the latency of each memory load. Here we analyze each of these factors in-turn to better understand the results in Figure 4.

4.1.1 Counting EPT-level walks

Figure 5 displays the number of EPT walks that occur per-TLB miss for the microbenchmark program under simulation (see §3.3). The number of EPT walks is determined by the hit-rate of the guest-level page structure caches and the size of the guest-level page mapping. For larger segments, the lower level (L1-L3) page structure caches will become overwhelmed, causing the walk to begin with either a hit in the L4 cache or even a read of the gCR3 register. On the other hand, the guest-level page mapping will determine when the walk will terminate (one level sooner if 2MB pages are used). For example, for our microbenchmark program a 64GB segment with 2MB pages performs 2 EPT walks per TLB-miss. The most likely scenario for such a result is a hit in the gL4 page structure cache resulting in gL3 and gL2 walks. The cache-hit rates are similar with 4KB pages at 64GB, but because of the 4KB mapping it performs one extra EPT walk.

4.1.2 Counting EPT-level memory loads

Figure 6 displays the number of EPT loads that occur per-TLB miss for the microbenchmark program under simulation (see §3.3). The maximum number of loads that occur for a 2MB segment is just over 3, while for 4KB segments it is just over 4. If we once again examine the results for the 64GB segment and 2MB pages, we see that the 3 loads occur within 2 EPT walks (as described in §4.1.1).

The first walk (gL3) will attempt to translate a guest physical address pointing to the L2 paging structure - a guest kernel address. Given that the entire page table of the 64GB segment can fit in less than 2MB of physical memory, this means that the gL3 walk should normally begin with a hit in the hL3 cache, resulting in just a single load.

The second walk (gL2) will translate the final guest physical address and thus spans over 64GB of guest physical address space, resulting in two loads assuming a hit in the hL4 cache.

Combining the EPT-level loads with the number of guest-level loads (one for each EPT walk), the maximum number of memory accesses incurred by the page walker are approximately 5 and 7 for 2MB and 4KB page sizes respectively.

4.2 Page walker memory loads

The latency of address translation is greatly impacted by where a particular load hits in the memory hierarchy. Here we focus our analysis on the memory loads that impact the TLB miss latency the most: those that hit in the L3 data cache or in main memory.

Figure 7 shows the average number of L3 data cache or memory loads per operation for the guest-level (native) portion of the walk. With a 64GB segment and 2MB pages, there are normally five total loads: two loads at the guest-level (§4.1.1) and three at the EPT-level (§4.1.2). One of those loads goes beyond the L2 data cache 70% of the time, and rarely hits memory.

With 4KB pages, the page tables will be significantly larger and can potentially overwhelm the data caches. However, we've noticed that the performance counters used in Figure 7 seem to be undercounting the number of page walker loads that hit main memory. For example, with a 256GB segment and 4KB pages we would expect a guest-level page table that is over 512MB in size and thus would expect a larger proportion of page walker loads missing the cache hierarchy. That expectation also correlates with the re-

30

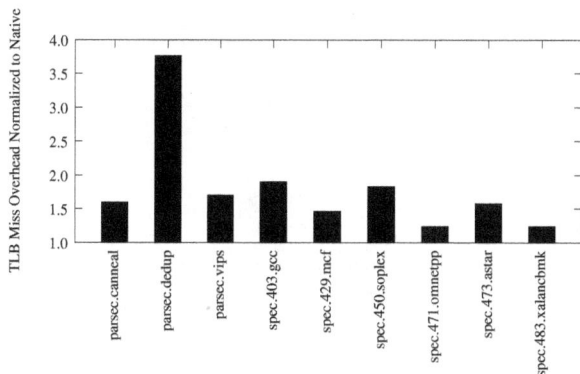

Figure 10. TLB miss overhead on virtual normalized to native

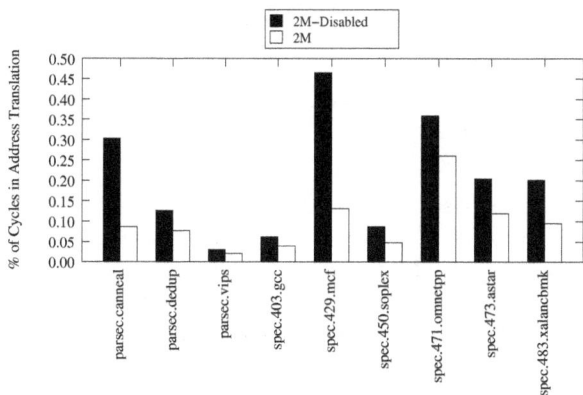

Figure 11. TLB miss overhead on virtual (with 4KB pages in the hypervisor) normalized to native

sults in Figure 4, where a difference in hundreds of cycles separates Virtual-4KB-2MB and Virtual-2MB-2MB at large segment sizes.

Figure 8 shows the average number of L3 data cache or memory loads per operation for the EPT portion of the walk. As we can see, the average number of loads that go beyond the L2 data cache is under 1 for both guest-level page sizes.

5. Evaluation

5.1 CPU-bound benchmarks

In order to better understand the cost of address translation in a virtual environment, we ran all programs from the Parsec [6], SPLASH-2 [24] and SPEC CPU2006 [10] benchmark suites. We executed the multi-threaded benchmarks using *pthreads* with 16 threads and ran all programs 20 times. The standard deviation for the relevant event counters was less than 5% for all programs.

The results shown in Figure 9 demonstrate that out of 49 benchmark programs, only six programs spend more than 5% of their cycles in TLB-miss processing even when exe-

cuting virtually. Figure 10 shows the average TLB miss cycles normalized to native for all 9 programs that spend more than one percent of their cycles on address translation. We can see that for all but one program the increase is between 1.25x and 1.9x. For *dedup*, the added virtualized execution overhead is caused by a dramatic increase in the number of TLB misses, particularly for instructions that never retire.

However, the important conclusion to draw from the results in Figure 9 is that only a single program experiences greater than a 2x increase in address translation cycles across nearly 50 programs.

The results in Figure 9 and Figure 10 use 2MB mappings at the hypervisor level and thus benefit from the reduced TLB pressure, smaller page tables and shorter EPT-level walks. Figure 11 shows the increase in TLB miss processing with 2MB mappings disabled in the hypervisor. The cost increases dramatically for some programs like *mcf*, which experience a 4.3x increase in TLB misses.

5.2 Database Benchmark Analysis

We implemented the TPC-C [21] workload on Oracle 12c R1. The results presented in this paper are not indicative of the absolute performance of Oracle DBMS. The benchmark used was a non-compliant implementation of TPC-C workload, and the results cannot be compared to published TPC-C results. We used the TPC-C on Oracle benchmark as a workload to exercise the address translation subsystem, not to report absolute database performance results.

We populated 32000 warehouses in a 3.8TB database on 72 SSDs. The DBMS shared memory segment, most of which is used for caching disk blocks, was 430GB. We ran with 600 threads of execution, and drove both native and virtual configurations to 85% CPU utilization.

This test is representative of the most demanding real world Tier 1 applications on large servers. Even when system-level benchmarks such as TPC benchmarks have been used in previous research [3, 4], it had been with small databases, which are easily cacheable and not representative of real world applications. Our implementation of TPC-C with 32000 warehouses resulted in 155K storage IOPS, 127K networking packets/second, 285K context switches/sec, and a load average of 311. Saturating the server required 600 processes, which place a heavy load on the TLB. The demands of this benchmark set it apart from the TLB micro-benchmark and the much simpler SPLASH-2, SPEC CPU, and PARSEC benchmarks.

Table 2 lists the processor event counts relevant to TLB miss processing. Each column is average of 5 runs at 85% CPU utilization for the native and the virtual cases, with virtual running at 90% of the native throughput. Here are the take-aways:

1. The overall time spent in TLB miss processing (the 3 WALK_DURATION events) is 15.4% of total cycles in native, 19.6% in virtual. The 4.2% increase is corrobo-

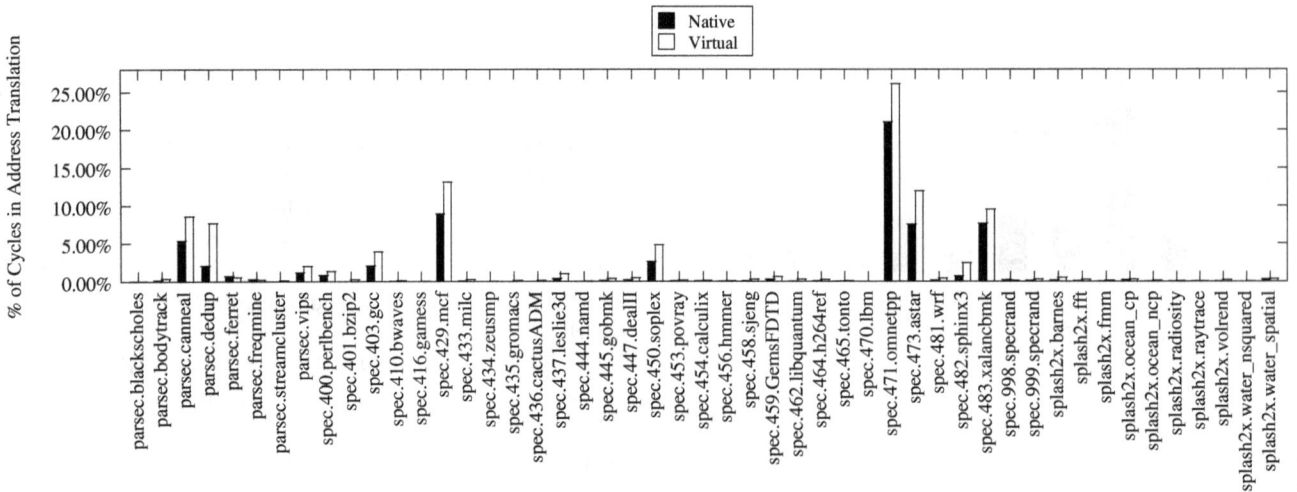

Figure 9. Average cycles spent in TLB-miss processing in Parsec[6], SPLASH-2[24] and SPEC CPU2006[10]

rated by the 5.4% of total time in EPT walk cycles in the virtual case.

2. The rise in LLC references is 13K/tran. The total TLB miss count is 10K/tran. Even if we ignore the contributions of the hypervisor to this rise, this means an upper bound of 1.3 LLC accesses/tran due to EPT page table lookups. Similarly, there is an increase of only 1.5K LL3 misses/memory accesses per tran, implying that most of the LLC accesses due to EPT are hits.

Previous research [7] had identified the cycles in EPT as the major contributor to a large overhead when virtualizing the TPC-C workload. That investigation had used an ESXi 5.5/RHEL 6.1/Oracle 11i software stack on Westmere processors. The results in this paper were observed on an ESXi 6.0/RHEL 7.1/Oracle 12c software stack on Haswell processors. Although we observed a significant drop in both the overall virtualization overhead and the percentage of cycles in EPT in comparison to results in [7], EPT cycles are still responsible for about half of the overhead we observed for TPC-C.

5.2.1 Effects of Page Splintering

Modern hypervisors typically use host 2MB pages to map guest pages of any size. However, the hypervisor may choose to splinter a host 2M page into its constituent 4K pages to facilitate its own operations. The common cases for ESXi are:

1. To estimate the size of a VM's working set, ESXi keeps a running count of touched pages, by choosing 100 pages per VM per minute, and tracking accesses to them for 4 minutes. This sampling is done on a 4K-page basis, so any selected large page has to be splintered first. So, theoretically, as many as 400 large pages with 800MB of data may have been splintered. If the number of splin-

tered pages approaches this worst-case upper bound, it could make a noticeable impact on a VM with a small memory allocation of a few GB.

2. The hypervisor may choose to splinter a large page to facilitate some other functionality. Examples are preparing a VM for Live Migration, ballooning in the VM to avoid swapping under memory pressure [13], swapping in the host under memory pressure, and migration of memory between NUMA nodes. But it is important to note that all of these conditions are a) unusual, and not expected in the normal course of execution; and b) transient, e.g., after live migration completes, the VM's large pages are reconstituted on the target machine.

3. Transparent Page Sharing: Although theoretically pages of any size may be shared among VMs, small pages are most likely to have matching checksums, and calculating a checksum for small pages is much cheaper. So the hypervisor only allows sharing of 4K pages. It is important to note that the hypervisor does not splinter large pages to facilitate page sharing. The user has to explicitly disable the use of large pages for a VM to make all of the VM's memory (not just the pages that had happened to map to small host pages) eligible for page sharing. So, the user has to make a conscious trade-off between performance and saving memory.

Of all these possibilities of splintering, only working set sampling may impact a VM on a continual basis and without an explicit decision on the user's part. So, we disabled sampling on ESXi, and re-ran TPC-C. As expected for a VM with 475GB of memory and no memory pressure, the results in Figure 12 show that removal of page sampling had little impact on most performance metrics, and no impact on TPC-C throughput.

Event	Oracle TPC-C on **2.3GHz CPU**		VMmark on *3.1GHz CPU*
Hardware event	*Native*	*Virtual*	*Virtual*
INST_RETIRED.ANY	727.76	710.28	1,338.10
CPU_CLK_UNHALTED.THREAD	2,352.00	2,338.95	2,867.48
CPU_CLK_UNHALTED.REF_TSC	1,968.46	1,957.51	2,782.37
DTLB_LOAD_MISSES.WALK_DURATION	163.09	233.21	237.26
DTLB_LOAD_MISSES.WALK_COMPLETED	1.78	1.79	1.84
EPT.WALK_CYCLES	0.00	126.20	124.09
DTLB_LOAD_MISSES.PDE_CACHE_MISS	1.52	1.54	1.32
DTLB_STORE_MISSES.WALK_DURATION	24.11	37.02	29.79
DTLB_STORE_MISSES.WALK_COMPLETED	0.27	0.27	0.23
DTLB_STORE_MISSES.PDE_CACHE_MISS	0.20	0.21	0.21
ITLB_MISSES.WALK_DURATION	175.16	189.36	83.04
ITLB_MISSES.WALK_COMPLETED	1.84	1.67	0.87
PAGE_WALKER_LOADS.DTLB_L1	1.01	1.02	1.24
PAGE_WALKER_LOADS.DTLB_L2	0.47	0.47	0.44
PAGE_WALKER_LOADS.DTLB_L3	1.30	1.24	1.15
PAGE_WALKER_LOADS.DTLB_MEMORY	0.08	0.07	0.13
PAGE_WALKER_LOADS.ITLB_L1	1.02	0.99	0.68
PAGE_WALKER_LOADS.ITLB_L2	0.35	0.32	0.18
PAGE_WALKER_LOADS.ITLB_L3	0.70	0.62	0.28
PAGE_WALKER_LOADS.ITLB_MEMORY	0.13	0.13	0.04
LONGEST_LAT_CACHE.REFERENCE	58.65	58.94	41.26
LONGEST_LAT_CACHE.MISS	5.59	5.44	9.21

Table 2. Detailed Performance Event Counts in *Millions of events per second*

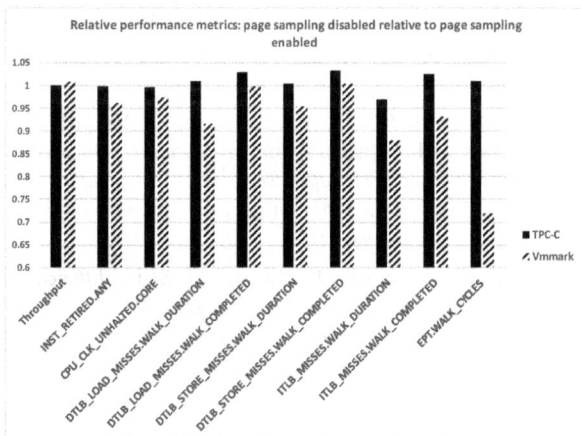

Figure 12. Disabling sampling of the working set avoids splintering large pages, and can result in improved performance

5.3 VMmark Analysis

All the earlier results in this section were with a single VM, which allows for native-virtual comparisons. But that is not a realistic use of virtualized servers. To study a realistic, multi-VM configuration, we used the VMmark benchmark [23], with is the de facto industry-standard benchmark for multi-VM server consolidation. Virtualization-specific benchmarks such as VMmark are unique in that there is no native equivalent to compare to. But we can still see the effects of two-dimensional page walks by looking at the events that measure the time in TLB miss processing.

Table 2 lists the averages of 22 collections of processor event counts relevant to TLB miss processing. The overall time in TLB miss processing is 12.3% of the total time, of which 4.3% is in EPT processing. Without matching native results, it is not possible to tease apart how much of the L3 and memory accesses are due to EPT. However, the low percentage in EPT suggests that most EPT accesses must be satisfied from L1/L2/L3 data caches.

5.3.1 Effects of Page Splintering

The VMmark benchmark has small VMs, over half of which are only 2GB in size. Thus, it sees a larger impact than TPC-C from working set sampling by the hypervisor. When we disabled the sampling, we saw a 33% drop in time in EPT cycles, and a corresponding drop in the sum of the TLB WALK DURATION events. The reduction in TLB miss processing cycles amounted to around 1% of the total CPU cycles per second. This drop explains the 0.8% increase in throughput as depicted in Figure 12. This is a much lower difference than noted in previous research [18].

6. Related Work

Some of the recent research has focused on avoiding the TLB miss altogether [2][4][9] by various schemes to use mappings that are larger than the native processor page sizes. Speculation is a common theme among this group [3], as is prefetching [5][14]. Page splintering has been the focus of some research although as we have shown here it may not as large a problem as reported in [18][19]. Redundant Memory Mappings in [15] uses a single TLB entry to translate a range of contiguous virtual addresses to a contiguous physical addresses. Such a scheme would benefit native and virtual environments similarly, which is the type of approach we advocate (as opposed to focusing on the additional overhead in virtual).

A recent paper showed a large drop in performance for TPC-C due to the overheads of two-dimensional page walks [7]. Although our results are similar to those in [7], we show that using more recent hardware and updated software results in a large reduction in this overhead. Large pages make a drastic impact on the TLB miss processing costs [11][17][18][20], but with memory sizes growing exponentially, and TLB sizes growing linearly, even a move to 1GB page won't be enough to avoid the TLB miss processing costs.

7. Conclusion

We have demonstrated, using an exhaustive set of workloads, that the performance impact of virtualization on TLB misses is not nearly as severe as one might expect. While the worst-case path through EPT seems prohibitively high, modern processors with larger TLBs and page structure caches at both the native and EPT levels substantially reduce the performance penalty.

Nonetheless, managing virtual memory remains expensive, and will only worsen with larger, multi-TB servers becoming mainstream while most x86 hardware and software stacks still use 4KB and 2MB pages. The memory size of servers is growing exponentially while the number of TLB entries grows linearly, and the dominant page sizes have not changed. Just as in a native execution environment, the most effective strategy for keeping address translation costs low in a virtualized system is avoiding the TLB miss in the first place.

8. Acknowledgements

We thank the anonymous reviewers for their detailed and insightful comments and feedback on the paper. The following individuals contributed to our work by running experiments, answering questions, or reviewing the analysis: Fei Guo, Bruce Herndon, Michael Ho, Seongbeom Kim, Jim Mattson, Sajjid Reza, Vish Viswanathan, and James Zubb.

References

[1] K. Adams and O. Agesen, "A comparison of software and hardware techniques for x86 virtualization," in *Proceedings of the 12th international conference on Architectural support for programming languages and operating systems (ASPLOS)*, 2006.

[2] T. Barr, A. Cox, and S. Rixner, *Translation Caching: Skip, Don't Walk the Page Table*, in *Proceedings of the 37th annual international symposium on computer architecture(ISCA)*, 2010.

[3] ——, *SpecTLB: A Mechanism for Speculative Address Translation*, in *Proceedings of the 38th annual international symposium on computer architecture (ISCA)*, 2011.

[4] A. Basu, J. Gandhi, J. Chang, M. Hill, and M. Swift, *Efficient Virtual Memory for Big Memory Servers*, in *Proceedings of the 39th annual international symposium on computer architecture (ISCA)*, 2012.

[5] R. Bhargava, B. Serebrin, F. Spadini, and S. Manne, *Accelerating two-dimensional page walks for virtualized systems*, in *Proceedings of the 13th international conference on Architectural support for programming languages and operating systems (ASPLOS)*, 2008.

[6] C. Bienia, S. Kumar, J. P. Singh, and K. Li, *The PARSEC benchmark suite: characterization and architectural implications*, in *Proceedings of the 17th international conference on Parallel architectures and compilation techniques (PACT) 2008*, 2008.

[7] J. Buell, D. Hecht, J. Heo, K. Saladi, and H. R. Taheri, *Methodology for Performance Analysis of VMware vSphere under Tier-1 Applications*, in *VMware Technical Journal*, 2013.

[8] X. Chang, H. Franke, Y. Ge, T. Liu, K. Wang, J. Xenidis, F. Chen, and Y. Zhang, *Improving Virtualization in the Presence of Software Managed Translation Lookaside Buffers*, in *Proceedings of the 40th annual international symposium on computer architecture (ISCA)*, 2013.

[9] J. Gandhi, A. Basu, M. Hill, and M. Swift, *Efficient Memory Virtualization: Reducing Dimensionality of Nested Page Walks*, in *Proceedings of the 47th Annual IEEE/ACM International Symposium on Microarchitecture (MICRO-47)*, 2014.

[10] J. L. Henning and SPEC, "benchmark descriptions, in ACM SIGARCH Computer Architecture News," vol. 34, Sep. 2006.

[11] J. Huck and J. Hays, *Architectural support for translation table management in large address space machines*, in *Proceedings of the 20th annual international symposium on computer architecture (ISCA)*, 1993.

[12] Intel, *Intel 64 and IA-32 Architectures Optimization Reference Manual*, 2015.

[13] ——, *Intel 64 and IA-32 Architectures Software Developer's Manual*, 2015.

[14] B. Jacob and T. Mudge, *Uniprocessor virtual memory without TLBs*, in *IEEE Transactions on Computers (Volume:50, Issue: 5)*, May 2001.

[15] V. Karakostas, J. Gandhi, F. Ayar, A. Cristal, M. Hill, K. McKinley, M. Nemirovsky, M. Swift, and O. Unsal, *Redun-*

dant Memory Mappings for Fast Access to Large Memories, in Proceedings of the 45thth annual international symposium on computer architecture (ISCA), 2015.

[16] C.-K. Luk, R. Cohn, R. Muth, H. Patil, A. Klauser, G. Lowney, S. Wallace, V. J. Reddi, and K. Hazelwood, "Pin: Building customized program analysis tools with dynamic instrumentation," in *Proceedings of the 2005 ACM SIGPLAN Conference on Programming Language Design and Implementation,* ser. PLDI '05. New York, NY, USA: ACM, 2005, pp. 190–200. [Online]. Available: http://doi.acm.org/10.1145/1065010.1065034

[17] J. Navarr, S. Iyer, P. Druschel, and A. Cox, *Practical, transparent operating system support for superpages, Proceedings of the 5th symposium on Operating systems design and implementation (OSDI) 2012,* 2012.

[18] B. Pham, J. Vesely, G. H. Loh, and A. Bhattacharjee, *Large Pages and Lightweight Memory Management in Virtualized Environments: Can You Have it Both Ways?, in Proceedings of the 48th Annual IEEE/ACM International Symposium on Microarchitecture (MICRO-48),* 2015.

[19] ——, *Using TLB Speculation to Overcome Page Splintering in Virtual Machines, in Rutgers University Technical Report DCS-TR-713,* Mar. 2015.

[20] T. H. Romer, W. H. Ohlrich, A. R. Karlin, and B. N. Bershad, *Reducing TLB and Memory Overhead Using Online Superpage Promotion, in Proceedings of the 22th annual international symposium on computer architecture (ISCA),* 1995.

[21] D. T.-C. D. TPC, *http://www.tpc.org/tpcc/detail.asp.*

[22] VMware, *Understanding Full Virtualization, Paravirtualization, and Hardware Assist.* [Online]. Available: https://www.vmware.com/files/pdf/VMware_paravirtualization.pdf

[23] ——, *VMmark Benchmark 2.* [Online]. Available: http://www.vmware.com/products/vmmark

[24] S. C. Woo, M. Ohara, E. Torrie, J. P. Singh, and A. Gupta, *The SPLASH-2 programs: characterization and methodological considerations,* 1995.

On Selecting the Right Optimizations for Virtual Machine Migration

Senthil Nathan, Umesh Bellur *, and Purushottam Kulkarni

Department of Computer Science and Engineering, IIT Bombay
{cendhu,umesh,puru}@cse.iitb.ac.in

Abstract

To reduce the migration time of a virtual machine and network traffic generated during migration, existing works have proposed a number of optimizations to pre-copy live migration. These optimizations are delta compression, page skip, deduplication, and data compression. The cost-benefit analysis of these optimizations may preclude the use of certain optimizations in specific scenarios. However, no study has compared the *performance* & *cost* of these optimizations, and identified the *impact of application behaviour* on performance gain. Hence, it is not clear for a given migration scenario and an application, what is the best optimization that one must employ?

In this paper, we present a comprehensive empirical study using a large number of workloads to provide recommendations on selection of optimizations for pre-copy live migration. The empirical study reveals that page skip is an important optimization as it reduces network traffic by 20% with negligible additional CPU cost. Data compression yields impressive gains in reducing network traffic (37%) but at the cost of a significant increase in CPU consumption ($5\times$). Deduplication needs to be applied with utmost care as the increase in CPU utilization might outweigh the benefits considerably. The combination of page skip and data compression works the best across workloads and results in a significant reduction in network traffic (40%).

1. Introduction

Live virtual machine (VM) migration [5] enables the movement of a VM from one physical server to another while the VM is executing. The migration process achieves this by transferring both memory pages and execution state of the VM. As VM's execution modifies memory state, memory pages are transferred over multiple iterations. After a certain number of iterations, the migration process suspends the VM's execution to transfer the residual pages and execution state. The performance metrics of migration are *migration time* (the time taken to complete the migration), *downtime* (the duration for which the VM is suspended), and *network traffic* (the amount of data transferred).

A data center employs VM migration for various management tasks including mitigating resource hotspots on an overloaded server [24], and evacuating a server for software/hardware upgradation. In each of these cases, an important requirement is to perform VM migration quickly. Further, it is necessary to reduce the network traffic generated during migration as this can cause performance degradation in other VMs [18]. Existing works [9, 18, 22, 23] have proposed various optimizations to reduce the migration time and network traffic. These optimizations are (i) delta compression—send only the modified page content instead of the entire page, (ii) deduplication—avoids the transfer of duplicate and zero pages, (iii) page skip—avoids transferring frequently dirtied pages, and (iv) data compression—compress pages by exploiting word level duplicate.

These optimizations come at the cost of increased CPU and memory utilization. The additional resources consumed by the migration process may become harmful in scenarios such as when the migration is being used to mitigate a resource hotspot. For example, employing page skip, data compression and deduplication during migration can increase the CPU utilization by $18\times$. Hence, all optimizations cannot be blindly applied to every migration scenario. A thorough understanding of the relation between *performance* and *cost* is necessary to decide a specific optimization that will yield more benefit than harm for a given scenario.

Further, the improvement in migration performance with each optimization is dependent on the application behaviour. Application behavior that may impact the performance gain (as identified in this paper) are page dirty characteristics — (page dirty frequency & page dirty rate), disk read/write rate, maximum writable working set size [17], and page content similarity. For example, if an application typically modifies most content of a page, employing an optimization which painstakingly sends only the modified portion of a page is overkill, and results in wastage of resources. To maximize

---

* Currently on a sabbatical and with Purdue University

VEE '16, April 02-03, 2016, Atlanta, GA, USA.
Copyright © 2016 ACM 978-1-4503-3947-6/16/04... $15.00.
http://dx.doi.org/10.1145/2892242.2892247

the performance gain and reduce resource cost, we need to select a suitable combination of optimizations with respect to a given application behaviour and migration scenario.

However, nowhere in the current literature, we have found evidence of such a study that: (a) understands how application behavior impacts the performance gain achieved by each otimization, and (b) provides a detailed *cost-benefit* analysis of different optimizations (which can aid us to select suitable optimizations for a given migration scenario such as hotspot mitigation). Our goal is to perform such a study. Specifically, the three major contributions of our study are:

1. A detailed empirical evaluation of four existing optimizations for pre-copy live migration that (i) quantifies the *performance* and *cost* using 294 migration instances (over 42 workloads[1]), and (ii) correlates application behaviour with the performance gain of optimizations.

2. Discovery of a new optimization component called **false dirty page** that helps in (i) identifying the impact of application behaviour on the performance gain, and (ii) finding the best optimization.

3. Recommendations on (i) how to combine various optimizations for reducing the impact of application behaviour, and the resource cost; (ii) which optimizations to employ for various migration scenarios.

The rest of the paper is structured as follows: Section 2 provides a background on vanilla live migration, describes existing optimizations, and motivates an empirical study. Section 3 explains our experimental methodology and expectations on the performance of existing optimizations. Section 4 empirically evaluates each optimization to understand the performance and cost tradeoff as well as relation between application behaviour and optimizations. Section 5 utilizes insights from empirical study to propose appropriate combinations of various optimizations. Section 6 lists a set of guidelines on the usage of these optimizations for various migration scenarios while section 7 concludes the paper.

2. Background

In this section, first, we provide background for vanilla pre-copy live migration technique and existing optimization techniques that improve its performance. Next, we motivate a comprehensive empirical study.

2.1 Vanilla Pre-Copy Live Migration

Pre-copy live migration [5] involves two phases—iterative pre-copy and stop-and-copy.

Iterative Pre-Copy Phase. Since an active VM can modify content stored in memory, the migration process transfers memory pages allocated to the VM over multiple iterations. In the first iteration, all memory pages are transferred to the destination server. In later iterations, memory pages that are modified (*a.k.a* dirtied) during the previous iterations are transferred. In order to identify dirtied pages, all pages al-

[1] The migration codes and logs are available at https://goo.gl/Ikycz9

Table 1. Performance gain as reported in literature. **MT**: Migration Time, **NT**: Network Traffic, —: not evaluated.

| Techniques | Workload | Reduction in | | additional |
		MT	**NT**	**CPU**
Delta Comp. [22]	LMbench	26%	—	0%
	SAP ERP	40%	—	
Page Skip [18]	RUBiS	30%	30%	—
	Kernel Compile	48%	48%	
Sub Page Dedup. [23]	Kernel Compile	15%	15%	—
	TPC-W	20%	20%	
Data Comp. [9]	MUMer	39%	48%	30%
	dbench	39%	80%	

located to the VM are marked as read only by the hypervisor before starting an iteration. As a result, a trap is generated when the VM tries to modify its memory content. The hypervisor, on receiving this trap, marks the corresponding pages as dirtied and provides write permission to the VM for that page (i.e., only the first write to a page is trapped during the course of an iteration). As the change in memory state is a continuous process for an active VM, the migration process employs the stop-and-copy phase.

Stop-and-Copy Phase. In this phase, the execution of VM is suspended to transfer all pages dirtied during the final pre-copy iteration and also the hardware state associated with the VM. The shift from iterative pre-copy phase to stop-and-copy phase occurs when certain pre-defined condition is satisfied at the end of an iteration. The migration process stops iterative pre-copy phase if the progress across two iterations is insufficient [19], i.e., the number of pages dirtied does not reduce by over 10%.

2.2 Optimizing Pre-Copy Live Migration

In this section, we explain the details of the four existing optimizations for pre-copy live migration, (i) delta compression [22], (ii) page skip [18], (iii) deduplication [23], and (iv) data compression [9]. For all optimizations, pages are considered one at a time, the optimization is applied, and then the page is transferred to the destination server. There are techniques [4, 8, 10, 12] which improve migration performance by avoiding the transfer of free pages and buffer caches but it requires guest OS modifications. Hence, we have omitted them from our study.

(1) Delta Compression. In every pre-copy iteration, instead of transferring the entire content of a dirtied page, the delta compression technique [22] transfers only the modified content of a page (called page delta—termed del as part of our study). To find the exact modified portion of a page, delta compression stores the content of the page in a cache before its transmission in an iteration. In the next iteration, while transferring a dirtied page, the migration process performs a bitwise XOR operation between the cached content of that page and the current content. Performing run length

Table 2. Components accounted in each optimization, parameters affecting the performance, and cost metrics.

Techniques	Account for								Parameters	Cost
	dirty characteristics			*content characteristics*						
	fdp	del	hdp	zp	szp	dup	sdup	wld		
Delta Comp. [22]	✓	✓							Cache size	CPU, Memory
Page Skip [18]	✓		✓						Build Frequency	CPU
Full Page Dedup. [23]	✓			✓		✓			—	CPU
Sub Page Dedup. [23]	✓	✓		✓	✓	✓	✓		Page Granularity	CPU, Memory
Data Comp. [9]				✓	✓			✓	—	CPU

encoding on XORed data results in a compressed page. Before transferring the compressed page, the cached content is replaced with the current content. On the destination server, the page content is updated by performing bitwise XOR between the received and stored content.

(2) Page Skip. A virtual machine can have memory pages that are modified frequently (called hot dirty pages—hdp). The page skip technique [18] avoids transferring frequently dirtied pages to improve the performance of migration. During an iteration, if pages that are scheduled for transfer are dirtied before their transmission, the page skip technique expects these pages to get dirtied again. Hence, after transferring every m pages in an iteration, the migration process retrieves the dirty bitmap to skip all dirtied pages that are yet to be transferred in the current iteration. The work in [17] establishes an analytical performance model for page skip.

(3) Deduplication. This technique [23] identifies and transfers only one copy of duplicate content to the destination server. Content similarity can be identified for either whole page (includes zero page—zp, duplicate page—dup) or fixed sub page (includes zp, sub zero page—szp, dup, sub duplicate page—sdup) by computing hash values.

In every iteration, before transferring a page, the migration process computes the SHA-1 value of the content stored in the page. Then, by employing the SuperFashHash[1] on the computed SHA-1 value, the migration process perform a look up on the hash table. On a unsuccessful lookup, the whole page is tranferred and the corresponding SHA-1 value is inserted into the hash table along with its page identifier (old entry is deleted from the hash table). On a successful hash lookup, only the page identifier of the original and duplicate pages is transferred. At the destination, either the newly received content or the existing content (in case the page is a duplicate) is used. The SHA-1 is the widely used hash function [11, 13, 14] for deduplication. For sub-page deduplication, SHA-1 value needs to computed for every sub-page of a page. To reduce collision in the hash table, we use a hash table of size equal to the number of pages allocated to the VM and the SuperFashHash[1].

(4) Data Compression. This optimization exploits word level duplicates (wld) in the data to reduce amount of data to be transferred. The migration process employs LZO compression algorithm [20] per page during migration to identify word level duplicates and reduce the network traffic.

2.3 Optimization Components

Our analysis reveals that each optimization improves the performance of pre-copy migration by eliminating overhead due to several distinct components. The original work that proposed these optimizations have not analyzed these components in detail but they are important since the presence or absence of these components are driven by application behavior. We can characterize these components into two distinct sets: those due to to either *page dirty characteristics* or *page content characteristics* of the application.

Table 2 shows the list of components that each of the optimization works on to improve the performance of migration. It is evident from Table 2 that different techniques overlap with each other in terms of the components they act upon. *Note that sub page deduplication technique aids in finding page delta only at a sub page size granularity.* We have discovered a new component called false dirty pages (fdp) which has been overlooked in all existing studies.

False Dirty Page . Ideally, the dirty logging for a page should be enabled only after that page is transferred to the destination. However, both Xen and KVM enable dirty logging for all pages allocated to the VM before every iteration. This is because, removing the write permission on a page (setting read only permission to corresponding page table entry) requires flushing of TLB entries. Frequently flushing the TLB can degrade application performance, and hence, all pages are set to read only before every iteration. As a result, in an iteration, a page that is already dirtied during the same iteration can be transferred. In the next iteration, this dirtied page is again transferred as it marked in the set of dirtied pages of the previous iteration. If this page is not dirtied again between the transfer in previous iteration and the current iteration, we end up transferring unmodified content unnecessarily. We term such pages as false dirty pages.

Existing studies failed to notice false dirty pages altogether. However, due to inherent nature of delta compression, page skip, and data deduplication technique, the redundant transfer of false dirty pages is avoided. It is necessary to identify the improvement due to fdp explicity to find the impact of application behavior on performance gain.

2.4 Why Do We Need Yet Another Empirical Study?

In existing studies [9, 18, 22, 23], the reduction in migration time (MT) and network traffic (NT) due to each optimization

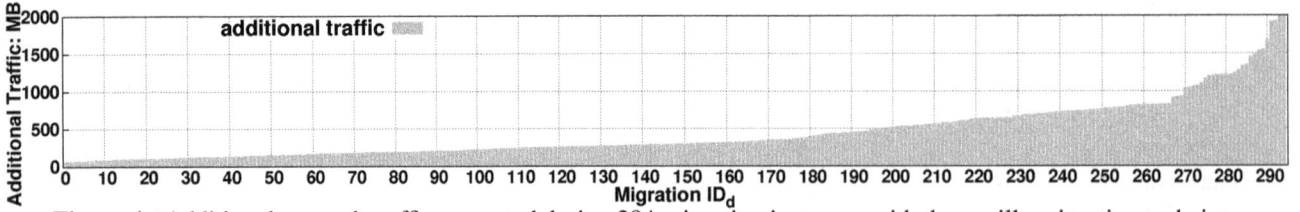

Figure 1. Additional network traffic generated during 294 migration instances with the vanilla migration technique.

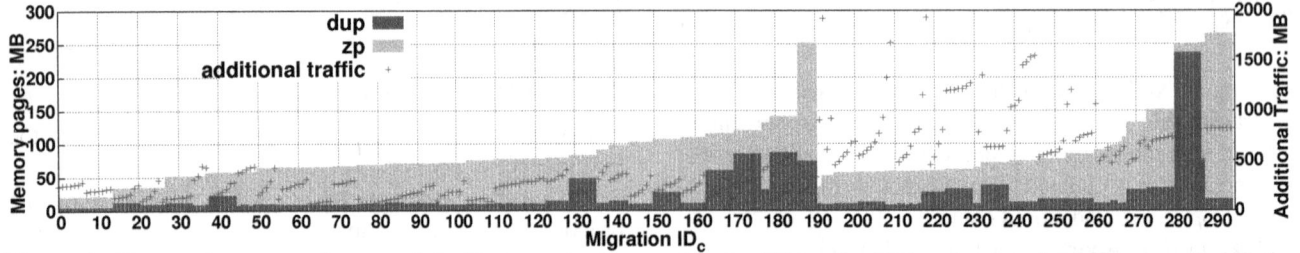

Figure 2. Expected amount of zero and duplicate content present in the VM and additional network traffic generated during 294 migration instances with vanilla migration technique.

is measured against the vanilla pre-copy live migration with only a limited number of workloads for a fixed migration rate (or transfer rate). Table 1 summarizes the improvement reported in existing studies. It is necessary to consider a wide range of workloads to obtain a variety of page dirty characteristics, and should use different migration rate (one of the major factor affecting the migration's performance [18]). Further, they have missed out on studying the effects of parameters on the performance gain. Hence, the best setting for these parameters is unknown.

Though the performance gain due to each optimization is presented in existing studies, the following two metrics are not reported: (i) the improvement due to individual components (which can help us to identify the impact of application behavior), and (ii) additional resource utilization with certain optimization (refer to Table 1). As there is no comprehensive empirical evaluation and comparison of these optimizations in terms of *performance* improvement and *cost*, answers to the following questions are also unclear.

- For a given migration scenario such as CPU or memory or network resource hotspot, which is the best optimization in terms of performance & cost? In other words, can we trade-off CPU for network resource?
- Is the increase in resource cost proportional to the performance gain?
- Does the performance gain depend on application behavior?
- How to combine various optimizations as there are overlap of components between optimizations?
- Can the combination of optimizations reduce the resource cost of individual optimization?

3. Experimental Methodology

In this section, first, we present the setup and workloads used. Next, we present our expectations on each optimization's performance, and steps employed for our study.

3.1 Setup and Workloads

Our setup consists of three servers, each equipped with a 2.8 GHz Intel Core i5 760 CPU (4 cores), and 4 GB of memory. One server acts as a controller that issues migration commands and generates load for the application executing in the VM. The other two servers execute *QEMU-KVM v1.7*. All servers are connected through a 1 Gbps switch. Each server and VM is installed with Linux kernel v3.8.0-29. Though our setup is small, our results remain valid for large setups. This is because, we assume that the network bandwidth is reserved between the source and destination server for migration process using SDN or managed hardware switches. Further, we assume that required CPU [17] is reserved for the migration process using `cpulimit` tool. Hence, the interference due to other VMs can be avoided in large setups.

The three parameters that impact the performance of pre-copy live migration are (i) page dirty rate, (ii) VM memory size, and (iii) migration rate [18]. To experiment with a variety of page dirty rates, we consider a wide variety of workloads (42 in total) that are commonly hosted in data centers. Further, we use different workloads to obtain a variety of application behaviors. The workload consists of (i) web and database services—HTTP file server, RUBiS [21], Mediawiki [15], OLTPBenchmark [6], (ii) multimedia and data mining benchmarks such as NU-MineBench [16], Parsec [2], and (iii) other multi-threaded benchmarks [3]. Refer to Appendix A for detailed description of these workloads.

All workloads are hosted on VMs of memory size 1 GB except for OLTPBenchmark and NU-MineBench which are assigned 1.5 GB and 600 MB, respectively. The VMs are migrated with 7 different transfer rates (as the migration performance is directly proportional to the transfer rate) ranging from 100 Mbps to 700 Mbps in steps of 100 Mbps to generate 294 migration instances. For each instance, we measure migration time, downtime and network traffic.

3.2 Expectations on Migration Performance

From Table 2, we have seen that the delta compression & page skip techniques account only for *page dirty characteristics*. Whereas, the data compression technique accounts only for *page content characteristics*. On the other hand, the deduplication technique accounts for both *page dirty and content characteristics*. Based on these facts, we present the following expectations on migration's *performance* and *cost* while employing each optimization.

(1) Expectation for delta compression and page skip techniques. For optimizations that account only for *page dirty characteristics*, we expect the performance improvement to be proportional to the page dirty rate. It is stated in [18] that the *additional network traffic* generated during migration (which is the difference between total network traffic generated during migration and VM's memory size) is proportional to the page dirty rate. Hence, we expect the performance improvement to be proportional to the additional network traffic generated with vanilla migration technique.

Figure 1 plots the additional network traffic generated during the 294 migration instances (using vanilla migration technique). Here, the migration instances are sorted in ascending order of additional network traffic and a migration identifier (ID_d) is assigned to each instance. When we employ either delta compression or page skip technique, we expect the performance improvement to increase with increase in the migration ID_d.

(2) Expectation for deduplication technique. For optimization that accounts for both *page dirty & content characteristics*, we expect the performance improvement to be proportional to both additional network traffic and amount of zero & duplicate content present in the VM's memory. Figure 2 plots the expected amount of zero and duplicate pages present in each of the 294 instances of migration (as determined by analyzing the memory snapshot of the VM).

As the deduplication technique is dependent on both *dirty and content characteristics*, we divided the 294 migration instances into two groups. The migration instances with less than 450 MB of additional network traffic belong to the first group (i.e., from 0 to 190 in Figure 2), whereas all other instances belong to the second group. For both groups, the migration identifier (ID_c) is assigned to each instance by sorting them in ascending order of the sum of zero and duplicate pages.

When we employ the deduplication technique, we expect the performance improvement to be proportional to both zero & duplicate pages and additional network traffic generated. Further, we also expect the number of sub zero pages and sub duplicate pages to be proportional to the number of zero pages and duplicate pages, respectively.

(3) Expectation for data compression technique. Though the compression technique accounts for *content characteristics* alone, the performance improvement is also dependent on the *dirty characteristics*. This is because, the

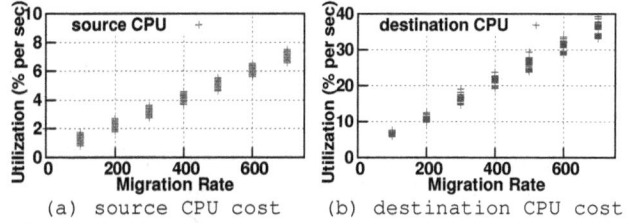

Figure 3. CPU utilization at source and destination server.

opportunity for compression increases with increase in the total network traffic. When we employ data compression, we expect the performance improvement to be proportional to number of zero page & word level duplicates and total network traffic generated with vanilla migration.

(4) Expectation on resource cost. For all optimizations, we expect the CPU utilization at both source and destination server to increase. Figure 3 plots the CPU utilization during migration. With increase in the migration rate, the CPU utilization increased as more pages are transferred and received per second. The CPU utilization at the destination server was five times higher than at the source. The reasons is that, at the source server, the TCP segmentation offload feature was enabled to reduce the CPU overhead of TCP/IP.

3.3 Methodology

We employed the following four steps:

1. With the 294 migration instances, we employ each optimization individually to quantify the improvement in migration time (MT), downtime (DT), and network traffic (NT) over the vanilla migration technique. We also quantify (a) the individual components (refer Table 2) due to which performance gain is observed, and (b) the increase in CPU utilization at the source and destination server.

2. If performance improvement is not as expected for certain migration instances, we identify the application behaviour that explains the anomaly. This helps in establishing a correlation between application behaviour and how well the optimization works.

3. We then compare these optimizations on the basis of resource cost (i.e., total CPU utilization at the source and destination server) and the performance improvement (i.e., total network traffic reduction).

4. Based on our observations from steps 1 and 3, we list the appropriate combinations of optimizations. For these combinations, we again employ step 1 to 3 until we find no more viable combinations.

4. Empirical Evaluation

In this section, we evaluate each optimization individually from the perspectives of performance gain over vanilla migration, resources used to achieve it, and the impact of application behaviour on this performance gain. Table 3 presents a summary of performance gains and cost increases (in terms of additional CPU used to apply the optimization).

Table 3. Performance and cost tradeoff of each optimization, and improvement due to individual component.

Techniques	Average reduction due to (in MB)									Average reduction in			Increase in CPU at	
	fdp	hdp	del	dd	zp	szp	wld	dup	sdup	NT (MB)	MT (s)	DT (s)	src. server	dest. server
Delta Comp.	131		92	54						277	7	2	3.2 x	1.2 x
Page Skip	289			20						309	10	0.73	1 x	1 x
Full Page Dedup.	104			33	79			46		262	7	0.44	11 x	1 x
Sub Page Dedup.	99		15	35	78	25		45	13	310	8	0.5	13 x	1.2 x
Data Comp.				62	510					572	16	0.79	5 x	1.3 x

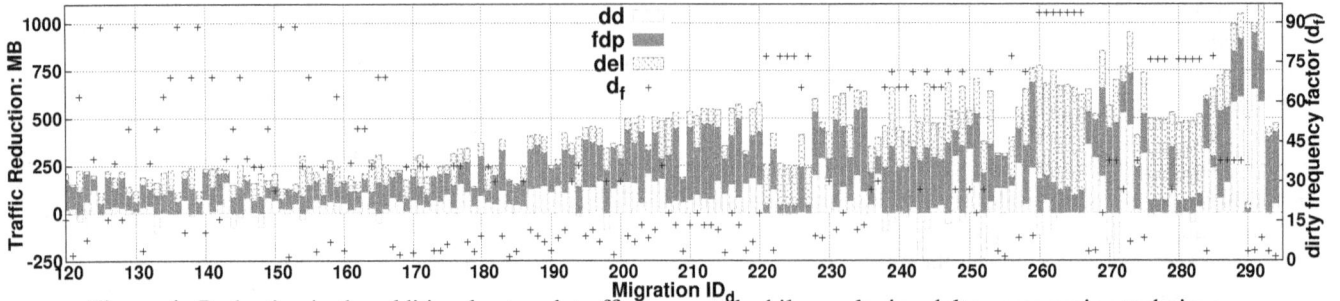

Figure 4. Reduction in the additional network traffic generated while employing delta compression technique.

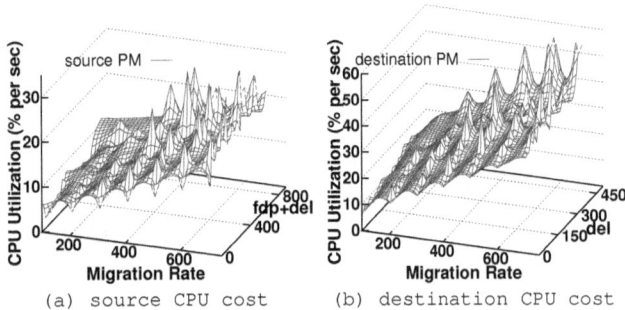

(a) source CPU cost   (b) destination CPU cost

Figure 5. CPU utilization at source and destination server during migration with delta compression technique.

4.1 Delta Compression

The delta compression technique identifies and transfers only the modified portion of a page instead of the entire page. The size of delta compression cache was set to VM's memory size to attain maximum performance.

Performance gain. On employing the delta compression technique on 294 migration instances, we observed an average reduction of 17% in the network traffic and 14% in the migration time. The improvement in performance was due to three components namely (i) false dirty pages—fdp, (ii) page delta—del, and (iii) reduction in total number of pages dirtied—dd. The reduction in dirtied pages was observed because of reduction in the iteration time caused by other two components, and we know from [18] that the number of pages dirtied is proportional to the iteration time. For certain workloads, the total number of pages dirtied increased as more number of iterations were executed (which means the enough progress between iterations were observed).

Impact of Application Behaviour. Every dirtied page is either a fdp or eligible for del but not both. This is because, if a page is dirtied after its transmission in an iteration (irrespective of its state before the transmission), it is definitely not a false dirty page but eligible for page delta depending on the modified portion of that page. The main factor which decided the improvement due to fdp and del was page dirty frequency. Figure 4 plots the improvement due to optimization components for each migration instance along with dirty frequency factor (d_f) associated with the workload. The value of d_f for a workload was calculated as

$$d_f = \frac{\left[\sum_{\forall i} dirty\_frequency(page_i)\right] - \#pages\ dirtied\ once}{total\ \#pages\ dirtied}$$

where, i denotes a page. The $dirty\_frequency(page_i)$ denotes the occurrence of dirty bit for page i in the collected bitmaps. As expected, the reduction in network traffic increased with increase in ID_d except for a few workloads. When the dirty frequency factor was low, improvement due to fdp was higher than del (refer to ID_d 190 to 220 in Figure 4). This is because, when a page is dirtied before its transmission in an iteration, the chance for the page getting dirtied again before the next iteration is low (when d_f is low).

On the other hand, when the page dirty frequency was high, the number of pages eligible for del was higher (ID_d 220 to 230, 260 to 267, 275 to 285). However, the improvement due to del was dependent on the size of modified portion of a dirtied page. Specifically, the improvement was low when pages were dirtied due to

1. frequent execution of malloc(), memset(), and free() operations which modified entire page—observed with minebench, parsec, and dacapo benchmarks.

2. disk read (as entire page was modified)— observed with *vips* and *file server* workload.

42

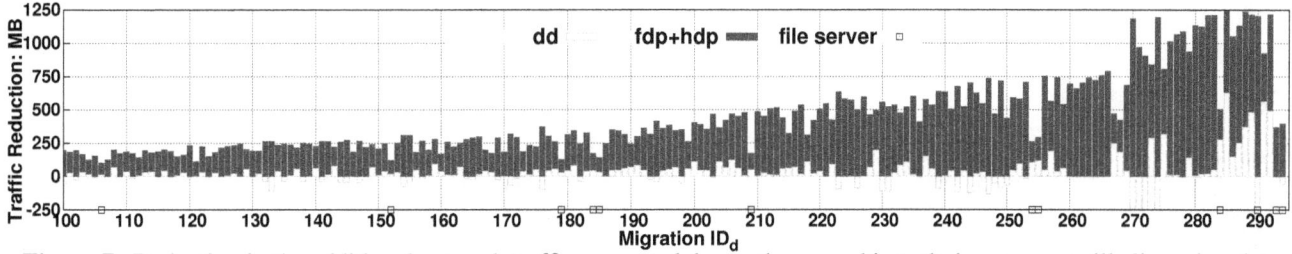

Figure 7. Reduction in the additional network traffic generated due to the page skip technique over vanilla live migration.

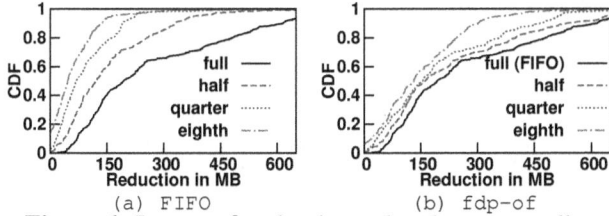

(a) FIFO   (b) fdp-of

Figure 6. Impact of cache size and replacement policy.

With a moderate value of dirty frequency factor, the improvement due to fdp and del was approximately equal for most of the workloads while for a few workloads, fdp was little higher than del.

Resource cost. The CPU and memory utilization are the two resource costs associated with delta compression technique. Figure 5 plots the CPU utilization at both source and destination server against the migration rate and performance gain. With increase in the performance gain (due to fdp & del), the CPU utilization at the source increased. This is because, when the reduction due to fdp and del was high, the amount of data to be transferred reduced and hence the number of pages processed per second increased (due to decrease in the network I/O waiting time). Similar behaviour was observed with CPU utilization at the destination server. Further, the processing time of pages were varied depending on the content, delta size, run length encoding, & number of overflows, and hence, some spikes in CPU utilization was observed. The reduction due to fdp did not impact the destination's CPU utilization as the destination had to work only on del. On average, the CPU utilization at source and destination with the delta compression technique was $3.2\times$ and $1.2\times$ higher than the vanilla migration's CPU utilization, respectively (refer to Figure 3 and 5).

Impact of Cache Size and Replacement Policy. In existing works, the cache replacement policy is set to first in first out (FIFO). Figure 6(a) plots the CDF of reduction in the network traffic while using FIFO replacement policy and four different cache sizes. Full implies that the cache is as large as the VM's memory size and the other three sizes were half, quarter and eighth of the VM's memory size, respectively. With decrease in the cache size, the performance gain decreased due to the low hit rate as expected.

We found out that the *FIFO cache replacement policy is not suitable for delta compression as it can retain pages which have zero or low dirty frequency while evicting important pages (i.e., pages with high dirty frequency)*. Hence,

we propose a new replacement policy called fdp-of. In fdp-of, the pages to be evicted are the ones which were either used to identify a false dirty page (means low dirty frequency) or the ones which resulted in overflow—of (while employing XOR and run length encoding) as most portion of pages were modified. When there is no such suitable page for eviction, we employ FIFO policy. Figure 6(b) plots the CDF of reduction in the network traffic while using fdp-of replacement policy. As expected, the performance gain improved over FIFO policy.

4.2 Page Skip

The page skip technique avoids transferring frequently dirtied pages to reduce the network traffic.

Performance gain. On employing the page skip technique on 294 migration instances, we observed an average reduction of 20% in both the network traffic and migration time. If a page gets dirtied before its transmission, it can be either a fdp or a hdp. However, the improvement due to individual components cannot be determined due to the nature of page skip technique and dirty tracking mechanism.

The traffic reduction due to fdp+hdp was significantly higher than dd (refer Table 3). Figure 7 plots each component due to which the reduction in network traffic was observed. The reduction due to dd was on average 2.6 times higher compared to the delta compression due to execution of more iterations for 48 instances. The downtime with skip technique was on average 1.27 times higher than delta compression. The reason is that the skip technique is not applicable for the stop-and-copy phase unlike delta compression.

Impact of application behaviour. As shown in Figure 7, performance gain increased with increase in the migration ID_d except for a few migration instances (for e.g., ID_d 284, 293, 294). The reason for poor performance gain with the certain workloads was that most pages were dirtied only after their transmission in an iteration, and hence the skip technique did not identify these pages. This behaviour was observed with migration instances where the page dirty rate was much lower than the migration rate. This is because, when pages were transferred rapidly, most pages were dirtied only after their transmission due to low page dirty rate.

With file server workload, irrespective of the migration rate, performance improvment was low due to very low page dirty rate. Further, the writable working set size [17], which is the total number of unique pages that can be dirtied, was

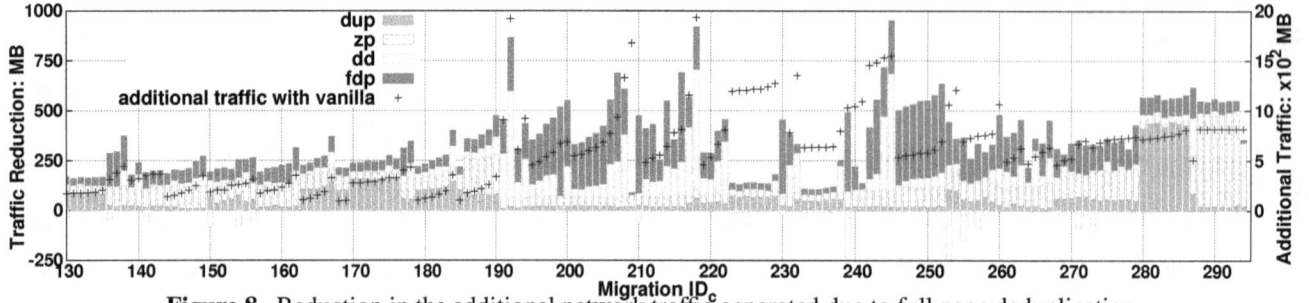

Figure 8. Reduction in the additional network traffic generated due to full page deduplication.

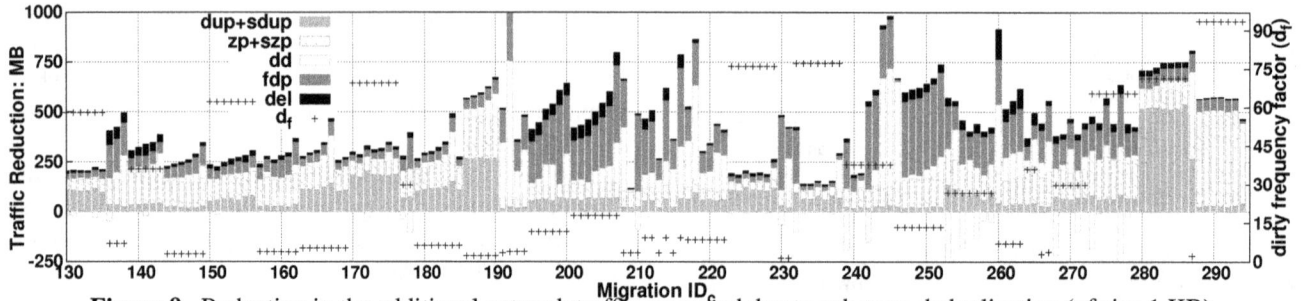

Figure 9. Reduction in the additional network traffic generated due to sub page deduplication (of size 1 KB).

equal to the VM size. On the other hand, when either the difference between page dirty rate and migration rate was low or the page dirty was large (irrespective of the migration rate), significant performance gain was achieved.

Resource cost and Impact of parameters. The additional CPU utilization with page skip is negligible as the only overhead is dirty bitmap collection. The dirty bitmap collection frequency (i.e., after transferring every m pages) is the only parameter associated with the page skip technique. We found the value of 1024 to be suitable for m. When the value of m was lower than 1024, CPU utilization increased a bit with negligible performance gain. When the value was greater than 1024, the performance gain reduced.

4.3 Deduplication

The deduplication technique identifies duplicate pages and transfers only one copy of that page to the destination. We can employ this technique either for full pages or sub pages.

Performance gain. On employing this technique for full pages (of size 4 KB) and sub pages (of size 1 KB) on each of the 294 migration instances, we observed an average reduction of 17% and 20% in the network traffic, respectively. The improvement with sub page deduplication was higher due to the additional components such as szp, sdup, and del.

Impact of application behaviour. The performance gain due to each component for both techniques are plotted in Figure 8 and 9. As expected, the performance gain due to zp and dup increased with increase in the migration ID_c (in both groups). As expected, the improvement due to szp and sdup was proportional to the amount of zp and dup. The fdp was also proportional to the additional network traffic except for a few migration instances (for e.g., ID_d 220 to

230 & 270 to 290). This is because of the high page dirty frequency associated with those workloads.

Resource cost & Impact of parameters. Compared to the vanilla live migration, the CPU utilization for full page deduplication was on average 11 times higher at the source server (due to hash computation and hash comparison), whereas there was no difference in the destination's CPU utilization. In the case of sub page deduplication, hashing is done on parts of a page and hence the CPU utilization increased ($13\times$ higher at the source server).

The sub page size is the only parameter associated with this optimization. We repeated all experiments with a sub page size of 2 KB and 512 bytes. On average, the network reduction with 2 KB and 512 bytes sub page was 2% lower and 2% higher, respectively, as compared to the sub page size of 1 KB. For the sub page size lesser than 1 KB, the migration rate did not go beyond 500 Mbps due to high CPU blocking time with frequent hash computation).

4.4 Data Compression

The data compression technique exploits word level duplicates to improve the migration performance. On employing the data compression technique on 294 migration instances, we observed an average reduction of 37% in both network traffic and migration time. Figure 10 plots dd and wld+zp+szp due to which the reduction in network traffic was observed. As expected, the performance gain was proportional to the total network traffic generated with the vanilla live migration except for the file server workload (refer Figure 10). This is because, text files used with the file server workload were created using dd if=/dev/urandom which did not introduce word level duplicates.

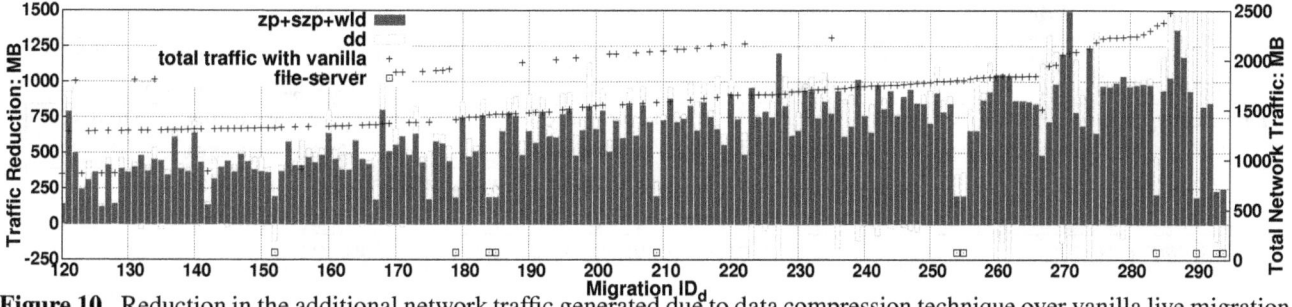

Figure 10. Reduction in the additional network traffic generated due to data compression technique over vanilla live migration.

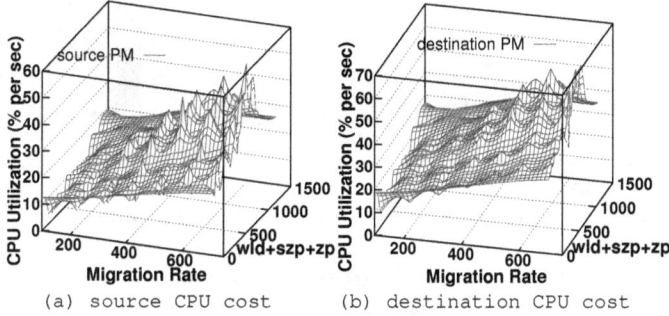

(a) source CPU cost   (b) destination CPU cost

Figure 11. CPU utilization at source and destination server during migration with data compression technique.

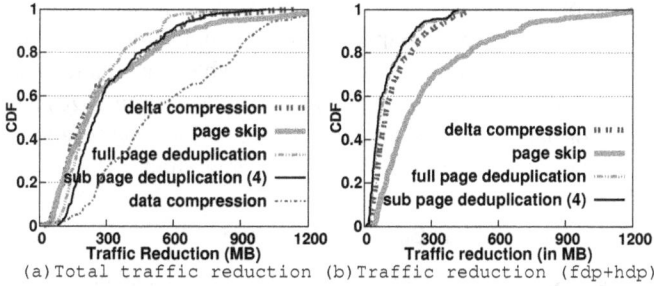

(a) Total traffic reduction (b) Traffic reduction (fdp+hdp)

Figure 12. Network traffic reduction.

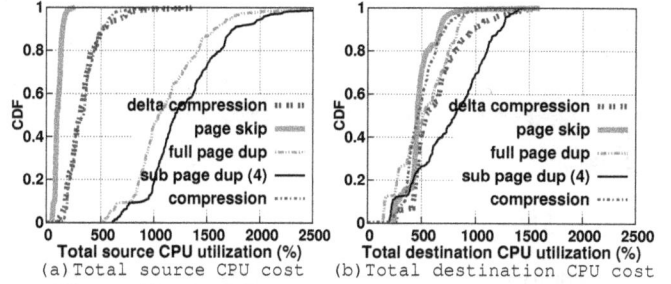

(a) Total source CPU cost   (b) Total destination CPU cost

Figure 13. Total CPU utilization during migration.

Figure 11 plots the CPU utilization at both source and destination server against migration rate and performance gain. With increase in migration rate and performance, the CPU utilization at both source & destination increased due to the increased page processing rate. The CPU utilization at the destination server was on average 1.5 times higher than at the source. Compared to the vanilla live migration, the CPU utilization at the source and destination was on average 5 times and 1.3 times higher, respectively (refer to Figure 3).

4.5 Comparison of Optimizations

In previous sections, we presented the results of evaluating each optimization in terms of performance gain and cost increases over the vanilla pre-copy migration. In this section, we compare optimizations with each other on the basis of total network traffic reduction and total CPU utilization to find the best optimization in terms of performance & cost. Further, this comparison will aid us to find the appropriate combinations of optimizations.

Performance and cost tradeoff. Figure 12(a), and Figure 13 plot the CDF of the total network traffic reduction and total CPU utilization for each optimization, respectively. Out of these five optimizations, page skip and data compression techniques reduced the total network traffic significantly while utilizing very little CPU at both source and destination server. The total CPU utilization at the source for both delta and data compression were approximately equal even when the CPU utilization per second with data compression was nearly twice as compared to delta compression (as the reduction in network traffic was twice). With deduplication, the total CPU utilized was significantly larger though the reduction in total network traffic was small.

Table 3 summarizes the average improvement due to each individual component. Out of nine components, the improvement due to fdp was higher than any other components. This is because, almost all workloads have pages which are dirtied less frequently. Figure 12(b) plots the CDF of traffic reduction only due to fdp and hdp. Page skip is the only optimization which identified both fdp and hdp while utilizing same amount of CPU as vanilla live migration.

Appropriate combination of optimizations. Every dirtied page is either a fdp or a hdp and the page skip technique identifies both. Further, the improvement due to fdp+hdp is high as compared to all other components (refer to Table 3). Therefore, we conclude that *the page skip technique should be employed irrespective of the application behavior*. Only in addition to the page skip technique, we should employ either deduplication or delta or data compression. Specifically, for unskipped pages during each iteration, we can employ one of the other optimizations.

Figure 15 plots the percentage of pages, which were dirtied during an iteration, got skipped, and the amount of pages

Table 4. Correlation between application behaviour and optimization techniques.

Individual Optimization	For individual optimization, performance gain will be low when	With page skip as base optimization, performance gain will be low when
Delta Compression	dirty frequency factor is high and then these pages are dirtied due to disk read or memset	unskipped pages are dirtied due to disk read or `memset`
Page Skip	page dirty rate $<<$ migration rate and writable working set size is large	
Deduplication	dirty frequency factor is high and `dup+zp` is low	`dup+zp` is low
Data Compression	word level duplicates and zero content are low	

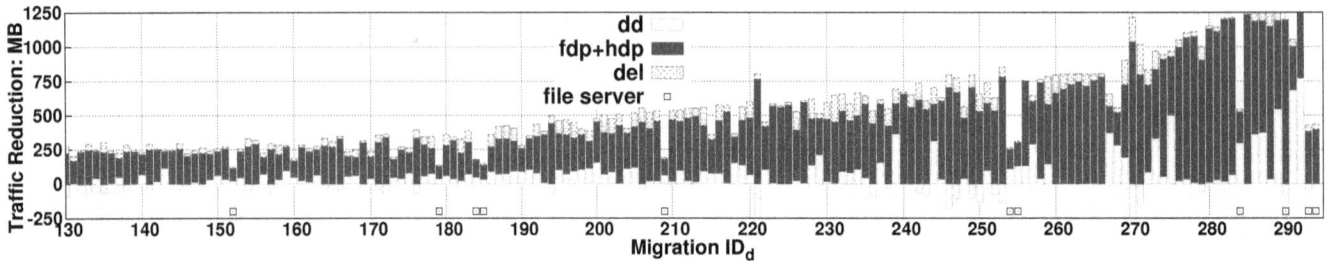

Figure 14. Reduction in the network traffic generated while employing both page skip and delta compression.

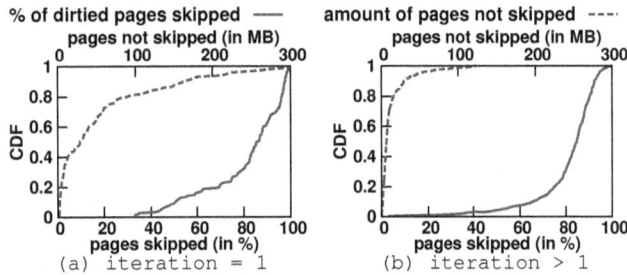

Figure 15. Skipped and Unskipped dirtied pages.

which were not skipped for both iteration 1 and other iterations. The percentage of pages skipped in the first iteration and other iterations was less than 50% for only 9% and 4% of 294 migration instances, respectively. The amount of pages not skipped in the iteration 1 was higher than other iterations (as all pages were scheduled to transfer in the iteration 1 as compared to only dirtied pages for other iterations).

The delta compression technique significantly reduced the downtime as compared to all other optimizations (refer Table 3). Hence, employing this optimization in addition to the page skip technique will reduce the downtime even more. Further, the data compression technique can be employed for every page before its transfer as it reduces the network traffic significantly. Zero content present in the VM is also handled by data compression. Hence, we need to apply deduplication very selectively by analyzing the expected amount of duplicate pages (but not zero pages) present in the VM as the cost in terms of CPU utilization will be high. Further, when page skip is the base optimization, we expect the impact of application behaviour on performance gain to change and are summarized in Table 4.

Based on these reasonings, we recommend the following three combinations of optimizations—with page skip as base optimization, employ either delta compression or deduplication or data compression.

5. Evaluation of Combinations of Optimizations

We employ each combination of optimizations on the 294 migration instances and present the performance gain and cost over vanilla live migration. First, we evaluate combinations in which page skip is the base optimization. Based on this evaluation, next we find other suitable combinations of optimizations that can be employed. Table 5 summarizes the performance and cost associated with various combinations of optimizations over the vanilla live migration.

5.1 Page Skip as Base Optimization

We employ delta compression, deduplication, and data compression individually along with page skip to quantify the effect of combined optimizations on the performance & cost, and also to study the impact of application behaviour.

(1) Page Skip with Delta Compression. On employing both page skip and delta compression techniques together, the average reduction in network traffic was 21.4% which was just 1.4% increment over page skip optimization (when applied alone). However, the average reduction in migration time was 4% higher as compared to the page skip optimization (when applied alone). This is because of small reduction in the CPU utilization which decreased CPU waiting time (.3x, refer to Table 3 and 5). The improvement due to `fdp+hdp` reduced as compared to page skip optimization because of increment in `dd`. As shown in Figure 14, with increase in the migration ID_d, the reduction in network traffic increased except for file server workload because of low page dirty rate (& large writable working set size which was equal to VM size) and high disk reads.

(2) Page Skip with Deduplication. On employing both page skip and deduplication techniques together, the average reduction in network traffic was 27% with full page deduplication (7% increment over only page skip) and 29% with

Table 5. With page skip as base optimization, performance and cost trade-off of each combination over vanilla.

Techniques	Average reduction due to (in MB)									Average reduction in			Increase in CPU at	
Page skip with	fdp	hdp	del	dd	zp	szp	wld	dup	sdup	NT	MT (s)	DT (s)	src. server	dest. server
Delta Comp.	277	43	32							353	10	1.18	2.7 x	1 x
Full Page Dedup.	275		32	69				50		426	12	0.91	10.8 x	1 x
Sub Page Dedup.	270	16	22	71	20			49	8	456	13	0.88	13 x	1.2 x
Data Comp.	238		71		377					686	20	1.23	4.7 x	1.3 x

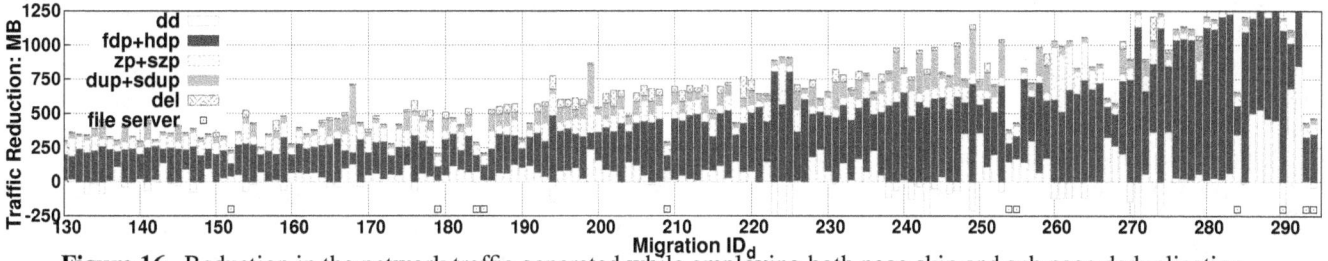

Figure 16. Reduction in the network traffic generated while employing both page skip and sub page deduplication.

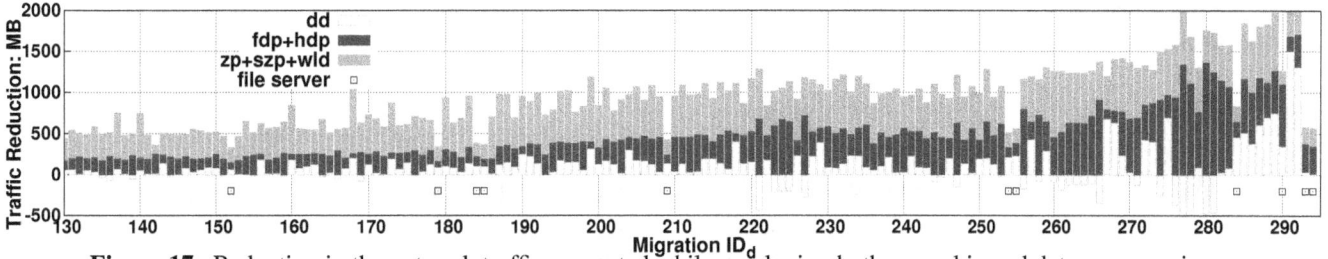

Figure 17. Reduction in the network traffic generated while employing both page skip and data compression.

sub page deduplication (9% increment over using just page skip). The CPU cost associated with deduplication technique was still high. It is advisable to avoid sub page deduplication as the average reduction in network traffic was only 2% higher than full page deduplication while doubling the CPU cost. Figure 16 plots the reduction in network traffic due to each component. With the file server workload, the reduction in network traffic was less due to a smaller page dirty rate and lower zero & duplicate content. For a few migration instances (between ID_d 199 and 249), the reduction in network traffic was large due to the copious amount of zero and duplicate content in the VM.

(3) Page Skip with Data Compression. On employing both page skip and data compression techniques together, the average reduction in network traffic was 41% which was just 4% increment over data compression but 21% increment over page skip. However, the CPU utilization (per second) at the source and destination did not reduce significantly. The improvement due to fdp+hdp reduced significantly due to increase in dd. The reduction in dd was observed due to reduction in the iteration time. Figure 17 plots the reduction in network traffic due to each component. Other than file server workload, significant reduction was observed.

Total CPU utilization with combined optimizations. Figure 18 plots the CDF of total CPU utilization at both source and destination server during migration when page

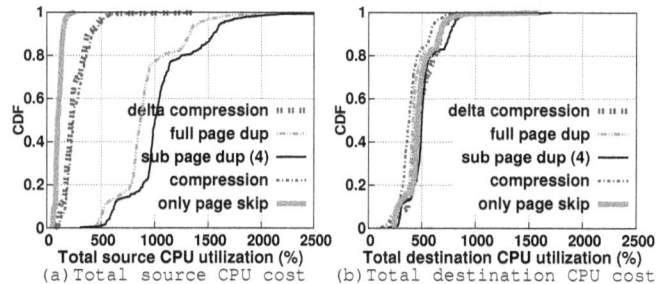

Figure 18. Total CPU utilization during migration with page skip as base optimization.

skip was the base optimization. The total CPU utilization at both source and destination decreased due to combination of optimizations (refer to Figure 13 and 18). For e.g., the average reduction in total CPU utilization at the source for page skip and data compression combination was 60%. *The combination of page skip and data compression is the best in terms of performance and cost.* Hence, in the next section, we consider page skip and data compression as the base optimizations and employ either delta compression or deduplication technique.

5.2 Page Skip and Data Compression as Base

(1) Page Skip and Data Compression with Delta Compression. On employing delta compression technique along with page skip and data compression, the average reduction in network traffic increased only by 3% and there was no reduction in migration time (over page skip and data compression optimizations). Further, the CPU utilization per second also increased and became the sum of CPU utilized by combination of (i) page skip & delta, and (ii) page skip & compression. This is because, when a page belongs to del, we did not employ data compression (as run length encoding was already employed by the delta compression).

(2) Page Skip and Data Compression with Deduplication. On employing deduplication technique along with page skip and data compression, the average reduction in network traffic increased only by 2% with full page deduplication. With sub page (of size 1 KB), the performance improvement got worsened (3% increase in the additional traffic) due to decreased migration rate (because of huge contention on CPU). Further, the CPU utilization per second also became the sum of the cost of individual optimization. This shows that any more combinations of optimizations is not useful.

Hence, we conclude that the page skip, and a combination of page skip and data compression are more appropriate.

6. Guidelines for Employing Optimizations

In this section, we present a list of guidelines on how to use these optimizations for various migration scenarios.

1. The page skip is the predominant optimization in terms of a performance and cost tradeoff. It would be the preferred optimization to apply first under any circumstance.

2. The deduplication technique must be applied with utmost care as the CPU cost associated with this technique is high. In our study, we estimated zero and duplicate content using memory snapshot of the VM. However, this may not be applicable for live data center applications. It is advisable to use a memory sharing tool such as KSM to estimate the amount of zero & duplication content, and then make the decision whether to employ this technique.

3. Determining whether to apply data compression is dependent on knowing the extent of word level duplicates in a page. This can often be difficult to estimate.

4. If reducing the downtime is main goal, delta compression is the best technique. However, if memory bandwidth or memory size is the bottleneck, this technique will worsen the situation even further. This is because, if the cache size is too small, delta compression will not result in any performance gain. The size of the cache should be equal to the maximum writable working set size [17] to achieve the maximum performance.

5. The combination of optimizations (with page skip as the base) reduces total CPU utilization as well as utilization per second at the source. Hence, this would be very useful while migration is employed to resolve resource hotspot mitigation.

6. If resource hotspot is due to the network bandwidth, it is advisable to employ both page skip and data compression

technique as this combination reduces network traffic immensely while consuming a moderate amount of CPU.

7. Conclusion and Future Work

In this paper, we performed a comprehensive empirical study to understand the performance/cost trade-off of various optimizations for VM live migration. Specifically, we found the page skip technique to be more efficient compared to all other optimizations. Further, we correlated application behaviour such as page dirty frequency factor, maximum writable working set size, page content similarity to performance improvement of each optimization. Further, we provided recommendation on how to combine various optimization such that the performance is improved while paying lesser CPU cost (compared to individual optimization).

As a part of future work, we would like to propose an analytical model for each of these optimization which takes into account of application behaviour and resource allocation for the migration process. Such a model will be useful to take precise decision on certain migration scenario.

A. Workloads

The following are workloads used in this paper:

Web Services: (a) HTTP File Server—where clients download files at two different rates of 80 Mbps and 160 Mbps (b) RUBiS [21]—an auction site prototype modeled after eBay.com which implements the following features: browse and bid on existing items, register and sell items. (c) Mediawiki [15]—an open source wiki package written in PHP, mainly used in all Wikipedia websites. The workloads (a), (b) and (c) are two tier applications, i.e., web server and a database server. The Apache Jmeter [7] was used to generate load for RUBiS and Mediawiki. For RUBiS, the Jmeter was configured with 50, 100, and 300 clients in three different runs, repetively. For mediawiki, the Jmeter was configured with 10 and 20 clients in two different runs, respectively.

OLTPBenchmarks [6]:—an open source testbed for benchmarking database management systems. It implements different set of workloads such as *ycsb*, *twitter*, *seats*, *votes*, *tpcc*, and *tatp*.

Multimedia, Data Mining and Multi-threaded Benchmarks: (a) Parsec [2]—a benchmark suite that consist of multi-threaded programs from different area such as computer vision, image and video processing, and animation physics. We used the following six applications: *bodytrack*, *ferret*, *fluidanimate*, *freqmine*, *vips*, and *x264*. (b) NU-MineBench [16]—a data mining workload which implements many mining algorithms such as *ECLAT*, *HOP*, *ScalParC*, and *UtilityMine*. (c) Dacapo [3]—an open source client-side JAVA benchmark suite consist of *avrora*, *eclipse*, *fop*, *h2*, *jython*, *luindex*, *lusearch*, *pmd*, *sunflow*, *tomcat*, *tradebeans*, *tradesoap*, and *xalan*. (d) Kernel compile—which compiles Linux kernel v2.6.39 with the default configuration.

References

[1] SuperFastHash: http://www.azillionmonkeys.com/qed/hash.html.

[2] C. Bienia, S. Kumar, J. P. Singh, and K. Li. The PARSEC Benchmark Suite: Characterization and Architectural Implications. In *PACT*, 2008.

[3] S. M. Blackburn, R. Garner, and C. Hoffmann. The DaCapo Benchmarks: Java Benchmarking Development and Analysis. In *OOPSLA*, 2006.

[4] J.-H. Chiang, H.-L. Li, and T.-c. Chiueh. Introspection-based Memory De-duplication and Migration. In *VEE*, 2013.

[5] C. Clark, K. Fraser, S. Hand, J. G. Hansen, E. Jul, C. Limpach, I. Pratt, and A. Warfield. Live Migration of Virtual Machines. In *NSDI*, 2005.

[6] D. E. Difallah, A. Pavlo, C. Curino, and P. Cudr-Mauroux. OLTP-Bench: An Extensible Testbed for Benchmarking Relational Databases. In *PVLDB*, 2013.

[7] E. Halili. *Apache JMeter*. Packt Publishing, 2008.

[8] K.-Y. Hou, K. G. Shin, and J.-L. Sung. Application-assisted Live Migration of Virtual Machines with Java Applications. In *EuroSys*, 2015.

[9] H. Jin, L. Deng, S. Wu, X. Shi, and X. Pan. Live virtual machine migration with adaptive, memory compression. In *CLUSTER*, 2009.

[10] C. Jo, E. Gustafsson, J. Son, and B. Egger. Efficient Live Migration of Virtual Machines Using Shared Storage. In *VEE*, 2013.

[11] R. Koller and R. Rangaswami. I/o deduplication: Utilizing content similarity to improve i/o performance. *ACM Transactions on Storage*, 2010.

[12] A. Koto, H. Yamada, K. Ohmura, and K. Kono. Towards Unobtrusive VM Live Migration for Cloud Computing Platforms. In *APSYS*, 2012.

[13] Y.-K. Li, M. Xu, C.-H. Ng, and P. P. C. Lee. Efficient hybrid inline and out-of-line deduplication for backup storage. *ACM Transactions on Storage*, 2014.

[14] B. Mao, H. Jiang, S. Wu, Y. Fu, and L. Tian. Read-performance optimization for deduplication-based storage systems in the cloud. *ACM Transactions on Storage*, 2014.

[15] MediaWiki. MediaWiki, 2011.

[16] R. Narayanan, B. Ozisikyilmaz, J. Zambreno, G. Memik, and A. Choudhary. MineBench: A Benchmark Suite for Data Mining Workloads. In *IISWC*, 2006.

[17] S. Nathan, U. Bellur, and P. Kulkarni. Towards a Comprehensive Performance Model of Virtual Machine Live Migration. In *SoCC '15*, 2015.

[18] S. Nathan, P. Kulkarni, and U. Bellur. Resource Availability Based Performance Benchmarking of Virtual Machine Migrations. In *ICPE*, 2013.

[19] M. Nelson, B.-H. Lim, and G. Hutchins. Fast Transparent Migration for Virtual Machines. In *USENIX ATC*, 2005.

[20] M. F. X. J. Oberhumer. oberhumer.com: LZO data compression library. http://www.oberhumer.com/opensource/lzo/, 2002.

[21] J. Spacco and W. Pugh. RUBiS Revisited: Why J2EE Benchmarking is Hard. 2005.

[22] P. Svärd, B. Hudzia, J. Tordsson, and E. Elmroth. Evaluation of Delta Compression Techniques for Efficient Live Migration of Large Virtual Machines. In *VEE*, 2011.

[23] T. Wood, K. K. Ramakrishnan, P. Shenoy, and J. van der Merwe. CloudNet: Dynamic Pooling of Cloud Resources by Live WAN Migration of Virtual Machines. In *VEE*, 2011.

[24] T. Wood, P. Shenoy, A. Venkataramani, and M. Yousif. Black-box and Gray-box Strategies for Virtual Machine Migration. In *NSDI*, 2007.

Urgent Virtual Machine Eviction with Enlightened Post-Copy

Yoshihisa Abe[†], Roxana Geambasu[‡], Kaustubh Joshi[•], Mahadev Satyanarayanan[†]

[†]Carnegie Mellon University, [‡]Columbia University, [•]AT&T Research

{yoshiabe, satya}@cs.cmu.edu, roxana@cs.columbia.edu, kaustubh@research.att.com

Abstract

Virtual machine (VM) migration demands distinct properties under resource oversubscription and workload surges. We present *enlightened post-copy*, a new mechanism for VMs under contention that evicts the target VM with fast execution transfer and short total duration. This design contrasts with common live migration, which uses the down time of the migrated VM as its primary metric; it instead focuses on recovering the aggregate performance of the VMs being affected. In enlightened post-copy, the guest OS identifies memory state that is expected to encompass the VM's working set. The hypervisor accordingly transfers its state, mitigating the performance impact on the migrated VM resulting from post-copy transfer. We show that our implementation, with modest instrumentation in guest Linux, resolves VM contention up to several times faster than live migration.

1. Introduction

As a means of load balancing, VM migration plays a crucial role in cloud resource efficiency. In particular, it affects the feasibility of oversubscription. Oversubscription is co-location of VMs on the same host in which their allocated resources can collectively exceed the host's capacity. While it allows the VMs to share the physical resources efficiently, at peak times they can interfere with each other and suffer performance degradation. Migration, in this situation, offers a way of dynamically re-allocating a new machine to these VMs. The faster the operation is in resolving the contention, the more aggressive vendors can be in deploying VMs. Without a good solution, on the other hand, those with performance emphasis must relinquish resource efficiency and use more static resource assignments, such as Placements on Amazon EC2 [1]. Although such strategies can guarantee VM performance, they lead to wasted resources due to conservative allocation. Migration for contending VMs thus has its own value, which can impact resource allocation policies.

However, migration of a VM under contention poses challenges to be solved because of its distinct requirements. It needs to salvage the performance of all the VMs being affected, namely their *aggregate performance*. The primary goal, therefore, is to evict the target VM from its host rapidly, allowing the other VMs to claim the resources it is currently consuming. This objective is achieved by transferring the execution of the migrated VM to a new host, so that its computational cycles are made available to the other VMs. Additionally, the duration of migration decides when the VM's state can be freed on the source host; reclaiming the space of memory state, which can be tens or hundreds of gigabytes, can be particularly important. While adhering to these priorities, the impact on the migrated VM should be mitigated to the extent possible, for its service disruption to be limited and the aggregate performance to recover fast.

These properties are especially desirable when the VMs provide services that need to sustain high overall throughput. Example cases include back-end servers or batch-processing applications, such as big data analytics. With these types of workloads, resolving the contention between VMs directly translates to optimizing their performance as a whole. Migration can also be more for saving the contending VMs than the target VM itself. The contending VMs can be running more latency-sensitive services, such as web servers, than those of the target VM. Or, the target VM may be malfunctioning, for example under a DoS attack, needing diagnosis in segregation. In all these situations, as illustrated in Figure 1, migration with appropriate characteristics would allow the VMs to be co-located under normal operation, and to be allocated new resources when experiencing a surge of loads.

Unfortunately, the requirements described above defy the trends in VM migration approaches. In particular, the current standard of live migration [12, 30] often results in elongated duration due to its design principles [19, 38]. This behavior leaves VMs under contention, delaying their performance recovery. In this paper, we present a design point that is fundamentally different and driven by *enlightenment* [28]. Enlightenment is a type of knowledge the guest passes to the hypervisor for improving the efficiency of its operation. Applying it to migration, we develop an approach called *en-

VEE '16 April 2–3, 2016, Atlanta, Georgia, USA.
Copyright © 2016 ACM 978-1-4503-3947-6/16/04...$15.00
DOI: http://dx.doi.org/10.1145/http://dx.doi.org/10.1145/2892242.2892252

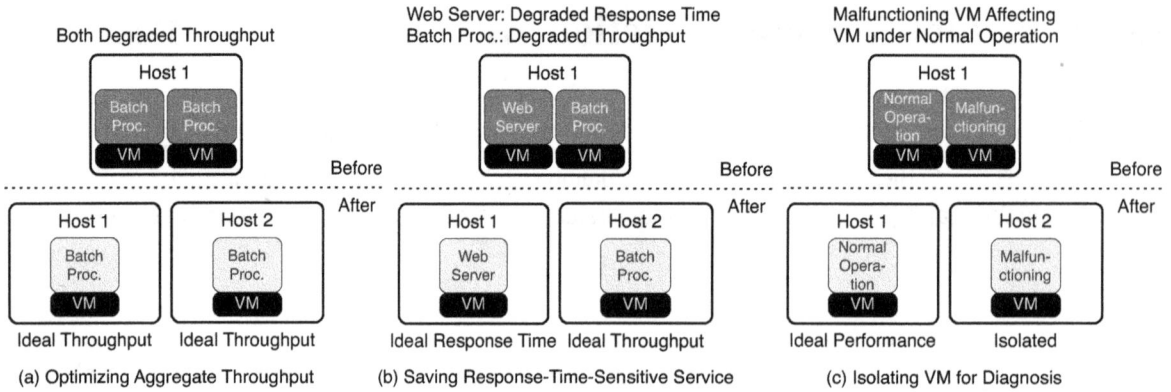

Figure 1. Scenarios for Urgent VM Eviction. The top and bottom rows illustrate VMs before and after migration, respectively.

lightened post-copy. It employs a post-copy style, in which the VM is resumed on the destination before its state has been migrated, and mitigates the resulting performance impact through enlightenment. Upon migration, the guest OS informs the hypervisor of memory regions that require high transfer priority for sustaining the guest performance. The hypervisor then transfers the execution of the VM immediately to a new host, while continuously pushing its state as instructed and also serving demand-fetch requests by the destination VM. Our implementation, with modest changes to guest Linux, shows the effectiveness of the guest's initiative in performing migration with the desired properties.

The main contributions of this paper are as follows:

- Explaining common behaviors of migration and deriving properties desired for VMs under contention (Section 2).
- Presenting the design and implementation of enlightened post-copy, an approach that exploits native guest OS support (Sections 3 and 4).
- Evaluating the performance and trade-offs of enlightened post-copy against live migration and other basic approaches (Section 5).

2. Analysis of VM Migration

VM migration has historically focused on the liveness, namely minimal suspension, of the target VM. Specifically, live migration is the current standard widely adopted by common hypervisors [12, 30]. The characteristics of live migration, however, deviate from those desired in the context of VMs under contention; it leads to extended duration of migration and thus continued interference of the VMs. Figure 2 illustrates this problem, with live migration by qemu-kvm 2.3.0 under the Memcached workload and experimental setup described in Section 5. One of the two contending VMs is migrated, with approximately 24 GB of memory state to be transferred, under varied bandwidth. Migration takes 39.9 seconds at 10 Gbps, and fails to complete at 2.5 Gbps. For the duration of migration, the VMs suffer degraded performance due to their mutual interference. In this section, we

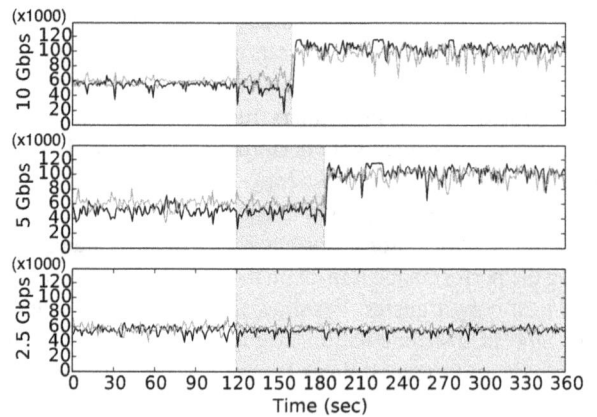

Figure 2. Live Migration Behavior of qemu-kvm under VM Contention. The y-axis indicates throughput in operations per second. The black and gray lines represent the migrated and contending VMs, respectively, and the shaded areas the duration of migration.

describe the algorithm and behavior of live migration causing this problem, and derive the properties desired in our solution.

2.1 Mechanics of Migration

Figure 3 illustrates aspects of VM migration including execution, state transfer, and performance. Migration is initiated on the source, on which the VM originally executes. The VM is suspended at one point, and then resumed on the destination. State transfer during the course of migration is categorized into two types: pre-copy and post-copy. Pre-copy and post-copy are phases performed before and after the VM resumes on the destination, respectively. Associated with the duration of these state transfer modes, there are three key time metrics:

- **Down time**: time between the suspension and resume of the VM, during which its execution is stopped.

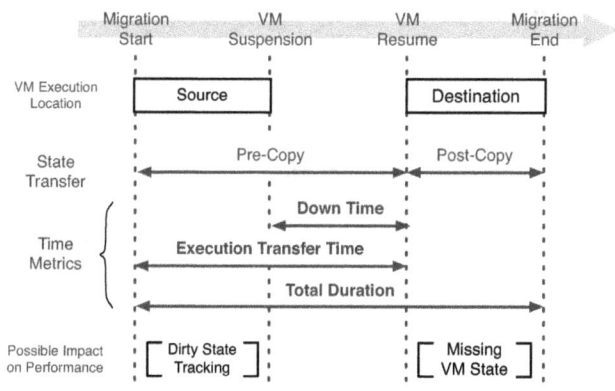

Figure 3. Overview of Migration Mechanics

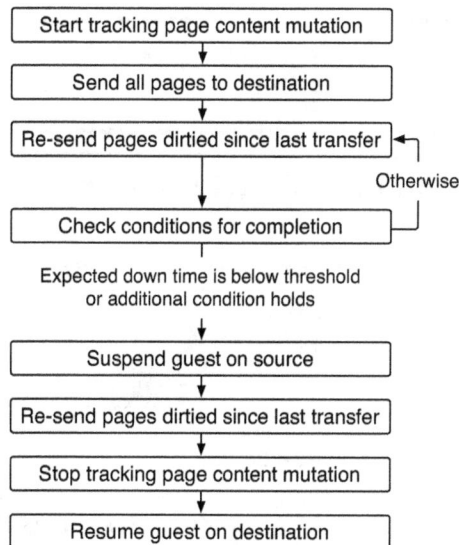

Figure 4. Live Migration Algorithm

- **Execution transfer time**: time since the start of migration until the VM resumes on the destination.
- **Total duration**: time since the start and until the end of migration.

Until execution transfer completes, contending VMs on the source continue to experience degraded performance. Thus, the faster execution transfer is, the more effective the migration operation is in salvaging the performance of both the migrated and other VMs. Reasonable down time also is important for mitigating the service disruption of the migrated VM. The VM execution halts during this time, rather than continuing with performance degradation. Finally, the hypervisor on the source needs to maintain the migrated VM's state until the end of total duration. Shorter total duration, therefore, means that allocated resources such as guest memory can be freed and made available to other VMs sooner.

Pre-copy and post-copy phases have associated performance costs. Pre-copy, when overlapped with VM execution, requires tracking state changes to synchronize the destination hypervisor with the latest VM state, a computational overhead known as migration noise [20]. Post-copy, on the other hand, can stall VM execution when the running guest accesses memory contents that have not arrived on the destination.

2.2 Live Migration

Live migration commonly employs pre-copy, and its algorithm works as shown in Figure 4. Upon initiation, live migration starts sending memory page contents while continuing the VM execution and keeping track of memory content changes. It then iteratively retransmits the pages whose content has been dirtied since its last transfer. The purpose of the iteration phase is to minimize down time, thereby optimizing for the liveness of the migrated VM. While iterating, the algorithm uses the current rate of state transfer to estimate down time, during which the last round of retransmission is performed. If the expected down time is short enough (e.g., 300 ms in qemu-kvm), the iteration phase completes and the VM is resumed on the destination. Implementations

can also have additional conditions for preventing migration from taking an excessive amount of time. Common examples include a limit on the number of iterations, and high expected down time that steadily exceeds a threshold. Regardless of the exact form in which these conditions are expressed, common to these parameters of live migration is that they aim to control the maximum duration of the iteration phase. Note that Figure 4 illustrates the migration of memory state; in this paper, we assume the availability of disk state through shared storage.

2.2.1 Impact of Workloads

Being pre-copy and optimized for down time, live migration handles state transfer while dealing with the guest state changes. Consequently, its behavior depends on the guest workload and the bandwidth available for migration traffic. Figure 5 shows the throughput of a Memcached server, hosted in a VM, during live migration by qemu-kvm. The memslap benchmark generates a load for the server, and its set-get ratio and the bandwidth available for migration traffic are varied. The other configurations for these measurements are the same as those described in Section 5, with the guest allocated 30 GB of memory and the server using 24 GB as its cache. Note that qemu-kvm zeroes out guest memory when setting it up, and live migration compresses each page whose bits are all zeros to one byte accompanied by a header; thus, it avoids sending the unused 6 GB in these measurements.

As the available bandwidth for migration traffic decreases, live migration takes more time to complete. This increase is non-linear; with set-get ratio of 1:9, migration finishes in approximately 40 and 90 seconds at 10 and 5 Gbps, respectively. At 2.5 Gbps, it fails to complete in a timely manner. With set-get ratio of 5:5, migration does not complete even at 5 Gbps. This is because expected down time never becomes short enough with the guest workload, and

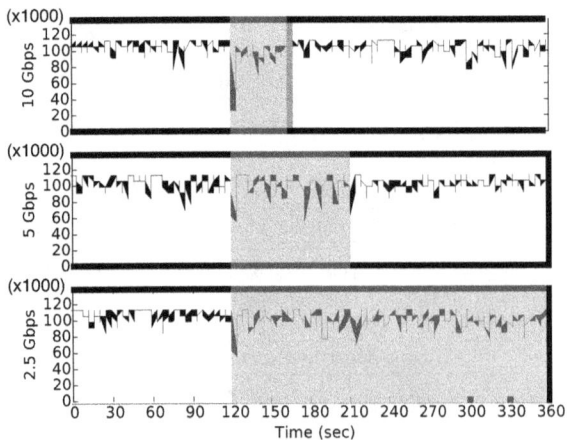

(a) Set-Get Ratio: 1:9

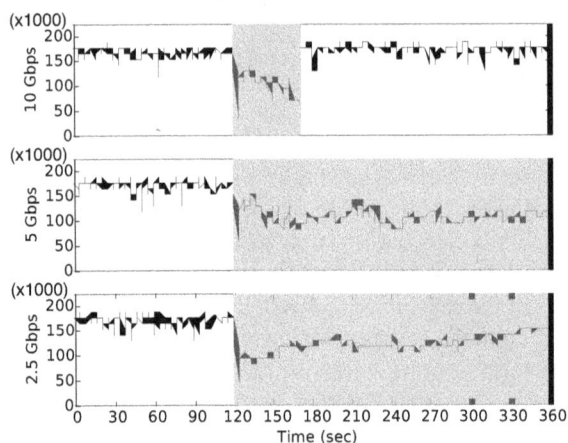

(b) Set-Get Ratio: 5:5

Figure 5. Behavior of Migrating a Memcached VM with qemu-kvm. The y-axis indicates throughput in operations per second, and the shaded areas the duration of migration.

qemu-kvm does not use a hard limit on the number of iterations. In addition, we can observe more throughput degradation during migration with set-get ratio of 5:5 than with 1:9. As the workload generates more memory content changes, dirty state tracking interferes more with it because of trapping memory writes, which are caught more frequently. Finally, even when live migration performs fairly well with set-get ratio of 1:9 and at 10 Gbps, it takes considerably longer than transferring 24 GB over that bandwidth (which takes less than 20 seconds). qemu-kvm's migration code is single-threaded, and it saturates a CPU core to transmit state at gigabytes speed while tracking dirty pages. Migration can thus easily be a CPU-bound procedure unless special care is taken, for example by parallelization of the code [39].

2.2.2 Commonality among Implementations

The characteristics of live migration explained above are inherent to its algorithm, and therefore shared by major implementations. Figure 6 shows the behavior of migrating a Memcached VM with common hypervisors, qemu-

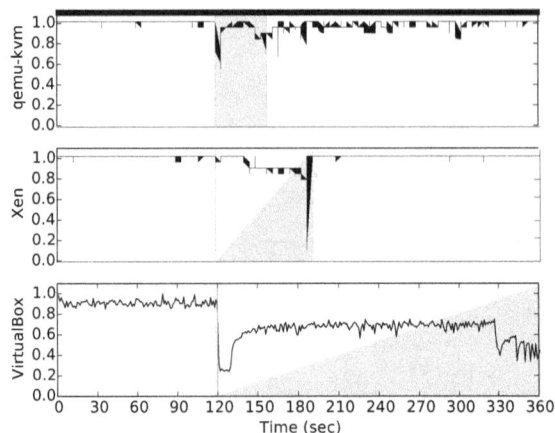

Figure 6. Behavior of Migrating a Memcached VM with Major Hypervisors at 10 Gbps. The y-axis indicates throughput normalized against the maximum in each measurement, and the shaded areas represent the duration of migration.

kvm 2.3.0, Xen 4.1.6, and VirtualBox 4.3.16[1]. The memslap benchmark is run with set-get ratio of 1:9. The VM memory size and server cache size are the same as explained previously: 30 GB and 24 GB. The VM is assigned 4 cores, and migrated over a 10 Gbps link. Note that we used machines different from those for the rest of our measurements, due to hardware accessibility reasons. They were equipped with an Intel Core i7-3770 CPU at 3.4 GHz and 32 GB of memory, running Ubuntu 12.04 with Linux kernel version 3.5.0.

As each implementation differs from one another, the performance cannot be directly compared between the hypervisors. In particular, the duration of the iteration phase is determined by parameters, and additional factors such as page content compression also lead to varying performance. For example, Xen takes longer than qemu-kvm, with its nature of throughput degradation during migration differing from that of qemu-kvm. Also, unlike the other hypervisors, VirtualBox does not complete migration under this workload. The key point of these results, however, is not the absolute performance differences, but the common behavior that the VM lingers on the source for tens of seconds or longer. This total duration exemplifies the cost paid in an effort to minimize down time.

2.3 Desired Properties of Migration under Contention

Live migration thus exhibits undesirable behavior when migrating contending VMs, for two fundamental reasons. First, it focuses on the down time of the target VM, rather than considering all the VMs affected. Second, it uses pre-copy and monitors the VM workload to achieve its objective, delaying execution transfer. Our goals, in contrast, are to 1) free resources on the source rapidly through fast execution transfer and short total duration, 2) handle loaded VMs

---

[1] Similar results with VMware ESXi 5 are publicly available in [7].

without relying on the reduction in their workloads, and 3) with these properties, salvage the aggregate performance of the VMs under contention. These requirements motivate the guest's active cooperation, which allows the departure from pre-copy and workload monitoring.

3. Enlightened Post-Copy Migration

Our approach to the above goals, called enlightened post-copy, exploits guest cooperation and post-copy-style state transfer. We derive the key ideas behind this approach specifically from our goals. First, minimizing execution transfer time requires that VM execution be immediately suspended on the source and resumed on the destination. This early suspension upon the start of migration also ensures minimal total duration, because the frozen VM state necessitates no retransmission as done in live migration. Therefore, post-copy follows naturally as the desirable method of state transfer. Second, fast performance recovery of the migrated VM requires that the part of its state needed for its current workload arrive at the destination as early as possible. The guest's enlightenment is the key that enables identifying this part of the VM state; with state transfer following the instructed prioritization, the VM on the destination can start recovering its performance without the completion of entire state transfer, and thus before the total duration of migration.

Figure 7 illustrates the workflow of enlightened post-copy. When migration is initiated, the hypervisor makes a request for enlightenment to the guest OS. The guest OS traverses its data structures and prepares priority information of the memory pages. Once the priority information is available, the guest OS notifies the hypervisor. The hypervisor then suspends the VM on the source, and resumes it on the destination immediately after sending the device state necessary for the resume operation. As the VM starts execution, the hypervisor parses the priority information and accordingly transfers the remaining memory page contents to the destination; it attempts to proactively push as many pages as possible before the access to them.

3.1 Guest's Enlightenment

In enlightened post-copy, the guest identifies those memory pages containing the working set of the currently active processes. As a design principle, the guest OS should be able to obtain a list of these pages without incurring noticeable overhead. Otherwise, the approach does not justify the guest instrumentation due to the resulting performance loss. As the types of memory page classification, therefore, we use straightforward notions such as the code and data of the OS kernel and running processes. Such bookkeeping information of memory pages is already available in the OS for its regular tasks, and re-usable without significant implementation effort for the purpose of migration.

For prioritized state transfer, the general idea is to transfer memory pages essential for running the guest OS, those for

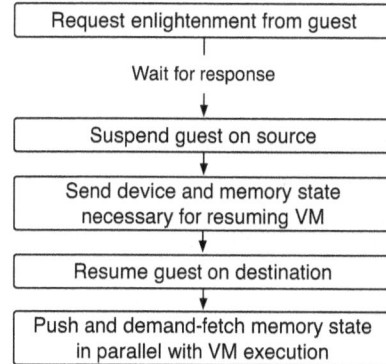

Figure 7. Enlightened Post-Copy Migration Algorithm

the actively running processes, and then the other less critical pages such as the kernel page cache and those for the non-active processes. Also, we can eliminate the transfer of the memory pages that are not allocated by the guest OS for any use, because the actual contents of such pages do not affect the correctness of guest execution [23].

The guest OS needs to prepare these types of information, as enlightenment to the hypervisor, in two distinct forms. The memory page priorities can be determined by a one-time operation upon the request by the hypervisor. There is no need for always tracking them during the course of the guest's normal operation. On the other hand, keeping track of allocated and non-allocated memory pages requires real-time processing, performed with or without migration, that maintains the information in a manner easily passed to the hypervisor. The reason is that the source hypervisor needs to know the exact allocation by the guest OS right at the time of VM suspension, for the destination hypervisor to construct a consistent memory image. For the one-time operation, the associated costs are that of guest-host communication delay upon migration start, and the impact of the in-guest processing on performance. For the real-time processing, the cost is the overhead added to relevant memory management operations of the guest OS. Minimizing these costs motivates the use of the above types of enlightenment, which are adequately informative but not excessively fine-grained.

3.2 Integration into State Transfer

The source hypervisor can integrate enlightenment into state transfer in a straightforward manner, because of the use of post-copy. Since the VM is frozen at the start of migration, enlightenment at that time reflects its latest state before execution transfer, from which the VM resumes on the destination. After receiving enlightenment and suspending the VM, the source hypervisor pushes the memory pages as instructed by the guest OS. While the destination hypervisor receives the memory pages, it also issues demand-fetch requests to the source for those that are accessed by the guest before their arrival. Although their arrival may incur delays due to the interference with the push traffic, these demand fetches help reduce VM execution stalls due to the divergence of the push order from the actual access order by the guest.

3.3 Design Trade-Offs

The design of enlightened post-copy is in sharp contrast to that of common live migration based on pre-copy. Enlightened post-copy targets VMs under load, while live migration expects idleness from them. Enlightened post-copy, therefore, employs a state transfer method that enables timely load balancing through fast physical resource reallocation. Down time and execution transfer time are expected to be instantaneous, and total duration corresponds to the one-time transfer of the entire state. At the same time, the disruption of the migrated VM's performance spans a longer period than down time itself, since post-copy is used. Guest cooperation is the key to alleviating this disruption.

On the other hand, live migration focuses on one aspect of the migrated VM's performance, down time. Being a guest-agnostic approach without an external source of knowledge, it relies on letting the VM stay on the source and tracking dirtied memory pages. Execution transfer time is equivalent to total duration; these time frames become longer when more iterations are done. The sole use of pre-copy ensures the migrated VM's performance on the destination, since all the state resides there on VM resume. Thus, down time approximately represents the duration of application-level disruption. However, dirty page tracking incurs a certain cost while the VM lingers on the source. Results in Section 5 demonstrate the effects of these trade-offs made by enlightened post-copy and live migration.

4. Implementation

We implemented enlightened post-copy on guest Linux 3.2.0 and hypervisor qemu-kvm 2.3.0. Figure 8 shows its architecture. When the source hypervisor initiates migration, it sends a request to guest Linux through a custom VirtIO device [6] (Step 1). The guest OS driver for this virtual device triggers enlightenment preparation, which scans data structures (Step 2) and writes priority information in the priority bitmap (Step 3). Page allocation information is always kept up-to-date in the free bitmap, so that its content is valid whenever the the hypervisor suspends the VM. These bitmaps maintained in the guest's memory facilitate the processing by the hypervisor; they are an abstract enough representation of the passed information, and the guest OS can avoid communicating it through the VirtIO device and instead have the hypervisor directly parse it. When the priority bitmap has been written, the guest OS notifies the hypervisor through the VirtIO device (Step 4). The hypervisor then sends to the destination the device state, including some in the guest memory, which is used by the destination hypervisor for the initial VM set-up. Finally, it starts transferring the remaining page contents in the prioritized order (Steps 5 and 6). On the destination, the hypervisor resumes the VM

Kernel	Kernel executable code
Kernel_Allocated	Allocated for kernel use
Memory_I/O	Used for memory-mapped I/O
Page_Table	Page table of active process
User_Code	Executable page of active process
User_Data	Non-executable page of active process
File_Active	Active cache of file
File_Inactive	Inactive cache of file
Other	Not belonging to any of the above

Table 1. Page Types Categorized by the Guest OS

once the device state has arrived. While receiving the pushed page contents, it writes them into the guest memory. When the guest OS accesses pages whose content has not yet been received, it generates demand-fetch requests to the source hypervisor. On the source, the hypervisor frees all the VM resources once all the page contents have been sent.

4.1 Guest OS

In our guest Linux, memory management and process scheduling code is instrumented to label each memory page with a priority level. The instrumentation follows naturally in the relevant existing parts of the source code, and requires only a modest number of changes to the original kernel.

4.1.1 Enlightenment Preparation

Taking advantage of memory management information that already exists, the guest OS classifies the memory pages in use into the priority categories shown in Table 1. The system-wide categories, such as Kernel, Kernel_Allocated, Memory_I/O, File_Active, and File_Inactive, are derived from kernel data structures or through the flags of page frame descriptors (e.g., `struct zone` and `struct page`). For the process-specific categories, the enlightenment preparation code parses the virtual memory area descriptors of each active process (`struct vm_area_struct`). These categories are each assigned a numerical value, in a descending order of priority from the top to the bottom in the above list. This order is decided such that the core system services, the active processes, and caching by the OS are given priority in that order. If a particular page belongs to multiple categories, it is treated with the highest of these priorities. Pages such as those belonging to the inactive processes and those used for the priority bitmap itself belong to the Other category. The bitmap simply contains the priority values, without the hypervisor needing to understand their exact semantics.

In order to decide the group of active processes, the scheduler maintains the last time each process was scheduled for execution (in `struct task_struct`). A process is considered active if it has been run recently at the time of generating enlightenment. In our implementation, we empirically use a threshold of the past 16 seconds for this purpose, considering the order of seconds migration is roughly expected to take.

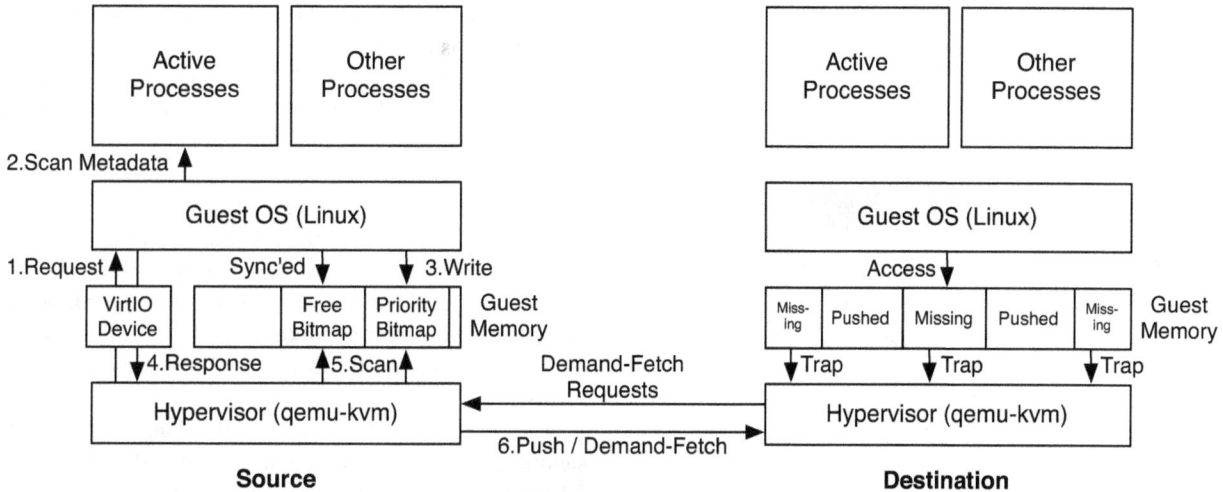

Figure 8. Implementation of Enlightened Post-Copy. The numbers represent the steps in order during the course of migration.

When the guest OS receives a request from the hypervisor, the guest OS runs code that generates the priority bitmap as explained above. Once it notifies the hypervisor, it is ensured that the guest can be suspended with the bitmaps available for parsing in its memory. Note that the free bitmap is always kept up-to-date and ready for processing. The response from the guest OS includes the addresses of the two bitmaps, and the hypervisor scans these locations while performing state transfer.

4.1.2 Implementation Cost

The modifications to the core Linux kernel code are minimal, mostly under `mm/` and `kernel/` in the source tree. Maintaining the free bitmap requires adding at most several lines of code in 16 locations. Keeping track of the last schedule time for each process requires a few variable assignments added in the scheduler code. Marking each page with kernel or user allocation needs less than 15 lines of code. These operations only add atomic variable assignments in the code paths of memory allocation and process scheduling. As shown in our experiments, compared to the original kernel, these minor modifications incur negligible performance overhead. The VirtIO device driver and the priority bitmap preparation code, which make use of the instrumentation, are implemented as loadable kernel modules.

4.2 Hypervisor

On the source, the hypervisor scans the bitmaps provided by the guest. It first scans the free bitmap and sends the corresponding page frame numbers in a packed format, along with the device and some memory state, right after which the VM is resumed on the destination. Next, the hypervisor traverses the priority bitmap and starts pushing the page contents over a TCP connection. The transfer is performed in rounds, starting with the Kernel pages and ending with the Other pages. While this push continues, a separate thread

services demand-fetch requests from the destination hypervisor over another TCP connection. Note that while we attempt to give a higher priority to the demand-fetched pages through the TCP_NODELAY socket option, the push transfer can still interfere with their arrival timings.

On the destination, the hypervisor registers userfault [5] handlers with the guest memory region. Userfault is a mechanism on Linux that enables a user process to provide a page fault handler of its own for specified pages. This interposition enables post-copy state transfer. The userfault handler is first registered for the entire main memory of the VM when the hypervisor starts on the destination. On the receipt of the unallocated page information, the handler is removed from the respective addresses. Then, as the memory page contents arrive, they are written to the corresponding addresses and the userfault handler is unregistered from these addresses. When the guest accesses these memory pages whose content is already available, no further interposition by the hypervisor is carried out. On access to a page whose content is still missing, the hypervisor issues a demand-fetch request to the source hypervisor.

5. Experiments

We performed experiments to demonstrate the effectiveness of enlightened post-copy in resolving resource contention and the performance trade-offs resulting from its design principles. Our experiments address the following points. First, we show how enlightened post-copy salvages the throughput of contending VMs through end-to-end results, while comparing them to those of original live migration of qemu-kvm 2.3.0. Next, we investigate the efficacy of our approach in robustly dealing with workloads by examining the performance of two baseline methods, stop-and-copy and simple post-copy, as reference points. Finally, we show the cost of enlightened post-copy in terms of state transfer amounts and guest OS overhead.

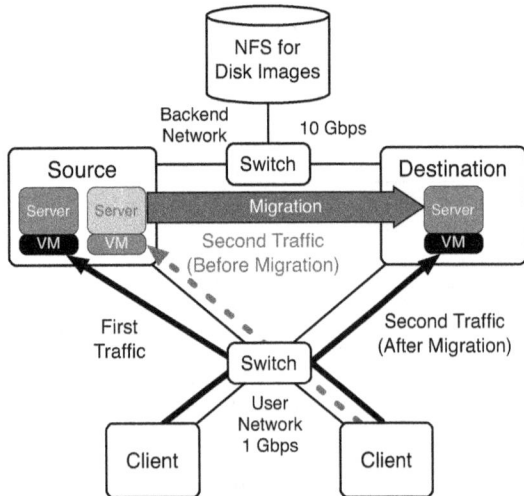

Figure 9. Experimental Set-Up

5.1 Set-Up and Workloads

Figure 9 shows our experimental set-up. VMs are migrated between a pair of source and destination hosts, which are connected through a backend 10 Gbps network for migration traffic. They are also connected on this network to an NFS server that stores VM disk images. The client machines use a separate 1 Gbps network for user traffic to and from the VMs. In the experiments except those with idle VMs, initially two VMs are running and contending with each other on the source machine. We migrate one of the VMs to the destination machine, after which each VM has its own dedicated machine. The VM hosts and client machines are each equipped with two Intel Xeon E5-2430 CPUs at 2.20 GHz and 96 GB memory, running Ubuntu 14.04. The VM hosts execute Linux kernel 4.1.0-rc3 with a userfault patch applied, while the other machines run version 3.16.0. As userfault currently does not support the use of huge pages, they are disabled in our measurements. Time on the machines is synchronized via an NTP server, and the backend bandwidth between the VM hosts is controlled using Linux Traffic Control for measurements at 5 Gbps and 2.5 Gbps. The VMs run Ubuntu Server 12.04 with unmodified kernel 3.2.0 in all the cases except those with enlightened post-copy, in which we use our modified version of the kernel.

We use the following workloads that exhibit different types of resource intensity and reveal performance trade-offs made by enlightened post-copy:

Memcached: The VMs run an in-memory key-value store, Memcached 1.4.13 [2], and the clients execute its bundled benchmark memslap 1.0, which is modified to report percentile latencies. The VMs are each allocated 30 GB of memory and 8 cores, with Memcached configured with 4 threads (due to its known scalability limitation) and 24 GB cache. We first run the benchmark against Memcached to fill up its cache, and then perform measurements with concurrency level of 96 and set-get ratio of 1:9. At the time of

migration, approximately 24 GB of memory is in use, almost all of which is by Memcached.

MySQL: The VMs run MySQL 5.6, and the clients execute OLTPBenchmark [3] using the Twitter workload with scale factor of 960. The VMs are each allocated 16 cores and 30 GB of memory, and MySQL is configured with a 16 GB buffer pool in memory. The concurrency of OLTPBenchmark is set to 64. After generating the database contents, we execute Tweet insertions for 25 minutes and then the default operation mix for 5 minutes as a warm-up. At the time of migration, MySQL uses approximately 17 GB of memory, and almost all of the 30 GB memory is allocated by the guest OS for use.

Cassandra: The VMs run a NoSQL database, Apache Cassandra 2.1.3 [4], and the clients use YCSB [8] 0.1.4 with 24 threads and core benchmark F, which consists of 50% read and 50% read-modify-write operations. The VMs are each configured with 16 cores and 30 GB of memory. Before measurements, the benchmark is run for approximately 10 minutes to warm the servers up. At the time of migration, the server uses around 8.4 GB of memory out of 12 GB in use by the guest OS.

In the above workload configurations, Memcached is the most memory- and network-intensive, while consuming relatively low CPU resources. Also, the VM's memory is almost exclusively used by the server process itself. MySQL is more CPU-intensive, and also less memory-intensive in terms of the access footprint per unit time. Finally, Cassandra is the most compute-intensive among these workloads, making CPUs the source of contention. In the MySQL and Cassandra cases, the guest OS uses a non-trivial amount of memory in addition to that allocated by the server processes themselves. These characteristics make Memcached the hardest case, and MySQL and Cassandra more winning cases for enlightened post-copy in comparison to live migration.

5.2 End-to-End Performance

In this section, we compare application-level performance of the three workloads during migration with enlightened-copy and live migration. In addition to the throughput of the server applications, we also report the impact of migration on application-level latency.

5.2.1 Memcached

Figure 10 (1) compares Memcached throughput of enlightened post-copy (labeled "EPC") and live migration (labeled "Live") under varied bandwidth. The y-axis shows operations per second in thousands (x1000), and the total duration of migration is shown as shaded areas. The dark lines indicate the performance of the migrated VM, and gray lines are that of the contending VM. The dotted lines represent the aggregate of the the two. The source of contention is user traffic handling by the source hypervisor. As Memcached accounts for almost all the guest memory pages in use (which

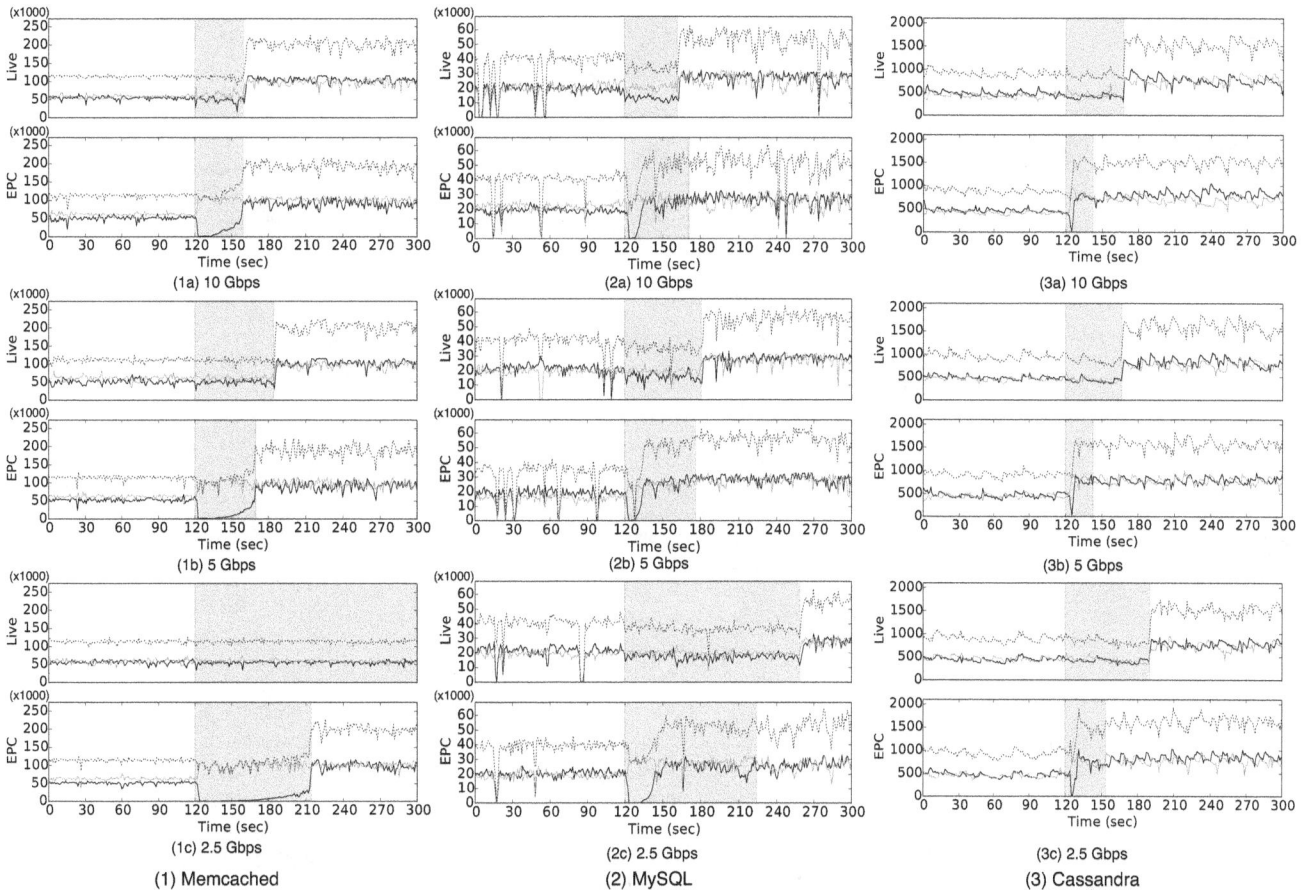

Figure 10. End-to-End Results with Enlightened Post-Copy and Live Migration. The y-axis indicates throughput in operations or transactions per second. The black and gray lines represent the migrated and contending VMs, respectively, and the dotted lines the aggregate of the two. The shaded areas show the duration of migration.

are categorized into User_Data) and accesses them at a great speed, it leaves little room for memory prioritization through enlightenment. Thus, the performance recovery during enlightened post-copy migration is not significant because it requires most pages for the Memcached server to be present. Immediate execution transfer, still, lets the contending VM recover its performance as soon as the migration starts. On the other hand, live migration handles the read-mostly workload relatively well. At 10 Gbps, it finishes almost as soon as enlightened post-copy does. However, it performs more state retransmission as bandwidth becomes lower, and at 2.5 Gbps it fails to finish while the benchmark continues. Note that, because of the migration thread causing the saturation of a core at 10 Gbps, the results at this speed are not as good as can be expected from the 5 Gbps results.

The latency characteristics of the 10 Gbps measurements are shown in Figure 11 (1). The top two graphs present the 90th percentile latency of the server responses over time. The latency stays roughly between 1 and 2 ms before migration, and around 1 ms once it completes. Live migration sustains mostly good latency until the end of migration. En-

lightened post-copy leaves the 90th percentile latency close to 1 second right after the start of migration, while it starts to decrease as more state arrives at the destination. The bottom two graphs show CDFs of the response times during the same 5-minute period. Despite its longer tail to the right side, enlightened post-copy still maintains the curve of the migrated VM close to that of the contending VM and those with live migration. While the differences in throughput should also be considered when interpreting these results, they indicate that the impact on latencies of the served requests is moderate at the 5-minute granularity.

5.2.2 MySQL

Figure 10 (2) shows the throughput results with MySQL. Although the workload is less network-intensive than Memcached, multiplexing user traffic between the VMs on the source causes contention. We also attribute to this bottleneck the ephemeral performance drops that are observed especially before migration. As the workload has more memory access locality, as well as memory allocated besides the cache of MySQL itself, enlightened post-copy gains signif-

59

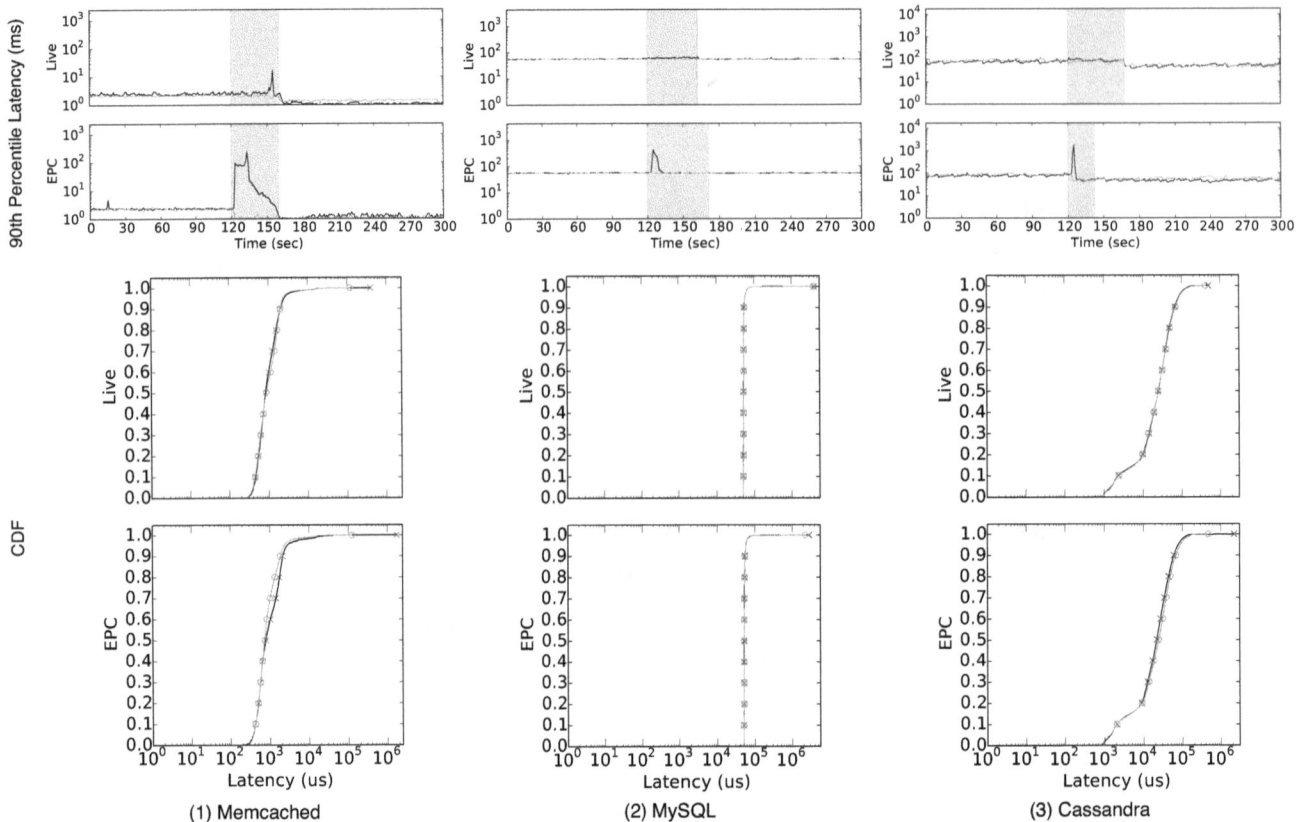

Figure 11. Latency with Enlightened Post-Copy and Live Migration at 10 Gbps. The black and gray lines correspond to the migrated and contending VMs, respectively. In each column, the top two graphs show the 90th percentile latency over time on a log scale, with the shaded areas indicating the duration of migration. The bottom two figures are CDFs of the response latencies during the 5-minute period, with markers at every 10th percentile.

icantly from prioritized state transfer. The throughput of the migrated VM starts recovering shortly after the migration start, and well before its total duration. In addition to taking longer as the workload size increases with respect to bandwidth (i.e., at lower bandwidth), live migration also exhibits more interference with the throughput of the migrated VM at higher bandwidth. The reason is that the workload is fairly CPU-intensive, and that the migration thread performs dirty state checking more frequently per unit time. Also, unlike all the other cases, live migration completes sooner than enlightened post-copy at 10 Gbps. As the interference of the hypervisor slows the guest, it consumes less computational resources besides those spent for network transfer than enlightened post-copy does. As a result, live migration can better utilize the bandwidth.

The latency results for the workload are shown in Figure 11 (2). The 90th percentile latency with enlightened post-copy recovers quickly as the throughput does, lowering to the level of a VM without contention before the completion of migration. The CDFs also indicate that the response time distributions are comparable between the two methods, including the tails to the right representing the maximum latency.

5.2.3 Cassandra

Finally, Figure 10 (3) shows the results with Cassandra. This workload makes the CPUs on the source the bottleneck for the VMs before migration. Its total duration not being affected by the resource intensity of the workload, enlightened post-copy finishes as soon as the amount of memory in use has been transferred. It also starts recovering the throughput of the migrated VM halfway through the migration process. With severe CPU contention on the source, live migration is prevented from performing dirty state checking and state transmission frequently. Thus, we do not observe its interference with the migrated VM's throughput, but instead see total duration heavily penalized at higher bandwidth; effective state transfer rate stays low enough that the duration differs only slightly between 10 and 5 Gbps. Overall, the difference in the duration between the two methods is more significant than with the other workloads.

As shown in Figure 11 (3), the good performance of enlightened post-copy is also reflected in the latency results. The 90th percentile latency increases for a short period with enlightened post-copy, and soon drops to the ideal level without the contention. Also, the response time distributions of enlightened post-copy and live migration compare well to each other. Except for the right tail of the migrated VM being a little longer with enlightened post-copy, the two methods show similar distribution curves.

5.3 Comparison with Baseline Approaches

We have so far compared enlightened post-copy with live migration based on pre-copy, which is predominantly used in today's virtualized environments. We further describe our design trade-offs by way of comparison to two fundamental approaches: stop-and-copy [36, 43] and simple post-copy. Stop-and-copy is an early form of migration that stops the VM, transfers all its state, and resumes the VM, in a sequential manner. It achieves the shortest total duration possible at the cost of making down time equivalently long. Simple post-copy solely uses demand fetches. It transfers only those memory pages that are being accessed by the guest on the destination, making each access incur an RTT between the hosts. These approaches can be considered as extreme design points: stop-and-copy as live migration that eliminates iterations for the sake of minimal duration, and simple post-copy as enlightened post-copy without, or with completely ineffective, enlightenment. They thus serve as baselines that reveal the benefits of using the sophistication in enlightened post-copy.

Figure 12 illustrates the behavior of stop-and-copy and simple post-copy with the Memcached and MySQL workloads at 10 Gbps. The two workloads exemplify cases in which they perform well or poorly compared to enlightened post-copy (whose corresponding cases are shown in Figure 10 1a and 2a). Stop-and-copy works relatively well for Memcached, and poorly for MySQL. Its performance is determined by the state transfer amount, regardless of the workload, while enlightened post-copy copes better with the MySQL workload than with the Memcached workload. The gain by enlightened post-copy, therefore, becomes clearer in the MySQL case. Simple post-copy is ineffective for Memcached and fairly adequate for MySQL. It significantly impacts the Memcached performance once the VM starts on the destination, as the cost of page retrieval is prohibitive for the memory-intensive workload. MySQL, on the other hand, exhibits enough memory access locality to prevent this cost from significantly affecting its performance. As a result, enlightened post-copy shows a clear advantage in the Memcached case. In summary, stop-and-copy and simple post-copy have cases they can handle and those they cannot; enlightened post-copy performs comparably to them in their best cases, and outperforms them considerably in the other cases.

5.4 Costs of Enlightenment

Enlightened post-copy targets VMs under load and makes explicit design trade-offs. One question that arises is the overhead incurred due to its design when used in other situations. Table 2 shows time and state transfer statics of mi-

(Unit: ms)	Enlightenment	Suspension	Execution Transfer	Total Duration
Live	-	6327	6548	6548
EPC	691	706	1280	2571

(a) Time Metrics

(Unit: KB)	Pre-Copy	Demand Fetch	Push	Free Memory Information	Total
Live	1029496 (100%)	-	-	-	1029496
EPC	36028 (4.0%)	892 (0.1%)	871188 (95.9%)	10 (<<0.1%)	908118

(b) State Transfer Amounts

Table 2. Costs of Idle VM Migration. The tables show time and state transfer statistics of migrating an idle VM, with no active applications inside. The numbers in parentheses in part (b) represent percentages of the total transfer amount.

grating an idle VM with 30 GB memory over 10 Gbps. The guest OS uses approximately 1 GB of memory, with no user applications actively running. In part (a), the columns from left to right indicate guest communication time for obtaining enlightenment, time until the VM is suspended on the source, execution transfer time, and total duration. Although enlightened post-copy pays the price of communicating with the guest OS, the cost is insignificant in this idle VM case. Live migration, even when the VM is idle, needs to scan the entire guest memory and thus takes some time until completion. Overall, enlightened post-copy is no worse than live migration in terms of the time metrics. Part (b) in the figure shows the amount of state transfer by the transfer method used. "Free memory information" for enlightened post-copy represents how much data is sent to inform the destination hypervisor of all the unallocated memory pages. Since enlightened post-copy performs one-time transfer and live migration needs little retransmission, they transfer similar amounts in total.

In order to measure the real-time cost of tracking page allocation in the free bitmap, we ran a microbenchmark program inside the guest. The program performs repeated memory allocation, as fast as possible, in chunks of 1000 individual 4KB malloc() and free() calls each. With the original Linux kernel and our modified kernel, one pair of these calls takes 1.394 us and 1.455 us (4.4% increase), respectively. As demonstrated in the preceding results, this difference typically has negligible impacts on regular applications because they do not allocate and free memory as frequently.

6. Related Work

VM migration has improved over the past decade, with previous work targeting different environments. Live migration focuses on minimizing the down time of migrated VMs, and exemplifies pre-copy approaches. Early work on VM transfer started with stop-and-copy, in which guest execution is suspended before, and resumed after, entire state transfer. It was used by Internet Suspend/Resume [22, 37], and adopted by μDenali [43]. Stop-and-copy was also augmented with partial demand fetch and other optimizations [36] for virtu-

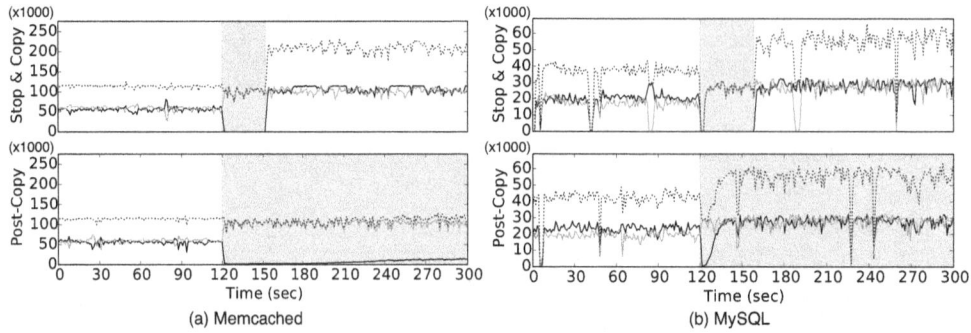

Figure 12. Behavior of Baseline Approaches. The y-axis indicates throughput in operations or transactions per second. The black and gray lines represent the migrated and contending VMs, respectively, and the dotted lines the aggregate of the two. The shaded areas show the duration of migration.

alizing the user's desktop environment, as *virtual desktops*, in Internet Suspend/Resume and Collective [11, 21, 34, 35]. The approach opposite to the pre-copy style is post-copy migration. VMs are resumed on their destination first, and then their state is retrieved. Examples of this approach include work by Hines et al. [16, 17] and by Liu et al. [24]. Post-copy migration is often desirable when migrating all state as fast as possible is prohibitive with respect to available network resources. Also in such situations, optimized techniques have proven to be effective that are based on a pre-copy approach [9, 44] and large-scale solutions such as VM distribution networks [31–33]. Hybrid approaches utilizing pre-copy and post-copy have also been proposed [26]. Finally, various optimizations to migration have been used, such as page compression [15, 40] and guest throttling [9, 27]. Page compression can considerably reduce the amount of state transfer, being effective when the migration process is not bottlenecked by CPUs. Guest throttling helps live migration to complete early by limiting the rate of page dirtying. In this work, on the other hand, we aim to let VMs that are already slowed down by contention consume as many physical resources as possible.

The other key aspect of our work is enlightenment, which has been used in various ways. Satori [28] uses the knowledge of guests about their reclaimable memory, for memory consolidation between multiple VMs. Ballooning [41] is another well-established form of explicit guest involvement in the memory reclamation by the hypervisor. Our work applied the concept of enlightenment to migration, and investigated how explicit guest support can improve migration performance. An alternative approach to full enlightenment through guest cooperation is to use hypervisor-level inference. Kaleidoscope [10] exploits memory semantics inferred from architecture specifications, and uses the obtained information for fast VM cloning. JAVMM [18] expedites migration of VMs containing Java applications, by having them inform the hypervisor of memory containing garbage-collectable objects and avoiding its transfer. There also exists previous work that takes the task of migration into the appli-

cation layer, instead of passing available knowledge down to systems software. Zephyr [14], Madeus [29], and ElasTraS [13] are examples of such approaches applied to databases. Imagen [25] targets active sessions for JavaScript web applications, migrating them between devices for ubiquitous access. Wang et al. [42] proposed a fault tolerance scheme for MPI applications that triggers their live migration.

7. Conclusion

We presented enlightened post-copy, an approach to urgently migrating VMs under contention. It addresses aspects of VM migration differing from the focus of the existing approaches: urgent execution transfer of the migrated VM, thereby recovering the aggregate performance of the contending VMs rapidly. Live migration, which is the current standard, exhibits undesirable characteristics in these aspects due to its design choices. Departing from its blackbox nature, we treat migration as a native functionality of the guest OS. Enlightened post-copy exploits this cooperation between the guest OS and the hypervisor, allowing prioritized post-copy state transfer that achieves the above objectives. Our prototype, implemented in guest Linux and qemu-kvm, requires only moderate changes to the guest kernel, and it demonstrates that the cooperative approach resolves the contention between VMs up to several times faster than live migration.

Acknowledgements

This research was supported by the National Science Foundation under grant number CNS-1518865, the Alfred P. Sloan Foundation, and the Defense Advanced Research Projects Agency under grant number FA8650-11-C-7190. Additional support was provided by the Intel Corporation, Vodafone, Crown Castle, and the Conklin Kistler family fund. Any opinions, findings, conclusions or recommendations expressed in this material are those of the authors and should not be attributed to their employers or funding sources.

References

[1] AWS | Amazon Elastic Compute Cloud (EC2) - Scalable Cloud Hosting. http://aws.amazon.com/ec2.

[2] memcached - a distributed memory object caching system. http://memcached.org.

[3] OLTPBenchmark. http://oltpbenchmark.com/wiki.

[4] The Apache Cassandra Project. http://cassandra.apache.org.

[5] userfaultfd v4 [LWN.net]. https://lwn.net/Articles/644532.

[6] Virtio - KVM. http://www.linux-kvm.org/page/Virtio.

[7] VMware vSphere vMotion Architecture, Performance and Best Practices in VMware vSphere 5. http://www.vmware.com/files/pdf/vmotion-perf-vsphere5.pdf.

[8] Yahoo! Cloud Serving Benchmark (YCSB). https://github.com/brianfrankcooper/YCSB/wiki.

[9] R. Bradford, E. Kotsovinos, A. Feldmann, and H. Schiöberg. Live Wide-Area Migration of Virtual Machines Including Local Persistent State. In *Proceedings of the Third International Conference on Virtual Execution Environments (VEE '07)*, San Diego, CA, USA, June 2007.

[10] R. Bryant, A. Tumanov, O. Irzak, A. Scannell, K. Joshi, M. Hiltunen, A. Lagar-Cavilla, and E. de Lara. Kaleidoscope: Cloud Micro-elasticity via VM State Coloring. In *Proceedings of the Sixth ACM European Conference on Computer Systems (EuroSys '11)*, Salzburg, Austria, April 2011.

[11] R. Chandra, N. Zeldovich, C. Sapuntzakis, and M. S. Lam. The Collective: A Cache-based System Management Architecture. In *Proceedings of the Second Conference on Symposium on Networked Systems Design & Implementation - Volume 2 (NSDI '05)*, Boston, MA, USA, May 2005.

[12] C. Clark, K. Fraser, S. Hand, J. G. Hansen, E. Jul, C. Limpach, I. Pratt, and A. Warfield. Live Migration of Virtual Machines. In *Proceedings of the Second Conference on Symposium on Networked Systems Design & Implementation - Volume 2 (NSDI '05)*, Boston, MA, USA, May 2005.

[13] S. Das, D. Agrawal, and A. El Abbadi. ElasTraS: An Elastic, Scalable, and Self-managing Transactional Database for the Cloud. *ACM Transactions on Database Systems*, 38(1), April 2013.

[14] A. J. Elmore, S. Das, D. Agrawal, and A. El Abbadi. Zephyr: Live Migration in Shared Nothing Databases for Elastic Cloud Platforms. In *Proceedings of the 2011 ACM SIGMOD International Conference on Management of Data (SIGMOD '11)*, Athens, Greece, June 2011.

[15] S. Hacking and B. Hudzia. Improving the Live Migration Process of Large Enterprise Applications. In *Proceedings of the Third International Workshop on Virtualization Technologies in Distributed Computing (VTDC '09)*, Barcelona, Spain, June 2009.

[16] M. R. Hines, U. Deshpande, and K. Gopalan. Post-copy Live Migration of Virtual Machines. *SIGOPS Operating Systems Review*, 43(3), July 2009.

[17] M. R. Hines and K. Gopalan. Post-copy Based Live Virtual Machine Migration Using Adaptive Pre-paging and Dynamic Self-ballooning. In *Proceedings of the 2009 ACM SIGPLAN/SIGOPS International Conference on Virtual Execution Environments (VEE '09)*, Washington, DC, USA, March 2009.

[18] K.-Y. Hou, K. G. Shin, and J.-L. Sung. Application-assisted Live Migration of Virtual Machines with Java Applications. In *Proceedings of the Tenth ACM European Conference on Computer Systems (EuroSys '15)*, Bordeaux, France, April 2015.

[19] K. Z. Ibrahim, S. Hofmeyr, C. Iancu, and E. Roman. Optimized Pre-copy Live Migration for Memory Intensive Applications. In *Proceedings of 2011 International Conference for High Performance Computing, Networking, Storage and Analysis (SC '11)*, Seattle, WA, USA, November 2011.

[20] A. Koto, H. Yamada, K. Ohmura, and K. Kono. Towards Unobtrusive VM Live Migration for Cloud Computing Platforms. In *Proceedings of the Third ACM SIGOPS Asia-Pacific Conference on Systems (APSys '12)*, Seoul, South Korea, July 2012.

[21] M. Kozuch, M. Satyanarayanan, T. Bressoud, and Y. Ke. Efficient State Transfer for Internet Suspend/Resume. *Intel Research Pittsburgh Technical Report IRP-TR-02-03*, May 2002.

[22] M. A. Kozuch and M. Satyanarayanan. Internet Suspend/Resume. In *Proceedings of the Fourth IEEE Workshop on Mobile Computing Systems and Applications*, Callicoon, NY, USA, June 2002.

[23] H. A. Lagar-Cavilla, J. A. Whitney, A. M. Scannell, P. Patchin, S. M. Rumble, E. de Lara, M. Brudno, and M. Satyanarayanan. SnowFlock: Rapid Virtual Machine Cloning for Cloud Computing. In *Proceedings of the Fourth ACM European Conference on Computer Systems (EuroSys '09)*, Nuremberg, Germany, April 2009.

[24] H. Liu, H. Jin, X. Liao, L. Hu, and C. Yu. Live Migration of Virtual Machine Based on Full System Trace and Replay. In *Proceedings of the Eighteenth ACM International Symposium on High Performance Distributed Computing (HPDC '09)*, Garching, Germany, June 2009.

[25] J. Lo, E. Wohlstadter, and A. Mesbah. Live Migration of JavaScript Web Apps. In *Proceedings of the Twenty-Second International Conference on World Wide Web (WWW '13 Companion)*, Rio de Janeiro, Brazil, May 2013.

[26] P. Lu, A. Barbalace, and B. Ravindran. HSG-LM: Hybrid-copy Speculative Guest OS Live Migration Without Hypervisor. In *Proceedings of the Sixth International Systems and Storage Conference (SYSTOR '13)*, Haifa, Israel, June 2013.

[27] A. J. Mashtizadeh, M. Cai, G. Tarasuk-Levin, R. Koller, T. Garfinkel, and S. Setty. XvMotion: Unified Virtual Machine Migration over Long Distance. In *Proceedings of the 2014 USENIX Annual Technical Conference (USENIX ATC '14)*, Philadelphia, PA, USA, June 2014.

[28] G. Miłós, D. G. Murray, S. Hand, and M. A. Fetterman. Satori: Enlightened Page Sharing. In *Proceedings of the 2009*

USENIX Annual Technical Conference (USENIX ATC '09), San Diego, CA, USA, June 2009.

[29] T. Mishima and Y. Fujiwara. Madeus: Database Live Migration Middleware Under Heavy Workloads for Cloud Environment. In *Proceedings of the 2015 ACM SIGMOD International Conference on Management of Data (SIGMOD '15)*, Melbourne, Australia, May 2015.

[30] M. Nelson, B.-H. Lim, and G. Hutchins. Fast Transparent Migration for Virtual Machines. In *Proceedings of the 2005 USENIX Annual Technical Conference (USENIX ATC '05)*, Anaheim, CA, USA, April 2005.

[31] C. Peng, M. Kim, Z. Zhang, and H. Lei. VDN: Virtual Machine Image Distribution Network for Cloud Data Centers. In *Proceedings of INFOCOM 2012*, Orlando, FL, USA, March 2012.

[32] J. Reich, O. Laadan, E. Brosh, A. Sherman, V. Misra, J. Nieh, and D. Rubenstein. VMTorrent: Virtual Appliances On-demand. In *Proceedings of the ACM SIGCOMM 2010 Conference (SIGCOMM '10)*, New Delhi, India, August 2010.

[33] J. Reich, O. Laadan, E. Brosh, A. Sherman, V. Misra, J. Nieh, and D. Rubenstein. VMTorrent: Scalable P2P Virtual Machine Streaming. In *Proceedings of the Eighth International Conference on Emerging Networking Experiments and Technologies (CoNEXT '12)*, Nice, France, December 2012.

[34] C. Sapuntzakis, D. Brumley, R. Chandra, N. Zeldovich, J. Chow, M. S. Lam, and M. Rosenblum. Virtual Appliances for Deploying and Maintaining Software. In *Proceedings of the Seventeenth USENIX Conference on System Administration (LISA '03)*, San Diego, CA, USA, October 2003.

[35] C. Sapuntzakis and M. S. Lam. Virtual Appliances in the Collective: A Road to Hassle-free Computing. In *Proceedings of the Ninth Conference on Hot Topics in Operating Systems - Volume 9 (HotOS '03)*, Lihue, HI, USA, May 2003.

[36] C. P. Sapuntzakis, R. Chandra, B. Pfaff, J. Chow, M. S. Lam, and M. Rosenblum. Optimizing the Migration of Virtual Computers. In *Proceedings of the Fifth Symposium on Operating Systems Design and Implementation (OSDI '02)*, Boston, MA, USA, December 2002.

[37] M. Satyanarayanan, B. Gilbert, M. Toups, N. Tolia, A. Surie, D. R. O'Hallaron, A. Wolbach, J. Harkes, A. Perrig, D. J. Farber, M. A. Kozuch, C. J. Helfrich, P. Nath, and H. A. Lagar-Cavilla. Pervasive Personal Computing in an Internet Suspend/Resume System. *IEEE Internet Computing*, 11(2), March 2007.

[38] A. Shribman and B. Hudzia. Pre-Copy and Post-copy VM Live Migration for Memory Intensive Applications. In *Proceedings of the Eighteenth International Conference on Parallel Processing Workshops (Euro-Par '12)*, Rhodes Island, Greece, August 2012.

[39] X. Song, J. Shi, R. Liu, J. Yang, and H. Chen. Parallelizing Live Migration of Virtual Machines. In *Proceedings of the Ninth ACM SIGPLAN/SIGOPS International Conference on Virtual Execution Environments (VEE '13)*, Houston, TX, USA, March 2013.

[40] P. Svärd, B. Hudzia, J. Tordsson, and E. Elmroth. Evaluation of Delta Compression Techniques for Efficient Live Migration of Large Virtual Machines. In *Proceedings of the Seventh ACM SIGPLAN/SIGOPS International Conference on Virtual Execution Environments (VEE '11)*, Newport Beach, CA, USA, March 2011.

[41] C. A. Waldspurger. Memory Resource Management in VMware ESX Server. In *Proceedings of the Fifth Symposium on Operating Systems Design and Implementation (OSDI '02)*, Boston, MA, USA, December 2002.

[42] C. Wang, F. Mueller, C. Engelmann, and S. L. Scott. Proactive Process-level Live Migration and Back Migration in HPC Environments. *Journal of Parallel and Distributed Computing*, 72(2), February 2012.

[43] A. Whitaker, R. S. Cox, M. Shaw, and S. D. Gribble. Constructing Services with Interposable Virtual Hardware. In *Proceedings of the First Conference on Symposium on Networked Systems Design and Implementation - Volume 1 (NSDI '04)*, San Francisco, CA, USA, March 2004.

[44] T. Wood, K. K. Ramakrishnan, P. Shenoy, and J. van der Merwe. CloudNet: Dynamic Pooling of Cloud Resources by Live WAN Migration of Virtual Machines. In *Proceedings of the Seventh ACM SIGPLAN/SIGOPS International Conference on Virtual Execution Environments (VEE '11)*, Newport Beach, CA, USA, March 2011.

SRVM: Hypervisor Support for Live Migration with Passthrough SR-IOV Network Devices

Xin Xu

VMware Inc
xinxu@vmware.com

Bhavesh Davda

VMware Inc
bhavesh@vmware.com

Abstract

Single-Root I/O Virtualization (SR-IOV) is a specification that allows a single PCI Express (PCIe) device (physical function or PF) to be used as multiple PCIe devices (virtual functions or VF). In a virtualization system, each VF can be directly assigned to a virtual machine (VM) in passthrough mode to significantly improve the network performance. However, VF passthrough mode is not compatible with live migration, which is an essential capability that enables many advanced virtualization features such as high availability and resource provisioning.

To solve this problem, we design SRVM which provides hypervisor support to ensure the VF device can be correctly used by the migrated VM and the applications. SRVM is implemented in the hypervisor without modification in guest operating systems or guest VM drivers. Our experimental results show that SRVM can effectively migrate all memory state, and there is no data loss or corruption in applications after live migration. SRVM does not increase VM downtime. It only costs limited resources (an extra CPU core), and there is no significant runtime overhead in VM network performance. In fact, since the VF can continue to be used during the pre-copy phase, it offers network throughput which is 9.6 times and network latency which is 98% lower compared to other solutions that switch to para-virtualization mode during live migration.

Keywords Virtualization; Live Migration; Passthrough; Virtual Network; SR-IOV

1. Introduction

Networking I/O performance is a crucial aspect when moving applications from bare-metal systems to virtualized en-

VEE '16,   April 2–3, 2016, Atlanta, Georgia, USA..
Copyright is held by the owner/author(s).
ACM 978-1-4503-3947-6/16/04.
http://dx.doi.org/10.1145/2892242.2892256

vironments, especially for those applications that are not traditionally hosted in virtualization systems. For example, in the High-Performance Computing domain, applications rely on technologies such as InfiniBand [1] and RDMA [2] to achieve sub-microsecond message passing latencies and multiple-Gbps throughput between systems. Similarly, telecommunications operators have specialized packet processing appliances that deal with packet rates in the millions of packets/second with low latency and jitter. Providing high-performance network for those applications in virtualization systems still remains a challenging task.

SR-IOV has been utilized in some commercial products to improve network performance [3, 4]. Figure 1 shows an architecture comparison between para-virtualization mode and SR-IOV in passthrough mode. Note that in this paper we assume a hypervisor contains both the virtual machine monitor as well as the control domain which provides drivers and management tools (as in VMware ESXi).

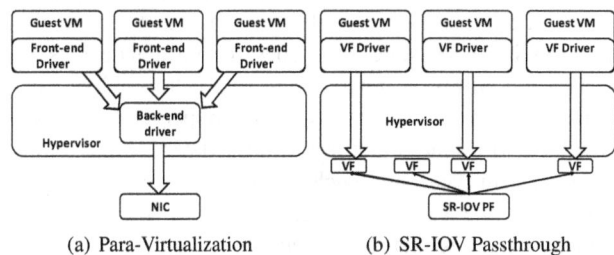

(a) Para-Virtualization   (b) SR-IOV Passthrough

Figure 1: Virtual Networking Architectures

Currently, para-virtualization mode is widely used for network I/O in virtual environments. As shown in Figure 1 (a), para-virtualized network I/O utilizes a back-end driver (also known as device emulation) in the hypervisor, between the guest VM and the physical device, to manage device sharing. This extra layer adds performance overhead compared to bare-metal machines.

In contrast, SR-IOV allows *self virtualization*, meaning that a single physical function (PF) can appear as multiple virtual functions (VF) in the hypervisor. Each VF can be directly assigned to a VM in passthrough mode as shown in Figure 1 (b). In passthrough mode, the hypervisor does only minimum management work to provision VFs for guest

VMs. The VF driver in the guest VM directly configures the VF for packet processing. This configuration greatly reduces I/O overhead compared to para-virtualization.

Figure 2 shows a performance comparison between para-virtualization mode and SR-IOV passthrough-mode. The numbers are normalized with respect to the results from the native machine. The performance is measured in terms of throughput and response time. The experiments are conducted using Intel Niantic 10GbE Ethernet Controller with VMware ESXi. Figure 2 (a) shows L3 packet forwarding rate using DPDK library for various packet sizes. SR-IOV passthrough mode closely matches the native packet forwarding rate. In contrast, the para-virtualization mode (VMware VMXNET3 driver) can only achieve 16.2% to 49.7% of native throughput. Figure 2 (b) shows the minimum, average and maximum latencies. The average latency of SR-IOV passthrough mode is only 13% higher than the native machine. In contrast, the latency of the para-virtualization mode is 107.7% higher than the native machine. The results demonstrate that SR-IOV passthrough mode significantly outperforms para-virtualization mode. Figure 2 (b) shows the SR-IOV normalized maximum latency (66.2%) is lower than the SR-IOV normalized average latency (113%), which is correct but counter-intuitive. This is because of normalization with respect to the results from the native machine. The SR-IOV absolute maximum latency is higher than the SR-IOV absolute average latency.

However, SR-IOV is not a perfect solution. A well-known limitation is that VMs with passthrough devices are not compatible with live migration, which seamlessly moves a running VM from one host machine to another. This is because the hypervisor cannot easily save and restore the passthrough device state as it does for virtual devices in the para-virtualization mode due to two factors. First, saving hardware state is difficult since the hypervisor does not know the entire state of the passthrough device. Most of the device state in data path, such as ring registers, is directly managed by the VF driver in the guest VM. And, second, restoring hardware state is difficult because the hypervisor cannot simply over-write the hardware state as it does to the software state. Some hardware state cannot be programmed by the hypervisor, and programming certain hardware state may trigger side-effects. For example, writing any value to the transmit ring tail register will cause packet transmission.

Another important reason why SR-IOV is not compatible with live migration is that the hypervisor cannot easily track the VM memory modified by the passthrough devices. Therefore, if the VF is receiving packets during live migration, the received data may not be migrated to the destination host, and the application will suffer from data loss.

Previous research addresses this issue mainly using two approaches: migrating hardware state [5, 6]) or migrating VMs without passthrough devices [7, 8]. The approach of migrating hardware state tries to do transitional checkpoint-

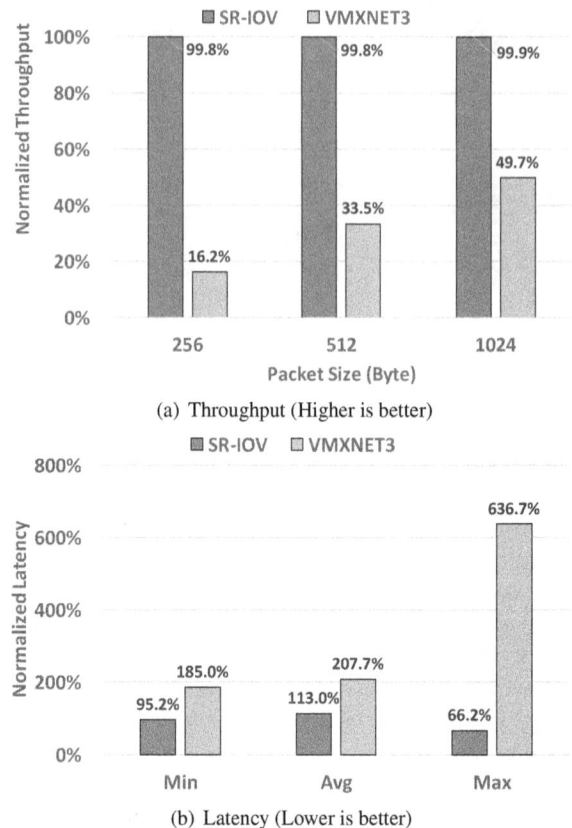

(a) Throughput (Higher is better)

(b) Latency (Lower is better)

Figure 2: Performance Comparison of Virtualization Network

and-restore to migrate as much hardware state as possible. For hardware state that cannot be checkpointed or saved, this approach utilizes an emulation layer to emulate them. It also requires major modifications to the guest OS or drivers. It is therefore difficult to adopt.

The other approach detaches the passthrough device before live migration, so VMs are migrated without passthrough devices. This approach generally relies on bonding two network adapters, one para-virtualized network adapter and one passthrough adapter, using a special driver (e.g., Linux bonding driver [9] or Microsoft NetVSC [8]). Those bonding drivers are OS specific, e.g. Microsoft Hyper-V only supports live migration with passthrough devices in Windows guest VMs. Also, the passthrough device is not available during live migration, which may affect network throughput. For large sized VMs, which may take a long time to migrate (tens of minutes), this performance degradation should be avoided, if possible. Moreover, some applications (e.g., Network Function Virtualization or NFV) commonly utilize Date Plane Development Kits (DPDK) to achieve high performance networking. DPDK requires direct hardware access to a single network interface, and therefore it is not compatible with bonding driver.

In this paper, we describe the design and implementation of SRVM, which provides hypervisor support to enable live migration for SR-IOV passthrough network devices. SRVM does not require modification in the guest driver or kernel, and allows the device to be used during live migration. The key observation is that it is not necessary to do traditional checkpoint and restore for passthrough devices. We only need to guarantee correct functioning of the device so that high-performance passthrough network activity can be maintained during and after live migration.

There are three technical challenges to design and implement SRVM. First, during live migration, the application that is receiving network packets may suffer from data loss, if received data are not properly handled. This is because received packets are placed in VM memory through direct memory access (DMA). DMA is directly issued from a VF device to guest VM memory, assisted by hardware IOMMU (e.g. Intel VT-d [10]). The hypervisor does not know which pages are modified by DMA, and therefore won't explicitly migrate modified VM memory.

Second, after live migration, the destination host must provision a new VF for the migrated VM. But the guest VF driver still has the original state. The hypervisor must make the new VF accessible to the guest VM and synchronize state between the guest VF driver and the new VF.

Third, SR-IOV can be used with user-level poll mode drivers (such as DPDK) to achieve high-throughput and low-latency networking. It is important that the proposed techniques work not only with traditional guest OS drivers (such as Intel IXGBEVF), but also with DPDK.

SRVM is designed to solve these problems. Specifically, we make three contributions in this paper:

- We develop a new technique to provide hypervisor support for tracking dirty memory pages. To the best of our knowledge, this is the first solution to dirty memory tracking without modification in the guest driver or OS kernel. It explicitly tracks and migrates the modified VM memory that may otherwise be lost after live migration.

- We also provide hypervisor support to provision VFs after live migration, which does not require modification in guest OS or driver. SRVM only saves a minimum set of the control path data (e.g., PCI configuration and MSI-X interrupt table), and restores it to a new VF in the destination host so that the guest VF driver can access the device and synchronize device state after live migration.

- We design and implement our techniques in both the Intel IXGBEVF driver and the DPDK user-level poll mode driver. To the best of our knowledge, this method is the first attempt to support user-level poll-mode driver.

We also conduct thorough evaluation to demonstrate the effectiveness and the performance overhead of our approach. This paper is organized as follows. Section 2 provides the background information on live migration and SR-IOV. Section 3 discusses existing work and explains the advantages of SRVM. Section 4 explains SRVM design details and imple-

mentation issues. Section 5 shows the evaluation results of SRVM in terms of effectiveness and performance overhead. Section 6 concludes the paper.

2. Background and Motivation

In this section, we explain the basics of live migration and SR-IOV device, and then explain the reason why live migration is not compatible with device passthrough mode.

2.1 Live Migration

Live migration is an important virtualization feature [11]. It allows a VM to be migrated from one machine to another while the VM is running. VM data to be migrated include CPU state, memory, and other virtual devices state such as virtual network devices. Live migration typically consists of the following steps [12].

Mark memory pages. In the beginning of live migration, the VM will be briefly paused. All memory pages of this VM will be marked as dirty, and will be migrated later.

Pre-copy. After all memory pages are marked, the pre-copy phase starts. Pre-copy iteratively scans the entire VM memory and migrate pages that have been marked as dirty. During the pre-copy phase, the VM is running. A page that has been migrated may be modified again (dirtied). The hypervisor needs to trap those modification and mark those pages as dirty, to make sure they are migrated. Tracking dirty pages can be done with hardware support (e.g., Intel EPT [13]) or without hardware support (e.g., shadow page table).

Pre-copy can have several iterations until only a small number of memory pages are left or the specified criteria are met (e.g., maximum time is reached). The pre-copy phase may be time-consuming (tens of minutes) if VM memory is large or the VM has memory-intensive workloads [12].

Checkpoint. After the pre-copy completes, the hypervisor will pause VM again and checkpoint the virtual device state and the virtual CPU state.

Switch-over. The checkpoint data and the remaining dirtied pages that are not copied by the pre-copy phase will be transferred to the destination.

Resume VM. After all data are transferred, the checkpoint data will be restored to the VM in the destination host. The VM is then resumed on the destination host.

2.2 SR-IOV Network Devices

SR-IOV network devices has been used in platforms requiring high performance network I/O [3]. A SR-IOV device can be used in full-function mode or in SR-IOV mode. When used in full-function mode, the device will be used as a single interface like other regular network devices. When used in SR-IOV mode, the hypervisor can configure the device to appear as multiple VFs in the host. For example, the Intel 82599 (codename Niantic) 10GB network controller supports a maximum of 63 VFs for each PF [14]. Kernel-level VF drivers (e.g., Intel IXGBEVF [15]) have already been in-

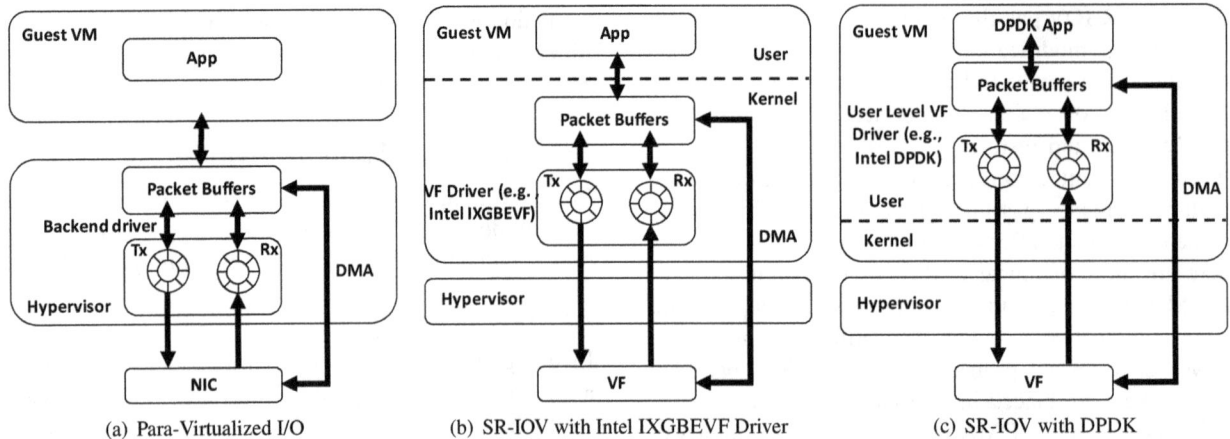

(a) Para-Virtualized I/O   (b) SR-IOV with Intel IXGBEVF Driver   (c) SR-IOV with DPDK

Figure 3: Packet Delivery Paths

tegrated into current OS so that the guest VM can easily use a VF in passthrough mode to achieve high performance.

Intel's Data Place Development Kit (DPDK) [16] is a user-level driver library that also supports SR-IOV VF passthrough mode. This software framework allows network applications to process packets in the user-level bypassing the kernel network stack. The network performance can be further improved by using DPDK with passthrough VF.

2.3 Live Migration with SR-IOV Passthrough VF

While SR-IOV provides high performance, the hypervisor does not have full control over the VFs in passthrough mode. The hypervisor only handles the control path, such as setting up PCI configuration, interrupt delivery, and memory mapped I/O (MMIO). The guest VF driver (Intel IXGBEVF or DPDK) directly manages the data path, such as setting up Tx/Rx rings and allocating data buffers. During packet transmission, the VF will directly access guest VM memory without assistance from the hypervisor. This causes a problem in the pre-copy phase, the checkpoint phase and the resume phase during live migration.

To better explain this problem, we compare the packet delivery paths of para-virtualization, SR-IOV passthrough with Intel IXGBEVF, and SR-IOV passthrough with DPDK user-level library, as shown in Figure 3. In para-virtualization mode, the back-end driver and hypervisor configure the packet delivery path of the physical device. Specifically, the ring buffers and packet buffers that are used to send and receive packets through the physical network interface are allocated by the hypervisor (through the bank-end driver). The hypervisor knows exactly when and where these packets are allocated or freed. Taking receiving packets as an example, the physical device writes all received packets to the packet buffers in the hypervisor. Then, the packet data is demultiplexed by a virtual switch in the hypervisor to determine which guest VM they should be delivered to. The back-end driver then delivers the packets to the guest VM.

The front-end driver in the guest VM thus only interacts with the back-end driver, rather than the actual physical device.

This configuration gives the hypervisor full control over the guest VM network. During the live migration pre-copy phase, the hypervisor can know which packets have been received, and can explicitly migrate them to ensure the destination host receives the up-to-date data. The hypervisor can also save and restore guest VM network configuration for since they are essentially state captured in the VM memory.

This is not the case in SR-IOV passthrough mode. Figure 3 (b) shows the architecture when Intel IXGBEVF is used in the guest VM. The packet processing path is moved up from the hypervisor to the guest VM. The guest driver directly configures the Tx/Rx rings and allocates the memory buffers within its own guest VM memory regions. The device can directly access these guest memory buffers through DMA. The only hypervisor intervention required is for interrupt delivery, assuming the VF is configured to deliver interrupts for I/O completion and other events. If the VF is used in poll mode as with DPDK, the hypervisor cannot even know when the packet is sent or received. Figure 3 (c) shows the architecture when a user-level poll mode driver (e.g. DPDK) is used. The packet delivery path is further moved up into the user-level. The packet buffers are managed and allocated in the user level memory regions within the guest VM.

In SR-IOV passthrough mode, the guest VF driver directly configures the VF for sending and receiving packets. For example, the guest VF driver should allocate memory buffers for packets and should configure the VF to access these buffers. DMA can only access memory through machine memory addresses, while the guest VF driver only provides guest physical addresses. Translation between guest physical addresses and machine addresses is done through a hardware IOMMU (e.g. Intel VT-d). The hypervisor only does a one-time configuration of IOMMU for VMs.

This SR-IOV passthrough mode (for both SR-IOV with Intel IXGBEVF driver and SR-IOV with DPDK driver) causes two problems for live migration. The first problem is that in the pre-copy phase, the hypervisor is not able to track the pages that have been modified by DMA, because the address translation for DMA is done by hardware IOMMU not the hypervisor. If a page has already been migrated and is then modified by DMA, it will not be migrated again. As a result, the application may end up using incorrect data after live migration.

Another issue comes from restoring passthrough VF state in the checkpoint phase. In general, virtual device state can be easily saved and restored because it is essentially software state. But a passthrough VF is a hardware device that is not entirely configured by the hypervisor. Some hardware state (e.g., stats registers) are read-only, and they simply cannot be programmed by the hypervisor. Moreover, writing to some registers may cause side effects. For example, writing any value to the tail register of the transmit ring buffer will trigger packet transmission on the device. Therefore, restoring VF state is not as simple as restoring virtual device state.

Because of these two problems, current hypervisors either disable live migration for passthrough devices [17–19] or prevent using passthrough devices during live migration [8].

3. Related Work

Efforts have been made in both research and industrial communities to resolve this issue. Existing solutions are typically based on one of three techniques: 1) NIC bonding; 2) Shadow driver; 3) VF driver support. NIC bonding migrates VMs without the passthrough device. The shadow driver approach and the VF driver support approach migrate VMs by migrating the hardware state. A comparison of these techniques with SRVM is shown in Table 1. We discuss each technique and solutions below.

NIC bonding is a technique that aggregates multiple network interfaces into a single interface through a special driver such as Linux ethernet bonding driver [9]. A VF can be bonded with another virtual network interface that is compatible with live migration. Before live migration starts, the VF can be detached from the VM and traffic will go through the virtual network interface. In this way, the network connectivity is preserved during live migration. The VF is not available during live migration, so there is no dirty memory page issue. A Linux bonding driver is used with a hotplug mechanism to provide live migration capability for Linux VMs with SR-IOV passthrough devices [7]. Microsoft Hyper-V also uses a similar technique in which removal of the VF interface is done by a Windows plug-in, the Microsoft Network Virtual Service Client (NetVSC). However, current bonding drivers are designed for OS kernel drivers. For user-level driver libraries like DPDK, which is not managed by the OS kernel, it is not clear how to utilize bonding drivers for live migration. DPDK is likely used in NFV workload because of its high performance. It is critical to provide support for DPDK. Also, in this approach the high-

performance data path of SR-IOV is not available during the pre-copy phase. For large-sized VMs, which may take tens of minutes to migrate, the network performance degradation is significant.

Research work has been proposed to enable live migration of SR-IOV passthrough device using a shadow driver [5]. As shadow driver is an extra layer in the guest OS between the kernel and driver, that monitors the driver state and operations. After live migration, the shadow driver can restore the driver state on the destination host and can emulate the state that cannot be migrated. Marking dirty pages is not explicitly discussed in the paper. While this approach supports live migration between hosts with different types of passthrough device, it requires major modifications in the guest OS, which makes it difficulty to utilize.

Guest VF driver support has been proposed to enable live migration to track dirty memory pages and to handle VF migration [6, 20]. Both use a similar technique to track dirty page, by explicitly writing dummy data into each received page so that the page modification can be captured by the hypervisor. The advantage of this approach is that it can be easily implemented in the guest VF driver. But this involves memory access and memory address translation in each received packet, which may significantly affect network performance. Many network applications that do not even access the packet data, such as bridging, may suffer performance degradation because of this approach. This is desirable since the most important advantage of SR-IOV passthrough is high performance. Also, this approach may cause security concerns since the guest VF driver explicitly modifies every received network packet. To handle VF migration, CompSC tries to migrate the entire VF state, which requires an emulation layer for the state that cannot be migrated (e.g. stats and ring registers) [6]; whereas in another work [20], they only migrate partial state by suspending and resuming the VF from the VF driver.

In general, providing guest VF driver support is less complicated to design than hypervisor support because the VF driver directly controls the data path. But it is not easy to adopt because users are required to replace original drivers with the modified version. We believe that hypervisor support for live migration of SR-IOV passthrough devices is necessary because it is easier for users to leverage this feature. Our solution requires no modification to the guest OS or drivers. It does not require any emulation layer after live migration, and allows the VF device to be used during the live migration pre-copy phase. The detailed design of SRVM is explained in the following section.

4. SRVM Design

Our goal is to provide hypervisor support for live migration of SR-IOV passthrough devices instead of modifying the guest OS or VF drivers. SRVM mainly consists of two components: the dirty memory tracking module and the SR-IOV

Table 1. Related Works Comparison with SRVM

	No Guest OS Modification	VF is Available during Live Migration	No Need to Access Packet Data	DPDK Support
NIC Bonding [7, 8]	Yes	No	Yes	No
Shadow Driver [5]	No	Yes	Yes	No*
VF Driver Support [6, 20]	No	Yes	No	No*
Hypervisor Support (SRVM)	Yes	Yes	Yes	Yes

* The approach may be made to work with DPDK driver library with major modifications, but currently there is no such support

VF checkpoint module. The architecture of our approach is illustrated in Figure 4.

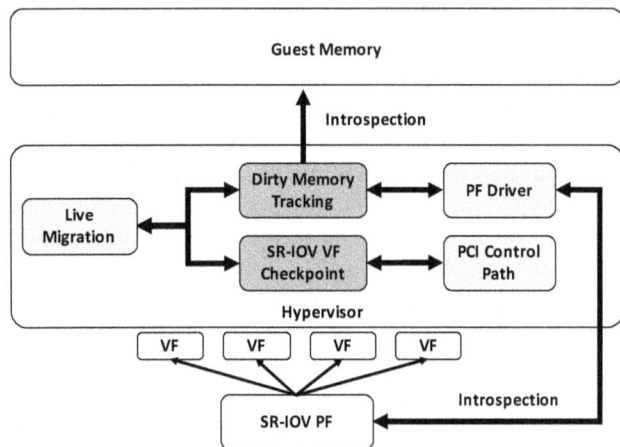

Figure 4: SRVM Design Framework

The dirty memory tracking module is enabled at the beginning of the pre-copy phase. It leverages the SR-IOV PF driver in the hypervisor to inspect the VF state, to obtain the addresses of received packets. Then, it sends these addresses to the live migration module for migration later on. The dirty memory tracking module ensures that all received data can be migrated, and it stops when the pre-copy phase is over.

Next, the SR-IOV VF checkpoint module starts to save the control path state of the VF (e.g., MMIO and the MSI-X interrupt vector table). At the destination host, this module provisions a new VF for the migration VM and restores the saved state to the control path of the newly provisioned VF. This module ensures that the guest VF driver can access the new VF in the destination host as if it were accessing the original VF. In the following, we discuss the design and major implementation issues for each module in detail.

4.1 Dirty Memory Tracking

Lifetime of Memory Tracking Module. The memory tracking module is only needed when live migration is started. It can be enabled by the live migration module at the beginning of the pre-copy phase and disabled after the pre-copy is done. This implementation means that there is no overhead during normal execution of the VM.

Tracking dirty memory cannot be easily done in the hypervisor because the hypervisor does not configure the data path of the passthrough VF. But the VF hardware state is stored in the PF hardware device, so we can inspect the VF state through the PF driver instead of using the VF driver. The next step is to determine which state to inspect to obtain the dirty memory information.

Obtaining Ring Information. Network I/O devices generally use ring structures for packet reception and transmission. Fig. 5 shows how a ring is used for receiving packets for a VF device. A ring is created in guest VM memory when the VF driver initializes the VF. The ring contains a limited number of entries (e.g., 512), and each entry specifies a packet data address. The network device finds the packet data through the addresses in the ring, and reads (writes) data via DMA for transmission (reception). To track dirty memory pages, we need to obtain the ring location and inspect the entries in the ring. A key insight is that only the receive ring is required because memory pages are only dirtied when VM is receiving packets (but not sending packets).

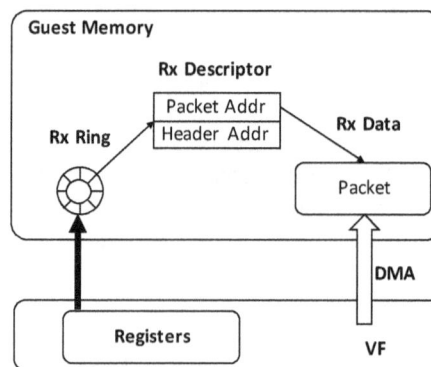

Figure 5: VF Receiving Ring

The ring information such as the ring base address and length is stored in several specific registers in the VF device. The PF driver can access those registers [14] and our dirty memory tracking module interacts with the PF driver to obtain this information. Note that this step should be done at the beginning of the pre-copy and it only needs to be done once during the entire live migration, because the ring information will not change until the VF device is reconfigured. If the VF is reset, we need to obtain the ring information again.

The resetting event will be handled by PF driver, and therefore the PF driver and the hypervisor can notify the module to refresh the ring information.

Introspecting Ring Memory. Once the receiving ring information is obtained, we need to examine the ring to find newly updated descriptors, which contain the packet addresses of received packets. We only need to obtain the packet addresses for migration, and we do not need to access the actual packet data. Therefore, our module only inspects a small piece of guest memory (approximately 2KB).

Packets can be received in two modes: interrupt mode or poll mode. The design of inspecting ring memory may vary depending on the receive mode. Interrupt mode is usually the default mode of the VF driver (e.g. Intel IXGBEVF). Packet arrival is notified by a hardware interrupt from VF. This interrupt will be delivered to the guest VM by the hypervisor. Therefore, we can use this interrupt delivery as the signal to activate the memory tracking module to inspect the ring. When there is no interrupt delivery, the dirty memory tracking module can be put to sleep to minimize resource utilization.

In poll mode, the VF driver will constantly examine the VF device to see if there are any new packet, and no receiving interrupt will be generated. This mode is used for high-performance and low-latency applications (e.g., DPDK user-level library). Interrupt-based inspection will not work with poll mode drivers, since packet arrival is not notified by an interrupt. To work with poll mode drivers, our module can also work in poll mode. That is, our module can constantly examine the ring for new packets instead of waiting for an interrupt. This approach will increase resource usage, but requiring this extra resource usage is reasonable because poll mode drivers like DPDK also sacrifice similar overheads by polling to achieve high-performance and low-latency networking. Also, the overhead is only incurred by the memory track module during live migration. For these two reasons, we use poll mode dirty page tracking in the current implementation.

Lockless Introspection. Ring memory is accessed by both the VF driver and our dirty memory tracking module and the VF driver is not aware that there is another module constantly reading the ring memory. A lock between the hypervisor and the VF driver might be used to prevent any potential race conditions. But a locking mechanism requires modifications in the VF guest driver. It also slows down packet processing and may even cause packet drops. Therefore, using a lock is not feasible, and we choose to use lockless inspection instead.

In fact, our module only does read access. As long as our module can process ring memory faster than VF packet processing, using a lock is not necessary. In fact, the inspection can be done very fast because it essentially just reads ring memory to obtain an address and then changes the corresponding bit in a bitmap. In Section 5.4, we evaluate the time spent in our module and VF packet processing to show that we can ensure our module processes faster than the packet arrival rate. Based on our experiments, SRVM performance is impacted by descheduling and interrupts. However, by assigning a dedicated core to SRVM and migrating interrupts out from the dedicated core during the pre-copy stage, this impact can be mitigated. Other sources of variance can be disabled by disabling power management and setting the host BIOS to maximum performance. We empirically found the above configurations can ensure SRVM processes data faster than the VF receives packets.

However, if the system is not properly configured, our module may be slowed down. Hardware support may be designed for such case to detect if SRVM misses any received packets. For example, a page fault behavior is described in PCI(e) address translation service specification [21]. PCI(e) devices and hardware IOMMU can leverage this page fault behavior to allow the hypervisor to track all the dirtied memory pages (by DMA) by raising a page fault. Current PCI(e) devices and hardware IOMMU do not support such page fault behavior, and future research and development effort is required. Note that even if this page fault behavior is supported by hardware in future, it alone cannot solve the dirty memory tracking problem while maintaining high performance. Because triggering a page fault for every received packet is likely too expensive, and the network throughput will be significantly affected. But IOMMU page fault may help us improve SRVM in other ways such as reducing required CPU resources for tracking dirty pages. With this hardware support, we may not need a dedicated CPU core for ring inspection. We will investigate this in our future work.

Also, two techniques can be employed to improve the processing speed of our module. One potential solution is deliberately slowing down the live migration VM if a high VF receiving rate is observed. This same approach has been used in VMware ESX when the memory dirty rate is too high during live migration [12]. Another potential solution is using multiple threads to process ring memory in parallel. Each thread can be assigned to a CPU core exclusively, which can further improve the processing performance. Since our evaluation shows that current single thread implementation can already process the ring fast enough, we use this single-thread implementation in the paper.

Network devices can be configured with multiple queues. SRVM currently uses one core per queue. Multiple queues would require multiple cores. SRVM can obtain VF configuration through PF driver to determine the required CPU cores. It is possible that SRVM cannot find an idle core for certain configurations (e.g. migrating too many VMs with VFs simultaneously). But such cases can be reliably detected and handled (e.g., alert users) by the hypervisor or management software, which manage live migration and its required CPU resources.

Introspect Ring Descriptor. A ring descriptor contains the address of packet data. Our module just needs to read the descriptor to identify the address. Our implementation is based on the Intel 82599 10GbB NIC card [14]. Its ring descriptor has two different formats: advanced descriptor format and legacy descriptor format. By examining the VF register, we can identify the currently used format. With the legacy format, the addresses of header and payload will be stored in the descriptor until the descriptor is recycled and over-written with a new descriptor by the VF driver. In this case, our module can directly read the descriptor to obtain the addresses.

The advanced descriptor format is different. The addresses are stored in the descriptor before the packet data is received. Once the packet data is received, the hardware will immediately over-write the descriptor with meta-data. In this mode, our module obtains the packet addresses of the allocated packet buffers that have not been written with new data through DMA, and marks them dirty. That is, our module is *pre-processing* the packet addresses before new data are written instead of *post-processing*. So our module does not rely the head and tail pointers for inspection. This is beneficial because accessing those device registers may slow down the inspection speed. In fact, this does not have any adverse impact on the correctness of the migrated VM or applications, because those allocated buffers eventually need to be migrated if they are filled with new received data in the future.

4.2 SR-IOV VF checkpoint

After live migration, the original passthrough VF is gone, and the guest VM has to use a newly provisioned VF on the destination host. However, the guest VM does not know about this change, and it will still try to access the VF with the original configuration. The access may fail without special handling in the hypervisor. Our SR-IOV VF checkpoint module must properly insert the new VF to solve two problems: 1) the control path of the new VF must be properly configured so that the VM can continue accessing this VF device through its original configuration; 2) synchronize the data path configuration state between the new VF and the guest VF driver so that the device can properly process packets.

Checkpoint the control path configuration. In general, PCI devices are first configured by the OS before they can be accessed by drivers. In the virtualization system, SR-IOV devices are configured by the hypervisor before they can be used by the guest VM in passthrough mode. The control path configuration mainly involves PCI(e) configurations (e.g., MMIO configuration) and interrupt delivery.

PCI(e) configuration is stored in a set of standard device registers in each PCI(e) device, no matter what type of PCI(e) devices they are. The OS or the hypervisor follows standard steps to configure the device [22], such as configuring memory mapped I/O (MMIO) and enabling the device.

After this configuration is done, the driver can access the device through MMIO. In our case, to allow the VF driver to access the new VF in the destination host, the MMIO configuration must be saved and restored.

In native machines, MMIO can be configured by the BIOS or OS. Mapped MMIO addresses will be stored in PCI base address registers (BARs). In current VMware ESXi, a virtual MMIO of SR-IOV passthrough VF is exposed to the guest VM. This virtual MMIO can be leveraged to checkpoint the control path configuration. The virtual MMIO design in the VMware ESXi is illustrated in Figure 6.

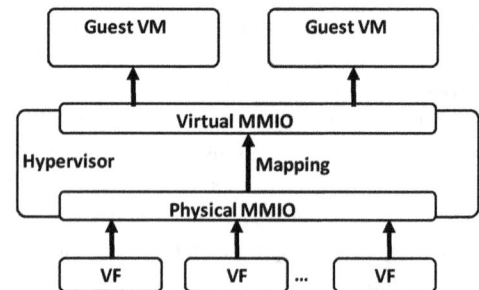

Figure 6: Virtual MMIO Mapping

The guest VM only sees a virtual MMIO, and the hypervisor manages the mapping between the physical MMIO of a VF and a virtual MMIO. After live migration, the guest VM will try to use the same virtual MMIO to access the VF. But the hypervisor on the new host will associate a new virtual MMIO with the newly provisioned VF. The consequence is that the guest VF driver cannot access the VF anymore, even though a new VF has been provisioned.

To allow the guest VM to access this new VF in the destination, the hypervisor needs to save and restore the original virtual MMIO. The virtual MMIO configuration can be obtained from the VF device through the VF's BARs. The design of the virtual MMIO greatly improves the flexibility of provisioning VFs. For example, the VF ID in the destination host and the source host can be different. If the VF ID in the source host has been taken by other VMs, we can provision any other available VFs for the migrated VM in the destination VMs.

Interrupt delivery should also be provisioned in the control path. The hypervisor is required to configure interrupt delivery for the VF even if it is in passthrough mode. Specifically, our module saves and restores the interrupt vector table (e.g., MSI-X in the Intel 82599 10GB NIC). The hypervisor then configures the interrupt delivery path according to the restored interrupt vector table to ensure that interrupts can be delivered to the correct VM. In this way, the migrated VM will be able to access the new VF through the original VF driver state. Configuring interrupt delivery is a one-time setup only when the VM is first powered on or migrated. The hypervisor is not involved in the MMIO accesses from guest VMs. SRVM does not rely on or change the VF interrupt delivery path, so it can work with DPDK which does not use interrupt to notify packet arrival.

Note that our approach requires that the destination host has the same SR-IOV device. This is the same requirement for using the VF driver support approach [6, 20]. To automate the live migration, modifications can be made in the virtualization management software (such as VMware vCenter) to automatically select a pool of available destination hosts with the same SR-IOV device. We plan to implement this feature as part of our future work.

Reset VF. At this point, the VF device will not correctly function because the data paths are not synchronized. That is, the new device has a clean state, but the guest VM driver still carries the old state of the original VF. To synchronize the data path, we set the VF device to a reset state from the hypervisor. This can be detected by the VF driver, which will then clean the driver state, allowing the device to function correctly. Note that by its nature, DPDK applications need to initialize and configure VFs through DPDK. To correctly handle VF reset for live migration, the application should include the status checking and resetting functions from the DPDK library. These are common routines that a robust DPDK application should do and can be easily implemented with unmodified driver library.

Note that our implementation is based on VMware ESXi and the Intel 82599 10GB NIC, but the design of SRVM essentially relies on PCI-SIG standard mechanisms such as SR-IOV VF interfaces and MMIO registers mapped via BARs. The concept of invoking a device-specific callback for tracking dirty pages can be applied to different I/O devices from different vendors for different technologies including storage (e.g. SAS controllers), networking, InfiniBand, etc. SRVM only needs to define high-level APIs to obtain information for live migration, e.g., dirtied page number. We plan to further investigate supporting these devices for future work. Other hypervisors such as KVM can leverage SRVM because they use similar live migration techniques and SR-IOV PF/VF driver interfaces.

5. Evaluation

We conduct a series of experiments to evaluate SRVM in terms of both effectiveness and performance impact. Essentially, we would like to use experiments to answer these questions:

- Can SRVM successfully track dirty memory pages?
- What is the downtime of live migration when using SRVM?
- What is the performance overhead of SRVM?

5.1 Experimental Setup

The experiment setup is as shown in Figure 7. We use two Dell PowerEdge T320 servers as the migration source and destination hosts. Each host has 24GB memory, one six-

core Intel Xeon E5-2440 CPU, and one two-port Intel 82599 10GB NIC. VMs are configured with 4 VCPU, 8GB memory, one VMXNET3 network interface (for live migration and management) and one VF passthrough network interface for application traffic. Both VMs are running RedHat Enterprise Linux Workstation 7.0. The migration VM on the source is used for live migration, and the testing VM on the destination host is used to generate network traffic and to measure downtime. The migration VM and the testing VM are connected through passthrough VFs. If our approach is effective, the testing VM should be able to connect to the migration VM through VFs before, during and after live migration (with downtime). Our prototype is implemented based on VMware ESXi.

For each experiment, we test two drivers, the Intel IXGBEVF driver (shipped with the OS) and DPDK 2.1.0 [16]. The Intel IXGBEVF driver is configured in interrupt mode by default. We use DPDK Pktgen 2.9.5 [23] to generate high packet rates. We also develop simple packet sending/receiving applications for DPDK and IXGBEVF for testing. The applications can send packets with data in specified formats so that we can easily verify if there are any missing packets.

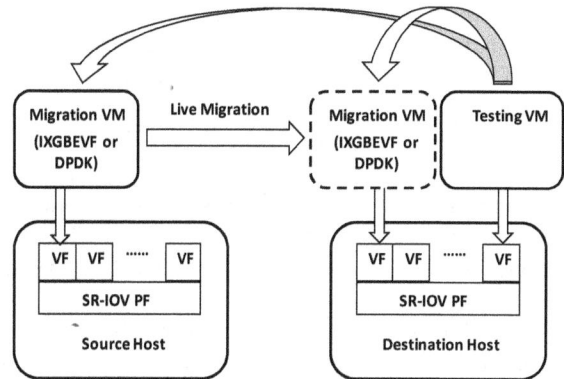

Figure 7: Experimental Setup

5.2 Packet Missing

Without SRVM, the packets that have been received during live migration may not be migrated to the destination. The consequence is that the application cannot know if its data are correct after live migration. To show the effectiveness of SRVM, we conduct experiments to compare those received packet buffers before and after live migration.

In the testing VM, we write a simple application to send packets from the test VM to the live migration VM. The packet is sent with a special format with an incrementing sequence number so that we can easily identify each packet.

For the DPDK driver, we allocate a large memory region containing 4KB buffers. This memory region is initialized with zero content and the DPDK application receives data directly into this memory buffer. The application does not update any data in the packet after the packet is received so the hypervisor won't consider them as dirty pages without SRVM. We compare the memory content before and after live migration. If there are no missing packets, the content should be the same. Any missing packet will show zero content in its buffer after live migration, whereas the same buffer before live migration should have data with a correct sequence number. An example is shown in Figure 8.

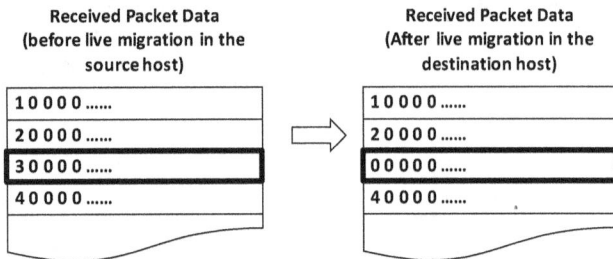

Figure 8: Missing Packet

We use the same test application for Intel IXGBEVF. To examine the received packets, we made modification to the driver in the related receiving functions. We examine the packet buffers in the receiving ring and also set he buffer size to 4KB. We compare the data in these buffers before and after live migration. If there are packets missing, the data in the same packet buffer are different. Note that this driver modification is solely for testing purposes, so that we can clearly see the missing packets. The memory tracking module does not require modifications to the Intel IXGBEVF driver.

To collect enough packets to compare, we run a simple application in the live migration VM that continuously writes dummy data into random memory pages. Running this application will increase the pre-copy phase of live migration to about two minutes, which is reasonable for our experiment. We repeat this experiment ten times. We always see packets missing when SRVM is not enabled and no packet missing with SRVM. As an example, Table 2 shows the result from one run of our experiments.

Table 2. Missing Packets After Live Migration

	SRVM	No SRVM
Intel IXGBEVF	0	86
DPDK	0	4

When using the Intel IXGBEVF driver, there are 111 received packets in total during the pre-copy phase. There are 86 packets missing after live migration. For DPDK, there are 4 packet missing out of 120 received packets. Note that the application or IXGBEVF driver will not be able to know if there is a missing packet. This essentially causes silent data corruption in applications. With SRVM, there is no data loss. The results effectively show that SRVM can track dirty memory pages and migrate them correctly.

High packet Rate. We use a lockless design for tracking dirty memory pages. If the packet receiving rate is higher

than the dirty memory tracking rate, some data may get lost. We conducted experiments to measure the dirty memory tracking rate. Specifically, we measure the time spent scanning an entire ring buffer (with 512 entries) and to mark those pages. We can scan and mark one packet in 28ns on average, including the time to inspect the ring memory and marking dirty pages. Comparatively, the packet processing rate is much slower than this. When using DPDK with SR-IOV passthrough mode, even if applications can run near line rate at 14.4 million packets (64KB) per second (mpps), and this translates to 69ns for processing each packet. Therefore, our module can track the packet much faster than a 10Gb NIC card can process packets. Also, note that usually near line rate speeds can only be achieved when the application is doing L2 forwarding, which basically does minimal packet processing. If the application does extra processing, the packet rate will drop. Moreover, there are more optimization that can be done to further improve the dirty memory tracking rate. For example, we can easily use multiple threads (CPU cores) for the dirty memory tracking module to improve the speed, and we can also separate inspection and marking tasks to future reduce the time spent on inspection. Therefore, we consider lockless inspection to be feasible.

5.3 Downtime

Downtime is an important metric for live migration. During the switch-over phase of live migration, there is a brief downtime for the migrated VM and its applications. This time should be as short as possible. We consider two types of downtime: VM downtime and network downtime. VM downtime is the period when the VM is paused. Network downtime is the period when the network is not available. SRVM needs extra time to set up the VF in the destination host, so the network will not be immediately ready after the VM is running, which means network downtime will be longer than VM downtime. We conduct experiments to examine both downtimes caused by SRVM.

For the Intel IXGBEVF driver, we use *ping* to measure network device downtime. We use another test VM to ping the live migration VM at short interval (100ms) through the VFs. Downtime is calculated as the total number of dropped ping packets multiplied by the ping interval. For the DPDK driver, *ping* won't work because the device is controlled by the DPDK application. Instead, we use the sending and receiving applications in Section 5.2 to measure network downtime. The test VM sends packets with sequence numbers at 100ms intervals. In the migrated VM, the receiving DPDK application examines the sequence number of the received packet to find dropped packets.

VM downtime is calculated by multiplying the number of missing packets by the interval, and is reported by examining the live migration logs in the source and destination hosts. We synchronize the time between two hosts and examine the time when the VM is paused in the source host and when it is resumed in the destination host.

Inside the migration VM, we run the memory dirtying application as the workload. As a comparison, we also measure the downtime of migrating the VM without a passthrough VF (with the VMXNET3 virtual device). We repeat experiments for three times and report the average downtime. Figure 9 shows the results of downtime for various configurations. The network downtime shown in the figure already includes the VM downtime. Note that the migrated VM is running a memory intensive application, so the measured results in this experiments may be longer than common cases.

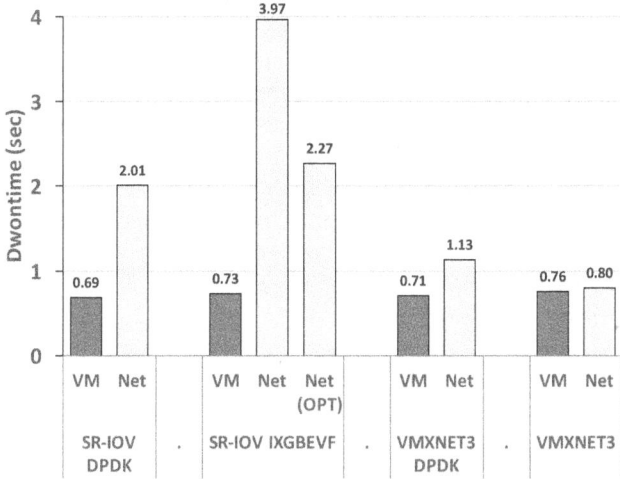

Figure 9: Comparison of VM and Network Downtime. For each configuration, VM downtime and network (Net) downtime are measured. For SR-IOV IXGBEVF, the downtime after optimization is shown as Net(OPT)

From the results, we can see our technique does not increase VM downtime. For example, migrating the VM with SR-IOV VF and DPDK driver results in 0.69s VM downtime. Comparatively, migrating the VM with VMXNET3 and DPDK driver results in 0.71s VM downtime. The VM downtimes are comparable. This is because SRVM may only affect VM downtime when it saves and restores VF configuration and we only save and restore minimum data.

But our technique did increase the network downtime. For the SR-IOV DPDK case, the downtime increases from 1.13s (VMXNET3) to 2.01s (SR-IOV). This is because it takes time for the driver to detect the device reset status and to reset the device (we set the interval of detecting device state to 0.1s). The extra downtime time (0.9s) involves device resetting and may have some other factors that we would like to investigate in the future. Note that during this extra time, VM is up and running.

For the SR-IOV IXGBEVF case, the downtime increases from 0.80s to 3.97s. We further examined the IXGBEVF driver and found that the extra downtime is due to the IXGBEVF watchdog timer that checks the device state with a 2s interval. Therefore, after VM is resumed the driver may not detect the reset event until the timer is fired. We change the timer interval from 2s to 0.01s, which allowed us to basically

remove this extra time and to understand the real downtime caused by resetting the device. After this simple optimization, the downtime was reduced to 2.3s. The network downtime overhead is about 1.5s. We plan to further investigate other sources of downtime and optimize it for future work. Note that our experiments show SRVM does not drop TCP connection. We believe TCP is resilient to transient changes to the underlying network like link state.

Previous approaches are evaluated in different hypervisors. Therefore, we cannot directly compare our downtime results with theirs. Also, the major difference of our approach is that it is completely designed and implemented in the hypervisor requiring no modifications to the guest OS and drivers. This is a very important design consideration for cloud service providers or infrastructure software providers, which greatly increases the portability of the approach.

5.4 Overhead

To understand the runtime performance overhead of SRVM, we conduct experiments to measure the network throughput and latency when network applications are running inside the migration VM. We also discuss the extra resource usage by our modules.

Network Throughput. To measure network throughput, we run DPDK in the VM. The application simply receives the packets that are sent from the testing VM through DPDK. Since SRVM only adds runtime overhead during the pre-copy phase, we measure the network throughput only in this phase. We compare the throughput in three different configurations.

- DPDK SRIOV with SRVM: DPDK uses the VF in passthrough mode with SRVM. This is the configuration we would like to test.

- DPDK SR-IOV without SRVM: DPDK uses the VF in passthrough mode without SRVM. Note that without SRVM, there might be missing packets and the VF won't be available after live migration. We just use this configuration to compare the throughput during the pre-copy phase.

- DPDK VMXNET3: DPDK uses the VMXNET3 driver that is backed by the PF in full function mode. Live migration is already supported in this configuration. The results are shown in Figure 10.

Comparing the results of DPDK SRIOV with or without SRVM, we see SRVM does not impact network throughput. This result is expected because SRVM runs on a separate CPU core without acquiring any lock from the VM.

Using SR-IOV VF passthrough mode allows high performance network, especially in a small packet size. VMXNET3 can only achieve about 1.1 to 1.2 mpps at various packet sizes. In contrast, using SR-IOV VF passthrough mode allows high throughput, e.g., with a 64-byte packet size the VF passthrough mode increases throughput by 9.6 times to

(a) Throughput (higher is better)

(b) Latency (lower is better)

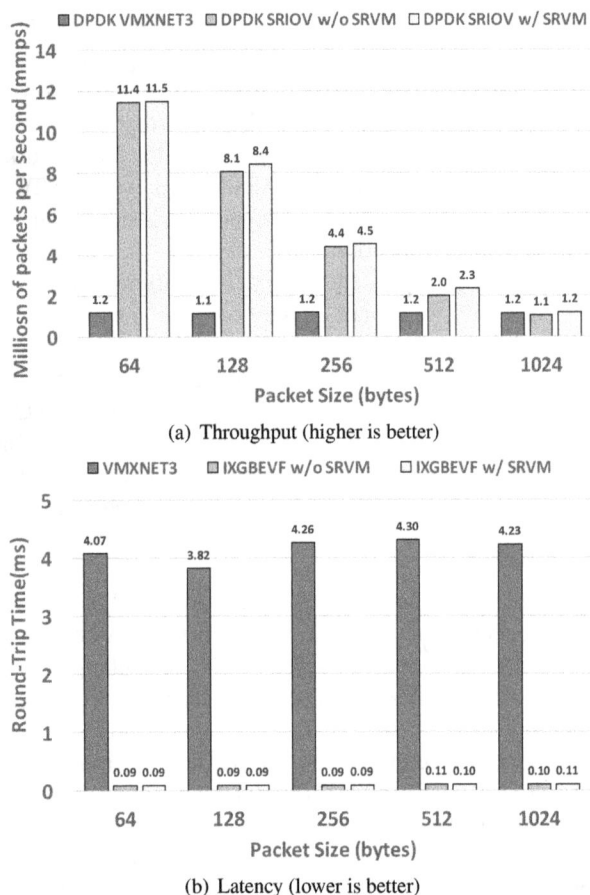

Figure 10: Network Performance During The Pre-Copy Phase

11.5 mpps. Note that this experiment is done during the pre-copy phase, so the throughput of VMXNET3 is affected by the pre-copy phase. The throughput of VMXNET3 during normal execution is higher than these numbers.

Network Latency. Another important network performance metric is latency. To measure latency, we run *ping* in the test VM with 1ms intervals. We compare round-trip time (RTT) in three configurations.

- IXGBEVF with SRVM: we use the Intel IXGBEVF driver in the migration VM with SRVM enabled. This is the configuration under test.

- IXGBEVF without SRVM: we use the Intel IXGBEVF driver without SRVM as comparison. Note that without SRVM, there might be packet loss and after live migration the VF device will not be available.

- VMXNET3: we use the VMXNET3 driver, which is backed by a PF in full-function mode.

The results are shown in Figure 10 (b). We find that the latencies when SRVM is enabled are between 0.09s and 0.11s, which is comparable to the latencies when SRVM is

disabled. The results show that SRVM does not affect VM network performance.

Compared with VMXNET3, using VF passthrough mode greatly reduces network latency (by 98% with a 64-byte packet size). This once again shows the advantage of enabling an SR-IOV VF for live migration.

Resource overhead. The memory tracking module is enabled only in the source host during live migration. Therefore, there is no runtime performance overhead for VMs before the live migration is started. However, during live migration the memory tracking module will use a separate CPU core to process and mark dirty pages. Therefore, CPU overhead is one core per live migration task. If multiple threads are used, the number of cores increases accordingly.

The memory tracking module does not copy any memory data from the ring buffer. Instead, it directly inspects the ring buffer. Therefore, it only require very small memory space for its local memory, which can fit into a single page. We also need some space to save PCI configuration for live migration and this can also fit into one page. Note that SRVM only inspects a small piece of guest memory (e.g., 2 pages for a 512-entry ring) and so the memory access overhead such as address translation and cache misses is also small.

6. Conclusion

In this paper, we presented the design and implementation of SRVM that enables live migration with passthrough SR-IOV VFs. Our experiment results show that SRVM can effectively migrate all received packets to ensure application data integrity. Also, SRVM does not increase VM downtime and does not affect the network performance. By leveraging hypervisor support provided by SRVM, the virtualization system users can take advantage of both high performance networking (SR-IOV VF passthrough mode) and advanced virtualization features (live migration) with their legacy VM configurations without having to modify their guest OS or drivers. For our future work, we plan to develop automation support in cloud management software (e.g. VMware vCenter) to facilitate SRVM.

Acknowledgment

We would like to sincerely thank all those engineers who provided great technical suggestions and comments for our project: Guolin Yang, Radu Rugina, Gabriel Tarasuk-Levin, Sreekanth Setty, Wei Xu, Michael Ho, Doug Covelli, Venkata Subhash Reddy Peddamallu, Xunjia Lu, Haoqiang Zheng, Josh Simons and Chris Rossbach. We would also like to thank all reviewers for their insightful comments and suggestions.

References

[1] "InfiniBand Trade Association," http://www.infinibandta.org.

[2] "RDMA Consortium," http://www.rdmaconsortium.org.

[3] "HIGH PERFORMANCE, OPEN STANDARD VIRTUAL-IZATION WITH NFV AND SDN," http://www.windriver.com/whitepapers/ovp/ovp_whitepaper.pdf, [Online; accessed 12-Oct-2015].

[4] "WIND RIVER TITANIUM SERVER," http://www.windriver.com/without-compromise/resources/pdf/CGCS_Product_Overview.pdf, [Online; accessed 12-Oct-2015].

[5] A. Kadav and M. M. Swift, "Live migration of direct-access devices," *SIGOPS Oper. Syst. Rev.*, vol. 43, no. 3, pp. 95–104, Jul. 2009.

[6] Z. Pan, Y. Dong, Y. Chen, L. Zhang, and Z. Zhang, "Compsc: Live migration with pass-through devices," in *Proceedings of the 8th ACM SIGPLAN/SIGOPS Conference on Virtual Execution Environments*, ser. VEE '12. New York, NY, USA: ACM, 2012, pp. 109–120.

[7] E. Zhai, G. D. Cummings, and Y. Dong, "Live migration with pass-through device for linux vm," in *OLS08: The 2008 Ottawa Linux Symposium*, 2008, pp. 261–268.

[8] "Microsoft Hyper-V," http://www.microsoft.com/en-us/server-cloud/solutions/virtualization.aspx, [Online; accessed 20-Aug-2015].

[9] "Linux ethernet bonding driver howto," https://www.kernel.org/doc/Documentation/networking/bonding.txt, 2011, [Online; accessed 20-Aug-2015].

[10] Intel, "Intel Virtualization Technology for Direct I/O," [Oct-2014].

[11] C. Clark, K. Fraser, S. Hand, J. G. Hansen, E. Jul, C. Limpach, I. Pratt, and A. Warfield, "Live migration of virtual machines," in *Proceedings of the 2nd conference on Symposium on Networked Systems Design & Implementation-Volume 2*. USENIX Association, 2005, pp. 273–286.

[12] VMware, "VMware vSphere vMotion Architecture, Performance and Best Practices in VMware vSphere 5," [Technical White Paper].

[13] Intel, "Intel 64 and IA-32 Architectures Software Developers Manual," [May-2011].

[14] ——, "Intel 82599 10 GbE Controller Datasheet," [Feb-2015 Revision 3.1 331520-002].

[15] ——, "Intel 82599 SR-IOV Driver Companion Guide," [May-2010 Revision 1.00].

[16] "Data Plane Development Kit," http://dpdk.org, [Accessed on Nov 17 2015].

[17] P. Barham, B. Dragovic, K. Fraser, S. Hand, T. Harris, A. Ho, R. Neugebauer, I. Pratt, and A. Warfield, "Xen and the Art of Virtualization," in *Proceedings of the Nineteenth ACM Symposium on Operating Systems Principles*, ser. SOSP '03. New York, NY, USA: ACM, 2003.

[18] "Kernel-based Virtual Machine," http://www.linux-kvm.org, [Online; accessed 15-Oct-2015].

[19] "VMware," http://www.vmware.com, [Online; accessed 15-Oct-2015].

[20] H. Z. Weidong Han, "Live Migration with SR-IOV Pass-through," [Presentation on KVM Forum 2015, Aug 2015].

[21] PCI-SIG, "Address Translation Services," [Jan-26-2009 Revision 1.1].

[22] ——, "PCI Express Base Specification Revision 3.0," [Nov-10-2010 Revision 3.0].

[23] "Pktgen-dpdk: Traffic generator powered by DPDK," http://dpdk.org/browse/apps/pktgen-dpdk/refs/, [Accessed on Nov 17 2015].

Enabling Efficient Hypervisor-as-a-Service Clouds with Ephemeral Virtualization

Dan Williams[†]   Yaohui Hu[‡]   Umesh Deshpande[*]   Piush K Sinha[‡]   Nilton Bila[†]
Kartik Gopalan[‡]   Hani Jamjoom[†]

[†]IBM T.J. Watson Research Center   [‡]Binghamton University   [*]IBM Almaden Research Center

Abstract

When considering a hypervisor, cloud providers must balance conflicting requirements for simple, secure code bases with more complex, feature-filled offerings. This paper introduces *Dichotomy*, a new two-layer cloud architecture in which the roles of the hypervisor are split. The cloud provider runs a lean *hyperplexor* that has the sole task of multiplexing hardware and running more substantial hypervisors (called *featurevisors*) that implement features. Cloud users choose featurevisors from a selection of lightly-modified hypervisors potentially offered by third-parties in an "as-a-service" model for each VM. Rather than running the featurevisor directly on the hyperplexor using nested virtualization, Dichotomy uses a new virtualization technique called *ephemeral virtualization* which efficiently (and repeatedly) transfers control of a VM between the hyperplexor and featurevisor using memory mapping techniques. Nesting overhead is only incurred when the VM is accessed by the featurevisor. We have implemented Dichotomy in KVM/QEMU and demonstrate average switching times of 80 ms, two to three orders of magnitude faster than live VM migration. We show that, for the featurevisor applications we evaluated, VMs hosted in Dichotomy deliver up to 12% better performance than those hosted on nested hypervisors, and continue to show benefit even when the featurevisor applications run as often as every 2.5 seconds.

1. Introduction

Modern commodity hypervisors increasingly implement complex *hypervisor-level services*, including rootkit detection [37], live patching [7], intrusion detection [13], high availability services [11], and a plethora of VM

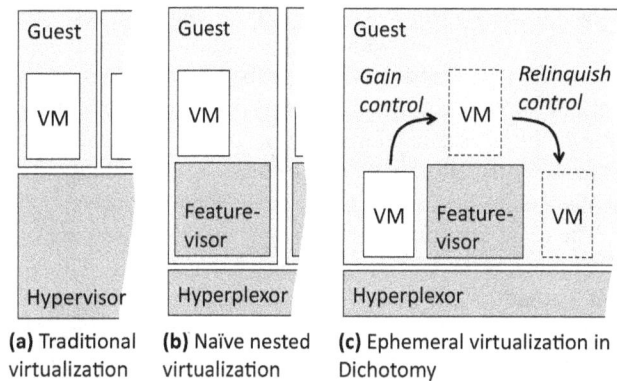

(a) Traditional virtualization (b) Naïve nested virtualization (c) Ephemeral virtualization in Dichotomy

Figure 1: Splitting the role of the hypervisor with ephemeral virtualization

introspection-enabled applications [12, 15, 24, 32, 34, 36]. As a result, when considering a hypervisor, cloud providers must balance desires for small, secure, and stable code bases with limited functionality (e.g., that simply multiplex hardware) against rich service offerings with increased complexity and potentially less security and stability. In this paper, we explore a step towards a *hypervisor-as-a-service* model, in which cloud providers can focus on maintaining a simple, secure and stable code base while simultaneously encouraging the further (potentially third-party) development of hypervisor-level services.

We propose *Dichotomy*, a new cloud architecture in which cloud providers have the best of both worlds. Dichotomy cleanly splits the role of the hypervisor into two parts: the *hyperplexor* and *featurevisor*. The hyperplexor, run by the cloud provider, is a small, secure, and stable hypervisor designed solely to multiplex physical hardware and support featurevisors. A featurevisor is a lightly-modified, full-fledged commodity hypervisor that runs on top of the hyperplexor, implements rich services, and performs management of a guest VM. A cloud user can potentially choose a different featurevisor for each VM depending on the services it requires. Furthermore, featurevisors may be developed by

VEE '16   April 2–3, 2016, Atlanta, GA, USA
Copyright © 2016 held by owner/author(s). Publication rights licensed to ACM.
ACM 978-1-4503-3947-6/16/04. . . $15.00
DOI: http://dx.doi.org/10.1145/2892242.2892254

many different (e.g., third-party) vendors and made available in an *as-a-service* model (e.g., hypervisor-as-a-service).

Dichotomy achieves the division of responsibilities described above through a new type of virtualization called *ephemeral virtualization*. Ephemeral virtualization, depicted in Figure 1, is similar to nested virtualization [5, 14, 16, 31, 47] in that it logically involves one hypervisor (the hyperplexor) managing a second hypervisor (the featurevisor), which manages the guest VM. However, ephemeral virtualization avoids the overhead of nested virtualization most of the time by enabling the second-layer hypervisor (the featurevisor) to voluntarily (and temporarily) relinquish control and management responsibilities of the guest VM to the hyperplexor. At these times, performance becomes indistinguishable from a single layer of virtualization. The featurevisor registers *triggers* with the hyperplexor in order to indicate when it next needs control over the VM. There are many featurevisor applications that do not need continuous control over the guest and therefore can benefit from ephemeral virtualization, including rootkit detection, guest patching, and sample-based logging, profiling, monitoring, or analysis.

The relative performance of a VM workload running on a featurevisor in Dichotomy (when compared to a traditional cloud or a hypervisor-as-a-service cloud using standard nested virtualization) is determined by four factors: (1) the amount of time the featurevisor needs to be in control of the VM to perform an action, (2) the frequency the featurevisor needs to regain control of the VM to repeat an action, (3) the overhead of nesting, and (4) the overhead of switching the VM between running directly on the hyperplexor to running under the control of the featurevisor and vice versa. The first two factors define the *duty cycle* for the featurevisor and are featurevisor dependent. The third factor is featurevisor and VM workload dependent. The design of Dichotomy centers around minimizing the fourth factor, switching overhead, therefore augmenting the circumstances in which ephemeral virtualization results in performance superior to standard nested virtualization.

Dichotomy achieves low switching overhead by ensuring that both the hyperplexor and featurevisor share an up-to-date view of most of the guest VM state. Importantly, Dichotomy avoids memory copies by mapping guest memory into both the hyperplexor and featurevisor. Remaining state (e.g., VCPU and I/O) are migrated similarly to VM migration. We have implemented Dichotomy using KVM/QEMU as the basis for both the featurevisor and hyperplexor, using timer-based triggers to switch between the two. We describe how to calculate—given a VM workload, featurevisor application, and switching overhead—when ephemeral virtualization outperforms nested virtualization. Furthermore, we have experimentally evaluated the performance of guest VMs running several benchmark workloads under Dichotomy, using featurevisors that perform rootkit detection and sample-based network monitoring. We found that Di-

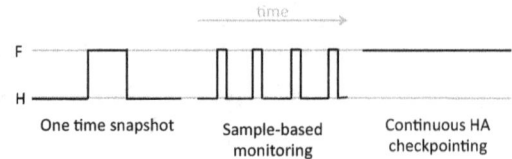

Figure 2: Duty cycles during ephemeral virtualization showing VM execution time on the featurevisor (F) vs. the hyperplexor (H)

chotomy delivers up to 12% better VM performance than nested virtualization. Dichotomy provides an improvement even for featurevisor applications that seize control of VMs as frequently as every 2.5 seconds. Switching VM control between the hyperplexor and the featurevisor is fast, averaging 80 milliseconds, because minimal amount of state is copied between hypervisors. Furthermore, in some realistic circumstances, the performance of VMs running on Dichotomy nears that of VMs on single-layer virtualization, unlike VMs on nested virtualization.

2. Featurevisors and the Duty Cycle

There are many hypervisor-level features that already exist in commodity hypervisors and many more that may appear in the future. In this section, we define the *duty cycle* [3] in the context of ephemeral virtualization and categorize specific hypervisor-level applications implemented in featurevisors in terms of their duty cycle.

A featurevisor can be thought of as any hypervisor-level service that exists in one or more commodity hypervisor (or may exist in the future). Featurevisor services may run in the control domain (e.g., Xen's Domain 0) as user applications or in the hypervisor proper. For example, featurevisors may be created to perform tasks as commonplace as VM snapshots, to more unusual services such as root-kit detection [37] or live guest OS patching [7].

We define a featurevisor's duty cycle as the fraction of one period during which the featurevisor has control of the guest. The *period* is the duration of time from one occurrence of a featurevisor gaining control over a VM to the next occurrence, including the time that it voluntarily relinquishes control. A higher duty cycle implies that a featurevisor spends more time exerting control over the VM.

Ignoring switching overhead for a moment, the duty cycle of a featurevisor provides an indication of the performance implications of ephemeral virtualization on a VM, as well as the lower and upper bounds on performance. In the best case, with a duty cycle of 0%, the VM always runs directly on the hyperplexor; performance will match traditional single-layer virtualization. With a duty cycle of 100%, the VM always runs nested on the hypervisor and the hyperplexor; performance will match nested virtualization.

Figure 2 shows the duty cycle for three example featurevisors. A one time VM snapshot featurevisor has a low duty

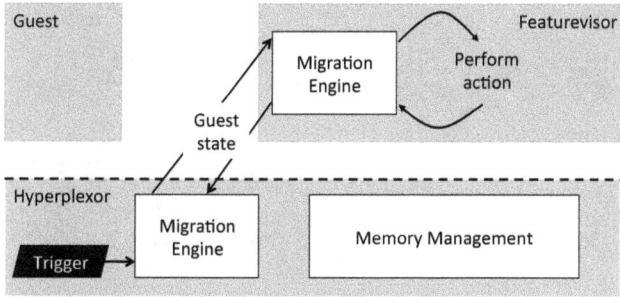

Figure 3: Design Overview of Dichotomy

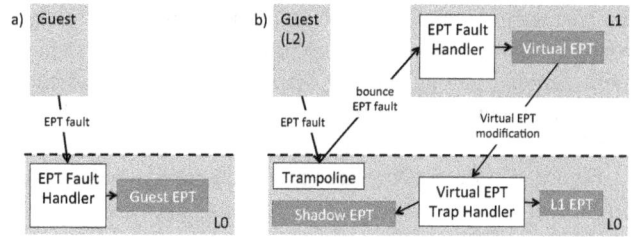

Figure 4: Memory management in a) single layer virtualization and b) standard nested virtualization

cycle because, despite the length of time the featurevisor manages the VM to compute the snapshot, it will run directly on the hyperplexor for the majority of the time. Other, more interesting featurevisors with similar duty cycles characterized by infrequent actions include live guest OS patching [7], VM management [33, 42, 48] tools, and specialized virtual devices that are irregularly accessed.

The second duty cycle shown in Figure 2 depicts sample-based monitoring, in which a very inexpensive operation (e.g., reading performance counters or statistics) occurs at a regular interval. The performance of these featurevisors depends highly on the period (or the frequency of the event). Other example featurevisors that will exhibit this type of pattern include sample-based event logging [25], root-kit detection [37], near field monitoring [36], and other VM introspection services [39, 43].

The final duty cycle shown in Figure 2 depicts a continuous snapshot mechanism for high availability, such as Remus [11]. In this case, the featurevisor maintains full control of the VM at all times to track memory access, buffer output and pause the VM during backup. The duty cycle is 100%, meaning that ephemeral virtualization in this case is equivalent to nested virtualization. Other example featurevisors of this type include memory deduplication [2, 17, 44] and intrusion detection with interrupt logging [13].

We target featurevisors with a duty cycle less than 100%. The goal of Dichotomy is to improve performance over pure nested virtualization by switching control of a VM back and forth between the hyperplexor and featurevisor. In the next section, we describe how we design Dichotomy with a low switching cost, which should be amortized away for realistic applications by the time the VM spends on the hyperplexor.

3. Design

The overall architecture of Dichotomy is shown in Figure 3. A guest initially runs directly on the hyperplexor. Dichotomy's *memory management* maps guest memory into the featurevisor so that switching control over the guest from hyperplexor to featurevisor (and vice versa) does not require expensive migration of guest memory contents. It also ensures that modifications to the memory map are synchronized as control over the guest changes.

Control over the guest is switched between hyperplexor and featurevisor via Dichotomy's *migration engine*. The featurevisor registers *triggers* – a list of events upon which it should gain control of the guest – with the hyperplexor. Upon a trigger event, the hyperplexor initiates migration of remaining guest state to the featurevisor. The featurevisor performs an action potentially scheduling or modifying the guest using its own data structures and virtual hardware. It then migrates the guest back to the hyperplexor.

In the simplest case, a hypervisor represents a guest VM as a set of physical memory pages, a memory map that translates guest-physical memory addresses to the addresses of these physical memory pages, CPU context (e.g., registers and control structures) and I/O information. We do not assume that the hyperplexor and the featurevisor maintain guest state in the same format, but that it is possible to translate between formats.

In the rest of this section, we describe in detail (1) how Dichotomy shares and maintains guest memory between the hyperplexor and featurevisor, and (2) how Dichotomy efficiently migrates control of the guest between them.

3.1 Memory management

In Dichotomy, the guest may run on either the hyperplexor or the featurevisor. To avoid memory copying while the guest transitions from one to the other, Dichotomy maps guest memory into both the featurevisor and the hyperplexor. The key challenge in memory management is ensuring that the shared guest memory and memory maps remain consistent as the guest transitions from the hyperplexor to featurevisor (or vice versa), even if guest pages are added to, removed from, or remapped in the guest memory map.

Background. Modern x86 hypervisors manage the physical memory resources a guest can access using a virtualization feature called *extended page tables* (EPT) [20]. As shown in Figure 4(a), in a standard (one-level) virtualization environment, the hypervisor manages a data structure that contains the memory map information about the guest, which is backed by an EPT (*guest EPT*). The EPT indicates to the hardware what the mapping should be between guest-physical pages and machine-physical pages. Whenever the guest attempts to access a guest-physical memory address that is not present (or not allowed) based on an EPT entry, the hardware generates an *EPT fault* and traps into the hypervisor. Using this mechanism, the hypervisor can implement demand paging (among other things) by interpreting EPT faults and updating the guest map and guest EPT accordingly.

Figure 4(b) depicts memory management in a nested environment. In a nested environment, guest pages are mapped into the second-layer hypervisor (L1). L1 manages memory for the guest as if it has direct control over the virtualization features of the hardware (i.e., single-layer virtualization). As such, it maintains a guest EPT. However, the guest EPT is virtualized; manipulations to the *virtual EPT* by L1 trigger a trap to L0. L0, in turn, will interpret the trap and maintain a *shadow EPT* that the guest actually runs with, which directly maps guest-physical addresses to the appropriate machine-physical addresses.[1] If the guest causes an EPT fault, L0 bounces the fault to L1 using a *trampoline*.

Sharing Memory. Figure 5 depicts how Dichotomy shares and manages guest memory between the hyperplexor and featurevisor. The hyperplexor has access to all of the physical memory on the machine and can assign some of it to a guest running directly on the hyperplexor in the normal way, maintaining an EPT for the guest called the *dual guest/shadow EPT* (Figure 5). Similarly, the hyperplexor assigns some physical memory to the featurevisor and maintains an EPT for it, depicted *F-EPT* in Figure 5. By including the physical pages corresponding to the guest (e.g., the targets specified in the dual guest/shadow EPT) in the F-EPT, the hyperplexor can share the guest memory with the featurevisor.

To avoid conflicts with the hyperplexor, the featurevisor must only use the shared guest memory for guest pages. As such, the hyperplexor and featurevisor agree upon a region of the featurevisor's physical memory that will be reserved for guest pages. This can be done through convention (e.g., a well-known memory region as in BIOS/OS interaction) or through an explicit handshake protocol using hypercalls. In Dichotomy, featurevisors allocate a reserved region for guest pages and register them with the hyperplexor upon initialization.

Managing the Guest Memory Map. As the guest runs on either the hyperplexor or featurevisor, the guest memory map may change. For example, a new page may be added to the guest memory map if the guest accesses part of its physical-memory space for the first time. Guest EPT faults are routed along either the hyperplexor path (denoted by "H" in Figure 5) or the featurevisor path (denoted by "F")

---

[1] This style of nested page table management is also known as *multi-dimensional paging* [29, 46]. Another approach to nested page table management, called *shadow-on-EPT*, creates a shadow page table in L1 for the guest's standard page tables. We do not discuss shadow-on-EPT further due to its performance overhead, caused by the more frequent standard-paging-related guest traps.

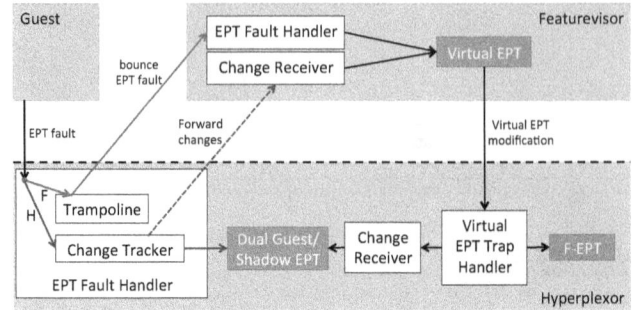

Figure 5: Memory management in Dichotomy

depending on whether the guest happens to be running on the hyperplexor or the featurevisor.

When the guest is running on the hyperplexor, memory management proceeds in a similar fashion to single-layer virtualization (Figure 4(a)). For the guest, the hyperplexor maintains the dual guest/shadow EPT in its "guest" role (its "shadow" role is described in the next paragraph in the context of the featurevisor). If the guest triggers an EPT fault (e.g., to trigger demand paging), the hyperplexor receives a trap. However, before updating the EPT, the EPT fault handler passes the fault through a *change tracker*. The change tracker records EPT modifications, which will be transferred to the featurevisor at some later time, before it begins running the guest. The featurevisor contains a *change receiver*, which interprets a list of recorded EPT modifications from the change tracker and updates the featurevisor's virtual EPT accordingly.

When the guest is running on the featurevisor, memory management proceeds in a similar fashion to standard nested virtualization (Figure 4(b)). The featurevisor does not need to implement a change tracker, because all EPT faults and updates already necessarily pass through the hyperplexor. When the guest is running on the featurevisor, guest EPT faults still enter the hyperplexor directly; the hyperplexor simply bounces the faults to the featurevisor via the trampoline. Then, the featurevisor handles the fault. If the featurevisor updates the virtual EPT due to the fault (or for any other reason), the hyperplexor will receive a trap. The hyperplexor passes the trap to its change receiver. The change receiver interprets the virtual EPT trap and updates the dual guest/shadow EPT (in its "shadow role" now). At this point, the hyperplexor dual guest/shadow EPT is synchronized with the virtual EPT in the featurevisor.

Encoding EPT Changes. When the hyperplexor makes a change to an EPT entry in the dual guest/shadow EPT, the change tracker encodes it in a format that will be later interpreted by the featurevisor's change receiver. In Dichotomy, the change tracker constructs a new EPT entry that specifies the mapping between a guest physical page and a featurevisor physical page. For an EPT entry in the dual guest/shadow EPT referring to the mapping $(x_{guest} \rightarrow y_{hyperplexor})$, the

```
forever:
  execute guest while waiting for a trigger

on_trigger:
  relinquish_guest
  wait_for_guest
```

Figure 6: Hyperplexor behavior

```
forever:
  wait_for_guest
  do action
  relinquish_guest
  finish action
```

Figure 7: Featurevisor behavior

change tracker first performs a reverse lookup in the featurevisor EPT to obtain the mapping $(z_{featurevisor} \rightarrow y_{hyperplexor})$. With this information, the change tracker can construct an entry that the featurevisor can directly interpret: $(x_{guest} \rightarrow z_{featurevisor})$. The change tracker also copies the flags (e.g., write protections, etc.) so that those in the new EPT entry match those in the dual guest/shadow EPT.

3.2 Guest Switching

Control of the guest switches between hyperplexor and featurevisor via a VM migration-like procedure, in which guest state is transferred between the migration engines in the hyperplexor and featurevisor. Specifically, one migration engine pauses the guest and transfers the guest VCPU state, I/O state, and any unsynchronized page table mappings to the other migration engine. As described above (and evaluated in Section 6), this transfer is efficient because only the EPT modifications need to be sent, not the page contents. The remaining state (CPU, I/O, etc.) is relatively small (about 16 KB).

The migration engines expose a simple interface to other programs (at the same level): `wait_for_guest`, which blocks until the migration engine at the other end issues a `relinquish_guest` call, which initiates the migration procedure.

The hyperplexor, which has control of the guest at the start of its execution, runs the guest until a *trigger* occurs. The hyperplexor conceptually runs the program specified in Figure 6. The featurevisor, on the other hand, conceptually runs the program specified in Figure 7. The action performed by the featurevisor is split into two segments to allow the featurevisor to relinquish the guest before completing its operation. For example, if the featurevisor is performing a snapshot-like activity, the featurevisor may compute an in-memory snapshot, relinquish the guest, then complete the action by writing the snapshot to disk.

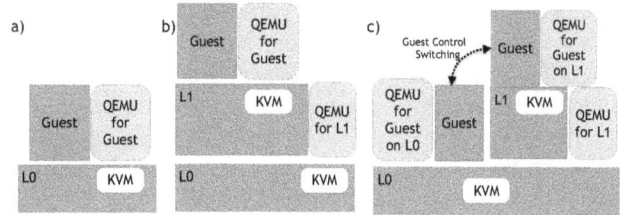

Figure 8: The position of KVM hypervisor as a Linux kernel module and QEMU as a user-level process, for a) single layer virtualization, b) standard nested virtualization, and c) Dichotomy.

Triggers. Each featurevisor in Dichotomy registers itself with the hyperplexor. As part of the registration process, the featurevisor specifies when it should be invoked from a set of hyperplexor *triggers*. The most trivial trigger is time based: for example, a featurevisor can specify a time interval detailing the frequency it should be invoked. To date, Dichotomy supports such a time-based trigger; further triggers, such as network events, or guest execution of a particular protected instruction or access to a particular part of memory, are discussed in Section 5.

4. Implementation

We have implemented Dichotomy using the KVM/QEMU virtualization platform in the Linux operating system. We begin with an overview of the roles of KVM and QEMU components, followed by implementation-specific details of guest memory sharing, fault handling, and control transfer.

Background. The KVM/QEMU [21] virtualization platform in Linux consists of two major components (a) KVM, which implements the core hypervisor functionalities as a Linux kernel module, and (b) QEMU which is a user-level management process, one per guest, that manages the life cycle of a guest, communicates with the KVM kernel module on behalf of the guest, and controls its I/O operations. Figure 8 shows the position of the KVM kernel module and the QEMU management process for non-nested, nested, and Dichotomy VMs. Figure 8(a) shows a non-nested guest running on the L0 KVM hypervisor and being managed by an associated QEMU process. When spawning a guest, the corresponding QEMU process designates a portion of its virtual memory address space as belonging to the guest, configures the guest's memory, virtual CPU and virtual I/O devices with the KVM kernel module, and launches the guest. Privileged operations by the guest result in `vmexits` or traps to the KVM hypervisor, which either handles the trap itself (such as for page faults) or forwards the trapping event to the QEMU process for further processing (such as I/O operations). Figure 8(b) shows a nested guest running on a L1 KVM hypervisor and being managed by an associated QEMU process which also runs on L1. The L1 hypervisor itself runs as a VM on the L0 hypervisor and has its own associated QEMU process on L0. vmexits by the guest are forwarded by the L0 KVM hypervisor to its L1 counterpart. Figure 8(c) shows a Dichotomy guest whose control switches back and forth between the L0 (hyperplexor) and L1 (featurevisor). At both levels, there is an associated persistent QEMU process that manages the Dichotomy guest's execution. These two QEMU processes coordinate with each other to exchange the guest execution state upon events that trigger the transfer of guest control. Depending on where the guest executes at any given instant, vmexits are handled as in standard non-nested or nested modes.

Memory Management. The guest's memory is shared between the featurevisor and hyperplexor dynamically during runtime as each page of the guest is accessed. To enable this dynamic sharing, however, the guest initialization operation must set up a sharing mechanism in the hyperplexor. Specifically, during initialization, the guest QEMU process on the hyperplexor registers the guest's memory map, i.e. QEMU's virtual memory address range associated with the guest, with its respective KVM. Similarly, the guest QEMU process on the featurevisor registers the guest's memory map with the KVM in the featurevisor, which in turn pre-allocates and registers a set of featurevisor physical addresses for the guest with the KVM in the hyperplexor. Since the guest memory is assigned from the virtual address space of the QEMU process, no physical memory is reserved in advance. Therefore, EPTs corresponding to the QEMU processes are empty at initialization.

The allocation and sharing of guest memory pages occurs when guest page faults are processed as described in Section 3.1 under the heading "Managing the Guest Memory Map". Our implementation differs from the design in the way we realize the *dual guest/shadow EPT*. To realize the ideal design – namely a single EPT that tracks guest memory map changes on both the hyperplexor and featurevisor – would have required extensive changes to the core memory management implementation in Linux and KVM. Instead, the hyperplexor maintains two EPTs for the guest – a guest EPT and a shadow EPT. The former is used when the guest executes over the hyperplexor and the latter is used when the guest executes over the featurevisor.

The guest EPT and shadow EPT are kept synchronized by the hyperplexor when handling guest EPT faults. Specifically, the EPT fault handling process described in Section 3.1 differs in the implementation in the following manner. Upon a shadow EPT fault (when the guest executes on the featurevisor), before allocating a new physical page to resolve an incomplete shadow EPT entry, the hyperplexor first checks if the faulting guest physical address has been already allocated in the guest EPT (as a result of the guest running previously on the hyperplexor). If the guest EPT mapping exists, then it is used to update the shadow EPT and F-EPT, else a new physical page is allocated. Conversely, upon a guest EPT fault (when the guest runs on the hyperplexor),

the shadow EPT is first consulted before a new physical page is allocated.

Guest Switching. The QEMU process includes a pre-copy [9] based live migration mechanism wherein the entire VM state is transferred from a source hypervisor to a destination over a TCP connection. We implemented guest switching in Dichotomy by modifying this migration mechanism in the QEMU of both the hyperplexor and featurevisor. Besides the primary modification of replacing guest memory transfer with memory sharing (described above), we also implemented an interface for triggering the guest switching. When the trigger is invoked, since the memory is shared, only the CPU and I/O states are transferred over the TCP connection between the two QEMU processes. After each switch, the featurevisor and hyperplexor QEMUs change their roles, from source to target or vice-versa. The QEMU which relinquished the guest now waits for the guest to return; while waiting, it maintains all the user and kernel data structures representing the guest state so they can be updated and reused once the guest returns.

Interestingly, we found that the use of certain virtualization features trigger the reinitialization of VM structures. For example, during migration, on the destination side, the load of VAPIC state will reinitialize the EPT. We found this had the side effect of imposing a "cold-start" penalty on the VM workload performance immediately after a guest switch due to the need to repopulate the virtual and shadow EPT entries from scratch. In our implementation, we presently disable usage of the VAPIC to avoid EPT reinitialization so that this cold-start penalty is avoided. In future work, we will investigate ways to avoid EPT reinitialization without disabling VAPIC.

5. Discussion and Future Directions

In this section, we discuss future work needed for a broader applicability of ephemeral virtualization. We focus the discussion on triggers, hyperplexor services, featurevisor composition, and featurevisor support.

Triggers. Dichotomy currently supports time-based triggers, for which featurevisors specify how often they should run. This is useful for sample-based featurevisor services, such as monitoring. However, a richer set of triggers in the hyperplexor may enable more interesting featurevisors.

For example, featurevisors could provide interesting network functionality in a similar style to software-defined networking (SDN) if they could be triggered every time a new network flow arrives. The featurevisor could then decide what to do with the flow, for example, it could block flows to act like a firewall, or record them for a network tomography application. Such a trigger could be implemented in the hyperplexor by augmenting or replacing the existing mechanism to call the SDN controller in open vSwitch.

As another example, featurevisors could provide interesting debugging or logging facilities if they could be triggered every time a guest accesses a particular part of memory. For example, the featurevisor could track changes to an important data structure in order to trigger replication of the data. This type of trigger could be implemented in the hyperplexor by modifying the permission bits on EPT entries and modifying the EPT fault handler to trigger a switch to the featurevisor.

Similarly, featurevisors could provide interesting debugging or logging facilities if they could be triggered every time a particular guest function is executed. Upon gaining control, the featurevisor could step through the function, emulating each instruction. One way to implement such a "guest program counter" trigger in the hyperplexor could be by temporarily rewriting guest code at load time to ensure that the guest traps at a specific program counter value.

Hyperplexor Services. There may be a set of common "featurevisor utilities" that are independently implemented in many featurevisors and can be implemented as services in the hyperplexor. For example, tracking guest memory writes (dirty page tracking) is useful for featurevisors performing a wide range of memory-related activities, including working set estimation and guest checkpointing. Gaining control on every guest write would result in a high duty cycle (near 100%) for these applications. Furthermore, switching so often would be unnecessary if the hyperplexor maintained and delivered a summary of guest pages written in the current epoch to the featurevisor. In other words, implementing a dirty page tracking utility in the hyperplexor may enable a class of featurevisors to become significantly more efficient. As the set of featurevisors grow, there is an opportunity to identify such utilities across featurevisors and explore their implementation in the hyperplexor.

Featurevisor Composition. To this point, we have described Dichotomy in terms of a one-to-one mapping between guest VMs and featurevisors. It is possible that this relationship be generalized in either direction.

First, a VM could be associated with multiple featurevisors. For example, the VM could infrequently switch to a featurevisor performing a backup service and more frequently switch to a featurevisor performing sample-based network monitoring. The main issues to consider when associating multiple featurevisors with a VM relate to how the featurevisors interact. For example, which featurevisor takes precedence if both are triggered by the same event? How can the hyperplexor ensure that triggers for one featurevisor are not lost when executing on a different featurevisor? Even with cooperative featurevisors, the mechanisms needed to enable a single VM to be associated with multiple featurevisors is a subject of future work.

Second, multiple VMs could be associated with a single featurevisor. For example, multiple VMs could temporarily use a high-speed shared memory communication channel [27, 45] implemented in the featurevisor. Conceptually, this requires straightforward changes to the guest memory

	Host	Featurevisor	Guest
Single	4 CPUs, 10 GB	N/A	2 VCPUs, 1-8 GB
Nested	12 CPUs, 128 GB	4 VCPUs, 10 GB	2 VCPUs, 1-8 GB
Dichotomy	12 CPUs, 128 GB	4 VCPUs, 10 GB	2 VCPUs, 1-8 GB

Table 1: System configuration (CPU, Memory) of single-layer, nested, and Dichotomy virtualization.

registration area and the communication channel (to identify which guest VM each message relates to).

Featurevisor Support. Finally, our implementation of both the hyperplexor and featurevisor is based on the KVM/QEMU hypervisor. It is conceptually straightforward to allow featurevisors to be based on different hypervisors (e.g., Xen) or built from scratch. The key design of sharing memory instead of migrating it can be maintained despite heterogeneous hypervisors; however, the remaining VM state and messages through the communication channel must be sent in a "canonicalized" form, with "drivers" at each featurevisor to translate them into their featurevisor-native structures.

6. Evaluation

In this section, we compare the performance of Dichotomy against alternative approaches for implementing hypervisor-level services, and use experimental results to show that Dichotomy is best suited for the task. Our results show that Dichotomy delivers low performance overheads due to fast switching times. The specific goals of our experiments are as follows:

- Investigate the operating region where the overheads of running VMs on Dichotomy are low and an improvement over running VMs on nested hypervisors full time.
- Demonstrate two featurevisors that implement hypervisor-level services–VM introspection and network monitoring–to manage unmodified guest VMs.
- Demonstrate that the switching times between the hyperplexor and the featurevisor are small and the associated penalty is minimal.

Our evaluation setup consists of a server containing six dual-core Intel Xeon 2.10 GHz CPUs and 128 GB memory. The L0 and L1 hypervisors run the 3.14.2 Linux kernel, KVM 3.14.2, and QEMU 1.2.0.

We compared the performance of a VM running on Dichotomy against a VM running on a single-layer hypervisor and a nested hypervisor. Table 1 shows the system configurations for the three approaches. The guest VM (column 4) is assigned 2 VCPUs and 1 to 8 GB memory in all three configurations. The featurevisor (column 3) is assigned 4 VCPUs and 10 GB memory in the nested and Dichotomy configurations. The physical host (column 2) is restricted in the single-layer virtualization configuration to use 4 physical CPUs and 10 GB memory, to match the featurevisor in the

	idle(s)	kernbench(s)	netperf(s)
volatility	3.42±0.15	3.43±0.25	3.34±0.10
netmon	1.08±0.05	1.079±0.006	1.084±0.009

Table 2: Service times t_f of featurevisor applications in seconds.

quicksort	Runtime(s)	Slowdown (α)	CPU(%)
base	60.6±0.547	1.0	100
no-op	62.8±0.44	0.96 (β)	99
volatility	63.4±0.89	0.95	99
netmon	62.8±0.44	0.96	99
kernbench	**Runtime(s)**	**Slowdown (α)**	**CPU(%)**
base	48.37±3.63	1.0	92
no-op	54.6±0.42	0.88 (β)	100
volatility	56±2.77	0.86	100
netmon	63.3±13.35	0.76	100
netperf	**Mbps**	**Slowdown (α)**	**CPU(%)**
base	941.1±0.014	1.0	4
no-op	853.0±14.7	0.91 (β)	40
volatility	725.5±5.58	0.77	32
netmon	830.5±16.34	0.88	40

Table 3: Workload performance, slowdown (α), and CPU usage. The slowdown for no-op is equivalent to standard nesting overhead (β).

other two configurations; in nested and Dichotomy configurations, the host uses all available CPUs (12) and memory (128 GB).

6.1 Workloads

The guest VMs used in our experiments were either idle or ran one of the three benchmarks below. We perform 5 iterations for each of the tests and report the average.

- **Quicksort** is the simplest of our benchmarks as it only stresses CPU and memory, but does not perform I/O after initialization. The quicksort benchmark consists of two phases: *initialization*, in which the benchmark allocates 800MB of memory and populates it with random data; and *sorting*, in which the benchmark sorts the data using quicksort. We measure the time taken to complete the sorting.
- **Kernbench** [22] is a multi-threaded benchmark that measures the time taken for repeatedly compiling the Linux kernel. kernbench stresses memory, CPU and I/O. It reads the kernel source code files from an external disk, compiles the code and writes the binary output files back to the disk. We used the default setting, in which kernbench uses two threads to compile the kernel and performs three iterations to measure the average compilation time.
- **Netperf** [30] is a single-threaded network benchmarking tool. It is primarily I/O bound. We use netperf to measure network throughput. We run a netperf client inside the guest and a netperf server on an external host. The machine hosting the guest and the external host are connected to the same switch with 1Gbps Ethernet links. During each test, the netperf client sends a TCP stream to the netperf server. We measure the average throughput of the TCP stream over 100 seconds.

For the experiments with Dichotomy and the nested hypervisor, we used three featurevisor configurations.

- The **no-op** featurevisor provides only standard VM management functions offered by KVM/QEMU. It immediately relinquishes control back to the hyperplexor.
- The **volatility** featurevisor implements a VM introspection application. volatility [43] is an introspection tool that saves a memory dump of a VM, then performs analysis on it. For our experiments, the output of the analysis is an accurate list of all processes running inside the

VM. We configured volatility to save the VM's memory dump in a memory-based filesystem (*tmpfs*) to avoid disk I/O overheads.
- The **netmon** featurevisor implements a network monitoring application using the tcpdump tool to capture packets traversing through the virtual network interface of the VM. To approximate sample-based monitoring, the featurevisor only runs tcpdump for 1 second before relinquishing the guest.

The guest VM is migrated between the hyperplexor and featurevisor at a given sampling rate. For the nested virtualization configuration, the featurevisor functionality is implemented in the L1 hypervisor, while in the single-layer virtualization configuration, it is implemented directly in the L0 hypervisor.

6.2 Application Characterization

We begin with a characterization of the featurevisor applications in terms of both their service times and their impact on the performance of workloads running within the guest VM. *Service time* is the length of time needed by the featurevisor to perform a task on the guest VM.

Table 2 shows the service times for the volatility and netmon applications, representing the theoretical minimum switching period for a Dichotomy VM with 2GB memory. Notice that the service times remain largely unaffected by the VM's workload because the featurevisor has sufficient vCPU and memory resources (as shown in Table 1) to run its application and, if necessary, to prioritize its execution over the VM.

Table 3 shows the slowdown of the quicksort, kernbench and netperf workloads when the guest runs on top of a featurevisor (with no switching). The slowdown

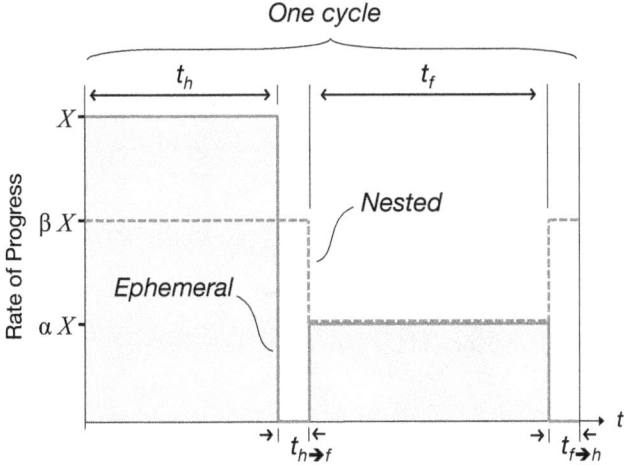

Figure 9: Analysis of one duty cycle

factor α represents the normalized performance of the workload compared to the guest running directly in an unmodified KVM L0 hypervisor (the row labeled 'base'). For featurevisors, the workload performance is measured with either an idle featurevisor (no-op) or one that continually executes the volatility or netmon tasks. The slowdown on the no-op featurevisor represents the minimum overhead of running a guest on a nested hypervisor (L1). We observe the most slowdown with kernbench and netperf due to I/O contention.

6.3 Expected Results

We do not expect Dichotomy to outperform nested virtualization for all featurevisor applications and all workloads. For instance, featurevisors that require a high duty cycle (especially with high switching frequencies) will incur prohibitive switching overhead. To build intuition and increase confidence in our experimental results, we first examine the operating region analytically.

Without loss of generalization, we only consider a single cycle (Figure 9). We focus on quantifying the progress that a guest VM workload makes during a full cycle, both in full nested mode and when switching back and forth between the hyperplexor and featurevisor. Let t_h be the time a VM spends on the hyperplexor. Let t_f be the time a VM spends on the featurevisor. During t_h, let X represent the expected rate at which the VM makes progress in $Units/t$. When a VM runs on top of a featurevisor, it can be slowed down in two ways. The first slowdown is purely due to nesting overhead. This is captured by β, resulting in a reduced rate of progress βX. The second slowdown is when a featurevisor application is running. There, the VM will be slowed down by rate α (i.e., due to nested virtualization overhead and contention for resources utilized by the featurevisor application). Thus, we expect the VM to make αX progress.

As depicted by the solid blue line in Figure 9, in ephemeral mode, the VM's rate of progress will switch between X and αX. There is, however, a non-zero switching time in which the VM is paused (i.e., makes no progress). This time is captured by $t_{h \to f}$ and $t_{f \to h}$, which represent the time to move the VM between the hyperplexor and the featurevisor, and vice versa. In contrast, Figure 9 also shows the VM's rate of progress in full nested mode (the red dotted line) which switches between αX and βX with no switching time.

A full cycle, t, can thus be expressed as $t_h + t_{h \to f} + t_f + t_{f \to h}$. The progress that a guest VM workload makes with ephemeral virtualization ($P_{ephemeral}$) is:

$$P_{ephemeral} = Xt_h + (0 \times t_{h \to f}) + \alpha Xt_f + (0 \times t_{f \to h}) \quad (1)$$

In contrast, the progress made by the VM in full nested mode (P_{nested}) is expressed as:

$$P_{nested} = \alpha Xt_f + \beta X(t_h + t_{h \to f} + t_{f \to h}) \quad (2)$$

Now, we calculate the range where the VM makes more progress during ephemeral mode when compared to nested mode (i.e., when $P_{ephemeral} > P_{nested}$). Performing direct substitution of the above equations and solving for t_h, we get:

$$t_h > \frac{\beta}{1 - \beta}(t_{h \to f} + t_{f \to h}) \quad (3)$$

The results confirm intuition: *it is better to switch back and forth as long as the VM stays on the hyperplexor long enough to amortize the switching cost.* In the next subsection, we experimentally find that ephemeral mode delivers lower performance overhead than full nested mode for periods as small as 2.5 seconds.

6.4 Macro Benchmarks

Figures 10, 11, and 12 show the relative performance of each VM workload (quicksort, kernbench, and netperf) compared to the the single level virtualization (Base), under each featurevisor (no-op, netmon, and volatility). Each graph shows the results when running the VM and featurevisor in Dichotomy, a standard nested virtualization environment, and a naïve ephemeral virtualization implementation using standard pre-copy live migration as the switching mechanism (denoted Pre-copy).

For these experiments, we vary the period length, or the frequency at which we run the featurevisor. We determine the actual period lengths at which ephemeral virtualization outperforms nested virtualization in a practical setting. Moreover, we are interested in the following general trends: 1) Dichotomy outperforms nested for sufficiently large period length, and 2) a fast switching mechanism is important for ephemeral virtualization.

All of the results confirm these general trends. In general, guest performance in Dichotomy converges more quickly to a better value than nested virtualization, up to 12% improvement. Regardless of the featurevisor application, as period

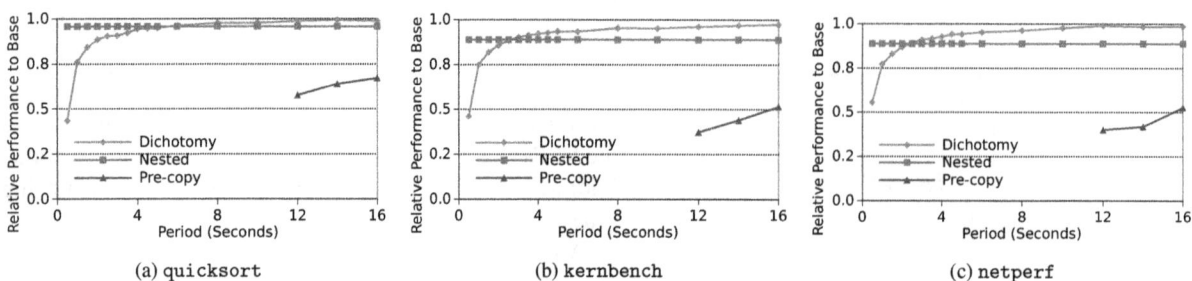

Figure 10: Workload runtimes when switching between hyperplexor and the `no-op` featurevisor.

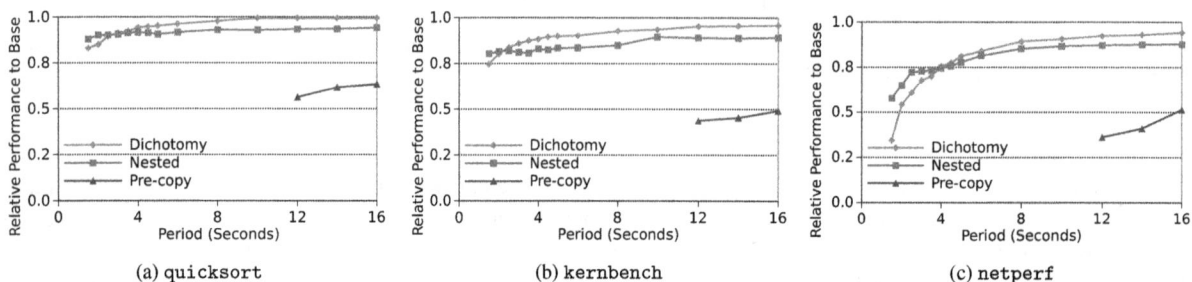

Figure 11: Workload runtimes when switching between hyperplexor and a featurevisor running the `netmon` task.

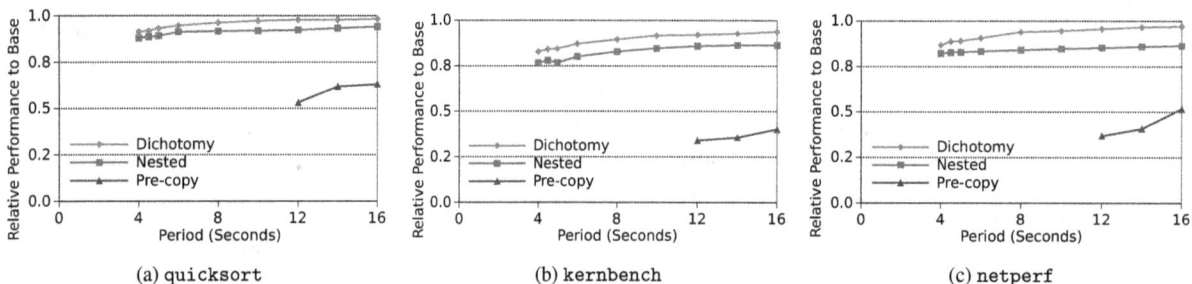

Figure 12: Workload runtimes when switching between hyperplexor and a featurevisor running the `volatility` task.

length increases, VM performance on Dichotomy converges to single-level virtualization (X from the analysis in Section 6.3), whereas VM performance on nested converges to base nested performance with no featurevisor running (βX from the analysis in Section 6.3). The importance of a fast switching time is dramatically emphasized by the poor performance of pre-copy live VM migration in all cases.

To explain the results in more detail, we first examine Figure 10. The `no-op` featurevisor does no work, but immediately yields the guest back to the hyperplexor. It does, however, incur switching overhead. The smallest period we test is about 160 ms, due to the fact that switching overhead (about 80 ms each direction) dominates at periods this small. As expected, Figure 10 shows that the performance of the workloads with Dichotomy suffers at short periods due to

the switching overhead, but the performance improves with longer periods. For comparison, pre-copy requires about 4s to switch the guest's execution. Therefore the workload performance can only be demonstrated for period durations greater than 10s ($> 2 * switch\ time + featurevisor\ service\ time$). Furthermore, the iterative memory copying during the workload execution adversely impacts the workload performance with pre-copy.

The performance of `kernbench` and `netperf` with Dichotomy matches the performance with the nested mode at 3 and 2.5 second periods respectively, while the performance of `quicksort` matches its performance with nested only after a 6 second period. Since `quicksort` does not stress I/O, as opposed to `netperf` and `kernbench`, it has lower nesting overhead in comparison, (i.e. βX from the analysis in Sec-

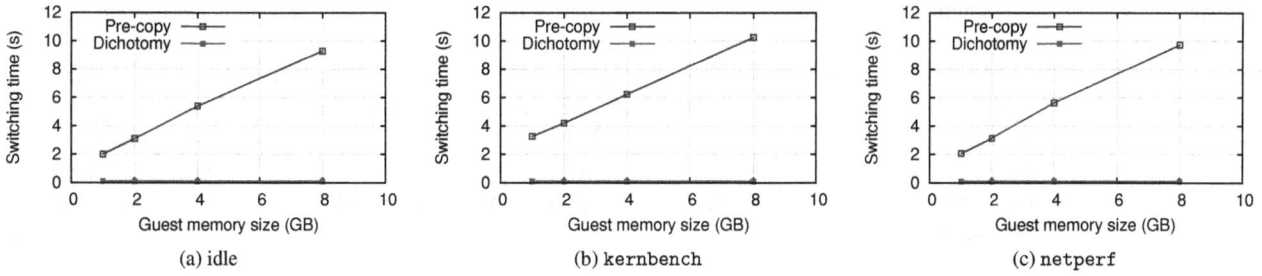

| (a) idle | (b) kernbench | (c) netperf |

Figure 13: Switching times of guest VMs with varying memory sizes between hyperplexor to featurevisor.

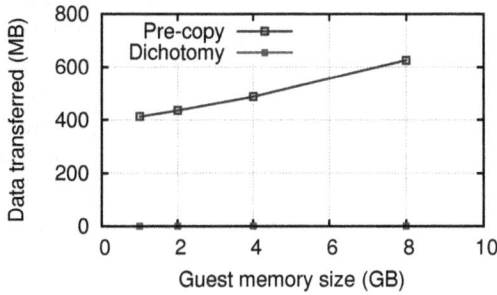

Figure 14: Data copied for switching

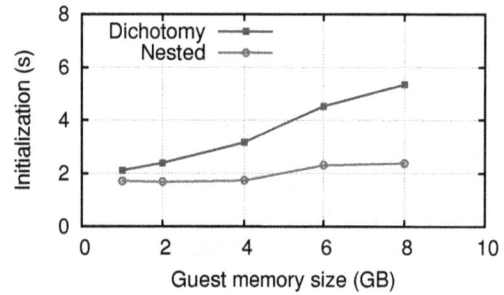

Figure 15: One-time initialization cost

tion 6.3 for quicksort is higher than that with kernbench and netperf). Therefore, for quicksort, Dichotomy can only amortize the switching overhead for longer period durations (i.e., when t_h is greater).

Figure 11 shows the performance of the all three workloads with netmon. In each period, the guest executes on the featurevisor for 1s before switching back to the hyperplexor. All three workloads show a similar pattern as with the no-op featurevisor, with an amortization point of 4 seconds or less. The performance of the VMs on Dichotomy remains fairly stable, except for the netperf workload. The netperf workload is most affected by the netmon featurevisor because it is a network-bound workloads.

Figure 12 shows the workload performance with the volatility featurevisor application. For each period, the guest executes on the featurevisor until the VM introspection is complete. Table 2 shows the service time of volatility for different workloads. Since the service time with volatility is longer than with netmon, we can demonstrate the workload performance for period lengths 4s or greater and as a result the crossing point of Dichotomy and nested is not visible. This result is important, as it indicates that for realistic featurevisors with service times of a few seconds, Dichotomy will always outperform standard nesting, even if they run frequently.

6.5 Micro Benchmarks

In the previous subsection, we showed that Dichotomy's low switching time played an important role in the system's performance. In this subsection, we quantify Dichotomy's switching times and its VM initialization overheads. Figure 13 compares VM switching times between the hyperplexor and a no-op featurevisor using Dichotomy and pre-copy live VM migration. Switching times to and from the hyperplexor—$t_{h \to f}$ and $t_{f \to h}$ —were observed to be similar, hence they are not distinguished here. The figure shows that, as the guest memory size is increased from 1 GB to 8 GB, the measured switching time for pre-copy also increases (ranging from 2 to 10 seconds), mainly due to memory copying overhead. In contrast, the switching time using Dichotomy is fairly constant around 80 ms, since the guest memory is shared in advance during initialization by the hyperplexor and the featurevisor.

We also measured the downtime experienced by a guest running kernbench when switching between the hyperplexor and the featurevisor when using pre-copy versus dichotomy. With pre-copy, the downtime remains within the range of 300ms to 350ms, whereas with Dichotomy the downtime is around 80 ms.

Figure 14 shows the number of data bytes copied as the VM size is increased; pre-copy shows an increase from 400MB to 625MB; Dichotomy transfers a constant amount of 15.8KB consisting of VCPU and I/O state.

Figure 15 compares the one-time initialization overhead for a nested guest against the Dichotomy guest. The nested guest initialization time increases slightly from 1.7 seconds to 2.3 seconds. However, Dichotomy guest initialization time increases from 2.1 seconds to 5.3 seconds since the initialization involves sharing the Dichotomy guest's memory between the hyperplexor and the featurevisor. In our current implementation, this requires the featurevisor to register the guest's memory address space with the hyperplexor through multiple hypercalls, the cost of which increases with increasing guest memory size. This cost can be potentially reduced by batching the registration operations into fewer hypercalls.

7. Related Work

Several lines of research have considered dynamic switching between execution environments: virtualized, bare-metal, and emulated. In this section, we discuss such switching approaches, and related work on hypervisor feature confinement and nested virtualization.

Ho et al. [19] use an on-demand approach to switch between single-layer guest VM execution (on Xen) and a QEMU-based emulator. Their system is tailored to a single application: performing taint tracking and the enforcement of a taint policy to disallow execution of tainted data. With Dichotomy, we are interested in a general approach to support a range of applications of which taint-based policy enforcement is an interesting use-case.

There has also been work examining dynamic switching between a "bare-metal" operating system and running the OS in a virtual machine. The on-the-fly introduction of a VMM underneath an operating system has been explored by on-demand virtualization [23]. It relies on OS hibernation mechanisms and the conversion results in about 90 seconds of downtime. Also, Mercury [8] proposes "self-virtualization", in which a VMM is dynamically attached or detached beneath an operating system only when needed with about 0.2 ms switching time. VMware offers products to convert between physical and virtual machines and vice versa [40, 41], but they do not target running systems. By targeting nested virtualization, Dichotomy leverages existing mechanisms to deal with the complexity of physical hardware, interrupt mapping, etc.

We propose a hypervisor-as-a-service environment in which many different hypervisors provide specialized features. In related work, there have been approaches that reduce the hypervisor's functionality to its essentials for a particular problem domain. A "microvisor" [26] does not virtualize all resources and is only applicable for the problem of online server maintenance. Similarly, CloudVisor [49] uses nested virtualization on a slim, trusted base hypervisor. Dichotomy's support for introducing and removing layers complements this work.

A related line of research relates to disaggregating the large administrative domain [6, 10, 28, 35] typically associated with a hypervisor, such as Domain 0 in Xen. The goal of these efforts to is replace a single large administrative domain with several small sub-domains (akin to privileged service-VMs) that are more resilient to attacks and failures, better isolated from others, and can be customized on a per-VM basis. Thus a VM could pick and choose the services of specific sub-domains which run at the same level as the VM atop the common hypervisor. Dichotomy's nested architecture essentially reduces the privilege of the featurevisor in addition to splitting them from the hyperplexor.

Dichotomy leverages existing work on nested virtualization and live VM migration. Nested virtualization was originally proposed and refined in the 1970s [4], has been studied in a microkernel environment [14], and has now become mainstream due to new implementations [5, 16] leveraging hardware support for virtualization on the x86 architecture [1, 38]. Dichotomy uses nested support in KVM [21]. Live VM migration [9, 18] enables VMs to migrate from one hypervisor to another with minimal downtime. Dichotomy both transfers control and completes migration faster than existing techniques by eliminating memory copying.

8. Conclusion

We presented Dichotomy, a new two-layer cloud architecture that splits the role of hypervisors between hyperplexors and featurevisors. This split enables cloud providers to focus on the security and stability, while at the same time allowing a third-party featurevisor ecosystem to grow in a hypervisor-as-a-service idiom. Experiments with our prototype show that, through ephemeral virtualization, Dichotomy delivers better VM performance than nested virtualization, even for featurevisor applications that access the VM as often as every 2.5 seconds. We attribute Dichotomy's performance to low VM switching times between hyperplexor and featurevisor, averaging 80 ms. In the future, we look forward to exploring the interaction and agility of featurevisors in a hypervisor-as-a-service model.

Acknowledgement

This work is supported in part by the National Science Foundation through grants 1527338, 1320689, and 0845832, and by the Air Force Rome Labs through grant CA01160915BINGU.

References

[1] AMD Virtualization (AMD-V). http://www.amd.com/us/solutions/servers/virtualization.

[2] A. Arcangeli, I. Eidus, and C. Wright. Increasing memory density by using ksm. In *Proc. of Linux Symposium, Ottawa, Canada*, July 2009.

[3] S. F. Barrett and D. J. Pack. *Microcontrollers Fundamentals for Engineers and Scientists*, chapter 4, pages 51–64. Morgan & Claypool Publishers, San Rafael, CA, July 2006.

[4] G. Belpaire and N.-T. Hsu. Formal properties of recursive virtual machine architectures. In *Proc. of ACM SOSP, Austin, TX*, pages 89–96, Nov. 1975.

[5] M. Ben-Yehuda, M. D. Day, Z. Dubitzky, M. Factor, N. Har'El, A. Gordon, A. Liguori, O. Wasserman, and B.-A. Yassour. The turtles project: Design and implementation of nested virtualization. In *Proc. of USENIX OSDI*, Vancouver, Canada, Oct. 2010.

[6] S. Butt, H. A. Lagar-Cavilla, A. Srivastava, and V. Ganapathy. Self-service cloud computing. In *Proc. of ACM CCS, Raleigh, NC*, pages 253–264, Oct. 2012.

[7] H. Chen, R. Chen, F. Zhang, B. Zang, and P. Yew. Live updating operating systems using virtualization. In *Proc. of ACM VEE*, Ottawa, Canada, June 2006.

[8] H. Chen, R. Chen, F. Zhang, B. Zang, and P.-C. Yew. Mercury: Combining performance with dependability using self-virtualization. In *Proc. of IEEE ICPP*, Xi'an, China, Sept. 2007.

[9] C. Clark, K. Fraser, S. Hand, J. G. Hansen, E. Jul, C. Limpach, I. Pratt, and A. Warfield. Live Migration of Virtual Machines. In *Proc. of USENIX NSDI*, Boston, MA, May 2005.

[10] P. Colp, M. Nanavati, J. Zhu, W. Aiello, G. Coker, T. Deegan, P. Loscocco, and A. Warfield. Breaking up is hard to do: Security and functionality in a commodity hypervisor. In *Proc. of ACM SOSP*, Cascais, Portugal, Oct. 2011.

[11] B. Cully, G. Lefebvre, D. Meyer, M. Feeley, N. Hutchinson, and A. Warfield. Remus: high availability via asynchronous virtual machine replication. In *Proc. of USENIX NSDI*, San Francisco, CA, Apr. 2008.

[12] A. Dinaburg, P. Royal, M. Sharif, and W. Lee. Ether: malware analysis via hardware virtualization extensions. In *Proc. of ACM CCS*, pages 51–62, 2008.

[13] G. W. Dunlap, S. T. King, S. Cinar, M. A. Basrai, and P. M. Chen. ReVirt: Enabling intrusion analysis through virtual-machine logging and replay. In *Proc. of USENIX OSDI*, Boston, MA, Dec. 2002.

[14] B. Ford, M. Hibler, J. Lepreau, P. Tullmann, G. Back, and S. Clawson. Microkernels meet recursive virtual machines. In *Proc. of USENIX OSDI*, Seattle, WA, Oct. 1996.

[15] T. Garfinkel and M. Rosenblum. A virtual machine introspection based architecture for intrusion detection. In *Proc. of NDSS Symposium, San Diego, CA*, Feb. 2003.

[16] A. Graf and J. Roedel. Nesting the virtualized world. In *Linux Plumbers Conference, Portland, OR*, Sept. 2009.

[17] D. Gupta, S. Lee, M. Vrable, S. Savage, A. C. Snoeren, G. Varghese, G. M. Voelker, and A. Vahdat. Difference engine: Harnessing memory redundancy in virtual machines. In *Proc. of USENIX OSDI*, San Diego, CA, Dec. 2008.

[18] M. Hines and K. Gopalan. Post-copy based live virtual machine migration using adaptive pre-paging and dynamic self-ballooning. In *Proc. of ACM VEE*, Washington, DC, Mar. 2009.

[19] A. Ho, M. Fetterman, C. Clark, A. Warfield, and S. Hand. Practical taint-based protection using demand emulation. In *Proc. of ACM EuroSys*, Leuven, Belgium, Apr. 2006.

[20] Intel 64 and IA-32 Architectures. Software Developers Manual, Combined Volumes: 1, 2A, 2B, 2C, 3A, 3B, 3C and 3D. http://www.intel.com/content/dam/www/public/us/en/documents/manuals/64-ia-32-architectures-software-developer-manual-325462.pdf.

[21] A. Kivity, Y. Kamay, D. Laor, U. Lublin, and A. Liguori. KVM: the linux virtual machine monitor. In *Proc. of Linux Symposium, Ottawa, Canada*, June 2007.

[22] C. Kolivas. Kernbench: http://ck.kolivas.org/apps/kernbench/kernbench-0.50/.

[23] T. Kooburat and M. Swift. The best of both worlds with on-demand virtualization. In *Proc. of USENIX HOTOS*, Napa, CA, May 2011.

[24] K. Kourai and S. Chiba. HyperSpector: Virtual Distributed Monitoring Environments for Secure Intrusion Detection. In *Proc. of ACM VEE*, Chicago, IL, June 2005.

[25] J. Levon. *OProfile: System-wide profiler for Linux systems, http://oprofile.sourceforge.net/about/*.

[26] D. E. Lowell, Y. Saito, and E. J. Samberg. Devirtualizable virtual machines enabling general, single-node, online maintenance. In *Proc. of ACM ASPLOS*, Boston, MA, Oct. 2004.

[27] A. C. Macdonell. *Shared-memory optimizations for virtual machines*. PhD thesis, University of Alberta, Edmonton, Canada, 2011.

[28] D. G. Murray, G. Milos, and S. Hand. Improving xen security through disaggregation. In *Proc. of ACM VEE*, Seattle, WA, Mar. 2008.

[29] G. Natapov. Nested EPT to make nested VMX faster. In *KVM Forum, Edinburgh, UK*, Oct. 2013.

[30] Netperf. http://www.netperf.org/netperf/.

[31] D. L. Osisek, K. M. Jackson, and P. H. Gum. ESA/390 interpretive-execution architecture, foundation for VM/ESA. *IBM Systems Journal*, 30(1):34–51, Feb. 1991.

[32] B. D. Payne, M. Carbone, M. Sharif, and W. Lee. Lares: An architecture for secure active monitoring using virtualization. In *IEEE Symposium on Security and Privacy, Oakland, CA*, pages 233 – 247, May 2008.

[33] RedHat CloudForms. *http://www.redhat.com/en/technologies/cloud-computing/cloudforms*.

[34] R. Riley, X. Jiang, and D. Xu. Guest-transparent prevention of kernel rootkits with VMM-based memory shadowing. In *Recent Advances in Intrusion Detection, Boston, MA*, pages 1–20, Sept. 2008.

[35] U. Steinberg and B. Kauer. Nova: A microhypervisor-based secure virtualization architecture. In *Proc. of EuroSys, Paris, France*, pages 209–222, 2010.

[36] S. Suneja, C. Isci, V. Bala, E. de Lara, and T. Mummert. Non-intrusive, out-of-band and out-of-the-box systems monitoring in the cloud. In *SIGMETRICS'14, Austin, TX*, 2014.

[37] J. Toldinas, D. Rudzika, V. Štuikys, and G. Ziberkas. Rootkit detection experiment within a virtual environment. *Electronics and Electrical Engineering–Kaunas: Technologija*, (8): 104, 2009.

[38] R. Uhlig, G. Neiger, D. Rodgers, A. Santoni, F. Martins, A. Anderson, S. Bennett, A. Kagi, F. Leung, and L. Smith. Intel virtualization technology. *Computer*, 38(5):48–56, 2005.

[39] vmitools. *https://code.google.com/p/vmitools/*.

[40] VMware, Inc. Virtual Machine to Physical Machine Migration. `http://www.vmware.com/support/v2p/doc/V2P_TechNote.pdf`, 2004.

[41] VMware, Inc. VMware Converter Users Manual. `http://www.vmware.com/pdf/VMware_Converter_manual.pdf`, 2006.

[42] VMWare vRealize. *https://www.vmware.com/products/vrealize-suite*.

[43] Volatility Framework. http://code.google.com/p/volatility/.

[44] C. A. Waldspurger. Memory resource management in VMware ESX server. In *Proc. of USENIX OSDI*, Boston, MA, Dec. 2002.

[45] J. Wang, K.-L. Wright, and K. Gopalan. XenLoop: a transparent high performance inter-VM network loopback. In *Proc. of ACM HPDC, Boston, MA*, pages 109–118, June 2008.

[46] O. Wasserman. Nested Virtualization: Shadow Turtles. In *KVM Forum, Edinburgh, UK*, Oct. 2013.

[47] D. Williams, H. Jamjoom, and H. Weatherspoon. The Xen-Blanket: Virtualize once, run everywhere. In *EuroSys, Bern, Switzerland*, Apr. 2012.

[48] Xen Cloud Platform. *http://wiki.xenproject.org/wiki/XCP_Overview*.

[49] F. Zhang, J. Chen, H. Chen, and B. Zang. CloudVisor: Retrofitting protection of virtual machines in multi-tenant cloud with nested virtualization. In *Proc. of ACM SOSP*, Cascais, Portugal, Oct. 2011.

Abstractions for Practical Virtual Machine Replay

Anton Burtsev   David Johnson   Mike Hibler   Eric Eide   John Regehr

University of Utah
Salt Lake City, UT USA
{aburtsev, johnsond, hibler, eeide, regehr}@cs.utah.edu

Abstract

Efficient deterministic replay of whole operating systems is feasible and useful, so why isn't replay a default part of the software stack? While implementing deterministic replay is hard, we argue that the main reason is the lack of general abstractions for understanding and addressing the significant engineering challenges involved in the development of a replay engine for a modern VMM. We present a design blueprint—a set of abstractions, general principles, and low-level implementation details—for efficient deterministic replay in a modern hypervisor. We build and evaluate our architecture in Xen, a full-featured hypervisor. Our architecture can be readily followed and adopted, enabling replay as a ubiquitous part of a modern virtualization stack.

1. Introduction

In the last decade, deterministic replay went through a full cycle of a blooming research field—from rapid growth, to its peak, and arguably into decline. Numerous applications of deterministic replay were suggested: e.g., debugging and analysis of complex software systems [15, 26, 27, 32, 33, 35, 40, 41], fault-tolerant replication [9, 43, 44], performance analysis [4], and forensics [11, 19, 22]). A number of deterministic replay systems were developed along with advanced techniques for reconstructing execution of parallel [1, 12, 13, 38] and distributed systems. However, despite academic success, deterministic replay did not become a de facto part of systems and virtualization stacks.

As a default component of the modern VMM stack, ubiquitous deterministic replay could change the way we develop and analyze complex software systems. The availability of complete system state, the guaranteed deterministic behavior of re-execution, and the absence of limitations on the run-time complexity of analysis algorithms collectively enable deep, iterative exploration of the run-time properties of whole systems, such as automatic debugging, explanation of cross-component performance anomalies, reconstruction of intrusion vectors, and more.

Why hasn't deterministic replay become a default part of the systems stack? Implementing deterministic replay is hard. We argue, however, that the main reason is the lack of general abstractions for developing replay mechanisms. In theory, system interfaces—OS system calls and VM hypercalls—are designed to provide a clean abstraction boundary and full encapsulation. In practice, abstractions are leaky due to a number of low-level optimizations aimed to deliver low-latency and high-throughput I/O for virtualized systems. In full-featured hypervisors like Xen and KVM, a replay interposition boundary built to capture the execution of a virtual machine cuts through multiple subsystems and layers of the software stack: hypervisor, host kernel, and host user-level. Without general abstractions for reasoning about nondeterminism, proper mechanisms for efficient recording, and tools for analyzing and debugging divergence, building replay into a full-featured hypervisor is impossible.

Abstractions for deterministic replay are badly needed. Existing replay prototypes either sidestep the complexity of a real environment and concentrate on a particular research topic, or develop an implementation that is challenging to generalize and reuse. It took the authors three person-years to implement a deterministic replay engine for uniprocessor guests running on Xen. Despite the existence of earlier replay implementations (one in Xen [23]), the reuse of code and strategies for replay did not appear to be possible. Having no reference design, and no clear abstractions or principles from prior work to follow, we had to re-analyze sources of nondeterminism, reinvent debugging tools, and rediscover a way to split Xen into deterministic and nondeterministic parts such that recording and replay have good performance.

The contribution of this paper is an effective collection of techniques and abstractions that provide a practical foundation for extending modern hypervisors with virtual machine replay. As our work is based on the experience of implementing deterministic replay in Xen, it fully reflects the complexity of a modern virtualization stack: parallel, asynchronous, and paravirtualized device I/O; a multi-layer device virtualization

VEE '16   April 2–3, 2016, Atlanta, Georgia, USA.
Copyright © 2016 held by owner/author(s). Publication rights licensed to ACM.
ACM 978-1-4503-3947-6/16/04...$15.00
DOI: http://dx.doi.org/10.1145/2892242.2892257

model; a fully preemptible, parallel hypervisor; and more. Our abstractions are clean and practical. We develop a general approach for capturing and coordinating the execution of a VM at multiple layers of the virtualization stack. We design general techniques for ensuring the determinism of larger nondeterministic components. Finally, our techniques keep recording mechanisms off the carefully optimized critical path of the hypervisor. We believe that deterministic replay is a useful part of the virtualization stack and that our blueprint can substantially simplify future replay implementations.

Although our work develops mechanisms essential for any replay engine, we focus on the replay of uniprocessor guest VMs. These are appropriate for many production use-cases where it is often acceptable to obtain scalability by running multiple guests on a powerful machine. A number of promising research efforts have addressed the problem of high overhead [13, 23] in recording multiprocessor guests. Still, these techniques require assumptions that are often unacceptable for production environments: e.g., the need to tolerate the overheads of whole-system binary translation [12], heavyweight execution-reconstruction techniques that are limited to several seconds of recording [1, 38], the inability to record a whole system due to strict limits on the amount of shared-memory nondeterminism [33], intrusive changes to the entire OS stack [7], or specialized hardware [29].

2. Deterministic VMMs Are Hard

The basis for deterministic replay is simple: the execution of a system is largely deterministic, and is only occasionally altered by external nondeterministic events. Being placed in identical initial conditions, and processing an identical instruction stream, the CPU deterministically generates the same values in registers and memory.[1] The determinism of execution holds until some external event, e.g., an external interrupt, or an I/O read from an external source, alters either the state of the CPU or the system's memory. Starting from the initial state, one can force the system to repeat its original execution by replaying external events.

Complex interposition boundary   Replay requires that all nondeterministic input be available for interposition during logging and replay. Although the virtual machine is designed to have a rigid isolation boundary, in a real system it has a number of architectural dependencies on multiple parts of the virtual machine monitor: the low-level state of the hypervisor (interrupt and exception handlers, timers, virtual CPUs and MMUs, and cross-VM shared memory), host device drivers (fully emulated and paravirtualized devices), a platform emulator (emulation of BIOS, legacy peripheral devices, and buses for unmodified guests), VM configuration and creation tools, and so on. Each of the parts contains some state of the VM and can affect its execution. Synchronized logging and orchestrated re-execution of the multi-level, multi-component

system require abstractions providing a general approach to nondeterminism in a complex system, as well as mechanisms that can (1) record a complex decentralized system without loss of performance and (2) re-execute it in a controlled lock-step manner during replay.

Concurrent, reentrant environment   Modern hypervisors are designed to provide low-latency virtualization of interrupts and device I/O. They run with minimal locking to ensure preemptive, concurrent, and parallel processing of high-priority interrupts and signals. Most components are reentrant, and under high load may create interleaving of low-level updates to the state of the replayed system in an order that is still acceptable for the system, but is impossible to replay at the level of recorded events. Deterministic replay must ensure the atomicity of recording across the entire VMM stack without introducing a "big lock" into a highly concurrent system.

Complex instruction-counting logic   Despite having a long development history, precise instruction counting—required for replaying asynchronous events—is still challenging on modern CPUs. Precise instruction counting requires tracking every exit from the replayed system. This is especially challenging in the face of the System Management Mode (SMM) interrupts, which exit straight into the BIOS firmware and are transparent to the hypervisor [46]. Instruction-accurate injection of asynchronous events requires support for emulating repeated string instructions, which do not change the instruction pointer or branch counter across multiple iterations, and careful emulation of the trace flag, which is used to single-step the replayed system.

Subtle divergence bugs   A change of a single bit in the state of the replayed system can potentially alter its execution path. An analysis of the divergence is further complicated by a period of execution that is common (unchanged) between the altering change and the observed divergence. In practice, without special debugging tools aimed at recording and comparing execution traces across original and replay runs, it is impossible to implement a replay engine that scales to replay enterprise workloads.[2]

3. Abstractions and Mechanisms for Replay

The main challenge of implementing a replay platform in the complex, concurrent, multi-layer environment of a VMM is ensuring the determinism of execution: mediating all sources of nondeterminism and guaranteeing controlled execution of the system in a lock-step manner between pairs of nondeterministic events. Several abstractions are critical for addressing the complexity of this task: a three-part model of the environment, a general approach to implementing interposition functions, a simple locking and event atomicity model, and a general execution scheduler.

---

[1] There are anecdotal examples of nondeterministic CPU behavior [9].

[2] The ReVirt team analyzed a replay-divergence bug caused by the order of page fault exceptions, which were required to emulate the "dirty" page bits, and external interrupts, for two months [21].

3.1 A Three-Part Model

A three-part model provides a general view of possible non-deterministic updates that affect the execution of the system. The model represents the entire replayed system as three components (Figure 1): (1) the replayed system, (2) a deterministic execution environment, and (3) the nondeterministic external world. This representation simplifies the development of interposition and replay execution-scheduling layers by classifying all interactions between the replayed system and its environment into the following three categories: deterministic, synchronous, and asynchronous. Also, the three-part split reflects the fact that the seemingly rigid boundary of a virtual machine monitor in practice is pushed well outside the narrow hardware interface of a VMM for the following reasons: (1) the flexibility to choose the interposition boundary that reduces the amount of recorded nondeterminism, and (2) the possibility of reusing complex, low-level VMM code for injecting asynchronous events and implementing device I/O. Most of the hypervisor code—e.g., memory management, page-fault handling, and the hypercall interface—is deterministic and can be classified as the deterministic environment. This often allows ensuring determinism by recording and replaying an invocation of a high-level function from the VMM code (Figure 1(d)). Device code, e.g., for disk, network, and console, can be forced to look deterministic to the replayed system with the help of a small layer of code, a *determinizing proxy*, that ensures the determinism of observed behavior (Section 3.2).

Deterministic updates A replayed system and its execution environment evolve together by updating each others' state (Figure 1(a)). For example, a replayed virtual machine starts through the normal VM-creation protocol that instantiates the VMM with a new VM (creates virtual CPUs, memory, paravirtualized or emulated device drivers, hardware emulator, etc.). In practice, it is simpler to ensure that the VM-creation protocol and its components are deterministic than it is to implement a new set of tools instantiating a replayed VM in a more controlled environment. Later, during VM execution, the VM updates the state of the deterministic environment, and vice versa. Deterministic interactions do not need to be logged, but they do need to be re-executed during replay to ensure that both parts of the system evolve in the same way they did in the original run.

Synchronous updates A guest system periodically invokes functions that might return nondeterministic results. For instance, reading the timestamp counter accesses nondeterministic data from otherwise deterministic code (Figure 1(b)). To ensure that the replayed machine follows the original execution path, synchronous events are replayed "in place." Replay interposition primitives query the replay engine and return to the system the value of the nondeterministic variable that was observed during the original run.

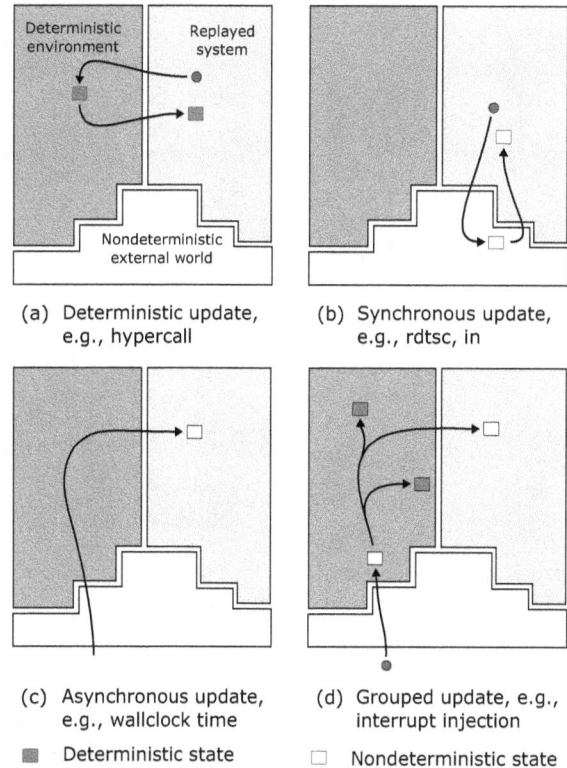

Figure 1. External world, deterministic environment, and replayed system.

Asynchronous updates Asynchronous events represent external updates to the replayed system (Figure 1(c)). These include interrupts and updates to shared memory from virtual device drivers running in parallel with the replayed system. In contrast to a synchronous event—where the replay machine effectively schedules the state update itself—an asynchronous event must be replayed in an instruction-accurate fashion by carefully scheduling execution of a replayed VM.

Dependent updates Figure 1(d) illustrates the common case where an asynchronous event triggers the execution of a function that performs multiple deterministic and synchronous updates. For example, an interrupt event updates the flags, registers, and stack of the guest system. While it is possible to record all these updates as asynchronous events, it is easier and more efficient to record a single asynchronous update, and treat the remaining updates as synchronous events originating from the code of the deterministic interrupt handler. Of course, the replay system must ensure the atomicity of the entire handler. In many cases this is easy, since the hypervisor is already designed to ensure that interrupt handlers are atomic.

3.2 Interposition Functions and Determinizing Proxies

Interposition functions Interposition functions implement a general logging, replay, and filtering interface for nondeterministic events (Figure 2). During the original run, interposition functions record all nondeterministic updates. During

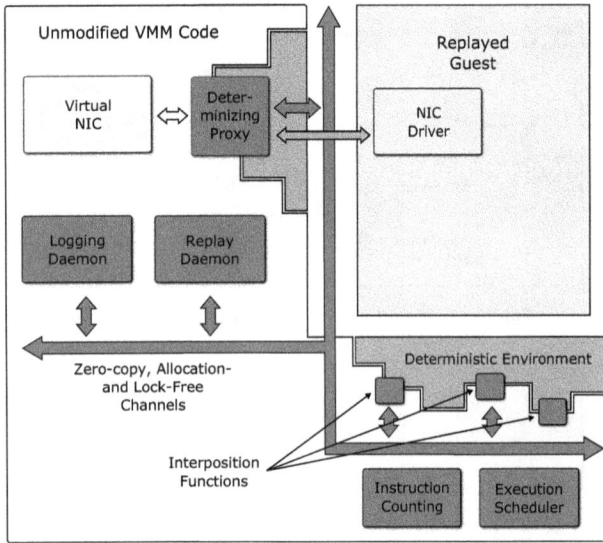

Figure 2. Components of the replay engine: pluggable interposition functions, logging and replay daemons, execution scheduler, instruction counting, and determinizing proxies.

```
int trace_<function>(...) {
  event_t event = {<EVENT_NAME>, ...};
  if(replayed_guest()) {
    if(synchronous(&event)) {
      // request replay of a specific event
      replay_current_events(..., &event, &ret);
      return ret;
    }
    // asynchronous event: suppress the
    // update but replay "optional" events
    replay_current_events(...);
    return OK;
  }
  // Pause all virtual CPUs
  pause_vm();
  trace_event(<event_type>, ...);
  // Emulate original event
  ret = <function>(...);
  unpause_vm();
  return ret;
}
```

Listing 1. Generic example of an interposition function.

replay, they serve two goals: (1) replay the original nondeterministic values and (2) prevent unscheduled nondeterministic events from updating the replayed system. Nondeterminism is generated by parts of the hypervisor and device drivers that were not modified to support replay and are therefore unaware that they are dealing with a replayed system. The interposition functions prevent nondeterminism from leaking into the replayed system.

An interposition function follows the pattern shown in Listing 1. When the system is under replay and the current event is synchronous, it asks the replay scheduler to replay the current event. If the event is asynchronous, it is suppressed, but the replay scheduler can replay optional events (Section 3.5). During the original run, the function first pauses all the virtual CPUs of the VM, traces the event, and then emulates it by either emulating the original operation or invoking one of the original functions in the hypervisor code. Note that it is critical to trace the event before emulating it, as emulation might trigger more nondeterministic events. By following this pattern during replay, events will be replayed in order.

Different interposition functions can be invoked in different contexts of execution, e.g., hypervisor, host kernel, and host user-level. If the function is invoked from outside the hypervisor, it relies on fast communication primitives to implement atomic tracing and replay of events that are coordinated from inside the hypervisor.

Determinizing proxies Virtual devices are not part of the deterministic environment. However, since their execution during replay is driven by requests from the replayed system, they are "nearly deterministic"—the only nondeterministic aspect of their execution is the time at which they respond, and order of replies. We use *determinizing proxies* to interpose on the communication protocol between the replayed

system and the device, ensuring that updates are propagated in a deterministic way. A virtual device accesses the state of the guest system through two mechanisms: (1) memory remapping and interrupt-signaling hypervisor calls, and (2) a region of shared memory. The determinism of hypervisor calls is ensured by the interposition layer inside the hypervisor. To ensure the determinism of direct memory updates, the determinizing proxy inserts itself between the guest system and the virtual device, and mirrors all updates to and from the guest system in a deterministic way. Some devices, e.g., network and console, require replay of the device I/O payload. The console device's proxy replays the console input itself. The more complex network device's proxy avoids emulation of the full device protocol. Instead, it replays the network payload into the guest device by using the device driver functions of the host kernel.

3.3 Precise Instruction Counting

A replay platform forces the replayed system to repeat its original execution by reproducing all nondeterministic updates to the state of the system and deterministic environment at the exact points of execution at which they happened during the original run. The position of each nondeterministic event is uniquely determined by the number of instructions executed by the replayed system since its start. While requiring compiler or binary translation support if done in software [36, 42], on modern CPUs, instruction counting can be implemented by utilizing the hardware performance monitoring interface [3, 31]. On the Intel architecture, two hardware performance counters can be utilized to implement an accurate instruction-counting algorithm: the branch instruction retired counter (`BR_INST_RETIRED.ALL_BRANCHES`) and the instruction retired counter (INST_RETIRED.ALL) [31]. A tuple of *{instruction pointer, branch counter}* is sufficient to identify the exact position in the instruction stream [24, 42]. On x86 systems, the tuple must be extended with the value of the RCX register, to account for cases when a string-copy instruction is preempted by an interrupt in the middle of the long copying loop. (The RCX register contains the last iteration of the loop.) Unfortunately, two problems complicate the implementation of a precise instruction counting: delay of the counter overflow interrupt, and nondeterminism.

Delay of the counter overflow interrupt The hardware performance monitoring interface of Intel CPUs provides support for preempting the execution of the system when a certain number of performance events is reached. In other words, it is possible to configure a performance counter to signal a nonmaskable interrupt when the counter overflows. Unfortunately, a nonmaskable counter overflow interrupt can be delayed for many cycles.[3] To address the interrupt delay problem, we configure the replay engine to preempt the execution of the system long enough in advance to account for the delay of the interrupt. After the interrupt is received, the system is single-stepped until the proper point in the instruction stream is reached.

Counter nondeterminism Both branch and instruction counters can become nondeterministic in the face of interrupts and exceptions. Specifically, certain instruction sequences change the behavior of the counter if preempted with an interrupt. In practice, this is a problem when the system is single-stepped for long periods during replay to compensate for the delay of the counter-overflow interrupt. During single-stepping, we implement a precise instruction-counting algorithm in software. If a counting anomaly occurs while the system is not in the single-step execution mode, we try to guess the correct value of the counter based on the value of the instruction pointer register. If the counter is only several instructions apart from the recorded value, we adjust it to match the value recorded during the original run.

3.4 Lightweight Interposition and Logging

Interposition code resides on the critical path of the guest system: inside interrupt and exception handlers, I/O paths of device drivers, and exit paths from the guest to the hypervisor. The main principle for implementing a fast interposition layer is to offload all tracing, processing, and saving of the trace data from the critical path. We implement this principle by utilizing a three-stage logging pipeline: pluggable interposition functions, ring channels, and a logging daemon (Figure 3).

The lightweight interposition layer must be designed to avoid memory allocations, data copying, and locking on the critical path. We implement our tracing mechanisms on top of a producer-consumer ring buffer. We allocate the memory

---

³ On our hardware, the counter interrupt is typically delayed by only several instructions. We have seen cases, however, in which the delay is more than a hundred cycles.

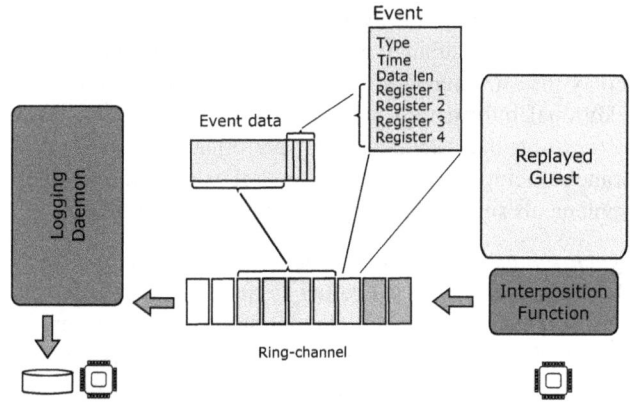

Figure 3. Lightweight interposition pipeline. Events and their payloads are allocated inside the ring.

for a new event record straight in the communication channel and log the event data into that memory. In the ring buffer, the pointer to the next element in the ring always points to the next available record, and thus it can be allocated by simply incrementing the pointer. Ring buffers are both lock-free and nonblocking; allocation, send, and receive operations are done with a single update of the producer and consumer pointers. To avoid blocking, a ring buffer provides flow control and tries to notify the receiver via an out-of-band mechanism when new records are available. For channels in which delay does not matter, ring channels notify the receiver only if the channel becomes critically full.

Atomicity of cross-CPU events To ensure the atomicity of recording nondeterministic events in a multi-CPU environment, we use *active messages*. We preempt and suspend the execution of the guest system. To record an asynchronous event between two physical CPUs—the CPU on which the event originates, and the CPU on which the recorded system is running—our primitives migrate the execution of the recording function between the CPUs. We request invocation on another CPU with an interprocessor interrupt (IPI). An IPI preempts execution of the guest system and invokes the requested function in the context of the IPI handler. Active messages allow us to avoid multiple cross-core round-trips required for suspending a VM.

Branch counter caching Frequent accesses to the relatively slow hardware branch-counter register introduce additional overhead when recording nondeterministic events. To minimize this cost, like ReVirt [22], our system accesses the hardware counter only once for each exit from the guest into the hypervisor.

3.5 Execution Scheduling

The replay engine induces a VM to reproduce a recorded execution path by injecting each nondeterministic event at its instruction-accurate position in the instruction stream. The execution scheduler implements controlled execution of the system from one nondeterministic event to the next.

Proper design of the event scheduler, and careful choice of the event scheduling types, ensures the extensibility of the replay infrastructure—allowing it to be modified to record additional information about the system: e.g., debugging information, the state of hardware performance counters, and branch-tracing store events. A general execution scheduler implements support for the following types of events.

Synchronous and asynchronous events To replay synchronous events, the scheduling engine lets the system run until it reaches the execution point at which it must replay that specific event. To replay asynchronous events, the execution scheduler configures branch counters to raise an overflow interrupt before the original event takes place, and then continues execution of the system in a single-step mode. This is done to address a hardware delay in receiving the interrupt [24, 37]. Upon reaching the target location in the execution, the replay engine replays the asynchronous event and continues execution by scheduling the execution of the system to the next nondeterministic event.

Optional events Optional events are useful to implement best-effort service. A scheduler will replay an optional event if it observes that the recorded guest is at a position in the instruction stream at which the event occurred in the original run; otherwise, it will discard the event. For example, we rely on the optional event type to replay performance information (Section 4.5) and turn on and off heavyweight debugging features like hardware branch tracing (Section 3.6).

Nonreplayable events Finally, nonreplayable events can record arbitrary information, e.g., debugging and performance analysis primitives like `printf`, tracing of real-time performance information during original and replay runs, and collecting BTS logs (Section 3.6).

Retyping asynchronous events as synchronous The replay engine benefits from recording as many synchronous events as possible. The replay of synchronous events does not require slow single-stepping—the system can just run to a point at which it exits into the hypervisor. Typically, several asynchronous events (e.g., device ring buffer updates) will be recorded while the guest system is inside the hypervisor that is servicing this synchronous exit. Although the synchronous exit itself does not need to be recorded since it is deterministic, it is possible to use the information about the synchronous exit to relabel all asynchronous events inside this exit as synchronous.

Replay on exit to guest It is reasonable to assume that the timestamp of the guest system changes only while it is running. In practice, this assumption is not true. The logic of instruction emulation implemented inside the hypervisor can change the instruction pointer of the guest system, moving its timestamp forward. Therefore, a scheduler should check if more events are ready to be replayed right before exiting into the guest system.

3.6 Scaling Development with Replay Analysis Tools

In our experience, the scalable development of deterministic replay is impossible without a range of debugging and analysis tools to aid the analysis of nondeterminism and the debugging of subtle replay divergence cases. Three mechanisms aid the development of replay: page guarding, hardware branch tracing, and run-time state comparison.

Page guarding Our system's run-time *page guarding* mechanism enables the detection of unrecorded updates to the guest system. Page guarding write-protects guest pages when the guest system exits into the hypervisor. To implement the guard, we extended the hypervisor to automatically protect and unprotect pages on every transition between the guest system and the hypervisor. Page guarding enables us to detect a large subset of all nondeterministic events at the processor and memory boundaries of the virtual machine interface.

Hardware branch tracing Any undetected nondeterminism or error in the replay implementation might *diverge* the execution of a guest system from its original run. Without additional information, subtle replay failures are difficult to debug. We implemented an efficient execution comparison tool using the Branch Tracing Store (BTS) facility provided by Intel CPUs [31]. The BTS interface allows us to configure a region of memory as a linear array in which the CPU records all taken branches. The BTS can be configured to send a nonmaskable interrupt when the array reaches a certain length. We flush the contents of the BTS buffer every time it traces a nondeterministic event. This way, we are able to see what code the system was executing between nondeterministic updates, and compare BTS traces across original and replay runs. We further built a set of tools that resolve raw branch addresses into human-readable symbol names. We rely on the GDB debugger to perform the symbol lookup. The BTS mechanism, coupled with automatic symbol resolution and trace-comparison tools, has proved to be a good mechanism for analyzing diverging executions.

Run-time state comparison Finally, to detect divergent state and nondeterminism in the hypervisor, the replay engine contains a run-time mechanism that can record and compare the state of the hypervisor across original and replay runs. We implement state comparison by extending our replay engine with a new optional event. This event carries the state information between original and replayed runs, and triggers a state comparison when it is replayed.

4. Deterministic Replay in Xen

We implemented our ideas in XenTT, a full-system deterministic replay engine for the Xen virtual machine monitor. Multiple reasons motivated the choice of Xen as the basis for XenTT. Xen is a full-featured, open-source virtualization platform [5]. It offers excellent virtualization performance; a fast, fully asynchronous, paravirtualized device driver architecture; and support for a wide variety of guest systems

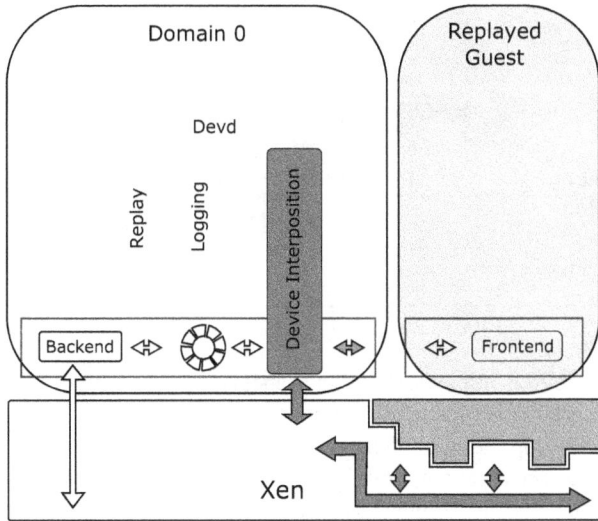

Figure 4. Architecture of the XenTT replay engine.

and hardware platforms. It is widely used as a virtualization provider in commercial datacenters [2] and large-scale academic research facilities [47].

4.1 XenTT Architecture

XenTT implements our replay architecture in Xen (Figure 4). Its replay engine consists of four main components and several high-bandwidth communication channels that connect them. The event-interposition layer utilizes pluggable interposition functions to implement logging and replay of the low-level VM interface exported by the hypervisor. The coordination layer relays events between the interposition functions and the logging and replay daemons. Logging and replay daemons run as user processes inside the privileged Xen domain; they process the log of recorded events and save it to a persistent store. The device-interposition layer implements determinizing proxies for each logged and replayed Xen device.

4.2 Hardware-level Virtual Machine Interface

Several Xen components require modification to record and replay nondeterministic events; we discuss them here.

Start info page The start_info page is shared between the guest system and the hypervisor at boot time. XenTT leverages the determinism of the domain-creation protocol, which recreates values in the start info page during replay.

Shared info page The shared_info page contains information required for initialization of the guest, delivery of interrupts (event channels), nanosecond and wall-clock time, etc. Shared info is updated asynchronously by the hypervisor. XenTT records and replays nondeterministic updates to the shared info page as simple memory-page updates.

Grant tables The grant tables store information for memory access permissions and in-flight sharing of pages between domains. Grant tables are typically updated asynchronously by the backend drivers. A grant table update has the form of a compare-and-exchange or a clear-flag operation. For compare-and-exchange, XenTT records a grant table operation as an index into the grant table array, the old value, the new value, and the result of the compare-and-exchange.

Event channels Event channels are Xen's analog to hardware interrupts. They are one-bit communication primitives used to send immediate notifications between virtual machines. To deliver an event, Xen preempts the execution of the guest, creates a special interrupt stack, and forces the execution of the interrupt handler. Although the event-delivery protocol requires several updates to the shared_info page, and the injection of an interrupt frame into the guest, its execution is deterministic. XenTT records and replays event notifications by simply invoking the event delivery function (evtchn_set_pending).

Copy-user interface The copy-user interface is used to return data from the hypervisor to the guest. XenTT wraps the copy-user function and records all asynchronous copy-user events. The recording of in-place copy-user events is optional, since they will be reinvoked as part of another action.

Privileged instructions The Xen hypervisor supports privileged CPU instruction emulation (e.g., cpuinfo and rdtsc). XenTT interposes on this emulation to detect instructions that return nondeterministic results.

EFLAGS register To single-step the guest during replay, XenTT uses the trace flag (TF) in the EFLAGS register of the guest. Obviously, TF can change the execution of the system during replay, if it is "leaked" into the guest. For example, TF changes the execution of the Linux kernel on the system-call entry path. To preserve the determinism of the guest, XenTT virtualizes the EFLAGS register. During replay, when the guest is single-stepped, XenTT parses the guest's instruction stream and detects instructions that save the EFLAGS register.

Optional events Some exits from the guest are in-place events (i.e., exceptions, hypercalls, and int 0x80 system calls) that are deterministically re-executed by the guest, if the determinism of all other events is preserved. To reduce interposition overhead, XenTT does not record these events.

Time Xen exports wall-clock time, system time since boot, and run-time state statistics to the guest system through a shared memory region that Xen updates periodically. To obtain the most recent time values, the guest system interpolates time values with nanosecond precision by reading a hardware timestamp (TSC) register that is used to compute the time passed since the last memory update. To ensure the determinism of time values, XenTT records updates of time values in the shared page, and implements emulation of the `rdtsc` instruction that accesses the timestamp counter. XenTT records and replays the guest's run-time state statistics that reflect the amount of time a guest system spends in each of four states: running, runnable, blocked, and idle. Finally, XenTT records the execution of periodic, polling, and single-shot timers.

4.3 Device Drivers

The major source of nondeterminism in any system is communication with external devices. Under Xen, a guest system accesses its virtual devices via a backend-frontend split device pair [14, 25]. To notify each other about new I/O requests, backend and frontend device drivers rely on a fast, lock-free, producer-consumer ring, which they share in a memory page. The backend and frontend devices add new requests to the ring by simply advancing the pointers in the shared ring, and sometimes notifying the other end via an event channel.

For high-bandwidth I/O devices, the shared ring contains only pointers to the memory pages with the actual I/O payload. The ring essentially holds a queue of I/O requests. Each I/O request contains a machine frame number of a page with the actual I/O payload. A typical I/O transfer relies on the memory-mapping mechanism, although other ways of communicating I/O data are possible, e.g., memory copy in and out of a large shared I/O buffer, hypervisor-supported memory copy operation, page flipping, etc.

There are two challenges in logging device driver communication. First, the overhead of logging every update to memory shared between virtual machines is prohibitive. XenTT leverages the semantics of the shared ring and logs only shared-ring pointer updates. (In theory, a guest could access the data in the shared memory before the pointer update; in practice, guest frontend device drivers do not.)

The second challenge is a result of the fact that a shared ring is updated inside the kernel of a device driver domain. XenTT must record the exact state of the guest at the update, but this state is only available inside the hypervisor. To avoid multiple context switches needed to read guest state, XenTT implements a new technique that ensures atomicity of the memory update *and* reading the guest state. Instead of updating a pointer in the ring, the device driver domain sends the hypervisor an active message (Section 3.4) describing the update. The hypervisor atomically performs the update and records guest state.

4.4 Determinizing Proxies

To preserve the determinism of replay, XenTT ensures the determinism of updates to the shared-ring buffers. To control all shared-ring updates from the backend devices, XenTT implements a device-driver interposition component: Devd, which is inserted between each pair of backend and frontend device drivers to mediate their communication (Figure 5). Devd implements determinizing proxies for the four most critical Xen devices: console, XenStore, disk, and network.

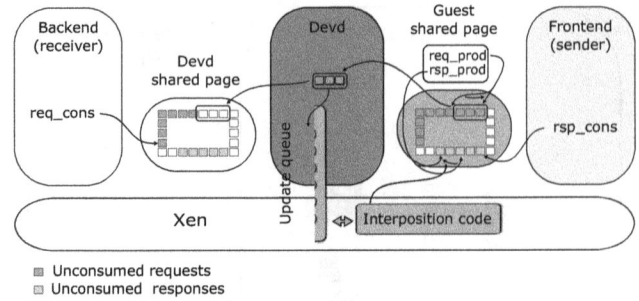

Figure 5. Details of ring interposition.

Devd is implemented as a user-level application that runs inside the device driver domain, i.e., Domain 0 in a typical Xen setup. Devd implements a device bus: by monitoring the XenStore database, Devd's bus driver discovers new devices connected to the guest system. For each newly discovered device, Devd walks through the list of registered drivers and tries to find a match for the device.

Instead of connecting to the event channels and shared rings of the frontend domain, backend devices connect to the shared rings created by Devd. Devd is transparent to the communication between backend and frontend devices: backend and frontend devices update their ring pointers as they do in case of noninterposed execution, and Devd reflects all updates between the two rings it mediates. In Figure 5, Devd mediates the update of the request producer pointer.

In-kernel payload logging Replay of the console, XenStore, and network devices requires logging of the data entering the guest during the original run. To shorten the datapath for high-throughput network devices, XenTT implements a payload logging mechanism, which allows it to save the payload of a backend device straight into a file without leaving the context of the device driver domain kernel.

Determinism of transactions in XenStore XenStore is a registry database fostering the exchange of device and domain configuration information; it implements a publish-subscribe interface across virtual machines. To support atomic updates, XenStore implements a transactional interface for updating its state. The determinism of the device-bootstrap protocol required deterministic XenStore transactions. XenTT implements this support by ensuring that transactions from replaying VMs always commit.

4.5 Extending Replay with Accurate Performance Information

Deterministic replay ensures that the replayed copy of execution is identical to the original run; i.e., during replay, the system repeats its original execution instruction by instruction. However, the performance information about the original execution is lost. Compared to the original run, the replayed system progresses at different speeds during replay. The two main factors that affect the performance of the replayed system are (1) eliminated periods of I/O waits and

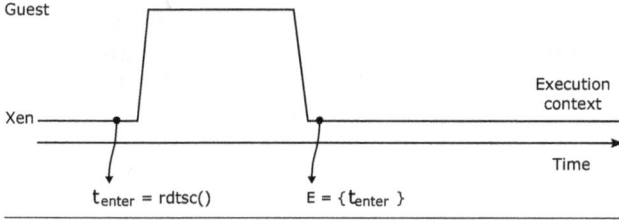

Figure 6. Saving and piggybacking the TSC information on exit to guest.

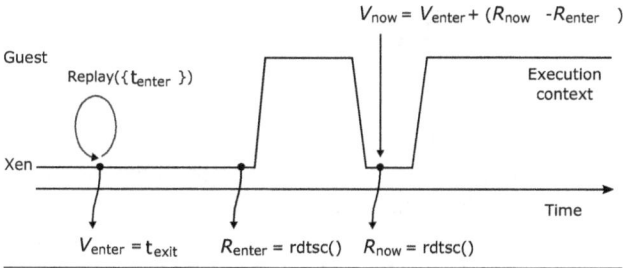

Figure 7. Replaying the TSC information.

CPU inactivity and (2) frequent periods of single-stepping required for replay of asynchronous events.

XenTT extends a traditional replay protocol with the ability to record and recreate a faithful view of performance of the original run during replay. During original execution, XenTT periodically records the value of the timestamp counter register (TSC). During replay, recorded values provide a basis for accurate approximation of performance at any moment of replayed execution with the help of a simple linear model.

XenTT records the value of the TSC on every transition from the hypervisor into the recorded system. The following optimization allows XenTT to make time recording more accurate. Every time the hypervisor is about to enter the guest, XenTT saves the current value of the TSC. The recording of this value is delayed until the guest returns to the hypervisor (Figure 6). During replay, the value of the original timestamp counter is replayed on every transition from the hypervisor into the guest (Figure 7). The current values of the TSC right at the entry point (R_{entry}) and at the moment the performance information is queried (R_{now}) allow XenTT to recreate the original value of the timestamp counter (V_{now}) as $V_{now} = V_{enter} + (R_{now} - R_{enter})$.

5. Evaluation

Can our replay abstractions and mechanisms be applied for recording complex software systems? In this section, we present several evaluation scenarios that demonstrate XenTT's ability to perform deterministic recording of real systems, on a variety of workloads, with overheads that are non-prohibitive for use in production environments.

Hardware setup We conducted our evaluation on a hardware platform that is representative of a production cloud environment. We performed experiments on a Dell PowerEdge R710 server equipped with a quad-core 2.4 GHz Intel Xeon

E5530 "Nehalem" processor with hyperthreading support, 12 GB of 1066 MHz DDR2 RAM, and four Broadcom NetXtreme II BCM5709 rev C 1 Gbps NICs. The machine is configured with four Western Digital WD1501FASS 1.5 GB SATA disks with a 64 MB buffer, 7200 RPM, and a sustained data transfer rate of 138 MB/s. One of these disks is the root disk. XenTT is based on a development version of the 32-bit Xen hypervisor (the closest corresponding Xen release is 3.0.4) and a 32-bit Linux 2.6.18 kernel.

To minimize test variability, we configured the system with the minimal set of resources required to fulfill the test task. For all experiments, we configured the Xen hypervisor to recognize only three CPU cores: two cores are allocated for Domain 0, and one core runs the XenTT guest VM. To reduce caching and buffering effects, we reduce the memory allocation for Domain 0 and the guest VM to be 2 GB and 192 MB, respectively.

5.1 Is Replay Faithful?

How do we know if the replayed system repeats the original execution? Deterministic replay naturally implements a self-checking mechanism through the replay of synchronous events. During replay, the system periodically asks for the replay of a synchronous event. At this point, the replay platform must provide the original value for a specific event. Replay detects divergence if the log does not contain the requested event, or if the timestamp of the event differs from the current position in the execution of the replayed system. In practice, synchronous events are frequent enough to provide a high degree of confidence that replay is faithful. A malicious system could possibly confuse the replay engine about its state (e.g., if replay is used for malware analysis or virtual machine accountability [28]). In these cases, hardware branch tracing can be used to compare executions at the level of taken branches.

5.2 Logging and Replay Overheads

CPU-intensive workloads To evaluate recording overhead on CPU-intensive workloads, we configured XenTT to run the open-source, multiplatform Freebench benchmarking suite. Freebench uses existing open source tools to implement ten tests that measure a system on a variety of workloads: scientific, 3D rendering, compression, encryption, database, photo processing, audio encoding, text processing, and AI.

Figure 8 presents our results from running Freebench benchmarks on a Linux guest and on a XenTT guest with recording enabled. For all but one test, the recording infrastructure introduced only a small overhead of 5.6%.

To evaluate the performance of a recorded system on a set of systems workloads, we configured XenTT to record the execution of the Phoronix benchmarking suite. The Phoronix suite provides a large library of benchmarks; we use nine that characterize whole-system performance and stress specific hardware components.

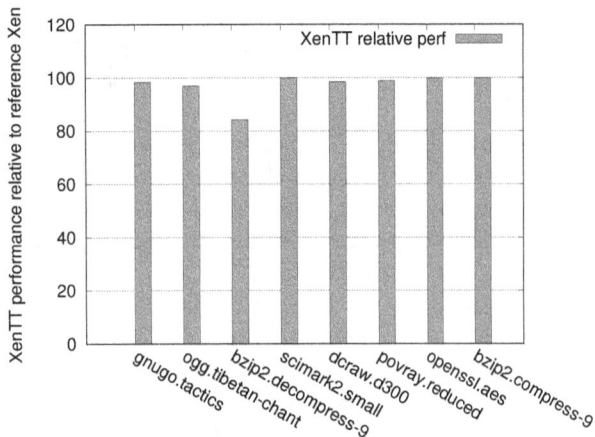

Figure 8. Freebench benchmarks.

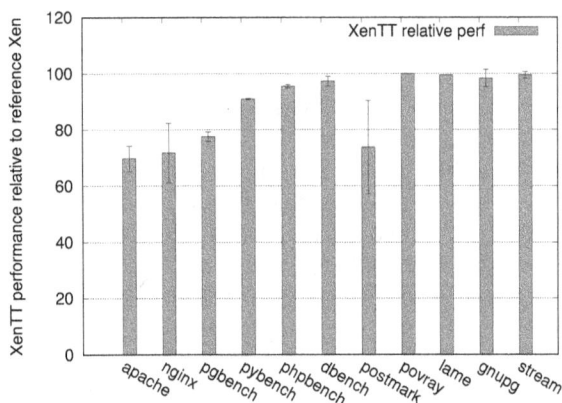

Figure 9. Phoronix benchmarks.

Figure 9 shows the performance of XenTT relative to the reference, non-XenTT performance, for each benchmark. LAME, GnuPG, and Stream remain within 2% of the performance of an unmodified Xen. Under XenTT, `apache` serves approximately 69% as many requests per second as the reference implementation. The `apache` benchmark incurs a large number of accesses to the timestamp counter register (TSC), via the `rdtsc` instruction. In an unmodified Xen, `rdtsc` is a non-privileged instruction. XenTT, however, forces the guest system to exit on `rdtsc` to record the returned TSC value. It is unclear if the large number of TSC events is inherent to the Apache workload or simply a side-effect of the benchmark. DBench and Postmark perform a large number of random disk operations. Higher delays of the disk interposition code penalize their performance.

Log sizes   We evaluated the space required to store deterministic logs by running XenTT on several representative tasks. A Linux kernel boot incurs a large number of exits to the hypervisor and nondeterministic events. XenTT logs performance information on every VM exit. An idle XenTT system generates a raw log at a rate of 167 MB/hr (4 GB/day), or 44 MB/hr (1 GB/day) if compressed with gzip. For the

Activity	Raw/Compressed Log Size	
Linux boot	903 MB	145 MB
Idle machine (12 hours)	2 GB	529 MB
	(167 MB/hr)	(44 MB/hr)
TCP receive (4 GB)		
Event log	1.8 GB	342 MB
Payload log	4.4 GB	(dependent)
TCP send (4 GB)	1.1 GB	211 MB
Disk write (4 GB file)	600 MB	145 MB
Disk read (4 GB file)	414 MB	62 MB

Table 1. Log size for various workloads.

TCP network receive test, we report both nondeterministic event and payload logs. We do not report the compressed size of the payload log, since it is payload-dependent.

Table 1 suggests that the system, which only reads and writes its disk at the highest speed, generates the compressed log at the speed of 5.5 GB/hr and 7.2 GB/hr, respectively. This implies that a 1 TB hard disk can only store 5.7 and 7.5 days of recording. The system, which sends and receives data over the network at the highest speed, will generate the compressed log at the speed of 18 GB/hr and 30 GB/hr, respectively. At such high rates, a 1 TB hard disk can only store 2.3 and 1.3 days of recording. The best case for deterministic replay is an idle system, which generates the compressed log at a rate of 1 GB/day. A 1 TB disk will store 3 months of deterministic recording.

Disk-intensive workloads   To stress sequential disk I/O, we used dd to read and write a 4 GB file (Figure 10). We used a 1 MB block size and averaged results over three runs. The Xen disk drivers provide little buffering on the I/O path and are therefore sensitive to the delays that XenTT introduces by routing all disk requests through a user-level device-interposition daemon. On a disk with a sustained data transfer rate of 138 MB/s, a vanilla Xen system achieves write and read throughputs of 101 MB/s and 130 MB/s, respectively. The XenTT interposition layer stays within 21% and 22% of the performance of unmodified Xen.

Network-intensive workloads   We evaluated network logging overhead by recording the execution of the `netperf` network benchmark (Figure 11). We set a TCP window size of 128 KB, ran `netperf` for 60 s, and averaged results over three runs. Compared to disk I/O, Xen's network drivers are more highly optimized to support high-bandwidth workloads and tolerate I/O delays. On send and receive operations, XenTT is able to stay within 8% and 14% of unmodified Xen.

To measure network delay, we used XenTT to record the execution of the `ping` tool (Figure 12). The tests report the overhead of interposition for both idle and loaded network paths. To load the network path, the guest system runs a `netperf` TCP stream test in the background, concurrently to the ping test. On a loaded connection, the measured delays

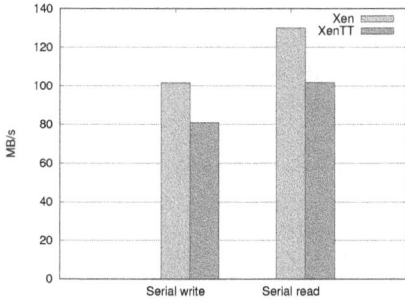

Figure 10. Disk throughput.

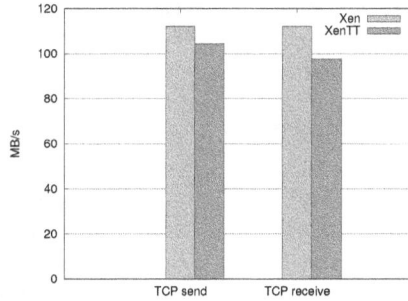

Figure 11. Network throughput.

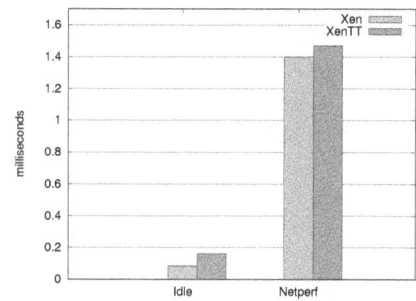

Figure 12. Network delay.

Test	Native	VMI/Perf Model	Error
nop1	120	212	1.77x
nop10	24	100	4.17x
nop100	68	128	1.88x
nop1K	352	420	1.19x
nop10K	3,568	3,808	1.07x
nop100K	34,924	35,976	1.03x
nop1M	349,068	350,300	1.00x
real10	28	116	4.14x
real100	80	168	2.10x
real1K	516	632	1.22x
real10K	5,224	5,260	1.01x
real100K	51,700	51,888	1.00x
real1M	516,756	517,680	1.00x

Table 2. Precision of the performance model.

for XenTT are within 5% of those measured for Xen. On an idle link, XenTT's interposition code adds an 80 μs delay.

5.3 Precision of the Performance Model

To characterize the precision of XenTT's performance model, we measured simple sequences of instructions. Table 2 lists our results. The "nopX" tests consist of X nop instructions; the "realX" tests consist of X simple instructions (e.g., pushl, inc, addl, etc.). To improve measurement fidelity, we removed the possibility of page faults while loading the test code pages. In the table, the "Native" cycle counts are obtained by directly instrumenting the test using the rdtsc instruction; the "VMI/Perf Model" values are obtained from the XenTT performance model via a virtual machine introspection (VMI) interface exported by XenTT at the beginning and end of the test sequence. The "Error" values are the ratios of VMI to Native cycle counts.

The performance model is noticeably less precise for very small instruction sequences. This is to be expected, given the fact that a combined entry and exit path to the hypervisor costs approximately 800 cycles, and the performance model must account for these and other expensive events as it virtualizes the TSC. However, its precision becomes much better over even a relatively small number of cycles (e.g., 10K nops or real instructions). Given this, we claim that the performance model provides reasonable precision.

6. Discussion

Although we implement deterministic replay for paravirtualized Xen guests, we argue that our ideas generalize to other hypervisors and types of virtualization. Paravirtualization and hardware-supported CPU virtualization require inherently similar replay interposition boundaries. A paravirtualized interface is designed to follow the shape of the hardware interface of the CPU—a pragmatic choice aimed at minimizing the changes necessary in the guest kernel. Compared to paravirtualization, hardware-supported virtualization defines a much cleaner and simpler protocol for injecting asynchronous interrupts into the guest system. As a result, the replay interposition boundary can rely on the same principles for injecting guest interrupts (i.e., determinism of low-level hypervisor functions), but does not require assembly programming to invoke interposition functions from an interrupt return path.

Full virtualization extends hardware-supported virtualization of the CPU with full emulation of a platform. This requires extending the interposition boundary into a hardware emulator: QEMU is a de facto standard emulator used by both Xen and KVM. Until recently, QEMU had a single-threaded, serialized device-emulation architecture that enabled relatively simple interposition and replay [12]. Components of a hardware emulator that are not performance-critical, such as BIOS emulation, can leverage this simple architecture, and thus can be trivially extended with replay. On the other hand, the emulation of high-throughput hardware devices would require fully asynchronous, parallel devices. Such devices will benefit from the techniques developed by our work: determinizing proxies, device interposition, fast communication primitives, centralized recording, active messages, and general replay scheduling. These same techniques can be applied to the replay of virtualization platforms that support direct device assignment and SR-IOV. In the case of direct assignment of a device, instead of full emulation of the device interface, a replay platform must implement a simpler interposition logic for the low-level device interface (the PCI configuration space, BAR regions, DMA engine, etc.).

KVM implements a hypervisor as part of the Linux kernel. While different than Xen, KVM is built on architectural ideas similar to those in Xen, and thus can benefit from the general mechanisms and principles presented here. Furthermore, we argue that our replay debugging and analysis techniques— page guarding of the VMCS region, BTS tracing, and runtime state comparison—can significantly aid in the analysis of nondeterminism. While originally dependent on QEMU-based device emulation, recent versions of KVM leverage virtio [39], a fast, paravirtualized device stack. Similarly to split-device drivers in Xen, virtio relies on shared-memory ring buffers for high-throughput communication. While having a different ring interface, virtio devices can leverage our ideas for implementing general device interposition.

7. Related Work

Techniques to log and replay state date back to the earliest computing systems. In 1948, the ENIAC relied on system checkpointing to recover computations interrupted by frequent component failures [34]. An excellent overview of the early work in the area of reversible execution is given by Leeman [34]. Several surveys provide taxonomies of early [20] and more recent work [16, 30] in the area of replay debugging. Chen et al. provide a good overview of recent approaches to multiprocessor replay [13]. Contemporary notions of system replay originated as parts of distributed checkpoint protocols [6], replay debuggers for parallel systems [18], and fault-tolerant replication approaches [8].

A major drawback of all early replay systems is their inability to handle asynchronous events. Mellor-Crummey and LeBlanc were the first to implement an instruction-counting algorithm in software [36]. Cargill and Locanthi were the first to advocate the implementation of a simple instruction-counting mechanism in hardware [10]. Bressoud and Schneider relied on one of the first hardware branch-counting implementations in their hypervisor-based, full-system replication solution [9]. Precise instruction counting on modern hardware is still a problem [37]. VMware has articulated the details of a precise branch-counting algorithm that operates in the face of System Management Mode (SMM) interrupts [46].

A process-level replay solution can be implemented inside [17, 41] or outside [26, 27, 40] of an operating system kernel, i.e., as an extension to a kernel or as a library within a process. Facing the complexity of implementing precise hardware branch counting, most existing process-level replay frameworks do not provide support for replaying asynchronous events [33]. Mozilla's rr is a notable exception that implements instruction counting and replay of asynchronous events for a process-level replay solution [37].

In contrast to process-level solutions, full-system replay can provide a complete implementation of replay that requires no simplifying assumptions about the replayed system, except those imposed by the virtualization platform [12, 19, 22, 48]. A commercial replay implementation from VMware can record and replay the execution of enterprise workloads, e.g., Microsoft SQL and Exchange servers, 1 Gbps streams, a

Hadoop cluster, etc., with an overhead of a few percent [43, 44].[4] QEMU-based replay solutions [12] simplify their implementation by relying on the inherently synchronized execution model of the QEMU emulator, which runs all structural parts—e.g., device and CPU emulation code—under the "big lock." As QEMU tries to depart from coarse-grained locking, those replay engines will require logging, locking, and orchestration mechanisms similar to the ones suggested by our recipe. Facing the challenges of the highly preemptive Xen environment, we implemented many concepts similar to those found in SMP-ReVirt [23, 24], which however lacked high-level abstractions and mechanisms that could help programmers to translate its implementation to other VMMs.

8. Conclusion

We have presented principles and mechanisms for implementing deterministic replay in a modern VMM. The contribution of this paper lies not in the implementation of a particular replay engine, but rather in laying out the issues that are common to all virtual machine replay systems and presenting a solution that we believe can be followed. Our architecture is the result of three person-years of effort spent implementing XenTT. We believe that if we had had a reference architecture to follow at the start of our XenTT project, our implementation effort would have been much smaller. By sharing our battle-won experience, we hope to encourage other implementations and thereby promote deterministic replay as standard equipment for VMMs.

Acknowledgments

We thank the anonymous VEE '16 reviewers for their helpful comments. We performed our experiments on machines provided by the Utah Emulab testbed [47]. This work was supported in part by the Air Force Research Laboratory and DARPA under Contract No. FA8750–10–C–0242. This material is also based upon work supported in part by the National Science Foundation under Grant Number 0524096.

References

[1] G. Altekar and I. Stoica. ODR: Output-deterministic replay for multicore debugging. In *Proc. SOSP*, pages 193–206, Oct. 2009. doi:10.1145/1629575.1629594.

[2] Amazon Web Services, Inc. Amazon EC2 – virtual server hosting, 2016. URL https://aws.amazon.com/ec2/.

[3] AMD Corporation. AMD64 Architecture Programmer's Manual Volume 2: System Programming, 2007.

[4] M. Attariyan, M. Chow, and J. Flinn. X-ray: Automating root-cause diagnosis of performance anomalies in production soft-

---

[4] Starting with version 8, VMware Workstation dropped support for replay debugging functionality. For a while, VMware continued using deterministic replay as a basis for their fault-tolerant VM replication solution in vSphere. However, vSphere 6.0 abandoned deterministic replay in favor of fast checkpointing [45].

ware. In *Proc. OSDI*, Oct. 2012. URL https://www.usenix.org/conference/osdi12/technical-sessions/presentation/attariyan.

[5] P. Barham, B. Dragovic, K. Fraser, S. Hand, T. Harris, A. Ho, R. Neugebauer, I. Pratt, and A. Warfield. Xen and the art of virtualization. In *Proc. SOSP*, pages 164–177, Oct. 2003. doi:10.1145/945445.945462.

[6] J. F. Bartlett. A nonstop kernel. In *Proc. SOSP*, pages 22–29, Dec. 1981. doi:10.1145/800216.806587.

[7] T. Bergan, N. Hunt, L. Ceze, and S. D. Gribble. Deterministic process groups in dOS. In *Proc. OSDI*, pages 177–192, Oct. 2010. URL https://www.usenix.org/legacy/event/osdi10/tech/full_papers/Bergan.pdf.

[8] A. Borg, J. Baumbach, and S. Glazer. A message system supporting fault tolerance. In *Proc. SOSP*, pages 90–99, Oct. 1983. doi:10.1145/773379.806617.

[9] T. C. Bressoud and F. B. Schneider. Hypervisor-based fault-tolerance. In *Proc. SOSP*, pages 1–11, Dec. 1995. doi:10.1145/224056.224058.

[10] T. A. Cargill and B. N. Locanthi. Cheap hardware support for software debugging and profiling. In *Proc. ASPLOS*, pages 82–83, Oct. 1987. doi:10.1145/36177.36187.

[11] A. Chen, W. B. Moore, H. Xiao, A. Haeberlen, L. T. X. Phan, M. Sherr, and W. Zhou. Detecting covert timing channels with time-deterministic replay. In *Proc. OSDI*, pages 541–554, Oct. 2014. URL https://www.usenix.org/conference/osdi14/technical-sessions/presentation/chen_ang.

[12] Y. Chen and H. Chen. Scalable deterministic replay in a parallel full-system emulator. In *Proc. PPoPP*, pages 207–218, Feb. 2013. doi:10.1145/2442516.2442537.

[13] Y. Chen, S. Zhang, Q. Guo, L. Li, R. Wu, and T. Chen. Deterministic replay: A survey. *ACM Comput. Surv.*, 48(2), Nov. 2015. doi:10.1145/2790077.

[14] D. Chisnall. *The Definitive Guide to the Xen Hypervisor*. Prentice Hall, first edition, 2007. ISBN 978-0132349710.

[15] J. Chow, T. Garfinkel, and P. M. Chen. Decoupling dynamic program analysis from execution in virtual environments. In *Proc. USENIX ATC*, pages 1–14, June 2008. URL https://www.usenix.org/legacy/event/usenix08/tech/full_papers/chow/chow.pdf.

[16] F. Cornelis, A. Georges, M. Christiaens, M. Ronsse, T. Ghesquiere, and K. D. Bosschere. A taxonomy of execution replay systems. In *International Conference on Advances in Infrastructure for Electronic Business, Education, Science, Medicine, and Mobile Technologies on the Internet*, 2003.

[17] F. Cornelis, M. Ronsse, and K. De Bosschere. TORNADO: A novel input replay tool. In *Proc. PDPTA*, 2003.

[18] R. Curtis and L. D. Wittie. BUGNET: A debugging system for parallel programming environments. In *Proc. ICDCS*, pages 394–400, Oct. 1982.

[19] D. A. S. de Oliveira, J. R. Crandall, G. Wassermann, S. F. Wu, Z. Su, and F. T. Chong. ExecRecorder: VM-based full-system replay for attack analysis and system recovery. In *Proc. 1st Workshop on Architectural and System Support for*

Improving Software Dependability, pages 66–71, Oct. 2006. doi:10.1145/1181309.1181320.

[20] C. Dionne, M. Feeley, and J. Desbiens. A taxonomy of distributed debuggers based on execution replay. In *Proc. PDPTA*, Aug. 1996.

[21] G. Dunlap. Personal communication, 2012.

[22] G. W. Dunlap, S. T. King, S. Cinar, M. A. Basrai, and P. M. Chen. ReVirt: Enabling intrusion analysis through virtual-machine logging and replay. In *Proc. OSDI*, pages 211–224, Dec. 2002. URL https://www.usenix.org/legacy/event/osdi02/tech/dunlap.html.

[23] G. W. Dunlap, D. G. Lucchetti, P. M. Chen, and M. A. Fetterman. Execution replay for multiprocessor virtual machines. In *Proc. VEE*, Mar. 2008. doi:10.1145/1346256.1346273.

[24] G. W. Dunlap III. *Execution Replay for Intrusion Analysis*. PhD thesis, University of Michigan, 2006.

[25] K. Fraser, S. Hand, R. Neugebauer, I. Pratt, A. Warfield, and M. Williamson. Safe hardware access with the Xen virtual machine monitor. In *Proc. 1st Workshop on Operating System and Architectural Support for the On Demand IT Infrastructure (OASIS)*, Oct. 2004. URL https://www.cl.cam.ac.uk/research/srg/netos/papers/2004-safehw-oasis.pdf.

[26] D. Geels, G. Altekar, S. Shenker, and I. Stoica. Replay debugging for distributed applications. In *Proc. USENIX ATC*, pages 289–300, May–June 2006. URL https://www.usenix.org/legacy/events/usenix06/tech/geels.html.

[27] Z. Guo, X. Wang, J. Tang, X. Liu, Z. Xu, M. Wu, M. F. Kaashoek, and Z. Zhang. R2: An application-level kernel for record and replay. In *Proc. OSDI*, pages 193–208, Dec. 2008. URL https://www.usenix.org/legacy/events/osdi08/tech/full_papers/guo/guo.pdf.

[28] A. Haeberlen, P. Aditya, R. Rodrigues, and P. Druschel. Accountable virtual machines. In *Proc. OSDI*, pages 119–134, Oct. 2010. URL https://www.usenix.org/legacy/event/osdi10/tech/full_papers/Haeberlen.pdf.

[29] N. Honarmand and J. Torrellas. RelaxReplay: Record and replay for relaxed-consistency multiprocessors. In *Proc. ASPLOS*, Mar. 2014. doi:10.1145/2541940.2541979.

[30] J. Huselius. Debugging parallel systems: A state of the art report. MTRC Report 63, Mälardalens University, Västerås, Sweden, Sept. 2002. URL http://www.es.mdh.se/publications/366-Debugging_Parallel_Systems__A_State_of_the_Art_Report.

[31] Intel Corporation. Intel 64 and IA-32 Architectures Software Developer's Manual, Volume 3 (3A, 3B, 3C, and 3D): System Programming Guide, 2015.

[32] S. T. King, G. W. Dunlap, and P. M. Chen. Debugging operating systems with time-traveling virtual machines. In *Proc. USENIX ATC*, pages 1–15, Apr. 2005. URL https://www.usenix.org/legacy/events/usenix05/tech/general/king.html.

[33] O. Laadan, N. Viennot, and J. Nieh. Transparent, lightweight application execution replay on commodity multiprocessor operating systems. In *Proc. SIGMETRICS*, pages 155–166, June 2010. doi:10.1145/1811039.1811057.

[34] G. B. Leeman, Jr. A formal approach to undo operations in programming languages. *ACM TOPLAS*, 8(1):50–87, Jan. 1986. doi:10.1145/5001.5005.

[35] G. Lefebvre, B. Cully, C. Head, M. Spear, N. Hutchinson, M. Feeley, and A. Warfield. Execution mining. In *Proc. VEE*, pages 145–158, Mar. 2012. doi:10.1145/2151024.2151044.

[36] J. M. Mellor-Crummey and T. J. LeBlanc. A software instruction counter. In *Proc. ASPLOS*, pages 78–86, Apr. 1989. doi:10.1145/70082.68189.

[37] Mozilla Foundation. rr: lightweight recording & deterministic debugging, Feb. 2016. URL http://rr-project.org/.

[38] S. Park, Y. Zhou, W. Xiong, Z. Yin, R. Kaushik, K. H. Lee, and S. Lu. PRES: Probabilistic replay with execution sketching on multiprocessors. In *Proc. SOSP*, pages 177–192, Oct. 2009. doi:10.1145/1629575.1629593.

[39] R. Russell. virtio: Towards a de-facto standard for virtual I/O devices. *ACM SIGOPS OSR*, 42(5):95–103, July 2008. doi:10.1145/1400097.1400108.

[40] Y. Saito. Jockey: A user-space library for record-replay debugging. In *Proc. AADEBUG*, pages 69–76, Sept. 2005. doi:10.1145/1085130.1085139.

[41] S. M. Srinivasan, S. Kandula, C. R. Andrews, and Y. Zhou. Flashback: A lightweight extension for rollback and deterministic replay for software debugging. In *Proc. USENIX ATC*, pages 29–44, June–July 2004. URL https://www.usenix.org/legacy/event/usenix04/tech/general/srinivasan.html.

[42] G. Venkitachalam, M. Nelson, B. Weissman, M. Xu, and V. V. Malyugin. Using branch instruction counts to facilitate replay of virtual machine instruction execution. U.S. patent 7,844,954, Nov. 2010.

[43] VMware. VMware vSphere 4 Fault Tolerance: Architecture and performance. White paper, Aug. 2009. URL https://www.vmware.com/resources/techresources/10058.

[44] VMware. Protecting Hadoop with VMware vSphere 5 Fault Tolerance. Technical white paper, Aug. 2012. URL https://www.vmware.com/resources/techresources/10301.

[45] VMware. VMware vSphere 6 Fault Tolerance: Architecture and performance. Technical white paper, Dec. 2015. URL https://www.vmware.com/resources/techresources/10514.

[46] B. Weissman, V. V. Malyugin, P. Vandrovec, G. Venkitachalam, and M. Xu. Precise branch counting in virtualization systems. U.S. patent 9,027,003, May 2015.

[47] B. White, J. Lepreau, L. Stoller, R. Ricci, S. Guruprasad, M. Newbold, M. Hibler, C. Barb, and A. Joglekar. An integrated experimental environment for distributed systems and networks. In *Proc. OSDI*, pages 255–270, Dec. 2002. URL https://www.usenix.org/legacy/event/osdi02/tech/white.html.

[48] M. Xu, V. Malyugin, J. Sheldon, G. Venkitachalam, and B. Weissman. ReTrace: Collecting execution trace with virtual machine deterministic replay. In *Proc. 3rd Annual Workshop on Modeling, Benchmarking and Simulation*, June 2007. URL https://labs.vmware.com/academic/publications/retrace.

Next Generation Virtual Memory Management

Kathryn S. McKinley

Microsoft Research

Abstract

The goal of virtual memory is an abstraction of infinite and private memory for every process. Unfortunately, the insatiable memory demands of modern applications increasingly violate this abstraction by exposing capacity, bandwidth, and performance limitations of modern hardware. Furthermore, emerging memory technologies are likely to exacerbate this problem. For instance, non-volatile memory differs from DRAM due to its asymmetric read/write performance and thus will likely be an addition rather than a drop-in replacement for DRAM. This talk will describe these problems and recent architecture and software innovations that address of some of them. If adopted, these solutions will impose substantial challenges for operating system memory management, which has evolved very slowly over the past 30 years. I will draw lessons from the past 15 years of garbage collection advances to suggest some promising directions for innovation.

Biography

Kathryn S. McKinley is a Principal Researcher at Microsoft. She was previously an Endowed Professor of Computer Science at The University of Texas at Austin. She is interested in creating systems that make programming easy and the resulting programs correct and efficient. She and her collaborators have produced several widely used tools: the DaCapo Java Benchmarks (30,000+ downloads), Hoard memory manager, TRIPS Compiler, MMTk memory management toolkit, and Immix garbage collector. Her awards include the ACM SIGPLAN Programming Languages Software Award and best paper and test-of-time awards from ASPLOS, OOPSLA, ICS, SIGMETRICS, IEEE Top Picks, SIGPLAN Research Highlights, and CACM Research Highlights. She currently serves on the CRA and CRA-W Boards. Dr. McKinley was honored to testify to the House Science Committee (Feb. 14, 2013). She is an IEEE and ACM Fellow and has graduated 22 PhD students. She and Scotty Strahan, her husband of 31 years, have three sons.

VEE'16, April 2–3, 2016, Atlanta, Georgia, USA.

ACM ISBN 978-1-4503-3947-6/16/04.

DOI: http://dx.doi.org/10.1145/2892242.2892244

Exploiting FIFO Scheduler to Improve
Parallel Garbage Collection Performance

Junjie Qian [§], Witawas Srisa-an [§], Sharad Seth [§], Hong Jiang [§†], Du Li [‡], Pan Yi [§]

[§]University of Nebraska Lincoln, [†]University of Texas Arlington, [‡]Carnegie Mellon University

{jqian, witty, seth, jiang, pyi}@cse.unl.edu, [‡]dawn2004@gmail.com

Abstract

Recent studies have found that parallel garbage collection performs worse with more CPUs and more collector threads. As part of this work, we further investigate this phenomenon and find that poor scalability is worst in highly scalable Java applications. Our investigation to find the causes clearly reveals that efficient multi-threading in an application can prolong the average object lifespan, which results in less effective garbage collection. We also find that prolonging lifespan is the direct result of Linux's Completely Fair Scheduler due to its round-robin like behavior that can increase the heap contention between the application threads. Instead, if we use pseudo first-in-first-out to schedule application threads in large multicore systems, the garbage collection scalability is significantly improved while the time spent in garbage collection is reduced by as much as 21%. The average execution time of the 24 Java applications used in our study is also reduced by 11%. Based on this observation, we propose two approaches to optimally select scheduling policies based on application scalability profile. Our first approach uses the profile information from one execution to tune the subsequent executions. Our second approach dynamically collects profile information and performs policy selection during execution.

1. Introduction

As the speed of microprocessors tails off, utilizing multiple processing cores per chip is becoming a common way for developers to achieve higher performance. To do this, developers shift from writing sequential code to employing multithreading to achieve execution parallelism by (i) evenly distributing the workload among all threads within the application [6] and (ii) minimizing the number of synchronization operations to promote higher execution parallelism among the threads. As such, many programming languages including Java, support threading as a language feature.

Unfortunately, effective workload distribution, alone, does not guarantee scalability because Java is a managed language and part of the overall execution time is spent on runtime systems such as garbage collection (GC), which usually exhibit a very different execution behavior from that of the actual program. Furthermore, studies have shown that garbage collection can take up to one-third of total execution time of an application [9, 26]. As such, any scalability study must decompose the overall execution time into at least two components: time spent in *executing the application* or *mutator time* and time spent in *performing garbage collection* or *GC time*.

Although the Java virtual machine (JVM) creates threads, it is the operating system that schedules them for execution. In JDK1.7, each thread in the JVM is mapped as one kernel thread in Linux and they are, by default, scheduled using Completely Fair Scheduler, which attempts to evenly divide the CPU time to all the processes in the running queue. Though the fairness between all the threads in an application is achieved, this scheduling policy also has adverse effects on garbage collection performance. Specifically, our investigation found that the garbage collector performs worse if the application's workload is evenly distributed among threads. A large number of concurrent threads create heap allocation competition that can lead to prolonged object lifespans. This phenomenon occurs because one thread is preempted before it can fully use the objects it allocated. As a result, although the objects of this thread would die soon, the heap becomes full and the GC is called as other threads compete to allocate objects on the heap. The lower GC efficiency makes the collector copy more objects from young to mature generation, which degrades the overall GC performance.

To the best of our knowledge, there has not been previous work that investigate the impact of scheduling policies on performance of multi-threaded Java applications. The key research question we want to investigate is: *how can different scheduling policies affect GC and application performances?* To answer this question, we conducted a series of investigations that make the following research contributions:

- We show that the completely fair scheduler in Linux prolongs the average object lifespan of scalable Java applications. The average longer object lifespan results in less efficient GC, which leads to poorer performance of both GC and whole application.
- We employ the first-in-first-out scheduler, instead, for the multi-threaded Java applications, which avoids allocating objects from all threads on the heap at the same time. Both GC and mutator performances show significant improvements with the first-in-first-out scheduler. Also, the GC scalability of the scalable applications is improved.
- We propose two approaches to select the best performing scheduling policy for an application based on its workload distribution profile. The first approach collects runtime information during a profile run and then selects a suitable scheduling policy based on the collected information for the subsequent runs. The second approach is to dynamically select an appropriate scheduling policy using on-the-fly profiling results.

The rest of this paper is organized as follows. Section 2 provides an overview of process schedulers and garbage collection. Section 3 explains the experimental methodology used in our investigation and reports the impact of the CFS scheduler on the applications performance. Section 4 presents the performance evaluations when using the first-in-first-out scheduler for the Java applications. Section 5 demonstrates two approaches we developed to automatically select an optimal scheduling policy for an application. Section 6 discusses the published works related to this topic. Section 7 discusses future work and concludes this paper.

2. Background

This section provides some background information on the process scheduling techniques in Linux and parallel garbage collection in Oracle OpenJDK 7.

2.1 Process Scheduling

During a life time of a process, it can be in many states that include ready, running, and blocked. When a process is created, it begins its life in the ready state waiting for its turn to execute. Once the process is scheduled, it enters the running state. Later, it may be swapped out as it waits for information from I/O devices or go back to ready state again if it is preempted due to quantum expiration. The number of threads that can run at the same time is often determined by the number of CPUs. The scheduler decides when to run which threads, and the order of the threads' execution has been shown to affect the overall performance of an application [19, 25, 27].

In Linux, at least two scheduling algorithms, *Completely Fair Scheduler* (*CFS*) and *First-In-First-Out* (*FIFO*) scheduler, are available. Within a system, *it is possible for one or more applications to use FIFO while the rest of the applications use CFS.*

Completely Fair Scheduler. CFS is currently the default scheduler in Linux [2] for system-level scheduling. Its goal is to provide balanced processing times among processes and avoid starvation. It is similar to round-robin scheduling, but with two major differences. First, CFS maintains process information in a red-black tree for constant time look up. Round-robin, on the other hand, uses a queue. Second, round-robin scheduler allocates a fixed execution period for each process while CFS uses a fair time period, with calculation based on several process parameters such as priority and percentage of CPU usage.

First-In-First-Out Scheduler. FIFO scheduler executes processes in the order that they are submitted to the run queue. The process keeps running until it finishes its work or it has to block as it awaits resources such as data being produced by other processes. In Linux, the FIFO scheduler exists on top of CFS. When an application is configured to use FIFO, threads within the application execute in a FIFO manner. However, threads in an application using FIFO are still subjected to preemption by the underlying CFS. To clarify the interplay between these two schedulers, we provide a simple example.

Assume that application A creates four threads: T_0, T_1, T_2, and T_3 in this particular order. If A is configured to use FIFO, its runtime behavior could be as follows:

- *Uni-processor—* T_0 is scheduled first. The other three remaining threads cannot run until T_0 finishes. For T_0, there is a maximum allowable time for it to run and if T_0 uses up this time, it is preempted so that *other threads from other applications can run*. The key point to take away from this example is that T_1 cannot run until T_0 is done. The execution order is from T_0 to T_3, respectively.
- *Multi-processor—* In Linux, there is a run queue per processor. Assume that our system has two processing cores so there are two run queues: R_0 and R_1. Even when FIFO is used, concurrent execution of two threads from the same application on two different cores is possible; e.g., T_0 is first placed on R_0 and T_1 is then placed on R_1. Note that T_2 and T_3 cannot be scheduled until T_0 or T_1 is done. The key point to take away from this FIFO policy example is that the number of concurrent threads from an application is determined by the numbers of cores and run queues in the system.

2.2 Garbage Collection

Currently, most state-of-the-art Java Virtual Machines use *Generational garbage collection* [13] to manage heap space. A generational collector segregates objects into "generations" using age as the main criterion. A typical generational garbage collector exploits the fact that objects have different lifetime characteristics; some objects are short-lived while others live for a long time. In terms of age distribution, past

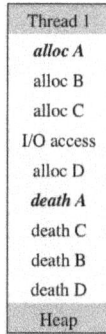

```
Thread 1
alloc A
alloc B
alloc C
I/O access
alloc D
death A
death C
death B
death D
Heap
```

Figure 1: Calculation Lifespan of Object A

studies, mainly based on single threaded applications, have shown that "most objects die young" (referred to as the weak generational hypothesis [13]); and thus, collection of objects in the youngest generation (minor collection) occurs more frequently than collection of objects from the entire heaps (mature collection). Note that the parallel GC in OpenJDK 1.7 HotSpot, which is the platform used in this study, parallelizes the process of identifying reachable objects to improve performance [1].

In a minor collection, live objects are copied from the young generation to the next older generation [13], the amount of work that must be done by a typical minor collector is proportional to the amount of live objects that must be copied. This implies that a small number of surviving objects would result in less GC effort, a shorter collection pause, and higher *GC efficiency*, which refers to the collected memory as a fraction of the allocated space prior to a collection [15], [13].

The lifespan of an object can be computed by observing the number of objects that have been created or the amount of available memory in the young generation that has been used between the creation of that object and the time that it dies (i.e., the object is no longer reachable because there are no more references to it) [23], [22], [11], [13]. Figure 1 illustrates a case in which there are three objects (B, C, and D) created during the lifetime of object A. Therefore, the lifespan of A is the total allocated size of these three objects.

An important consideration is that *object allocations consume the available heap space, but operations on those objects (execution) progress them toward their deaths*. If these two factors are not balanced (e.g., a long allocation burst that fills up the heap without sufficient execution efforts), generational GC would be ineffective because each minor GC invocation would need to copy a large number of live objects, resulting in poor garbage collection performance. Next, we conduct experiments to observe the relationship between object lifespans and number of threads and how it can affect scalability.

3. Scalability of Parallel Garbage Collection

In this section, we evaluate the scalability of parallel GC in OpenJDK 1.7. We then investigate the relationship between the workload distribution among threads and the average object lifespan as we varied the number of threads and CPUs.

Benchmark	Suite	Version	Heap size(MB)	Scalable
avrora	DaCapo	2009	75	No
eclipse	DaCapo	2009	330	No
fop	Dacapo	2009	90	No
jython	DaCapo	2009	90	No
h2	DaCapo	2009	900	No
lusearch	DaCapo	2009	90	Yes
pmd	DaCapo	2009	210	No
sunflow	DaCapo	2009	210	Yes
tomcat	DaCapo	2009	135	No
xalan	DaCapo	2009	150	Yes
compiler.compiler	SPECJVM	2008	4000	Yes
compiler.sunflow	SPECJVM	2008	2500	Yes
compress	SPECJVM	2008	2500	Yes
crypto.aes	SPECJVM	2008	2500	Yes
crypto.rsa	SPECJVM	2008	2500	Yes
crypto.signverify	SPECJVM	2008	2500	Yes
derby	SPECJVM	2008	4000	Yes
scimark.fft.large	SPECJVM	2008	2500	No
scimark.lu.large	SPECJVM	2008	2500	No
scimark.sor.large	SPECJVM	2008	2500	No
scimark.sparse.large	SPECJVM	2008	2500	No
mpegaudio	SPECJVM	2008	2500	Yes
xml.transform	SPECJVM	2008	4000	Yes
xml.validation	SPECJVM	2008	4000	Yes

Table 1: Benchmarks used in this paper. The last column identifies whether the application is scalable based on our empirical study.

3.1 Experimental Methodology

We conducted our experiments on a NUMA machine with four AMD 6168 chips; each chip contains 12 processing cores and the total RAM is 64 GB. We used Ubuntu 14.04.2 LTS and the kernel version is 64-bit 3.16.0-30 as the operating system and OpenJDK 1.7 HotSpot as the Java Virtual Machine (JVM). We configured HotSpot to use the stop-the-world throughput-oriented parallel scavenge garbage collector. This collector is based on a two-generational scheme (young and mature), previously described in Section 2 [13], [1]. The collector utilizes multiple threads to scavenge the nursery generation. Objects that survive the young generation are copied to the mature generation. This particular collector, by default, uses as many threads as the number of available cores to perform nursery (young-generation) collection, therefore, in presenting results, we use *cores* to reflect this constraint.

We chose 24 benchmarks from Dacapo-9.12-Bach [4] and SPECJVM2008 [21] as listed in Table 1. The unselected benchmarks from both suits either cannot run on our platform (tradesoap and tradebeans [1]) or run too short because of small workloads (startup.* and *.small benchmarks). The workloads and number of driver threads (64) are fixed for all benchmarks with different settings, and the actual number of

---
[1] http://sourceforge.net/p/dacapobench/mailman/message/29144190/

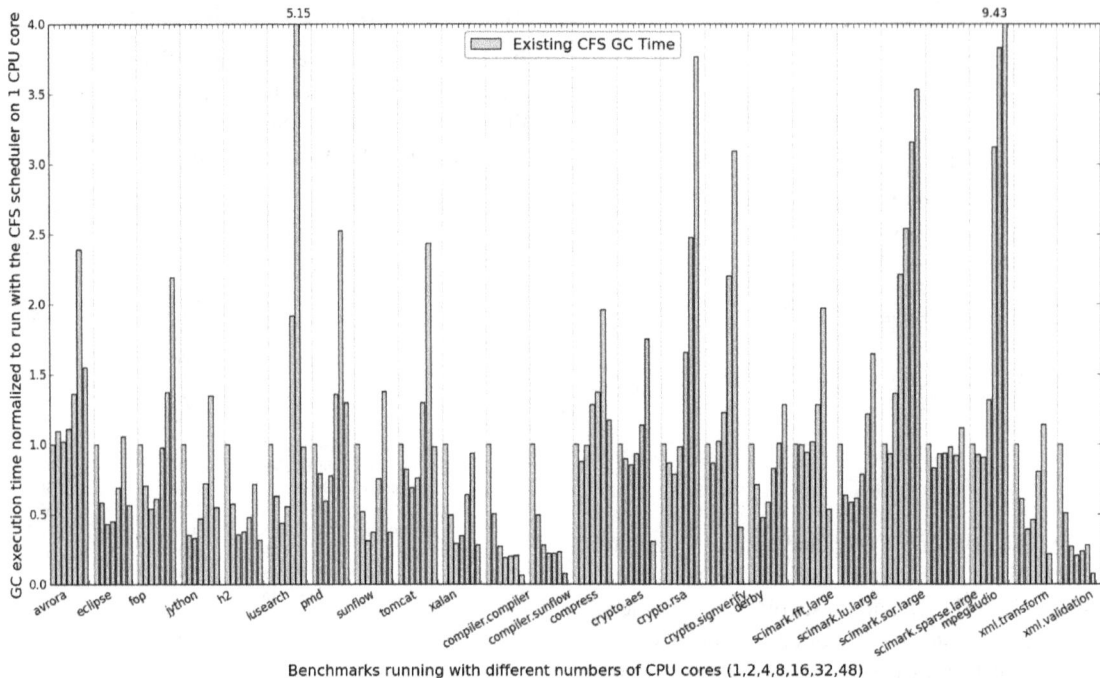

Figure 2: Effect of multiple threads/multiple cores on garbage collection scalability. For each application, there are seven bars. Each bar, from left to right, represents the GC execution time when 1, 2, 4, 8, 16, 32, and 48 threads and cores are used.

threads can be larger than the specified number of threads in each application.

Because the overall performances of Java applications can be sensitive to the workload and available heap space, we used the default input set and the same heap size for each run of an application (e.g., heap is set to 210MB for *sunflow* while the number of available CPU cores ranges from 1 to 48) as indicated in the Table 2. To set the heap size, we first identify the minimum heap requirement for an application using one mutator thread (i.e., if the heap is set to a smaller size, the application would crash). We then multiply this heap size by three (i.e., 3X of minimum heap size) [26]. Because there exists execution non-determinism due to threading, we ran each application 6 times to calculate the average value of each performance metric.

Table 2: Number of objects allocated (in million)

Benchmark	Number of mutator threads					
	2	4	8	16	32	48
eclipse	5308.5	5305.2	5306.8	5297.0	5304.7	5315.2
h2	3890.3	3897.6	3900.9	3906.4	3910.7	3914.1
jython	2217.8	2219.5	2217.7	2225.3	2225.6	2217.9
lusearch	5337.0	5336.5	5336.4	5336.4	5336.5	5336.9
pmd	*306.9*	*310.9*	*317.2*	*329.5*	*357.0*	*384.5*
sunflow	2529.3	2529.5	2529.9	2530.8	2532.7	2534.6
xalan	975.6	975.9	976.6	977.9	981.1	984.3

In JVM related studies, the experiments can be conducted with or without warm-up. Warm-up periods can provide time for the dynamic compilation system to generate op-

timized code. The approach with no warm-up periods has also been used in prior performance studies of application and garbage collection [5], [3]. In this study, we did not employ the warm-up approach in order to reduce the amount of traces. To validate the effects of using no warm-up periods, we verified our results with those reported by Du Bois et al. [6]. In that work, they attempt to distinguish scalable and non-scalable applications and evaluate garbage collection performance on multicore systems. Their methodology includes warm-up periods. We found our results and theirs to be nearly identical.

3.2 Scalability of Parallel GC

Previous studies have shown that parallel garbage collector can have poor scalability [6, 8–10, 17, 18]. As our first step, we conducted investigation to reconfirm the previously reported results for our setup. The results appear in Figure 2.

As shown, the GC times for most benchmarks are the smallest for four or eight threads/cores. Once we get to 16 threads/cores and beyond, we see that the GC times increase significantly for most applications. However, we also notice that increasing the number of threads in these application only slightly increases the number of allocated objects as shown in Table 2. As such, the additional garbage collection time is *not due to an increasing number of objects that must be collected*.

Based on this observation, we hypothesize that ineffective garbage collection, in which each collection invocation is not able to collect many objects, is the main reason for higher

112

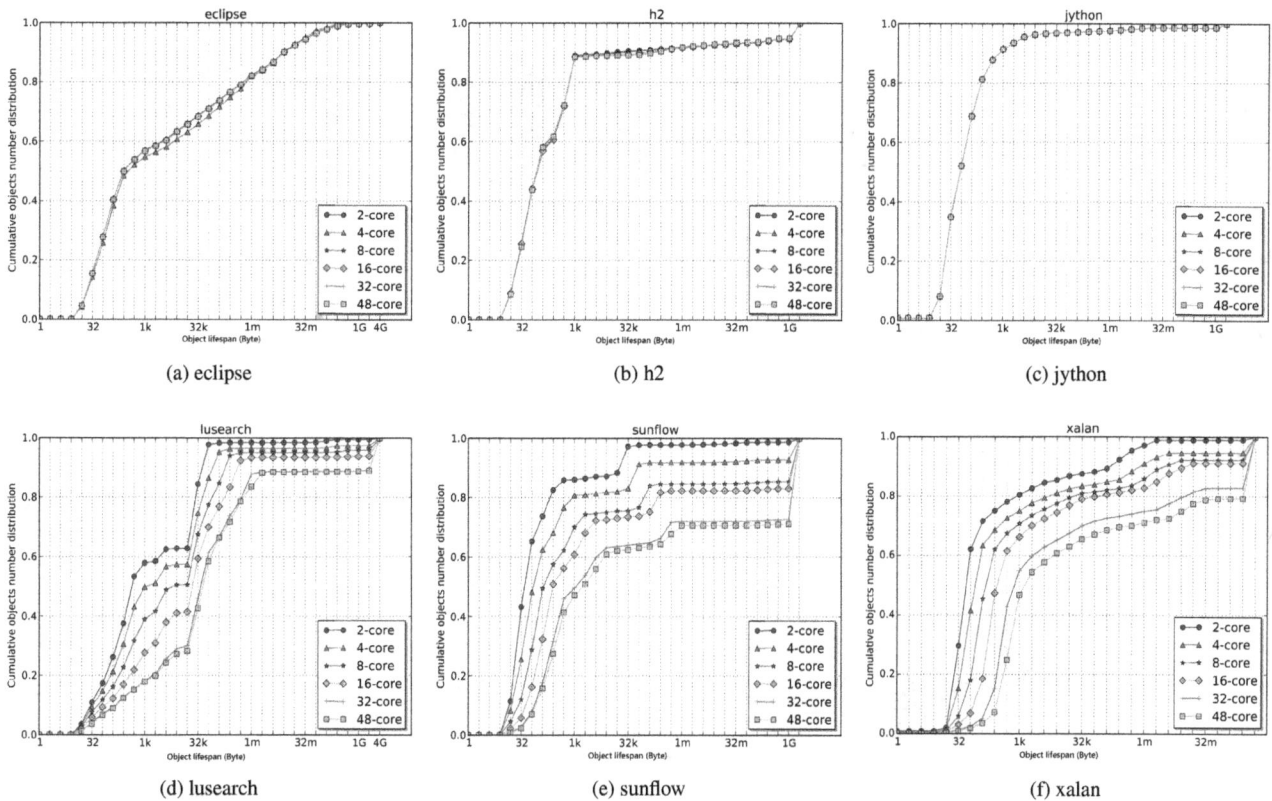

Figure 3: Object lifespan characteristics of scalable and non-scalable applications. The x-axis represents the object lifespan in bytes. The y-axis indicates the percentage of total objects that have a particular lifespan.

garbage collection overhead when 16 or more threads are used. Our hypothesis is based on the fact that generational collection performs well if most objects die young. However, a large number of surviving objects would results in higher copying cost [20], and therefore, higher garbage collection overhead. To validate our hypothesis, we conducted another experiment to evaluate the effects of increasing threads/cores on object lifespans.

Our results indicate that in some applications, object lifespans are sensitive to the numbers of threads and CPU cores while others show no sensitivity at all. Due to space limitation, we illustrate both characteristics in Figure 3 through six applications. The first three applications, *eclipse*, *h2*, and *jython*, show no change in object lifespans as we increase the number of threads. For the remaining three applications, *lusearch*, *sunflow*, and *xalan*, object lifespans are affected by increasing the number of the CPUs.

For *lusearch*, approximately 60% of all created objects have lifespans of 1KB or less when running with 2 mutator threads. When we set *lusearch* to run with 48 threads, less than 20% of all created objects have lifespans of 1KB or less. For *sunflow* and *xalan*, we observed a similar increase in lifespan. Over 80% of objects have the lifespans of 1KB or less when running with 4 mutator threads. However,

only 50% of objects have the lifespans of 1KB or less when running with 48 threads. Such increased lifespans resulted in more objects surviving the nursery collection. Therefore, more time is spent copying these surviving objects to the mature generation and more full garbage collection invocations are needed as the mature region fills up more quickly.

Next we characterize these applications to better understand why their lifespan characteristics are so much different. As part of this investigation, we observe the workload distribution among threads. Using the same six benchmarks, we report the amount of work done by each thread in Figure 4. The first three applications, *eclipse*, *h2*, and *jython* employ only a small number of threads regardless of the number of available threads to help perform the work. For example, *jython* mainly uses three to four threads to do most of the work. In the case of *h2*, only four to twelve threads perform most of the work. As we increase the number of threads, these additional threads perform very little work. This uneven workload distribution greatly limits scalability because adding more threads does not reduce the amount of work that the main threads must do.

On the other hand, *lusearch*, *sunflow*, and *xalan* show nearly uniform distribution of workload among threads. As more threads are added during our experiment, each thread

113

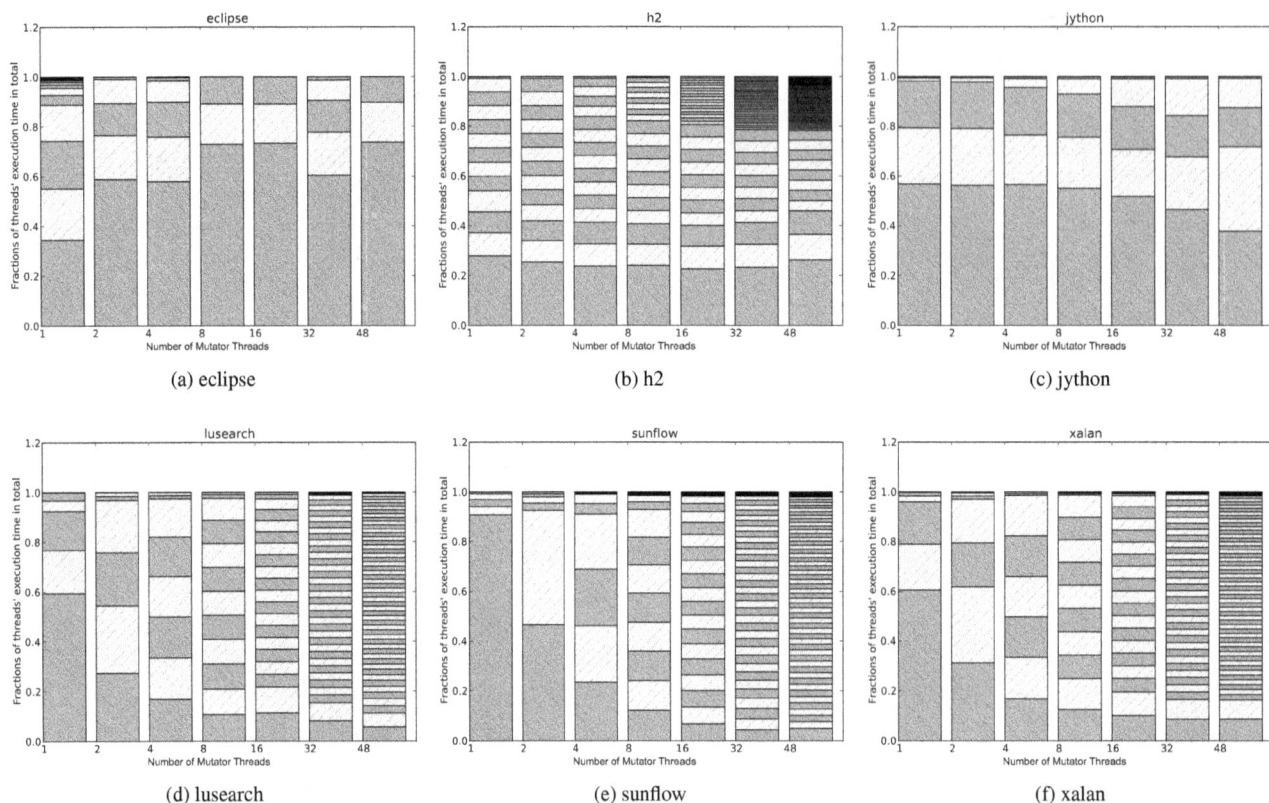

| (a) eclipse | (b) h2 | (c) jython |
| (d) lusearch | (e) sunflow | (f) xalan |

Figure 4: Fractions of threads' execution time as the number of employed threads increases. We sort each bar by placing the thread that spends the most time on the bottom of the bar and the one with the least time at the top of the bar.

would perform proportionally less work. So, these three applications achieve the first objective of being scalable. The last column of Table 1 identifies whether an application is scalable based on the results of our experiment.

3.3 Discussion

When the heap is shared by multiple threads, thread scheduling performed by the underlying operating system can affect lifespans of objects belonging to a thread. In our example shown in Figure 1, a thread, $(T1)$ allocates *object A*, *object B*, *object C*, and *object D*. Subsequently, $T1$ would access these objects but before doing so, it needs to perform an I/O operation. At this point, the operating system would suspend the execution of $T1$ and perform the requested I/O access on its behalf. If there are no other threads allocating objects from the same heap as $T1$, the lifespan of every object in $T1$ can be easily calculated based on the object allocation pattern of $T1$. Thus thread scheduling by the operating system has no effect on lifespans in a single-threaded environment.

On the other hand, consider a scenario where three threads, $T1$, $T2$, and $T3$ share the same heap. When $T1$ is suspended by the operating system during the I/O access, the scheduler may pick $T2$ to run next and then subsequently $T3$. At this point, the calculation of the lifespan of *object A*

must include objects created by $T2$ and $T3$. While the execution of $T1$ does not depend on any objects created by $T2$ and $T3$, these objects can greatly prolong the lifespans of objects created by $T1$. Furthermore, they also create additional allocation pressure that would eventually result in a minor collection invocation.

For the three scalable applications, evenly distributed workload means that the heap is shared by many threads, causing these applications to suffer from significantly prolonged lifespans due to scheduling and more threads allocating/using objects concurrently. This can result in poorer GC effectiveness as more time is spent on moving surviving objects from one generation to the next. For the remaining applications, additional threads perform little work and therefore, they have little effects on lifespans. In the next section, we describe our approach to reduce the effect of scheduling on object lifespan.

4. Effects of FIFO vs. CFS

In this section, we compare GC scalabilities and overall performances of the two scheduling policies: FIFO and CFS using the 24 benchmarks.

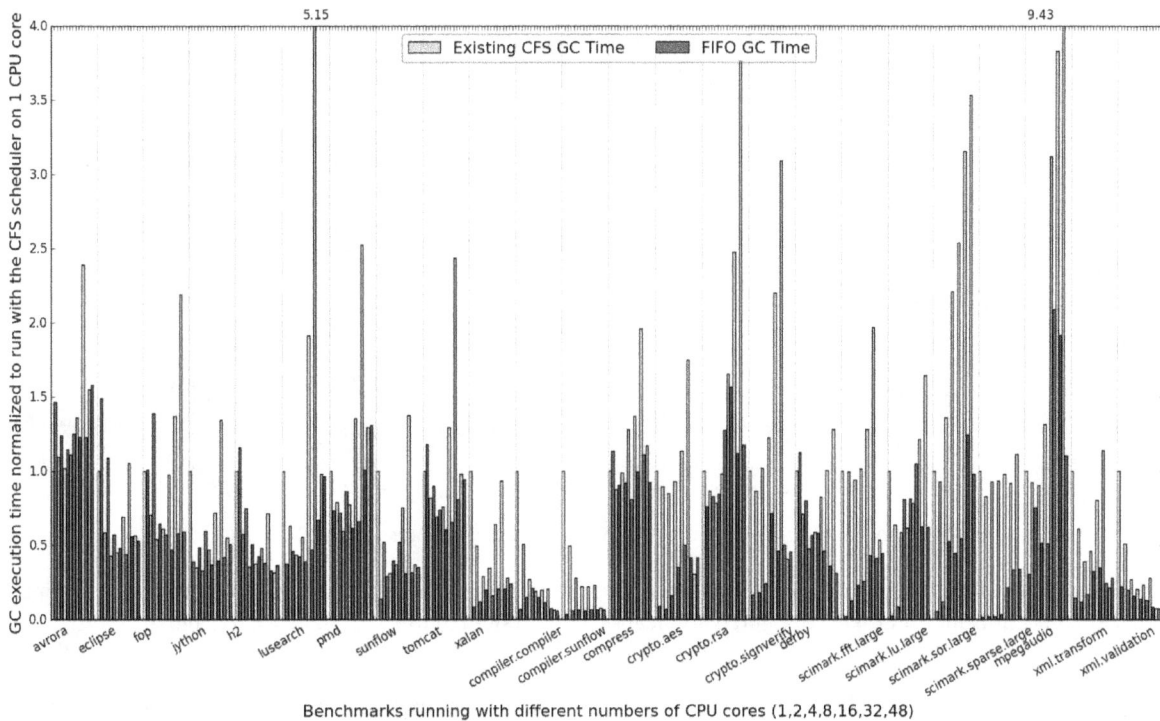

Figure 5: GC scalability with the CFS and FIFO schedulers. Each application has 14 bars. The gray bars represent CFS and the black bars represent FIFO. From left to right for each application, the pairs of gray and black bars indicate GC execution times for the number of cores = 1, 2, 4, 8, 16, 32, and 48, respectively.

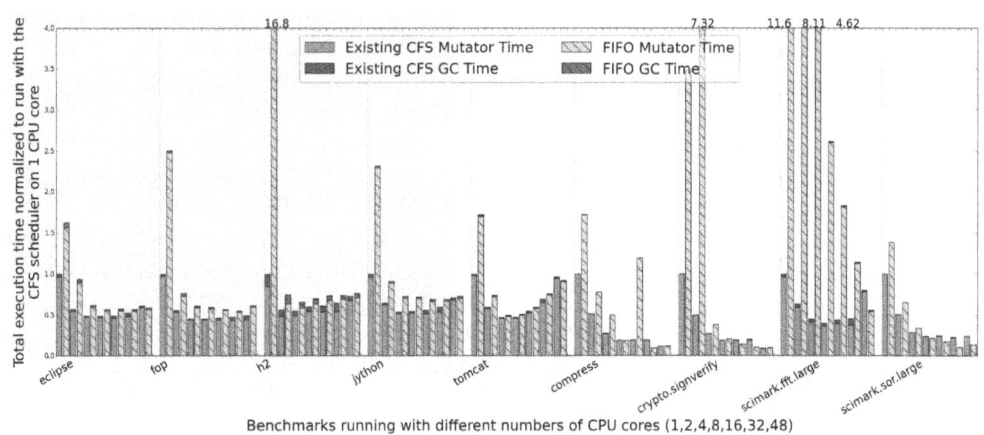

Figure 6: Comparison of the total execution times for CFS and FIFO schedulers for applications that do not benefit from FIFO. The bars for each application, from left to right, are for runs with 1, 2, 4, 8, 16, 32, and 48 cores.

4.1 GC Scalability Study

Figure 5 reports the CG scalabilities of each application when CFS and FIFO are used. The GC times of each application using CFS and FIFO are normalized to that of the same application using CFS running on a single CPU. We observe that the GC execution times when FIFO is used are smaller than those when CFS is used. The average GC execution time is reduced by 52%, while the biggest GC time re-

duction is nearly 90% for *scimark.fft.large*. Further, although GC performance for FIFO can degrade for higher numbers of threads/cores, it is still better than that for CFS. We find that the reason for the better performance is shorter object lifespans in FIFO due to less heap competition. FIFO also has fewer context switches during the GC period.

115

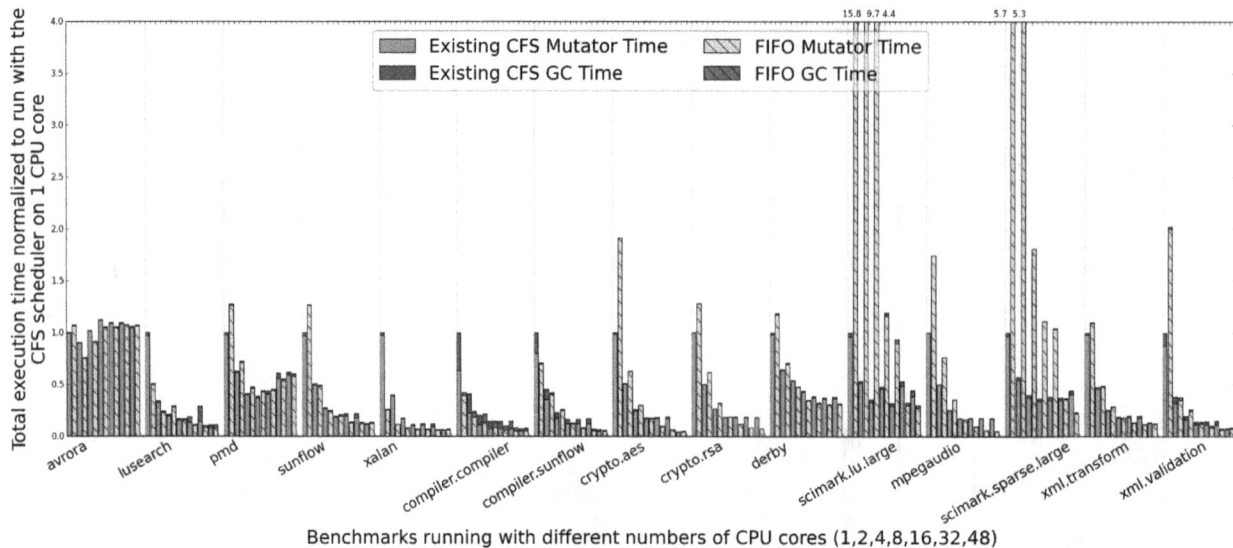

Figure 7: Comparison of the overall performances when CFS and FIFO are used. This figure reports the performances of applications that benefit from FIFO. We configured applications and system to use 1, 2, 4, 8, 16, 32, and 48 cores.

4.2 Study of Mutator and GC Performances

Although FIFO improves the GC performance over CFS with more CPUs, some mutator times become longer in comparison as shown in Figure 6. We note, however, that the benchmarks that work better with the CFS scheduler are all non-scalable, as previously characterized in Figure 4. Most of the threads in these benchmarks are helper threads and perform very little work and can finish within the CFS quanta. As such, the FIFO scheduler does not have any advantage over the CFS scheduler for these benchmarks. This is also true for *avrora* and *pmd*, which have been identified as non-scalable. However, in these two applications, FIFO and CFS performances are very similar, as shown in Figure 7.

Figure 7 presents the scalable benchmarks that show performance improvement when FIFO is used. The average improvement of the overall performance is 45% with 74% as the maximum improvement in *crypto.aes*. We also observed context switching behaviors of these scalable applications when FIFO is used. On average, FIFO reduces context switching by 90% over CFS. Fewer context switches result in better cache locality for threads. On the other hand, when only a few threads in an application do most of the work, more context switches occur when helper threads need to run and therefore they preempt the major threads [16].

4.3 Effects of FIFO on Other Applications Using CFS

By using two scheduling algorithms in a system, it is possible that a policy used in one application can affect schedulability of other applications, and therefore, affect their overall performance. To evaluate the impacts of FIFO on the performance of applications configured to use CFS, we con-

duct a set of experiments. First, we measure (i) performance of an application when FIFO is used, (ii) performance of an application when CFS is used, (iii) performances of two instances of the same application both running FIFO, (iv) performances of two instances of the same application, one using FIFO and the other using CFS, (v) performances of two instances of the same application, both running CFS. We set these programs to use 48 threads/cores. For brevity, we report the results of a scalable (*sunflow*) and non-scalable (*eclipse*) applications.

In Figure 8 (top), *sunflow*, which is a scalable application, performs best when FIFO is used. When we run two instances using FIFO, we see a slight increase in execution times. This is expected as there are more threads in the system. When we run two instances with two different schedulers, we also see a slight increase in execution time for FIFO but a more significant increase for CFS (about 27% higher than that of running alone with CFS). When both instances use CFS, all 96 or more threads from these instances can run in any order without having to wait for others to finish. This intensifies the competition to create objects in the heap, resulting higher GC overhead and execution time. When FIFO is paired up with CFS, the competition becomes less intense so the performance of CFS does not degrade as much as when both instances run CFS.

In Figure 8 (bottom), *eclipse*, which is a non-scalable application, shows that the impact of the scheduler change is very little when two instances run concurrently. One reason is that FIFO yields no benefit in non-scalable applications so the performance difference between FIFO and CFS is small. Another reason is that few threads in the non-scalable applications do most of the work; thus, there are idle CPUs that other applications can use. Fewer working threads also means less heap competition among threads within the application.

4.4 Discussion

In nearly all benchmarks (scalable or non-scalable), FIFO can provide benefit if used in a system with a large number of cores. It tends to perform worst when the number of cores is fewer than eight. This is to be expected as FIFO can achieve parallelism with more cores. In scenarios with a few processing cores, threads that are scheduled earlier would prevent other threads from running.

While FIFO can work well in most applications when more than 8 cores are used, there are also benchmarks that perform better with CFS. In addition, large server applications that rely on working threads polling for work would also perform poorly with FIFO. Up to now, we need to manually identify whether an application can benefit from using FIFO. The selection criteria include scalability and clearly defined amount of work. Next we introduce two approaches to automatically detect applications that can benefit from using FIFO. These mechanisms are only enabled when more than 8 processing cores are used. Otherwise, the system continues to use the CFS policy.

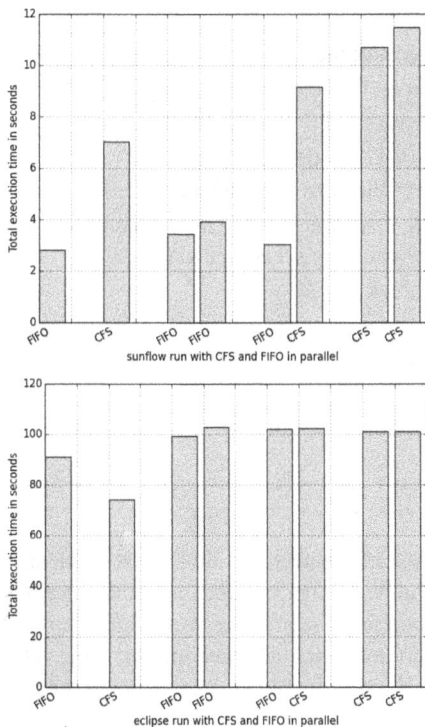

Figure 8: Comparison of the overall performances when CFS and FIFO scheduled same applications run in concurrent on 48 CPUs

5. Automatic Selection of Scheduling Policies

The analysis and results presented in the previous section indicate that the workload distribution between threads can help select a more suitable scheduling policy. In this section, we present two approaches to automatically select an optimal scheduling policy for an application.

5.1 Using Cross-run Profiles

The first approach transparently collects workload distribution information in the background of one execution run (profiling run) and uses it to select a better scheduling policy for the subsequent runs. Algorithm 1 describes the steps used in the approach. We measure the execution time of each thread as the workload. The collection of the threads' information is done by reading the system file */proc/$pid/stat*, which requires one thread pinned to a CPU to monitor the file. Figure 9 compares the performance degradation when the profiling script is executed concurrently with the application. As shown, in the worst case, the profiling thread adds 8% to the execution time. Keep in mind that this is a one time cost as it only incurs in the profiling run.

Algorithm 1: Proposed sampling based algorithm

---

1 **Initialization**: launch the multi-threaded Java application (J) and the helper script (H) concurrently;
2 **while** *J still runs* **do**
3   collect the active threads;
4   record current timestamp;
5 **end**
6 calculate the execution time of each thread;

Figure 10 demonstrates the three types of profiles, indicating whether CFS or FIFO should be selected or both schedulers should have similar performances. If most work is done by few threads (*jython*, the first bar in the figure), CFS performs better because few involuntary context switches are needed as explained in the previous sections. Otherwise, if the workload is well distributed among most or all threads (*lusearch*, the last bar in the figure), FIFO performs better as it improves the memory locality. For some applications, the workload is distributed between some threads (*avrora*, the middle bar), the performance difference between using CFS and FIFO policies is small.

5.2 Adaptive Runtime Selection

Because many factors such as underlying architecture, heap size configuration, and phase changes in application behaviors, it would be more efficient to adaptively select a better performing scheduler at the runtime, instead of employing a profiling run. In this section, we present a low-overhead sampling based scheduler selection mechanism that can adaptively switch between the CFS and FIFO schedulers according to the execution profiles of an application.

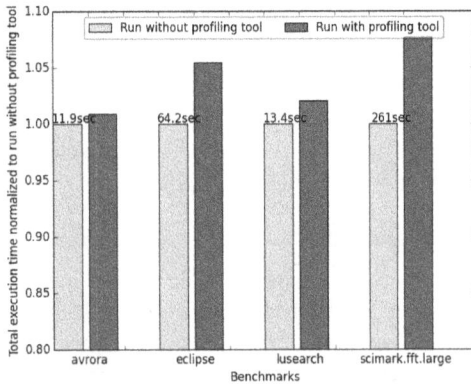

Figure 9: Overhead of the Profiling Thread.

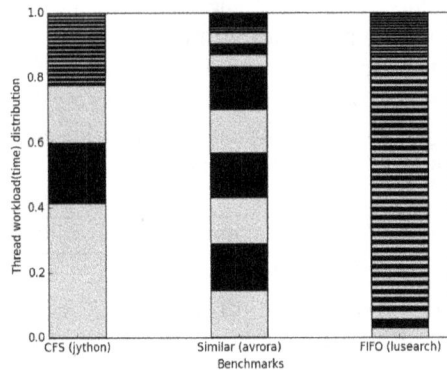

Figure 10: Three Different Workload Distribution Patterns.

Algorithm 2 describes the steps using in the proposed mechanism. The design exploits our observation that non-scalable applications tend to employ a small number of threads to do most of the work. As such, these threads are often long running. On the other hand, scalable applications tend to use threads more uniformly, and therefore, they often have similar execution times. In our approach, we start the profiling thread runs along side the application threads. The tool collects Thread IDs (TIDs) of running and suspended threads every n seconds. Currently, n is predefined as a fixed number (i.e., 2 seconds) for all the benchmarks. The selection process is explained later in this section. However, we can speculate that dynamically changing n for each application can provide more accurate profiles. We leave this part as future work.

Our mechanism compares the TIDs of two successive collections. If the TIDs are mostly the same, the mechanism selects CFS as the scheduler. If the TIDs are different, the mechanism selects FIFO scheduler. With this sampling approach, our system can deal with phase changes in an application. For example, an application, by default, starts with CFS. After a few sampling, the mechanism may switch it to FIFO. Toward the end when most threads have died and only a few threads remain, it can switch back to CFS. While

it is possible that the same application can start a thread, let it die, and then start another thread that has the same TID as the first thread, it is very unlikely. For that to happen, 2^{22} threads must be created in the system and the same application is assigned the same TID twice.

The sampling thread incurs very low-overhead because it often performs sampling only a few times during an application execution and the amount of work required to read the system file names in the process tree provided by the Linux is quite small. The comparison of TIDs between two successive sampling is done with the hash-table container which is done in constant time. The small number of TIDs also means that the amount of memory required to store these TIDs is small.

In addition to using the TIDs, we also explore the following strategies: monitoring the number of context switches and execution time distribution among threads. We found the performance results to be either similar to the proposed approach of using TID, as in the case of using context switching, or worse due to the high overhead (e.g., I/O and computation) or sampling noises that can degrade the selection accuracy, as in the case if using execution time distribution among threads.

Algorithm 2: Proposed adaptive runtime selection algorithm

---
1 **Initialization**: launch the multi-threaded Java application (J) and the helper script (H) concurrently;
2 J starts with the FIFO scheduler;
3 **while** *J still runs* **do**
4   collect the active threads into a hash-table;
5   **if** *one thread is already in the hash-table* **then**
6   Switch the scheduler to the CFS;
7   break;
8   **else**
9   Switch the scheduler to the FIFO;
10   **end**
11   wait for period time n;
12 **end**

The decision of value n. In this work, n is selected as 2 seconds. But we experimented with other values ranging from 1 second to 16 seconds as well which shows 2 seconds is the best number for all benchmarks. The value of n is determined quasi-dynamically, which needs the tuning in the executions. As stated previously, the future improvement is to adaptively change the scheduler based on dynamic value of n.

5.2.1 Evaluation

The proposed adaptive mechanism is used to adaptively select policies. We then compare its performance with the ap-

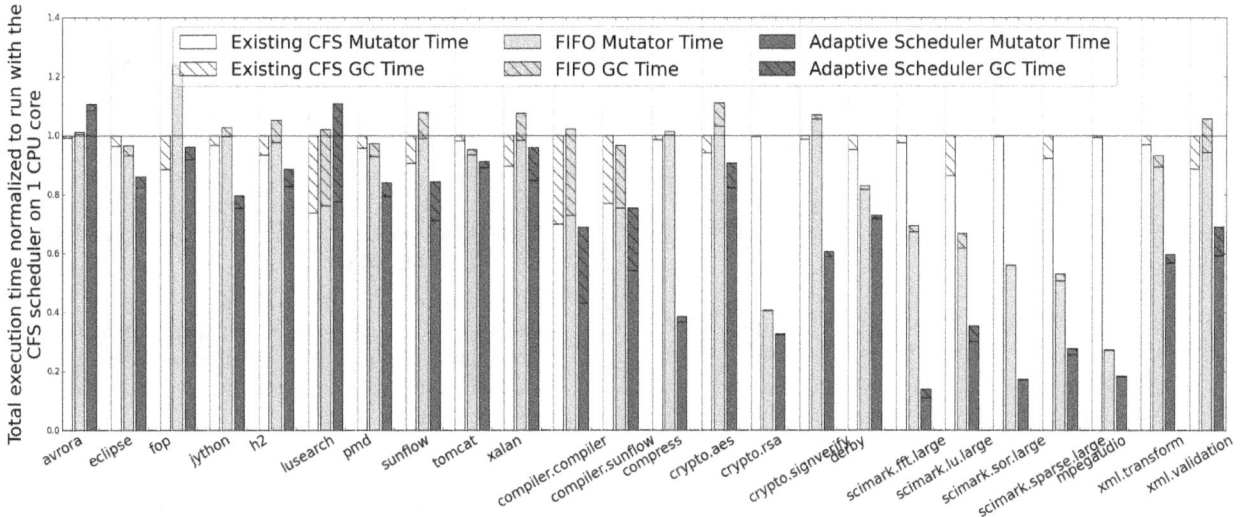

Figure 11: Evaluation of the proposed sampling algorithm.

proach of manually setting the policy to be CFS of FIFO. Figure 11 reports the results of our investigation.

Except for *eclipse* and *avrora*, the proposed adaptive policy selection mechanism performs better than the manually selected CFS and FIFO schedulers. We see that the adaptive mechanism can remain in CFS based on the detection of long running threads, implying that most work is done by those threads, in non-scalable applications. We also see that when an application uses many helper threads to prepare work for the main threads, there is a phase in this application that can benefit from FIFO. However, once this phase has passed, only a few worker threads remain and the system should switch back to CFS. Our mechanism is able to make the initial switch from CFS to FIFO, and then the subsequent switch from FIFO back to CFS.

6. Related Work

This section discusses some of the prior related work on performance improvement of multi-threaded Java applications from various aspects.

Design of scheduling algorithms for Java application. Xian et. al [24–27] design several types of schedulers for Java applications, including object allocation phase aware and contention aware schedulers. The allocation phase aware scheduler schedules the threads according to their allocation rate or preempt threads with the memory consumption instead of the running time which is used in the CFS. The contention aware scheduler avoids the threads with possible shared data running at the same time to reduce the lock contention, which improves the parallelism and so the execution time. Sartor et. al [19] investigate the performance difference when mapping the JVM threads and Java applications' threads to different and same CPU sockets on NUMA. The insights in their work include there is a cost for map-

ping, remote memory traffic degrades the performance and pinning threads to different sockets does not always improve the performance.

Performance limited by resources and synchronizations. Main sources of contention include architecture resources such as processor cores and memory bus. Chen et al. [5] study the scalability of Java applications on different numbers of processor cores and threads. They measure hardware performance and use the findings to explain the scalability issues. The solution they proposed is thread-local allocation buffer that is for application instead of VM. Unlike our work, their focus is mainly on the application performance and not the combined performances of application and GC, and so is Huang's work [12]. Prior studies and our work show that garbage collection and heap usage can also negatively impact scalability. Kalibera et al. [14] study the non-scalable issue of DaCapo benchmarks and they focus on concurrency issues by measuring the memory usage, synchronization, and communication among threads. Their work provides a good insight into thread management in JVM but pay very little attention to the GC subsystem as a potential factor that limits scalability.

Performance of mutator and garbage collection in Java. Esmaeilzadeh et al. [7] report that not all multi-threaded Java applications are running shorter with more threads. Their work focuses on the performance improvement with respect to architecture such as increased processing cores, instead of program's characteristics that can limit scalability. Gidra et al. [9, 10] compare the scalability of various garbage collection algorithms in JVM and report that time spent on stop-the-world GC increases with number of GC threads. This is the same observation as ours. However, they attribute this overhead to heap synchronization and objects movement on NUMA. Du Bois et al. [6] use Bottle Graphs to characterize work done by JVM and application threads when different numbers of threads/cores are used. They conclude that GC needs to do more work when there are more mutator threads. However, they do not further explore why more GC work is needed. Our work investigates the reasons for this observation in much greater details. We believe that both application and JVM need to be scalable in order to achieve the highest possible scalability.

7. Conclusion

Execution parallelism can be a double-edged sword. It can improve execution performance by having more threads collaborate on performing the work, but the collaboration makes threads compete for heap resource and degrade GC performance. Such contentions become aggravated with the CFS scheduler in the Linux. Without changing either the application, the JVM or the system, our investigation shows that many Java applications perform better with FIFO than with CFS. The improvement is gained through higher GC efficiency and mutator performance.

Based on this observation, we propose two approaches to optimally select scheduling policies based on application scalability profile. Our first approach uses the profile information from one execution to tune the subsequent executions. Our second approach dynamically collects profile information and performs policy selection during execution. Our evaluation result indicates that the dynamic selection process works well in our test subjects and can effectively switch scheduling policies based on dynamic application behaviors.

Acknowledgment

This material is based on research sponsored by NSF, DARPA and Maryland Procurement Office under agreement numbers CNS-1116606, FA8750-14-2-0053 and H98230-14-C-0140, respectively Any opinions, findings, conclusions, or recommendations expressed here are those of the authors and do not necessarily reflect the views of the funding agencies or the U.S. Government.

References

[1] Memory Management in the Java HotSpot Virtual Machine. http://www.oracle.com/technetwork/java/javase/memorymanagement-whitepaper-150215.pdf, 2006.

[2] Completely Fair Scheduler in Linux. https://www.kernel.org/doc/Documentation/scheduler/sched-design-CFS.txt, 2015.

[3] S. M. Blackburn, P. Cheng, and K. S. McKinley. Myths and Realities: The performance Impact of Garbage Collection. *ACM SIGMETRICS Performance Evaluation Review*, 32(1):25–36, 2004.

[4] S. M. Blackburn, R. Garner, C. Hoffmann, A. M. Khang, K. S. McKinley, R. Bentzur, A. Diwan, D. Feinberg, D. Frampton, S. Z. Guyer, et al. The DaCapo Benchmarks: Java Bench-

[5] K.-Y. Chen, J. M. Chang, and T.-W. Hou. Multithreading in Java: Performance and Scalability on Multicore Systems. *Computers, IEEE Transactions on*, 60(11):1521–1534, 2011.

marking Development and Analysis. In *ACM Sigplan Notices*, volume 41, pages 169–190. ACM, 2006.

[6] K. Du Bois, J. B. Sartor, S. Eyerman, and L. Eeckhout. Bottle Graphs: Visualizing Scalability Bottlenecks in Multi-threaded Applications. In *ACM SIGPLAN Notices*, volume 48, pages 355–372. ACM, 2013.

[7] H. Esmaeilzadeh, T. Cao, Y. Xi, S. M. Blackburn, and K. S. McKinley. Looking Back on the Language and Hardware Revolutions: Measured Power, Performance, and Scaling. In *ACM SIGARCH Computer Architecture News*, volume 39, pages 319–332. ACM, 2011.

[8] L. Gidra, G. Thomas, J. Sopena, and M. Shapiro. Assessing the Scalability of Garbage Collectors on Many Cores. In *Proceedings of the 6th Workshop on Programming Languages and Operating Systems*, page 7. ACM, 2011.

[9] L. Gidra, G. Thomas, J. Sopena, M. Shapiro, et al. A Study of the Scalability of Stop-the-world Garbage Collectors on Multicores. In *ASPLOS 13-Proceedings of the eighteenth international conference on Architectural support for programming languages and operating systems*, pages 229–240, 2013.

[10] L. Gidra, G. Thomas, J. Sopena, M. Shapiro, and N. Nguyen. NumaGiC: a Garbage Collector for Big Data on Big NUMA Machines. In *ASPLOS 15-Proceedings of the eighteenth international conference on Architectural support for programming languages and operating systems*, 2015.

[11] M. Hertz, S. M. Blackburn, J. E. B. Moss, K. S. McKinley, and D. Stefanović. Error-Free Garbage Collection Traces: How to Cheat and Not Get Caught. In *Proceedings of the 2002 ACM International Conference on Measurement and Modeling of Computer Systems (SIGMETRICS)*, pages 140–151, Marina Del Rey, California, 2002.

[12] W. Huang, J. Lin, Z. Zhang, and J. M. Chang. Performance Characterization of Java Applications on SMT Processors. In *Performance Analysis of Systems and Software, 2005. ISPASS 2005. IEEE International Symposium on*, pages 102–111. IEEE, 2005.

[13] R. Jones and R. Lins. *Garbage Collection: Algorithms for automatic Dynamic Memory Management*. John Wiley and Sons, 1998.

[14] T. Kalibera, M. Mole, R. Jones, and J. Vitek. A Blackbox Approach to Understanding Concurrency in DaCapo. In *Proceedings of the ACM International Conference on Object Oriented Programming Systems Languages and Applications*, OOPSLA '12, pages 335–354, 2012.

[15] C.-T. D. Lo, W. Srisa-an, and J. M. Chang. A Quantitative Simulator for Dynamic Memory Managers. In *Performance Analysis of Systems and Software, 2000. ISPASS. 2000 IEEE International Symposium on*, pages 64–69. IEEE, 2000.

[16] M. K. McKusick, G. V. Neville-Neil, and R. N. Watson. *The design and implementation of the FreeBSD operating system*. Pearson Education, 2014.

[17] J. Qian, D. Li, W. Srisa-an, H. Jiang, and S. Seth. Factors Affecting Scalability of Multithreaded Java Applications on

Manycore System. In *2015 IEEE International Symposium on Performance Analysis of Systems and Software (ISPASS)*, pages 167–168. IEEE, 2015.

[18] J. Qian, W. Srisa-an, D. Li, H. Jiang, and S. Seth. SmartStealing: Analysis and Optimization of Work Stealing in Parallel Garbage Collection for Java VM. In *Proceedings of the 12th International Conference on Principles and Practice of Programming in Java*, pages 170–181. ACM, 2015.

[19] J. B. Sartor and L. Eeckhout. Exploring Multi-threaded Java Application Performance on Multicore Hardware. In *ACM SIGPLAN Notices*, volume 47, pages 281–296. ACM, 2012.

[20] R. Shahriyar, S. M. Blackburn, and K. S. McKinley. Fast Conservative Garbage Collection. In *Proceedings of the 2014 ACM International Conference on Object Oriented Programming Systems Languages & Applications*, pages 121–139. ACM, 2014.

[21] J. SPEC. Client2008 Suite. *URL: https://www. spec.org/ jvm2008/*, 2008.

[22] D. Stefanović, M. Hertz, S. M. Blackburn, K. S. McKinley, and J. E. B. Moss. Older-First Garbage Collection in Practice: Evaluation in a Java Virtual Machine. *SIGPLAN Notices*, 38(2 supplement):25–36, 2003.

[23] D. Stefanović, K. S. McKinley, and J. E. B. Moss. Age-Based Garbage Collection. In *Proceedings of the ACM SIGPLAN Conference on Object-Oriented Programming, Systems, Languages, and Applications (OOPSLA)*, pages 370–381, Denver, Colorado, United States, November 1999.

[24] F. Xian, W. Srisa-an, C. Jia, and H. Jiang. AS-GC: An Efficient Generational Garbage Gollector for Java Application Servers. In *ECOOP 2007–Object-Oriented Programming*, pages 126–150. Springer, 2007.

[25] F. Xian, W. Srisa-an, and H. Jiang. Allocation-phase Aware Thread Scheduling Policies to Improve Garbage Collection Performance. In *Proceedings of the 6th international symposium on Memory management*, pages 79–90. ACM, 2007.

[26] F. Xian, W. Srisa-an, and H. Jiang. Microphase: An Approach to Proactively Invoking Garbage Collection for Improved Performance. In *ACM SIGPLAN Notices*, volume 42, pages 77–96. ACM, 2007.

[27] F. Xian, W. Srisa-an, and H. Jiang. Contention-aware Scheduler: Unlocking Execution Parallelism in Multithreaded Java Programs. In *ACM Sigplan Notices*, volume 43, pages 163–180. ACM, 2008.

Performance Analysis and Optimization of Full Garbage Collection in Memory-hungry Environments *

Yang Yu‡¶, Tianyang Lei§, Weihua Zhang‡¶†, Haibo Chen§, Binyu Zang§

‡ School of Computer Science, Fudan University
¶ Shanghai Key Laboratory of Data Science, Fudan University
§ Institute of Parallel and Distributed Systems, Shanghai Jiao Tong University
† Parallel Processing Institute, Software School, Fudan University
{yu_y13, zhangweihua}@fudan.edu.cn, {sky1young, haibochen, byzang}@sjtu.edu.cn

Abstract

Garbage collection (GC), especially full GC, would non-trivially impact overall application performance, especially for those memory-hungry ones handling large data sets. This paper presents an in-depth performance analysis on the full GC performance of Parallel Scavenge (PS), a state-of-the-art and the default garbage collector in the HotSpot JVM, using traditional and big-data applications running atop JVM on CPU (e.g., Intel Xeon) and many-integrated cores (e.g., Intel Xeon Phi). The analysis uncovers that unnecessary memory accesses and calculations during reference updating in the compaction phase are the main causes of lengthy full GC. To this end, this paper describes an incremental query model for reference calculation, which is further embodied with three schemes (namely optimistic, sort-based and region-based) for different query patterns. Performance evaluation shows that the incremental query model leads to averagely 1.9X (up to 2.9X) in full GC and 19.3% (up to 57.2%) improvement in application throughput, as well as 31.2% reduction in pause time over the vanilla PS collector on CPU, and the numbers are 2.1X (up to 3.4X), 11.1% (up to 41.2%) and 34.9% for Xeon Phi accordingly.

1. Introduction

Managed programming languages like Java have been steadily adopted in parallel computing due to its ease of pro-

---

* This work is supported by National High Technology Research and Development Program of China (No. 2012AA010905), NSFC (No. 61572314 and 61370081), National Youth Top-notch Talent Support Program of China and Singapore NRF (CREATE E2S2). Related patches have been upstreamed to OpenJDK (JDK-8146987). Yang Yu was a visiting student at IPADS, SJTU when doing this work.

graming thanks to its inherit threading, portability and automatic memory management. Actually, many big-data frameworks like Hadoop and Spark [26, 30] use Java virtual machines (JVMs) to run their tasks. There is also a steady momentum to adopt Java-like programming language to high-performance computing (HPC) domains to increase program productivity [17, 27, 29].

While the volume of memory for a single machine has been steadily increasing, memory is still a scarce resource. First, many data-intensive Java applications with a large working set suffer from a general phenomenon called memory bloat [6] due to processing a large amount of data. This is especially true for a shared-cluster design inside many companies like Google [31] such that each application is only accompanied with a limited amount of memory. Second, the increasing number of cores per-machine usually results in limited per-core memory. This problem especially exists in the Many Integrated Core (MIC) architecture (e.g., Intel Xeon Phi), which has an excessive number of cores/hardware threads sharing only a small amount of memory (e.g., 60 cores/240 threads sharing only 8GB memory).

Efficiently running Java applications on such memory-hungry environments requires efficient garbage collectors. There have been a number of algorithmic designs that try to mitigate memory pressure and improve scalability for such environments [4, 23, 25]. Recent work also shows that GC would occupy non-trivial proportion of execution time [13] and the accumulated stragglers due to GC would lead to increased overall execution time [15] as well as amplified tail latency [9] for big-data applications.

In this paper, we present an in-depth study on the performance behavior of Parallel Scavenge, the default garbage collector for HotSpot JVM in OpenJDK. PS is a throughput-oriented, stop-the-world garbage collector that uses a variant of Mark-Compact algorithm [14]. While less frequently, full GC would cause longer pause time than minor GC and thus incur more performance impact to applications. With the assist of a detailed profiling, our analysis shows that full GC may still cause a non-trivial impact to application performance (e.g., more than 50% for *JOlden.TreeAdd*).

A detailed profiling reveals that the bottleneck lies within the reference updating period of the compacting phase. The

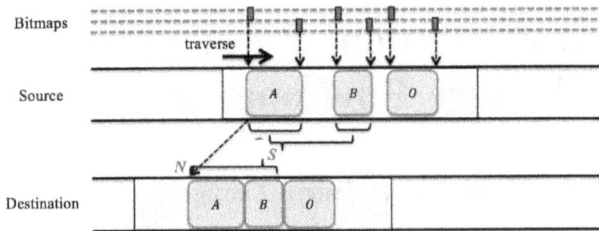

Figure 1: Update references using mark bitmaps

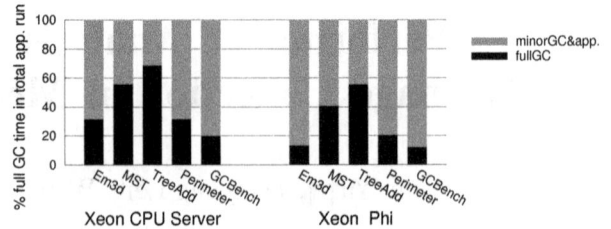

Figure 2: Proportion of full GC time in total application run

updates need to query two globally-preserved bitmaps mapping to the heap space that is segregated into multiple regions. The bitmap is searched from a specific region start as a reference is updated, which results in a lot of redundant calculations and memory accesses and contribute to more than 70% of full GC time. To this end, we propose a general *incremental query* (IQ) model to dynamically reuse the result of last query, which can significantly minimize the ranges for bitmap searching. According to different query patterns of runtime object references, we further design three IQ-based schemes (namely optimistic, sort-based and region-based) to maximize the reusability and query efficiency.

We have implemented the above designs in the HotSpot virtual machine of OpenJDK 7u and 8and perform a set of experiments using both standard benchmarks like *JOlden* [7], *Dacapo* [5], *SPECjvm2008* [1] as well as real-world big-data frameworks like *Spark* [26] and *Giraph* [3]. Our evaluation shows that our incremental query achieves up to 2.9x and 3.4x speedup in full GC throughput and 57.2% and 41.2% improvement in application throughput on a Xeon CPU server and a Xeon Phi coprocessor accordingly.

This paper makes the following contributions:

- A thorough profiling-based analysis of the full GC in Parallel Scavenge, which uncovers that reference updating in the compact phase is the most time-consuming bottleneck (§ 2).

- An incremental query model and three different schemes to accelerate the bitmap searching and improve the full GC throughput in Parallel Scavenge (§ 3).

- A detailed performance evaluation confirms the effectiveness of our design on both Intel Xeon and Xeon Phi MIC architectures (§ 4).

2. Performance Analysis of Parallel Scavenge

2.1 Parallel Scavenge

The HotSpot VM in OpenJDK leverages the well-known *generational collection* [14] to segregate the heap into multiple areas on the basis of different objects' ages, i.e., *young*, *old* and *permanent* generations. Parallel Scavenge is the default garbage collector with a *stop-the-world* fashion, i.e., the application will be suspended during GC. Here, we briefly introduce minor collection and review the design of full GC in greater details.

Young/Minor GC: The young collector in PS uses a copying algorithm by dividing heaps into several areas: an *eden* space and two *survivor* spaces. Most objects are initially allocated in the eden space (except for some large

ones). After a minor collection, some objects are moved to one of the survivor spaces, with other aged live objects being promoted to the old generation.

Full GC: The full GC leverages a mark-compact algorithm to collect the whole heap. The compaction process slides all live objects towards the starting side, thus could effectively avoid fragmentation and allow the *bump-the-pointer* technique for efficient memory allocation.

The full collection consists of three phases: *marking*, *summary* and *compacting*. In the *marking phase*, the collector utilizes an important data structure called *mark bitmap* to map the whole heap space. PS maintains two bitmaps, one for the beginning address of an object and the other for the end address. The corresponding bits in the two bitmaps are set to identify if an object is alive. The heap space is partitioned into a lot of regions (each with a size of 4KB). A piece of metadata is maintained for each region. As an object within a region is marked alive, the corresponding metadata for the region will be updated.

The *summary phase* is responsible for calculating the new location for each compacting region and the live objects within it, e.g., the new location of the region that a live object will be copied to. This phase is done very quickly and contributes little to the full GC time.

The essential work of the *compacting phase* is to move live objects to their new locations and update all the references contained in the objects. Initially, a set of empty regions are maintained as the destination regions, whose corresponding source regions have already been determined during the summary phase. The collector sequentially moves the live objects from the source region to the destination region.

For each live object, all its references will be updated as long as it is moved to the destination region. As illustrated in Figure 1, for a referenced object, e.g., O, its new location could be calculated by using the mark bitmaps and the metadata of the region it resides in. Since the region metadata records the new location of the first live object in the region (denoted as N), any live object in this region could be located by adding the total live objects' size between the first object and itself, e.g., S, to N. S can be computed by searching the mapping range on the mark bitmaps of this region. After the compacting phase, all live objects are compacted to the beginning of the space.

2.2 Impact of GC on Big Data Applications

While GC usually should have only small impact on application performance, there are several cases where the GC time would constitute a non-trivial portion of application execution time. Actually, a recent study shows that TPC-H Q17 and "shopper" workflows in Naiad [19] spend 20~40%

of their total runtime on GC regardless of the heap size for young generation [13]. Besides, the full GC is always claimed to be a key constraint to the throughput of stop-the-word collectors [16, 20, 28] like the Parallel Scavenge.

To confirm this, we measured a set of data-intensive Java applications to demonstrate the significant impact of full GC on both normal CPU and Xeon Phi (detailed evaluation setup in § 4). As shown in Figure 2, a considerable proportion of full GC time can be observed for all the applications with multiple GC threads on both CPU and Xeon Phi. The full GC time of *TreeAdd* could even exceed half of the whole execution time. This is because that an insufficient heap space caused by the memory-hungry environment may bring a high probability of full GC.

2.3 Detailed Performance Analysis

To further discover the most time-consuming part in the full GC of Parallel Scavenge, we designed and implemented a detailed profiling tool to attribute the full GC execution into individual operations. For simplicity, we utilize one GC thread to focus on the key operational logic.

Algorithm 1 Calc_new_pointer

Require: $addr \leftarrow$ old referenced object address
1: $region \leftarrow getRegion(addr)$
2: $dest \leftarrow region.destination()$
3: **if** $region.allAlive()$ **then**   # dense path
4:     **return** $dest + offset\_in\_region(addr)$
5: **else**   # sparse path
6:     **return** $dest + region.partial\_obj\_size() +$
         $live\_words\_in\_range(region.partial\_obj\_end, addr)$
7: **end if**

We first differentiate the full GC time in terms of the three different phases. Figure 3 shows that the compacting phase constitutes a majority of the total time for almost all applications, while the marking and summary phases only constitute a very small percentage. As mentioned in section 2.1, the compacting phase mainly does two thing: copy objects to their new locations and update all the references. From the graph we can see a much larger proportion for the reference updating (*sparse_update* and *dense_update*), which is reasonable because each time a reference is updated, the mark bitmaps need to be traversed from the region start for calculation of the new location, no matter how far the object lies from the start. Moreover, the amount of references is usually far greater than that of live objects in a Java application.

When profiling deeply into the reference updating procedure, we find that most time is spent on calculating the new location of the referenced objects. The new address is calculated by accumulating the live objects' sizes within the range, as illustrated in Algorithm 1, there are two paths: *dense path* and *sparse path*. When all data in the region is alive, it enters the dense path, where the new offset of the object is exactly the same with the offset in the current region. Otherwise, it enters the sparse path, in which the *live_words_in_range()* method will search the bitmaps from the end of the object that partially extends onto the region to the current object's location for total live sizes. Figure 3 reveals that for most benchmarks, the time spent on the sparse path significantly exceeds that on the dense path.

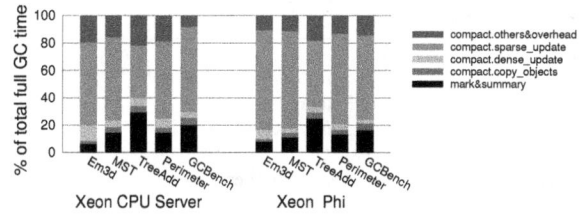

Figure 3: Decomposition of full GC time

Using our profiling tool, we can observe a substantial proportion of the "sparse path" of total full GC time. Hence, it is critically important to optimize the sparse path in the compacting phase for an overall reduction of full GC time.

3. Incremental Query

3.1 Basic Idea

According to our analysis, the key issue to optimize the full GC is to minimize the unnecessary memory accesses and calculations during reference updating period. However, the original *sparse path* in PS collector's compacting GC is very time-consuming and inefficient. For example, as shown in Figure 1, for two sequentially searched objects A and B in the same region, the range from the region start to A is repeatedly searched for both A and B.

To eliminate such redundant searches, we propose an incremental query scheme, which dynamically reuses the previous result for the next calculation. This idea is based on a key observation on Parallel Scavenge that each query is initialized from a fixed region start and confined within the current region.

Specifically, when the objects that two sequentially updated references point to lie in the same source region, the calculation for the latter object's new offset could be reduced by keeping track of the former's result. With the former object's address and new offset (i.e., the total size of live objects from region start), the latter object only needs to traverse the range from the former object, which could reduce a lot of redundant memory accesses and calculations.

Our basic idea is illustrated in Algorithm 2. The *beg_addr* and *end_addr* refer to the start and end of the searching range, respectively. In line 2 we first check if the *beg_addr* of current object matches that of last recorded object, if matches, they are considered in the same region. Line 3~13 compare the *end_addr* and *last_end_addr* to determine the new searching range. For example, in line 5, the current *end_addr* lies to the right of *last_end_addr*, it thus only needs to search the live words between them, then line 7 will add the result *delta* to *last_result* to get the total live words within the range from *beg_addr* to the current *end_addr*. Finally, it updates the variables for the reusing of next object.

However, how to effectively reuse previous results is not straightforward but depends on the query patterns of the references before the compaction. Based on our observations, the query patterns can be divided into two categories. The first one is a local pattern that the sequentially referenced objects tend to reside in the same region. For this pattern, the results of last queries could thus be easily reused. The second one is a random pattern that the referenced objects always lie in random regions, which makes it incapable to

Algorithm 2 Calculate live words within a range

Require: *beg_addr, end_addr*
1: *retrive last_beg_addr, last_end_addr, last_result*
2: **if** *beg_addr = last_beg_addr* **then**
3:     **if** *end_addr = last_end_addr* **then**
4:         *live_bits ← last_result*
5:     **else if** *end_addr > last_end_addr* **then**
6:         *delta ← live_words_in_range(last_end_addr, end_addr)*
7:         *live_bits ← last_result + delta*
8:     **else**
9:         *delta ← live_words_in_range(end_addr, last_end_addr)*
10:        *live_bits ← last_result − delta*
11:     **end if**
12:     update *last_end_addr, last_result* with *delta*
13:     **return** *live_bits*
14: **end if**
15: *live_bits ← live_words_in_range(beg_addr, end_addr)*
16: update *last_beg_addr, last_end_addr, last_result*
17: **return** *live_bits*

reuse last results directly. Most applications are mixed with these two query patterns, differentiated by their respective proportions. To this end, we further propose three optimizing schemes accordingly to handle different situations.

3.2 Optimistic IQ

Targeting the applications with a high proportion of local query patterns, we propose a straightforward implementation of our basic idea: the optimistic incremental query. This approach complies with Algorithm 2, with each GC thread maintaining only one global result of last query for all the regions. Besides, when the object lies between the region start and the last object, which corresponds to the condition in line 8∼10 of Algorithm 2, its distances to both sides will be checked to make sure the shorter path is selected.

The optimistic IQ relies heavily on the local pattern to take good effect, while its advantage lies in the minimal overhead for both memory utilization and calculation.

3.3 Sort-based IQ

For the applications with most random query patterns, the optimistic IQ is not the best choice since the sequentially referenced objects tend to reside in various regions. We thus propose an approach called sort-based incremental query, whose key idea is to dynamically reorder the references based on their addresses with a lazy update.

The sort-based IQ employs a buffer with a fixed size. All the references are first filled into the buffer in batches before their updating. Each time the buffer fills up, the references within the buffer will be reordered according to the region index, and then be updated in their new sequences after the sorting. The buffer size is typically set close to the size of an L1 cache line for good locality.

With the sorting scheme, the references in the same region are gathered periodically, making it possible to effectively apply Algorithm 2. However, this approach may impose some overhead due to the extra sorting procedure.

3.4 Region-based IQ

Based on the insights of the two schemes as well as their deficiencies, we propose a region-based incremental query

to embrace the best of the two schemes. This approach maintains a result of last query for each region per GC thread, thus can reasonably fit for both local and random query patterns. The region-based IQ applies Algorithm 2 within a region's bound.

We additionally employ a *slicing* scheme based on the concern that in some cases, the searching distance for a reference could span a large portion of the region width even with the reuse of the last result. Therefore, we reduce the searching range by dividing each region into multiple slices, maintaining the result of last query for each slice. For each referenced object, the region-based IQ checks the distances between it and last queried objects of two slices respectively: the current slice it resides in and the neighboring slice on the other side. The shortest searching path can thus be guaranteed with the slice-grained reuse of last queried result.

Minimize Overhead The region-based IQ is more aggressive than other two schemes and may impose some memory overhead due to the employment of slicing, especially with multiple GC threads. To minimize this overhead, we use a 16-bit integer to store the calculated size of live objects since it must be smaller than the region size (e.g., 4KB). Moreover, considering the region start will never be altered, we thus replace the 64-bit full-length address of the last queried object with the address offset to the region start, which only needs 12 bits and can perfectly fit in a 16-bit integer as well. By this way, the memory overhead is minimized to 0.09% of the entire heap size using the region-based IQ with one slice for each GC thread.

3.5 Parallelism

In our design, the results of last queries maintained by each GC thread are independent from each other, which can fundamentally eliminate the contention for updating the results after a bitmap searching completes. Our approach has no side effect to the multi-threading mechanism of the Parallel Scavenge GC.

4. Evaluation

4.1 Experimental Environments

Hardware/software platforms: We have implemented our optimization for OpenJDK 7u and later port it to version 8. The porting effort is trivial, which shows the portability of our optimization across versions. We evaluate our optimization on both Intel Xeon and Xeon Phi platform. The Xeon Phi Java support is based on OpenJDK 7u from our previous work [29]. The Xeon platform is an Intel Xeon E5-2620 CPU server with 6 cores at 2.0GHz frequency and 32GB memory space. The Xeon Phi coprocessor has 60 in-order cores at 1GHz, each of which has 4 hardware threads. There is no traditional shared last-level cache and the memory size is 8GB.

Benchmarks: We use standard benchmarks like JOlden, Dacapo, SPECjvm2008 as well as emerging big-data frameworks like Spark and Giragh for our study. We evaluate the memory-intensive applications from the suites to evaluate the GC behavior. As memory bloat is common for big-data applications [6, 13], we set the heap size (e.g, 1GB) close to

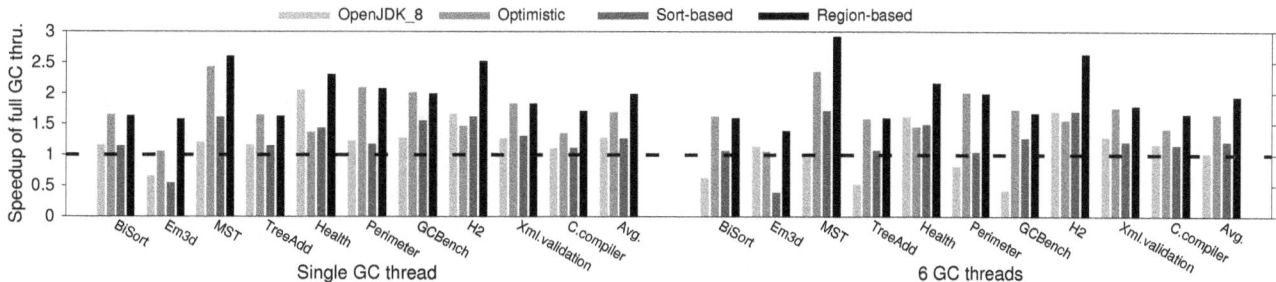
Figure 4: Speedup of full GC throughput with 1&6 GC threads on CPU.

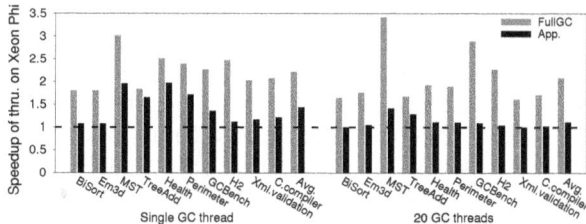
Figure 5: Speedup of full GC & app. thru. with 1&20 GC threads using region-based IQ on Xeon Phi

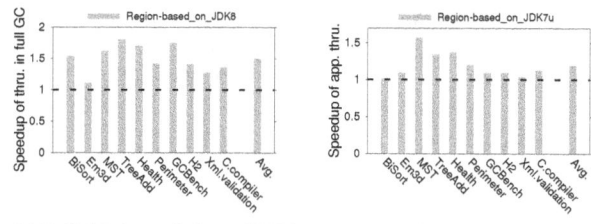
(a) Full GC thru. relative to JDK 8   (b) App. thru. relative to JDK 7u

Figure 6: Speedup of throughput with six GC threads on CPU

the workload size to emulate a memory-hungry environment for most of them to tax the GC, similar to prior work [11]. Besides, we evaluate Spark and Giraph with larger input and heap sizes (e.g., 10GB) as well to confirm the effectiveness of our optimization alone with increase of heap size.

GC setup: We present the throughput comparison of both full GC and application running with single and six GC threads on CPU and twenty for Xeon Phi. Twenty is the most appropriate thread count for Xeon Phi since the Parallel Scavenge does not scale well under a large number of GC threads [10]. Meanwhile, the memory overhead for the region-based IQ is about 3~4% with twenty threads which is modest and acceptable. The performance is normalized to that of the original OpenJDK 7u version. We also provide the reduction in full GC time and the total pause time.

Application	Heap Size (GB)	Description
JOlden.BiSort	1	A bitonic sort
JOlden.Em3d	1	Models electromagnetic waves
JOlden.MST	1	Computes minimum spanning tree
JOlden.TreeAdd	1	Recursive DFS of a binary tree
JOlden.Health	3	Simulates health-care system
JOlden.Perimeter	1	Computes perimeter in image
GCBench	1	Build arrays and trees
Dacapo.H2	1	Executes transactions in H2
SPECjvm2008.X.v.	1	Validates an XML tree
SPECjvm2008.C.c.	1	Test javac compiler
Spark.pagerank	1&10	Rank websites
Giraph.sssp	1&10	Shortest path compution

Table 1: Benchmarks. (X.v & C.c in SPECjvm2008 refer to Xml.validation & Compiler.compiler)

4.2 Improvement on Standard Benchmarks

4.2.1 Speedup in Full GC

Figure 4 depicts the speedup of full GC throughput on Xeon server. The results cover the three different schemes (region-based with 2 slices). Besides, OpenJDK 8 has made some

revision in region management by separating each region into multiple blocks. To study its performance impact, we provide a performance comparison with our optimization.

We can see that the optimistic and region-based IQ could both achieve significant speedup for most benchmarks. The two schemes perform similarly except for Em3d, Health, H2 and C.compiler. This is because these four applications mainly consist of random query patterns during compaction, which do not fit well for optimistic IQ. The sort-based IQ has inferior performance compared to the other two, which indicates: 1) a majority of sequentially updated references conform to a local pattern; 2) the overhead of sorting is significant, which makes the sort-based IQ less attracting.

When scaling up to six GC threads, there shows no significant reduction in speedup. This confirms that our approach has no side effect to the multi-threading mechanism. The region-based IQ achieves up to 2.9x and averagely 1.9x speedup for full GC throughput on CPU. Besides, by using the optimization in section 3.4, the memory overhead can be reduced to only 1.1% with six GC threads.

As illustrated Figure 5, the best-performed region-based IQ achieves a full GC speedup of 3.4x for *MST* and averagely 2.1x with twenty GC threads on Xeon Phi. The results are mostly consistent to those of the Xeon server.

Portability of our optimization: We also compared the port of our region-based IQ to OpenJDK 8 with the vanilla GC. As shown in Figure 4, the new revision of OpenJDK 8 performs even worse with multiple GC threads for many benchmarks than the original 7u version. However, as shown in Figure 6a, our region-based IQ could still achieve significant performance improvement, which can reach up to 1.8x for *TreeAdd* and averagely 1.5x speedup. This result confirms the portability of our optimization.

4.2.2 Application Performance Improvement

The three approaches have incremental performance, e.g., region-based IQ outperforms the other two. Despite some minor overhead, we believe that in most cases, the region-

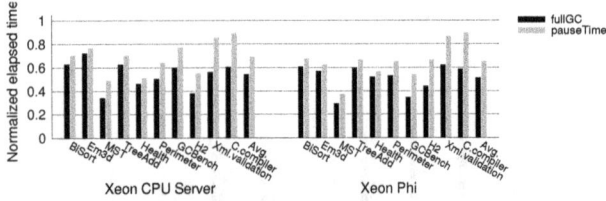

Figure 7: Normalized elapsed time. Lower is better

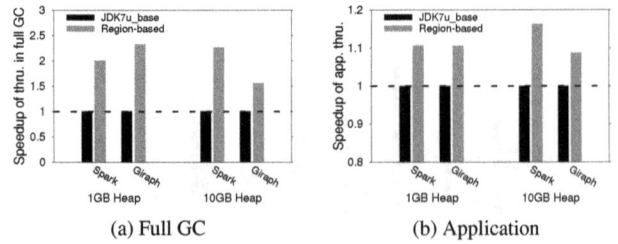

| (a) Full GC | (b) Application |

Figure 8: Throughput speedup of big-data applications with varying input and heap sizes

based IQ performs best and should be the default choice. Thus, we mainly use the it to demonstrate the speedup in the applications' throughput.

Figure 6b plots the improvement with six GC threads on CPU. While the proportions of full GC time vary across different applications, the performance improvement is remarkable for most benchmarks, which is up to 57.2% and averagely 19.3% with six GC threads.

As shown in Figure 5, the region-based IQ can bring up to 41.2% improvement in the application's throughput for the MST program with twenty GC threads on Xeon Phi. In general, we could achieve averagely 11.1% improvement for the applications under the multi-GC-threading environment.

Reduction in pause time: Figure 7 depicts the reduction in full GC time and total pause time by using the region-based IQ with multiple GC threads, compared to the original Parallel Scavenge in OpenJDK 7u. Due the significant performance improvement in full GC, the total pause time is notably reduced, which can reach averagely 31.2% and 34.9% for CPU and Xeon Phi respectively.

4.3 Improvement on Big-data Applications

We further use Spark and Giraph to show the effectiveness of our optimization for real-world applications, with both normal (i.e., 1GB) and larger (i.e., 10GB) heap sizes. The input data size is also increased, which is from 100MB to 2.6GB for Spark, and 400MB to 4GB for Giraph. The normalized throughputs relative to the original PS collector in OpenJDK 7u are provided in Figure 8 for both full GC and application execution.

A significant performance speedup comparable to the standard benchmarks in full GC can be observed with varying heap sizes. For the application execution time, the improvement can steadily reach about 10%, which is typically up to 16.3% for Spark with 10GB heap size.

Our optimization is orthogonal to distributed execution. To confirm this, we conducted a small-scale evaluation on a 5-node cluster. Each machine has two 10-core Intel Xeon E5-2650 v3 processors and 64GB DRAM. We ran Spark PageRank with 100 million edges and configured 10GB heap size on each node. We recorded the accumulated full GC time for all nodes and the elapsed application time on master. The improvement on full GC and application throughput is 63.8% and 7.3%, respectively. The speedup is smaller due to network communication becomes a more dominating factor during distributed execution. Yet, a still significant reduction in full GC time may help a lot in reducing tail latency [9, 15].

5. Related Work

There is a long thread of research to improve the performance of garbage collection, especially the mark-compact collector [2, 8, 18, 24]. For example, Abuaiadh et al. [2] proposed a heap compaction algorithm for SMP platforms, which saves information for a pack of objects instead of using standard forwarding pointer mechanism for updating references. Chung et al. [8] proposed a sweeping approach that traverses only the live objects so that the sweeping time depends only on the number of live objects in the heap. Our approach also only scans live objects but further reuses the prior scanning result. Morikawa et al. [18] described an adaptive scanning method between scanning bitmap and scanning heap for Lisp2 compactor collector. However, they did not consider the reuse of previous scanning result. Our optimization aligns with this thread of research by pinpointing a major bottleneck of the compaction phase and designing a novel solution to significantly boost the performance.

Some efforts have been made on the throughput-oriented Parallel Scavenge garbage collector. Gidra et al. [11, 12] studied the scalability issues of Parallel Scavenge on NUMA systems, and presented a NUMA-aware design which can maximize the memory access locality during collection. Some recent work advocates of using coordination to mitigate garbage collection for big data runtime [15, 19]. Specifically, Murray et al. [19] leveraged event information to partition objects into different regions for better memory management. Maas et al. [15] showed that coordination of GC among multicore nodes may reduce the impact of GC on big data performance. Our work is orthogonal to such work and could further reduce the GC impact.

Xu et al. [21, 22] performed a lot of work based on the problem of runtime bloat. They witnessed significant performance impact and severe pressure on the garbage collector, which is caused by the memory bloat in a managed runtime like JVM. They proposed an application-level approach to tackle this problem, such as a bloat-aware design paradigm towards the development in GC enabled languages to eliminate the bloat for large-scale data-intensive applications [6].

6. Conclusion

This section presented a detailed study on the full GC performance using standard and big-data applications. Our study found that full GC still contributes a non-trivial portion of application execution time. Our profiling found that the reference updating in the compaction phase is a major performance killer. To this end, this paper presented an incremental query model with three schemes. Our evaluation confirms the benefit of our optimization.

References

[1] SPECjvm2008. https://www.spec.org/jvm2008/, 2015.

[2] D. Abuaiadh, Y. Ossia, E. Petrank, and U. Silbershtein. An efficient parallel heap compaction algorithm. In *Proceedings of the 19th Annual ACM SIGPLAN Conference on Object-oriented Programming, Systems, Languages, and Applications*, OOPSLA '04, pages 224–236, New York, NY, USA, 2004. ACM. ISBN 1-58113-831-8. . URL http://doi.acm.org/10.1145/1028976.1028995.

[3] Apache. Apache giraph: an iterative graph processing system built for high scalability. http://giraph.apache.org/.

[4] S. M. Blackburn and K. S. McKinley. Immix: A mark-region garbage collector with space efficiency, fast collection, and mutator performance. In *Proceedings of the 29th ACM SIGPLAN Conference on Programming Language Design and Implementation*, PLDI '08, pages 22–32, New York, NY, USA, 2008. ACM. ISBN 978-1-59593-860-2. . URL http://doi.acm.org/10.1145/1375581.1375586.

[5] S. M. Blackburn, R. Garner, C. Hoffmann, A. M. Khang, K. S. McKinley, R. Bentzur, A. Diwan, D. Feinberg, D. Frampton, S. Z. Guyer, M. Hirzel, A. Hosking, M. Jump, H. Lee, J. E. B. Moss, A. Phansalkar, D. Stefanović, T. VanDrunen, D. von Dincklage, and B. Wiedermann. The dacapo benchmarks: Java benchmarking development and analysis. In *Proceedings of the 21st Annual ACM SIGPLAN Conference on Object-oriented Programming Systems, Languages, and Applications*, OOPSLA '06, pages 169–190, New York, NY, USA, 2006. ACM. ISBN 1-59593-348-4. . URL http://doi.acm.org/10.1145/1167473.1167488.

[6] Y. Bu, V. Borkar, G. Xu, and M. J. Carey. A bloat-aware design for big data applications. In *Proceedings of the 2013 International Symposium on Memory Management*, ISMM '13, pages 119–130, New York, NY, USA, 2013. ACM. ISBN 978-1-4503-2100-6. . URL http://doi.acm.org/10.1145/2464157.2466485.

[7] B. Cahoon and K. S. McKinley. Data flow analysis for software prefetching linked data structures in java. In *Proceedings of the 2001 International Conference on Parallel Architectures and Compilation Techniques*, PACT '01, pages 280–291, Washington, DC, USA, 2001. IEEE Computer Society. ISBN 0-7695-1363-8. URL http://dl.acm.org/citation.cfm?id=645988.674177.

[8] Y. C. Chung, S.-M. Moon, K. Ebcioğlu, and D. Sahlin. Reducing sweep time for a nearly empty heap. In *Proceedings of the 27th ACM SIGPLAN-SIGACT Symposium on Principles of Programming Languages*, POPL '00, pages 378–389, New York, NY, USA, 2000. ACM. ISBN 1-58113-125-9. . URL http://doi.acm.org/10.1145/325694.325744.

[9] J. Dean and L. A. Barroso. The tail at scale. *Commun. ACM*, 56(2):74–80, Feb. 2013. ISSN 0001-0782. . URL http://doi.acm.org/10.1145/2408776.2408794.

[10] L. Gidra, G. Thomas, J. Sopena, and M. Shapiro. Assessing the scalability of garbage collectors on many cores. *SIGOPS Oper. Syst. Rev.*, 45(3):15–19, Jan. 2012. ISSN 0163-5980. . URL http://doi.acm.org/10.1145/2094091.2094096.

[11] L. Gidra, G. Thomas, J. Sopena, and M. Shapiro. A study of the scalability of stop-the-world garbage collectors on multicores. In *Proceedings of the Eighteenth International Conference on Architectural Support for Programming Languages and Operating Systems*, ASPLOS '13, pages 229–240, New York, NY, USA, 2013. ACM. ISBN 978-1-4503-1870-9. . URL http://doi.acm.org/10.1145/2451116.2451142.

[12] L. Gidra, G. Thomas, J. Sopena, M. Shapiro, and N. Nguyen. Numagic: A garbage collector for big data on big numa machines. In *Proceedings of the Twentieth International Conference on Architectural Support for Programming Languages and Operating Systems*, ASPLOS '15, pages 661–673, New York, NY, USA, 2015. ACM. ISBN 978-1-4503-2835-7. . URL http://doi.acm.org/10.1145/2694344.2694361.

[13] I. Gog, J. Giceva, M. Schwarzkopf, K. Vaswani, D. Vytiniotis, G. Ramalingan, D. Murray, S. Hand, and M. Isard. Broom: Sweeping out garbage collection from big data systems. In *Proceedings of the 15th USENIX Conference on Hot Topics in Operating Systems*, HOTOS'15, pages 2–2, Berkeley, CA, USA, 2015. USENIX Association. URL http://dl.acm.org/citation.cfm?id=2831090.2831092.

[14] R. Jones, A. Hosking, and E. Moss. *The Garbage Collection Handbook: The Art of Automatic Memory Management*. Chapman & Hall/CRC, 1st edition, 2011. ISBN 1420082795, 9781420082791.

[15] M. Maas, T. Harris, K. Asanovic, and J. Kubiatowicz. Trash day: Coordinating garbage collection in distributed systems. In *Proceedings of the 15th USENIX Conference on Hot Topics in Operating Systems*, HOTOS'15, pages 1–1, Berkeley, CA, USA, 2015. USENIX Association. URL http://dl.acm.org/citation.cfm?id=2831090.2831091.

[16] S. Microystems. Memory management in the java hotspot virtual machine, 2006.

[17] J. E. Moreira, S. P. Midkiff, M. Gupta, P. Wu, G. Almasi, and P. Artigas. Ninja: Java for high performance numerical computing. *Sci. Program.*, 10(1):19–33, Jan. 2002. ISSN 1058-9244. . URL http://dx.doi.org/10.1155/2002/314103.

[18] K. Morikawa, T. Ugawa, and H. Iwasaki. Adaptive scanning reduces sweep time for the lisp2 mark-compact garbage collector. In *Proceedings of the 2013 International Symposium on Memory Management*, ISMM '13, pages 15–26, New York, NY, USA, 2013. ACM. ISBN 978-1-4503-2100-6. . URL http://doi.acm.org/10.1145/2464157.2466480.

[19] D. G. Murray, F. McSherry, R. Isaacs, M. Isard, P. Barham, and M. Abadi. Naiad: A timely dataflow system. In *Proceedings of the Twenty-Fourth ACM Symposium on Operating Systems Principles*, SOSP '13, pages 439–455, New York, NY, USA, 2013. ACM. ISBN 978-1-4503-2388-8. . URL http://doi.acm.org/10.1145/2517349.2522738.

[20] R. M. Muthukumar and D. Janakiram. Yama: A scalable generational garbage collector for java in multiprocessor systems. *IEEE Trans. Parallel Distrib. Syst.*, 17(2):148–159, Feb. 2006. ISSN 1045-9219. . URL http://dx.doi.org/10.1109/TPDS.2006.28.

[21] K. Nguyen and G. Xu. Cachetor: Detecting cacheable data to remove bloat. In *Proceedings of the 2013 9th Joint Meeting on Foundations of Software Engineering*, ESEC/FSE 2013, pages 268–278, New York, NY, USA, 2013. ACM. ISBN 978-1-4503-2237-9. . URL http://doi.acm.org/10.1145/2491411.2491416.

[22] K. Nguyen, K. Wang, Y. Bu, L. Fang, J. Hu, and G. Xu. Facade: A compiler and runtime for (almost) object-bounded big data applications. In *Proceedings of the Twentieth International Conference on Architectural Support for Programming Languages and Operating Systems*, ASPLOS '15, pages 675–690, New York, NY,

USA, 2015. ACM. ISBN 978-1-4503-2835-7. . URL http://doi.acm.org/10.1145/2694344.2694345.

[23] N. Sachindran, J. E. B. Moss, and E. D. Berger. Mc2: High-performance garbage collection for memory-constrained environments. In *Proceedings of the 19th Annual ACM SIGPLAN Conference on Object-oriented Programming, Systems, Languages, and Applications*, OOPSLA '04, pages 81–98, New York, NY, USA, 2004. ACM. ISBN 1-58113-831-8. . URL http://doi.acm.org/10.1145/1028976.1028984.

[24] V. Sarkar and J. Dolby. High-performance scalable java virtual machines. In *Proceedings of the 8th International Conference on High Performance Computing*, HiPC '01, pages 151–166, London, UK, UK, 2001. Springer-Verlag. ISBN 3-540-43009-1. URL http://dl.acm.org/citation.cfm?id=645447.652938.

[25] S. Soman, C. Krintz, and L. Daynès. Mtm2: Scalable memory management for multi-tasking managed runtime environments. In *Proceedings of the 22Nd European Conference on Object-Oriented Programming*, ECOOP '08, pages 335–361, Berlin, Heidelberg, 2008. Springer-Verlag. ISBN 978-3-540-70591-8. . URL http://dx.doi.org/10.1007/978-3-540-70592-5_15.

[26] Spark. Apache spark is a fast and general engine for large-scale data processing. http://spark.apache.org/, 2015.

[27] G. L. Taboada, S. Ramos, R. R. Expósito, J. Touriño, and R. Doallo. Java in the high performance computing arena: Research, practice and experience. *Sci. Comput. Program.*, 78(5):425–444, May 2013. ISSN 0167-6423. . URL http://dx.doi.org/10.1016/j.scico.2011.06.002.

[28] D. Vengerov. Modeling, analysis and throughput optimization of a generational garbage collector. In *Proceedings of the 2009 International Symposium on Memory Management*, ISMM '09, pages 1–9, New York, NY, USA, 2009. ACM. ISBN 978-1-60558-347-1. . URL http://doi.acm.org/10.1145/1542431.1542433.

[29] Y. Yu, T. Lei, H. Chen, and B. Zang. Openjdk meets xeon phi: A comprehensive study of java hpc on intel many-core architecture. In *Parallel Processing Workshops (ICPPW), 2015 44th International Conference on*, pages 156–165. IEEE, 2015.

[30] M. Zaharia, M. Chowdhury, T. Das, A. Dave, J. Ma, M. McCauley, M. J. Franklin, S. Shenker, and I. Stoica. Resilient distributed datasets: A fault-tolerant abstraction for in-memory cluster computing. In *Proceedings of the 9th USENIX Conference on Networked Systems Design and Implementation*, NSDI'12, pages 2–2, Berkeley, CA, USA, 2012. USENIX Association. URL http://dl.acm.org/citation.cfm?id=2228298.2228301.

[31] X. Zhang, E. Tune, R. Hagmann, R. Jnagal, V. Gokhale, and J. Wilkes. Cpi2: Cpu performance isolation for shared compute clusters. In *Proceedings of the 8th ACM European Conference on Computer Systems*, EuroSys '13, pages 379–391, New York, NY, USA, 2013. ACM. ISBN 978-1-4503-1994-2. . URL http://doi.acm.org/10.1145/2465351.2465388.

Leveraging Managed Runtime Systems to Build, Analyze, and Optimize Memory Graphs

Rebecca Smith

Rice University

rjs@rice.edu

Scott Rixner

Rice University

rixner@rice.edu

Abstract

Optimizing memory management is a major challenge of embedded systems programming, as memory is scarce. Further, embedded systems often have heterogeneous memory architectures, complicating the task of memory allocation during both compilation and migration. However, new opportunities for addressing these challenges have been created by the recent emergence of managed runtimes for embedded systems. By imposing structure on memory, these systems have opened the doors for new techniques for analyzing and optimizing memory usage within embedded systems. This paper presents GEM (Graphs of Embedded Memory), a tool which capitalizes on the structure that managed runtime systems provide in order to build memory graphs which facilitate memory analysis and optimization. At GEM's core are a set of fundamental graph transformations which can be layered to support a wide range of use cases, including interactive memory visualization, de-duplication of objects and code, compilation for heterogeneous memory architectures, and transparent migration. Moreover, since the same underlying infrastructure supports all of these orthogonal functionalities, they can easily be applied together to complement each other.

1. Introduction

Managed runtime systems, already common in traditional computing systems, are increasingly being adopted by embedded systems programmers to increase productivity. Modern embedded runtime systems such as eLua [2], p14p [5], Micro Python [7], and Owl [4] raise the abstraction level of embedded systems programming by providing interpreters for high-level languages and automating tasks such as thread scheduling, garbage collection, and inter-process communication. While the adoption of runtime systems has primarily been motivated by aspirations of productivity, these systems also provide new opportunities for improving memory analysis and optimization by imposing structure on memory.

Embedded systems exhibit a combination of resource constraints and heterogeneity which makes it difficult, yet essential, to carefully analyze and optimize memory. In terms of resource constraints, a typical mid-range microcontroller may have only 32–256 KB of SRAM and 128 KB–1 MB of flash, necessitating thoughtful management of memory at both compile-time and runtime.

The task of memory management is further complicated by heterogeneity; a single embedded system may consist of multiple microcontrollers with varied proportions of SRAM and flash. As an example, one member of STM32's Cortex-M series of microcontrollers has 256 KB of flash and 32 KB of SRAM [39], while another has only 128 KB of flash, but 64 KB SRAM [38]. In a heterogeneous system, allocation and data layout schemes could simply cater to the lowest common denominator of each type of memory. However, this is impractical due to the scarcity of memory; a more flexible solution is needed.

Outside the domain of embedded systems, tools have been developed to leverage the structure imposed by managed runtime systems to model memory as a graph [8, 16, 26, 30, 32, 43]. By providing a clear and intuitive representation of the relationships between objects, graphs facilitate visualization, analysis, and transformations across multiple nodes. This is hugely valuable to memory transformation, as inter-object references make it nearly impossible to operate on a single object in isolation. Yet, existing tools use memory graphs solely for visualization and analysis, transforming only insofar as is necessary to display the graph.

The challenges faced by embedded systems motivate the development of tools which use memory graphs not only for analysis, but also for optimization. However, embedded applications have traditionally been written in C, where the unstructured memory layout and presence of unidentifiable pointers inhibits the construction of memory graphs. In contrast, runtime systems for high-level languages organize

VEE '16, April 2–3, 2016, Atlanta, GA, USA
Copyright © 2016 ACM 978-1-4503-3947-6/16/04...$15.00
DOI: http://dx.doi.org/10.1145/http://dx.doi.org/10.1145/2892242.2892253

memory in a way that is amenable to graph-based analysis and transformation.

This paper introduces GEM, a memory configuration tool for embedded runtime systems which builds, analyzes, and transforms graphs of the entire memory space of a program. At its core is a set of fundamental transformation passes that can be combined into high-level use cases. Additionally, GEM includes a mechanism for installing a transformed graph in memory, allowing these abstract graph transformations to impact the actual memory layout of the system. Due to its flexible and extensible infrastructure, GEM has proven valuable in a variety of scenarios. In particular, this paper presents four key contributions:

- A versatile framework for combining low-level graph transformations to achieve high-level use cases.

- A mechanism for installing graphs in memory.

- Four novel low-level transformations: splicing, splitting, unpacking, and generic fine-grained de-duplication.

- Four high-level use cases: interactive visualization, object and code de-duplication, compilation for heterogeneous memory architectures, and transparent migration.

Evaluation of the four representative use cases showed that GEM is instrumental in improving memory analysis and optimization. For instance, its visualizer uncovered systemic inefficiencies, and its de-duplication capability reclaimed up to 24% of the flash consumed by language-level libraries.

The next section describes the context in which GEM operates. Section 3 presents GEM's infrastructure and transformations. Section 4 explains the workflow for each high-level use case, and Section 5 evaluates these use cases. Section 6 discusses related work, and Section 7 concludes the paper.

2. Context

Memory optimization tools are particularly valuable at the intersection of embedded systems and managed runtime systems. Embedded systems have much to gain from memory optimization; runtime systems establish the order within the memory space needed to achieve these gains.

GEM requires the memory organization to satisfy two properties. First, all data must be stored in objects of well-defined types known to the runtime system. Second, all objects must have explicit or implicit type and size identifiers. The fundamental concepts behind GEM are generalizable, and could be implemented for any runtime system which meets these requirements, such as the Oracle JVM or CPython. Because embedded systems face particularly stringent memory constraints, a prototype was built for Owl [4, 9], an embedded Python runtime system representative of managed runtime systems for embedded microcontrollers.

Like CPython, Owl includes both a compiler and an interpreter. Python source code is first compiled into code ob-

jects, which contain bytecodes. These bytecodes are then executed by the interpreter at runtime. Owl stores the entire Python program, including the code objects, as Python objects. Each object includes a 4 B object descriptor specifying its type and size, and has fields containing data and references to other objects.

These Python objects are distributed across SRAM and flash. All runtime state, including threads and stack frames, is allocated on the Python heap which resides in SRAM. At compile-time, modules of Python library code are stored in flash. Owl first compiles the modules using the standard CPython compiler, generating one Python code object for each module. Each code object includes the code itself — a series of bytecodes, in the form of a string of bytes — as well as metadata such as the filename and variable names. Next, the Owl toolchain converts the compiled modules into a "packed" format, using two special types: packed code objects and packed tuples. Packed objects do not reference other objects, instead storing constituent objects internally as a contiguous array. This saves space by eliminating references; further, this eliminates the need for a dynamic linker, as each module is completely self-contained.

Finally, at boot-time, Owl allocates a global object on the heap to hold the runtime state, including "module paths" consisting of the addresses of the code objects for each module. The module paths serve two purposes: they are used to import modules at runtime, and they ensure that all of the Python objects in flash are reachable from the heap.

Because Owl stores Python objects in both SRAM and flash, GEM's memory graphs have two components, one for each memory region. These graphs could easily be expanded to include components for additional memory regions, to support systems with more complex memory hierarchies.

3. Tool Organization

Due to resource constraints, GEM operates offline, so that it can build and manipulate graphs without using any of the microcontroller's precious memory space. This requires a "host" machine with sufficient resources to run GEM. A single host can serve a system of multiple microcontrollers, and could be connected via either a serial port or a wireless network. Further, this host need not be dedicated to GEM; for instance, the host could also be used to perform other deployment and management tasks required by the system.

GEM is composed of three layers. First is the memory transfer layer, which transports memory contents to and from the microcontroller in a raw byte format using two primitives, dump and memset. Next is the memory conversion layer, which uses an auto-generated parser and unparser to convert between two representations of memory: the raw byte format from the previous layer and a graph format used by the final layer. Last is the graph transformation layer, which consists of transformation passes that operate on a

Figure 1. GEM architecture

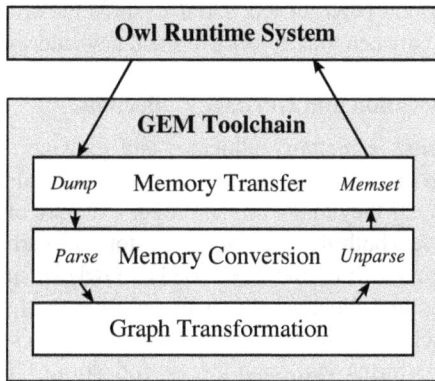

memory graph. Figure 1 depicts the GEM toolchain architecture.

Across these three layers, GEM uses two representations of memory. First, a PyMem, which is an intermediate representation of the microcontroller's entire memory space. This simple container is used by the parser to aggregate objects prior to building the graph. It includes a mapping for each region of memory — in Owl, SRAM (heap) and flash (library code objects) — which associate memory addresses with PyObjects. Each PyObject o has a type, a size, and two name-to-value mappings of its fields: data(o): data_names(o)$\mapsto$data_vals(o), for primitive types, and pyptrs(o): pyptrs_names(o)$\mapsto$pyptrs_vals(o), for pointers to other Python objects.

Frame objects include a third mapping: cptrs, which includes pointers that are not base addresses of Python objects. These are not arbitrary pointers, but well-defined pointers into other Python objects. In particular, there are three: the instruction pointer, the stack pointer, and a pointer to the last stack slot. The first of these points into a separate bytecode object; the others point within this same frame object.

Ultimately, GEM's graph transformation layer operates on a MemGraph. This is a directed graph of memory which, like the PyMem, encompasses multiple regions of memory. Each node corresponds to a PyObject, and edges run from a given PyObject to the nodes of each of the objects in its pyptrs_vals set. Formally, a MemGraph is a graph $G = (V, E)$ such that $V(G) = \{u \mid u \text{ is a PyObject}\}$ and $E(G) = \{(u, v \mid address(v) \in \text{pyptrs\_vals}(u)\}$.

3.1 Memory Transfer Layer

GEM provides two commands, dump and memset, which transfer a byte string representation of the memory space between the microcontroller and the host machine. These operations allow the memory transformations made by GEM to affect the actual layout of memory on the microcontroller.

The first of these, dump, consists of three stages. In each stage, GEM compiles and sends over the connection a function call which, upon execution by the interpreter on the microcontroller, causes the microcontroller to send heap data

back to GEM. GEM first queries for metadata including the base address of the heap. It then requests the heap contents, beginning at this base address. Last, GEM fetches all of the Python code objects stored in flash.

The reverse of dump is memset, which overwrites the heap on the microcontroller. The heap being memset need not have originated from the destination device. However, if the source and destination are different microcontrollers, the base addresses of the heaps and the contents of flash may also be different. Therefore, memset does not blindly replace the heap. Instead, GEM first dumps the memory of the destination device, and then splices the SRAM (heap) component from the source into the flash component from the destination using a technique that will be described in greater detail in Section 3.3.5. Finally, GEM prepares to place the heap on the destination device by shifting all intra-heap references by the difference between the source and destination base addresses, using a reference-updating technique that will be described in Section 3.3.1.

After constructing the spliced graph, GEM unparses this graph and initiates an overwrite by compiling and sending a custom MEMSET bytecode to the destination device. Unlike dump, memset cannot be implemented as a function call, since overwriting the heap obliterates the call stack. GEM then sends the heap contents and metadata over the connection in a byte format. In executing the MEMSET bytecode, the microcontroller reads the heap contents and metadata, overwriting both. Once MEMSET completes, the program automatically resumes execution from the exact point at which its memory was dumped.

3.2 Memory Conversion Layer

While graphs are highly amenable to analysis and transformation, they are not compact enough to serve as the memory format on the microcontroller. Instead, objects in memory are laid out as a contiguous array of bytes. GEM provides a parser and unparser to convert between the byte format and the MemGraph format. These include top-level parse and unparse functions which take in a byte string or graph, respectively, as well as parse_<type> and unparse_<type> functions for each Python object type and for free blocks.

The top-level parse function first builds an intermediate PyMem representation by reading the byte string and processing one object at a time. It interprets the first four bytes of each object as an object descriptor, extracts the size and type, and dispatches a call to the appropriate type-specific function, which creates a PyObject or free block. It then maps the object's address to the newly-created PyObject. Once the entire string has been processed, the parser builds the MemGraph by iterating over the PyObjects, inserting them as nodes, and adding edges for each of their pyptrs.

Conversely, unparse receives a MemGraph and outputs a byte string. It first constructs a sorted list of the addresses of all heap nodes in the graph. None of GEM's transformations introduce gaps in the address space, so these addresses will be contiguous assuming that GEM was given a valid image when it initially built the graph. It then unparses each object in order by invoking the appropriate `unparse_<type>` function to obtain a byte string representation of that object. Last, it concatenates the byte strings for the individual objects to form a complete representation of the heap.

Moreover, GEM auto-generates all of the type-specific functions at compile-time. It passes the header files containing the type definitions through pycparser [6], and uses a custom visitor to process each type definition. For each type, a list of tuples of (field name, field type, field size) is output to an intermediate file. This metadata is used by the parser generator to auto-generate the `parse_<type>` and `unparse_<type>` functions. The parse functions classify each field into `data`, `pyptrs`, or `cptrs` according to type, and advance the index into the byte string based on the field's size and the amount of padding between fields. The unparse functions fetch and unparse each field in order, concatenating the results together and adding padding as needed.

This auto-generation adds robustness to the parser and unparser. As new types are introduced to the runtime system, or fields are added or removed from existing types, no maintenance is required. Likewise, Owl accepts configuration options, specified as C defines, which may affect the type definitions; GEM's parser generator ensures that the parser and unparser are always consistent with the current configuration. Further, this auto-generation makes GEM extensible to other systems. With minor modifications to the parser generator, GEM could generate a parser and unparser for any system whose memory layout adheres to the principles outlined in Section 2.

3.3 Graph Transformation Layer

Converting the memory space into a graph unlocks a multitude of possible transformations; this section presents seven that are currently supported by GEM. Strategic composition of these transformations enables use cases including, but by no means limited to, the four that will be presented in Section 4.

3.3.1 Updating References

Moving even a single object in memory requires updating all references to it to reflect its new address. GEM provides two means of updating references. First, GEM can be given an offset by which to shift the entire heap; this involves shifting all intra-heap `pyptrs` and `cptrs` by this offset.

Second, given a mapping of old to new addresses, GEM can relocate all objects to their new addresses. To accomplish this, GEM iterates over the `pyptrs` and `cptrs` of each object. If it encounters a `pyptr` that is a key in the old-to-new mapping, it updates the reference to point to the corresponding new address. Updating the `cptrs` is slightly more complicated; while these references may not match any of the keys in the old-to-new mapping, they may point into an object whose base address is a key in the mapping. Thus,

GEM checks if the base address of the object into which each `cptr` points has been shifted, and if so shifts the `cptr` by the difference between that object's old and new addresses.

3.3.2 Allocation and Garbage Collection

GEM requires a memory allocator and garbage collector. These need not use the same algorithms as the runtime system, as long as they maintain the proper structure of the free list. However, both the memory allocator and garbage collector within GEM mimic those used by Owl, for simplicity.

The memory allocator is first fit, splitting the free block if it significantly exceeds the requested size. Owl's garbage collector performs mark-and-sweep collection. GEM supplements this with an optional compacting pass, effectively providing mark-compact collection. Compaction moves all live objects into contiguous addresses, aided by the reference updating technique from Section 3.3.1, and then coalesces the free list.

3.3.3 Eliminating Duplicates

To identify duplicates, GEM builds a set of object "pools" using a deep equality checker. This equality checker takes a pair of `PyObjects`, directly compares their `data` and `cptrs`, and recursively compares their `pyptrs`. Objects deemed equal are placed in the same pool. Finally, pools of size one — representing unique objects — are filtered out.

Using the remaining pools of duplicates, GEM can free large chunks of memory by eliminating redundancies. For each pool, GEM chooses one representative object, and uses the technique from Section 3.3.1 to update all references to other objects in the pool to point to the representative. It then uses the garbage collector described in Section 3.3.2 to free the non-representative duplicates.

While GEM can consolidate all types of objects, in practice it only does so for immutable objects, as combining distinct mutable objects would violate the semantics of Python. Despite this, GEM finds substantial opportunities for deduplication, as Python has many immutable types including booleans, integers, floating points, strings, and tuples.

3.3.4 Unpacking Objects

As described in Section 2, Owl contains packed types which embed their constituents within themselves. During graph construction (Section 3.2), GEM generates individual nodes for the top-level object and each constituent, drawing edges from the top-level object to each constituent.

Unpacking a packed object consists of allocating an equivalent unpacked object and freeing the original object. First, GEM allocates the top-level unpacked object using the memory allocator from Section 3.3.2. Second, GEM creates references from the unpacked top-level object to the existing nodes for the constituents. Constituents which are themselves packed are unpacked recursively. As an example, figure 2 shows the same tuple before and after being unpacked.

Figure 2. Unpacking a packed tuple

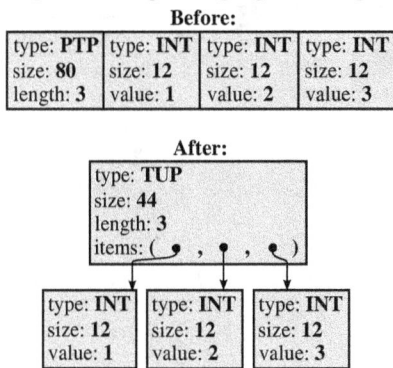

Before:

type: **PTP**	type: **INT**	type: **INT**	type: **INT**
size: **80**	size: **12**	size: **12**	size: **12**
length: **3**	value: **1**	value: **2**	value: **3**

After:

type: **TUP**
size: **44**
length: **3**
items: (• , • , •)

type: **INT**	type: **INT**	type: **INT**
size: **12**	size: **12**	size: **12**
value: **1**	value: **2**	value: **3**

Taken alone, unpacking consumes additional space, due to the extra layer of indirection. However, unpacked objects present opportunities for fine-grained de-duplication. Thus, unpacking can be a valuable asset when taken in conjunction with de-duplication, as will be shown in Section 5.2.

3.3.5 Splicing and Splitting

In addition to the intra-graph transformations discussed in Sections 3.3.1–3.3.4, GEM offers two transformations which operate on multiple graphs: splicing and splitting.

Splicing takes a source and destination graph and fuses one or more components of the source into one or more components of the destination. Splicing can be done with or without de-duplication; this section describes GEM's default behavior, which includes de-duplication. As an example, Figure 3 depicts splicing the entire source graph with the destination flash.

To accomplish this, GEM classifies the objects in the source component(s) to be spliced into two categories: those for which equivalent objects are present in the destination component(s), and those that have no equivalent in the destination component(s). This is achieved via an inter-graph duplicate search, using the procedure from Section 3.3.3. Once again, duplicates are only sought amongst immutable objects, to preserve program semantics.

For objects in the former category, no allocation is needed; GEM simply constructs a mapping from source addresses to destination addresses. For each unique object in the latter category, GEM allocates an equivalent object within the SRAM portion of the spliced graph, using the memory allocator from Section 3.3.2. During allocation, GEM updates the aforementioned mapping to map the original addresses of these objects to the addresses of the newly-allocated equivalents. Finally, GEM updates all references within the spliced graph according to this mapping, using the second technique from Section 3.3.1.

Splitting takes a single-component graph and partitions its objects into multiple components. GEM's splitting framework allows the user to input a custom algorithm for partitioning the objects. However, several different partitioning

Figure 3. Splicing source graph into destination graph

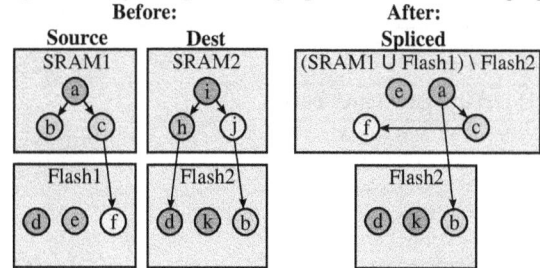

algorithms are already built into GEM, one of which will be presented in Section 4.3.1. GEM uses the input algorithm to split the objects into two disjoint subsets, and then constructs new graphs representing each subset. To eliminate the gaps introduced by partitioning the objects, GEM applies the compaction pass from Section 3.3.2 to each new graph.

4. Use Cases

The transformations and mechanisms described in Section 3 serve as building blocks which can be combined to support a multitude of use cases. To illustrate the versatility of GEM, this section presents four sample use cases. First, GEM can be augmented with a GUI to visualize the memory space. Second, it can be used to de-duplicate at compile-time, substantively decreasing code size. Also at compile-time, GEM can customize the layout of code across SRAM and flash, allowing the same runtime system to be deployed on a wide spectrum of memory architectures. Fourth, GEM can be used at runtime to transparently migrate a running program.

4.1 Memory Visualization

Extracting meaningful information from a raw heap dump is quite challenging. Thus, GEM supports a graphical visualizer which provides an organized view of the entire memory space of the microcontroller. This visualizer allows the user to easily view how objects are laid out in memory, see which objects are live at a given point in execution, and identify the most costly objects. The techniques from Section 3.3 are used to find and display duplicate objects and unreachable objects. GEM's visualizer is highly interactive, allowing the user to sort, search, navigate, and inspect objects.

4.1.1 User Interface

The GUI for GEM's visualizer is divided into three vertical panes, as shown in Figure 4. The left pane is a glossary of all objects in memory. It contains two sub-panes, one for SRAM and one for flash. Objects can be sorted by address, size, type, or value. A search bar enables lookup by address, and menu options allow for moving sequentially to the previous or next address. Selecting an object in the left pane updates several object-specific facets of the middle and right panes.

The middle pane offers six different display options. Three of these are specific to the selected object: textual

135

Figure 4. Graphical display for GEM's interactive memory visualizer

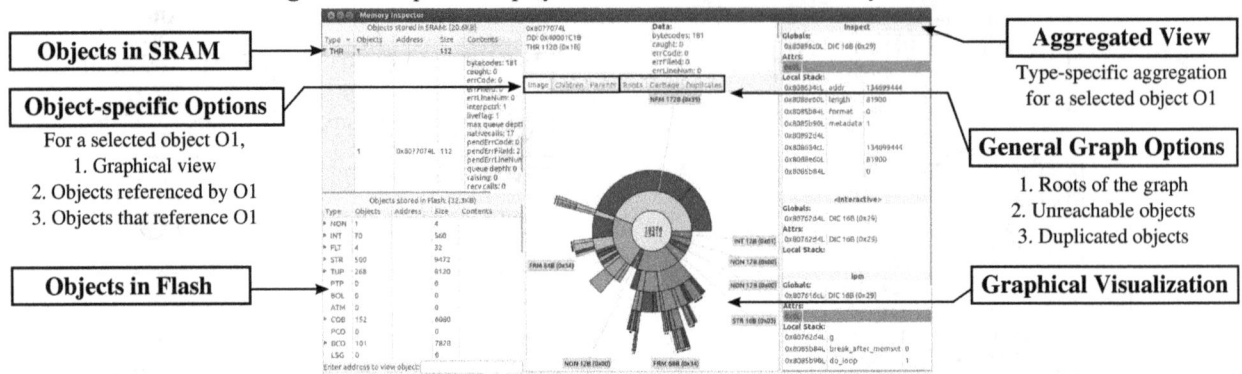

"parent" and "child" displays, plus a graphical "ringschart" display. An object's parent set consists of objects that reference it; its child set contains those objects that it references.

The graphical display is based on the open-source Linux Graphical Disk Usage Analyzer [1]. It displays a subset of the graph as a ringschart centered around the selected item. The center of the ringschart shows the total size of the weakly-connected component rooted in the selected object, broken down into SRAM and flash consumption. Each sector of the ringschart represents a reference to an object, and has an arc length proportional to the size of that object relative to sizes its "sibling" objects.

Hovering over a sector of the ringschart highlights that sector and spawns tooltips from its children, annotating them with type and size. If there are aliases, only one reference to the aliased object (sector in the ringschart) is colorized, with the rest displayed in grey. Hovering over a sector highlights all of its aliases. Rather than displaying the entire component rooted in the selected object, the GUI limits the depth of the rings to a number that can be configured via "zoom in" and "zoom out" options in the drop-down menu. It then annotates branches of the ringschart that are deeper than can be displayed. Clicking on a sector in the ringschart is equivalent to selecting the corresponding object from the left pane: the ringschart is re-centered around the selection, and all other object-specific panes are re-rendered.

The middle pane also includes three views of general properties of the graph: "roots", garbage, and duplicates. The roots view lists the addresses and types of the roots of the graph: global objects in memory which are not referenced by any other objects, and from which jointly all live objects are reachable. The garbage view lists objects that are not reachable from these roots. Last, the duplicates view displays each object pool — found using the technique from Section 3.3.3 — by listing the addresses of all objects in that pool.

The contents of the right pane are also specific to the selected object. This pane serves as an aggregated display for compound objects. It has special display modes for lists, tuples, sets, dictionaries, frames, threads, and code objects.

For instance, in Figure 4, the selected object is a thread, and the right pane displays the stack of frames running in that thread. Each frame is tagged with the name, attributes, global variables, and local variables of the function to which it corresponds; each variable is tagged with its name, address, and current value.

4.2 De-duplication

The standard CPython compiler generates code objects that are fraught with duplicates. These code objects are then placed in read-only memory, from which they cannot be consolidated at runtime. The duplicates are relatively harmless on a desktop machine with vast resources. However, in an embedded system where memory is precious, eliminating duplicate objects within the Python code is critically important. GEM uniquely applies de-duplication to code objects at compile-time. Thus, the savings that GEM achieves are completely orthogonal to those of runtime de-duplication techniques such as interning.

For correctness, GEM limits de-duplication to immutable objects. In reality, this is no limitation at all, as all of the constants referenced by the Python code objects belong to immutable types. Due to the prevalence of duplicates, GEM's de-duplication yields substantial memory gains, as will be shown in Section 5.2.

4.2.1 Workflow

At a high-level, de-duplication proceeds as follows:

1. Build a graph of the library code, in Owl's default packed format, using the parser from Section 3.2.

2. Unpack the library modules, as described in Section 3.3.4.

3. Eliminate duplicates, as described in Section 3.3.3, using the compacting garbage collector to eliminate any gaps.

4. Unparse the graph using the unparser from Section 3.2.

5. Output the unparsed image to a C file, which will then be compiled into the runtime system by the Owl toolchain.

6. Post-compilation, find the base runtime address of the image and shift all references by this base address, again using the technique from Section 3.3.1.

In greater detail, de-duplication begins after Owl's image creator builds a binary representation of the Python library code. GEM parses this binary representation into a graph, using a base address of 0 since the runtime memory address of the library has not yet been determined.

The packed objects that Owl's image creator produces by default cannot be de-duplicated, since they directly contain their constituent objects. Therefore, the next step is to unpack these objects. GEM provides two levels of unpacking. It can indiscriminately unpack all objects; however, while the conversion to unpacked objects enables de-duplication, it introduces an overhead by reinstating references. Thus, GEM also provides a more sophisticated hybrid approach: selectively unpacking only those objects for which the projected savings due to de-duplication exceed the projected overhead due to reference reinstatement. Section 5.2 will show that either level of unpacking, in conjunction with de-duplication, yields significant savings, but the latter approach consistently surpasses the former.

After unpacking, GEM finds and consolidates duplicates, using the compacting garbage collector to regain a contiguous sequence of objects. Next, GEM determines the module paths — the addresses of the code objects representing the library modules. The graph is now in the correct structure, but its base address is still 0. Therefore, GEM stores the graph and its module paths, to be adjusted once the C linker has placed the image. It then passes unparsed versions of the graph and its module paths back to the image creator.

For now, GEM is done, and normal compilation resumes. The Owl toolchain auto-generates a C file containing the unparsed library image and module paths and compiles this file into the runtime system. At this point, the base runtime address of the library has been assigned, so GEM can adjust the intra-library references. It uses `readelf` to find this base address, reloads the de-duplicated graph that was stored previously, and shifts all references by an offset equal to the base runtime address. It likewise increments each module path by the base address. Finally, GEM unparses the library and the module paths back into binary representations and overwrites the ELF file with the adjusted versions.

4.3 Heterogeneous Compilation

Enabling a runtime system to fit within a broad spectrum of microcontroller memory architectures eases the construction of heterogeneous embedded systems. GEM uniquely supports customization of the runtime system to a particular memory architecture by partitioning the Python library code amongst SRAM and flash. The amount of SRAM and flash available for these libraries can be specified at compile-time; given these constraints, GEM will compile and partition the runtime system, failing only if the capacity is too low.

4.3.1 Workflow

To increase the likelihood of meeting the given memory constraints, heterogeneous compilation is bracketed by the de-duplication procedure outlined in Section 4.2.1. Thus, its complete compile-time workflow is as follows:

1. Build a graph of the library code in Owl's default packed format, using the parser from Section 3.2.

2. Unpack the library modules, as described in Section 3.3.4.

3. Eliminate duplicates, as described in Section 3.3.3.

4. Partition the library code between SRAM and flash, using the technique from Section 3.3.5.

5. Unparse both graphs using the unparser from Section 3.2.

6. Output the unparsed image to a C file, which will then be compiled into the runtime system by the Owl toolchain.

7. Post-compilation, find the base runtime address of the image and shift all references by this base address, using the technique from Section 3.3.1.

In addition, the objects designated for SRAM are installed in the heap at runtime using a six-step process:

1. Boot the runtime system.

2. Dump the memory using the technique from Section 3.1.

3. Parse the memory into a graph, as in Section 3.2.

4. Splice the SRAM modules into the current memory graph using the technique from Section 3.3.5.

5. Unparse the augmented graph, as in Section 3.2.

6. Memset the augmented graph using the technique from Section 3.1.

As with de-duplication, GEM enters the compilation process just after Owl's image creator builds the binary representation of the packed Python library code. GEM then performs the same parsing, graph construction, unpacking, and duplicate elimination as it did for de-duplication. However, rather than compacting the objects into a single contiguous chunk of memory, it partitions these objects into two components, one for flash and one for SRAM.

For this use case, the partitioning algorithm must adhere to three constraints. First, it must respect the upper bounds on each memory region's size specified at compile-time. Second, since the SRAM modules will not be loaded until the end of boot-time, it must ensure that all modules necessary to boot the runtime system are relegated to flash. Third, it must guarantee that nothing placed in flash references anything placed in SRAM, since the runtime SRAM addresses are not known prior to boot time. Some microcontrollers cannot overwrite flash memory during execution, and it's expensive for those that can; additionally, references from flash into SRAM would become dangling references upon reboot, potentially causing the runtime system to crash.

GEM currently uses a greedy algorithm to satisfy these constraints, which the evaluation in Section 5.3 proves effective. This algorithm begins by placing only those objects that are required to boot the runtime system in flash, and assuming that all other objects are in SRAM. To satisfy the third constraint, the algorithm promotes objects to flash on the granularity of components, where each candidate component consists of a given object plus all other objects still in SRAM that are reachable from that object. It greedily chooses the largest component in SRAM that will fit in flash without exceeding capacity, terminating when even the smallest component left in SRAM is larger than the remaining capacity. If the size of the remaining SRAM component exceeds the specified bounds, the algorithm reports failure; otherwise, GEM proceeds with compilation.

After executing this algorithm GEM builds and compacts two new graphs, one for each memory region, and assigns a temporary base address to each. GEM then stores both graphs and their module paths for later reference adjustment and resumes the normal compilation process. As in de-duplication, it adjusts references to objects in flash once the runtime address of the flash library has been established.

Finally, the SRAM modules must be allocated on the heap. The runtime system is first booted into a special SRAM installation mode which imports only the modules needed to perform `dump` and `memset`. The mode minimizes the set of modules that are required to be placed in flash at compile-time, widening the range of flash sizes that GEM can accommodate. The memory space is then dumped and parsed into a graph format, using the techniques from Sections 3.1 and 3.2, and the SRAM graph built during compile-time is spliced in. During this splicing process, GEM keeps track of the addresses assigned to any top-level modules. Last, GEM unparses and memsets the graph, overwriting the current heap and augmenting the module paths with the addresses of the SRAM modules.

4.4 Transparent Migration

Transparent migration, which preserves the runtime state, is valuable in many scenarios. For instance, if a device fails, migrating a pre-crash checkpoint to another device prevents complete loss of work. Likewise, a system with substantial startup delays may benefit from migration of a pre-booted image [28]. While many existing systems support transparent migration, the value of GEM's approach lies in the ease with which it harnesses graph transformations — in particular, its novel splicing technique — to enable migration between devices with disparate hardware and software.

4.4.1 Workflow

In theory, a program running upon a runtime system can be migrated by transplanting the heap. However, as described in Section 3.1, the base address of the heap is not guaranteed to be identical across all instances of the runtime system. Further, the contents of flash may not be the same at the source and destination, which is problematic as objects on the heap may reference flash. GEM's `memset` command automatically corrects for these differences by adjusting all intra-heap references and allocating all missing flash objects in SRAM — since, as mentioned in Section 4.3.1, many microcontrollers do not support mutating flash at runtime.

Because `memset` automatically addresses these challenges, GEM's migration process is quite simple:

1. Dump the source memory, as described in Section 3.1.

2. Parse the memory into a graph, as in Section 3.2.

3. Optionally perform any desired transformations such as de-duplication or free list compaction.

4. Save the snapshot of the transformed graph.

5. Memset the snapshot onto the destination using the technique from Section 3.1.

In the prototype implementation, the `dump` and `memset` are initiated by the user, though they could be automated. To allow the user to initiate a `dump` or `memset`, GEM includes two mechanisms by which the user can pause the program and access the interactive prompt. First, if the programmer knows the point in the program at which he or she wishes to migrate in advance, he or she can insert a call to a built-in function which pauses execution.

However, the programmer may not always anticipate wishing to migrate. Thus, GEM extends Owl's interpreter to support pausing at any time by pressing a button on the microcontroller. Once the program is paused, the user can access the interactive prompt to perform migration. While manual activation serves as an effective proof-of-concept, the same pause/resume logic could be combined with Owl's message-passing capabilities to enable remote triggering.

5. Evaluation

Each of the use cases from Section 4 was evaluated on a series of benchmarks, where each benchmark is a snapshot of a specific workload running on a specific platform, named in the form <platform>_<workload>. GEM was evaluated on three platforms: a Stellaris LM3S9B92 microcontroller ("Stellaris"), an STM32F4-Discovery microcontroller ("STM32"), and a desktop machine ("Desktop"). The LM3S9B92 has 96 KB of SRAM and 256 KB of flash; the F4-Discovery board has 192 KB of SRAM and 1 MB of flash. The workloads include two that are not application-specific — compile time ("compile") and boot time ("boot") — as well as an application that uses an accelerometer and TFT display to present an artificial horizon display ("ahd").

5.1 Memory Visualization

GEM's memory visualizer has exposed multiple opportunities to improve the system design of Owl. For instance,

Table 1. Duplicate Objects in Unpacked Library Code

Type	All Objects		Intra-Module Duplicates		Inter-Module Duplicates		All Duplicates	
	Count	Total Size (B)	Count	Total Size (B)	Count	Total Size (B)	Count	Total Size (B)
None	132	528	108	432	23	92	131	524
Integer	111	888	17	136	27	216	44	352
Float	5	40	1	8	0	0	1	8
String	1418	23156	711	11212	213	2776	924	13988
Tuple	604	11340	284	2708	58	692	342	3400
Bytecode	111	7876	37	852	11	244	48	1096
Code Object	148	5920	0	0	0	0	0	0
Native Object	121	968	0	0	0	0	0	0
Total	2687	51568	1158	15348	332	4020	1490	19368

Table 2. Size of Python Libraries (KB)

Platform	Unpacked	Packed	Unpacked, De-duplicated	Hybrid
Desktop	50.4	41.1	31.5	31.3
Stellaris	86.4	71.4	62.7	60.3
STM32	97.1	80.9	70.3	68.9

GEM's memory visualizer inspired new memory formats for storing the Python library code in flash. Originally, Owl used the same unpacked, duplicated object format as CPython. However, using GEM to analyze the contents of flash revealed considerable wasted space. Therefore, two new library formats were proposed: the packed format described in Section 2, and the de-duplicated format from Section 4.2.

A comparison of the original and packed formats, which will be presented in Section 5.2, validates the intuition that the references in the unpacked version consume an exorbitant amount of space. Yet, further analysis using GEM's memory visualizer exposed many duplicates within these packed code objects, as shown in Table 1. GEM indicated that the gains to be had by eliminating duplicates would outweigh the losses associated with adding references. Both proposed formats were incorporated into Owl, and the user may now choose which format is used at compile-time.

5.2 De-duplication

Since de-duplication occurs at compile-time, it was evaluated on the *_compile benchmarks. For each benchmark, the Python library code was stored in four formats: the unpacked format output by the CPython compiler, the packed format inspired by GEM's visualizer, and two de-duplicated formats which utilize the procedure described in Section 4.2, first with naive unpacking and second with selective unpacking based on a heuristic that approximates the potential savings. Table 2 shows the space consumed by the library code in each of these four formats.

The modules included in the Python library vary across platforms. Many modules are platform-independent, such as `math`, `time`, and `types`. The desktop platform is smallest, as it consists solely of these platform-independent modules.

Stellaris and STM32 include additional platform-specific modules to support hardware peripheral access.

Across all three platforms, GEM's de-duplication consistently saved memory. Compared to the unpacked format used by CPython, the savings amounted to 19.1 KB, 26.1 KB, and 28.6 KB for desktop, Stellaris, and STM32, respectively; in each case this was a decrease of more than 29%. Table 1 breaks down the de-duplication performed by GEM by type. Strings accounted for over 72% of the de-duplication savings; the next largest sources of redundancies were tuples and bytecodes. Note that significant duplication occurs even amongst nested objects such as tuples.

Even as compared to the compact packed format, de-duplication yielded savings of 9.8 KB, 11.1 KB, and 12.0 KB for the three platforms: improvements of 14.8–23.8%. The percent improvement was greatest for the desktop version. However, Stellaris and STM32 yielded better absolute decreases. This is due to the fact that the extra platform-specific modules within Stellaris and STM32 primarily contain constants such as register addresses, and thus have an unusually small proportion of duplicate objects.

The presence of modules with a low proportion of duplicate objects motivated the creation of the hybrid format described in Section 4.2. The difference in size between the third and fourth formats in Table 2 indicates that GEM's hybrid approach elected to leave some low-redundancy modules packed, as it found insufficient duplicates to offset the overhead of unpacking. This selectivity proved profitable for each platform, saving up to an additional 2.4 KB.

5.3 Heterogeneous Compilation

By default, the Owl toolchain places the Python library code in a separate region of memory from the heap. On the microcontroller platforms, this region is flash; on the desktop platform, it is a read-only region of RAM. For the purposes of brevity, both types of read-only regions will be referred to as "flash" in this section.

GEM enables custom code placement to accommodate systems with varied memory shapes. Figure 5 presents examples of valid (flash, SRAM) divisions supported by GEM for each platform. Note that flash has a lower bound of ap-

Table 3. Intra-Platform Migration, Sizes (KB)

	Migration			Size Before			Size After			% Change
Benchmark	Flash Cap Before	Flash Cap After	De-duplicated?	SRAM	Flash	Total	SRAM	Flash	Total	Total
Stellaris_ahd	∞	80.0	No	34.2	109.4	143.7	64.1	80.0	144.1	0.3%
Stellaris_ahd	∞	80.0	Yes	34.2	109.4	143.7	61.2	80.0	141.2	-1.7%
Stellaris_ahd	80.0	∞	No	60.5	80.0	140.5	60.8	109.4	170.2	21.2%
Stellaris_ahd	80.0	∞	Yes	60.5	80.0	140.5	30.7	109.4	140.1	-0.3%

Figure 5. Valid (Flash, SRAM) Configurations

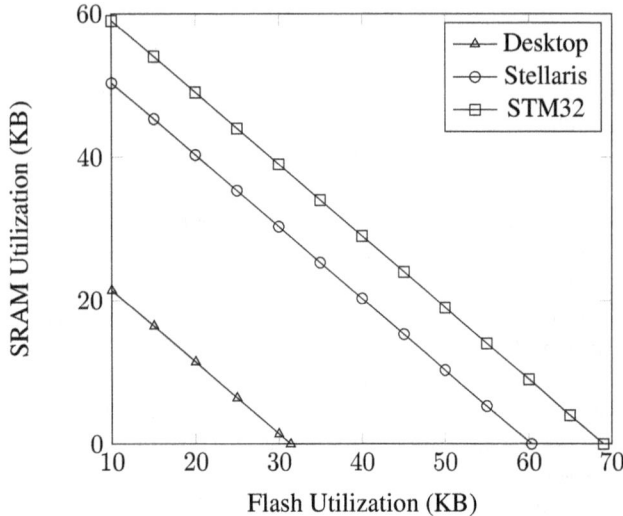

proximately 10 KB, as a small set of modules needed to boot the virtual machine must reside in flash.

GEM's heterogeneous compilation process de-duplicates not only within flash, but across SRAM and flash. Therefore, the total amount of space consumed by a given platform's library code is constant regardless of the flash/SRAM breakdown; there is no net disadvantage to moving code to SRAM. Further, collecting the data in Figure 5 revealed that the greedy algorithm described in Section 4.3 successfully partitions the objects without wasting memory. Out of 30 datapoints, flash was always filled to within 4 B of capacity, and was filled exactly to capacity 83.3% of the time.

5.4 Transparent Migration

GEM facilitates migration across different memory architectures and across different platforms. Such heterogeneity complicates migration; since the contents of flash may be different at the source and destination, blindly migrating the SRAM may result in missing or duplicated objects. As described in Section 4.4, GEM handles missing objects by allocating these objects within the SRAM component of the graph prior to overwriting the heap. Redundancies can in turn be eliminated by de-duplicating just before memsetting.

Table 3 shows the results of migration across the same platform (Stellaris), but between different memory architectures. It presents the memory distribution of the artificial

horizon display application before and after migration between a system with sufficient space to fit all of the code in flash memory (flash cap of ∞) and a system with only 80 KB of flash. Further, it shows the resultant memory layout with and without de-duplication. Note that for these experiments the library modules were previously de-duplicated during compilation; all savings due to de-duplication during migration result from consolidating runtime structures.

Even without de-duplication, migration from a system with more flash to one with less introduced virtually no overhead (0.3%). Objects in the source flash that were absent from the destination flash were simply placed in the destination SRAM; thus, while the memory breakdown at the destination is different, the total consumption is roughly the same. The negligible overhead comes from a small amount of build-specific information. Performing de-duplication during migration re-gained 2.9 KB, more than compensating for this overhead.

In contrast, migration from a system with less flash to one with more flash resulted in a 21.2% overhead without de-duplication. This is because the complete contents of the source heap were placed at the destination, with no regard for the fact that much of what was relegated to SRAM on the source already resided in flash at the destination. This was easily solved with de-duplication, which eliminated the extraneous modules as well as some redundant runtime structures, reclaiming over 30 KB for a net gain upon migration.

Migration of the artificial horizon display application between the Stellaris and STM32 platforms highlights GEM's cross-platform capabilities. Chosen for its realistic workload, this application requires hardware peripherals at the source and destination. However, the peripherals at the source and destination need not be identical, so long as they are both compatible with the application. For these experiments the same model of LCD display was used for both Stellaris and STM32, but the Stellaris board was connected to an external accelerometer whereas the STM32 board utilized its on-board accelerometer. Table 4 presents the results of this migration with and without de-duplication. Without de-duplication, migration added an overhead of approximately 1–2%; however, de-duplication once again regained all of the overhead and then some.

Table 4. Inter-Platform Migration, Sizes (KB)

Migration		Size Before			Size After			% Change
Benchmark → Platform	De-duplicated?	SRAM	Flash	Total	SRAM	Flash	Total	Total
Stellaris_ahd → STM32	No	34.4	128.2	162.5	37.2	128.5	165.7	2.0%
Stellaris_ahd → STM32	Yes	34.4	128.2	162.5	33.0	128.5	161.5	-0.6%
STM32_ahd → Stellaris	No	34.3	128.5	162.8	37.4	128.2	165.5	1.7%
STM32_ahd → Stellaris	Yes	34.3	128.5	162.8	33.2	128.2	161.4	-0.8%

6. Related Work

Considerable past work has used memory graphs for program visualization [8, 16, 26, 30, 32, 43]. However, GEM's visualizer diverges from past work by catering to a different domain and audience.

First, existing tools were designed to profile applications running on systems with extensive resources. Such applications may have over a million live objects on the heap [10]. Thus, many existing tools abstract away details to make the graph manageable. Some do not include nodes for primitive types [8, 26]; others collapse individual objects of the same type into a single node [32]. In contrast, GEM targets resource-constrained embedded systems, which have far fewer live objects. With a minimum object size of 12 B, Owl's default 80 KB heap fits only a few thousand objects. This makes it tractable for GEM to provide a finer level of detail by including a node for each object on the heap. Yet, GEM still provides aggregated views of compound objects.

Second, the primary audience of existing tools is the application developer. While GEM also benefits the application developer, it primarily targets the system developer. Many design choices made by existing tools are not optimal for GEM's target audience. For instance, one tool constructs a graph using logging data that is unavailable at boot-time [30]. This is suitable for application profiling, but insufficient for system profiling, as it excludes objects created during start-up that persist unmodified. Another extracts the heap by querying GDB from the roots, thereby excluding garbage and unused code [43]. GEM includes both, as they highlight opportunities for system-level improvements.

Those tools that do capture a full snapshot of the heap perform the aforementioned abstractions. Sacrificing detail for simplicity is a reasonable choice when presenting a million-object heap to a programmer who has no interest in system-level details. However, this conceals information that, when displayed by GEM, inspired improvements such as the de-duplicated code object format. Further, since the programmer has no control over the layout of the code, existing tools uniformly focus on the runtime data and only snapshot the heap [8, 16, 26, 30, 32, 43]. GEM captures a snapshot of both the data on the heap and the code in flash.

Additionally, GEM provides a mechanism by which the user can obtain a snapshot at any point in execution, without advance warning. Several existing tools provide similar flexibility, but at the cost of slowing execution by continuously logging [16, 30], or excluding unreachable objects [43]. Other tools sacrifice flexibility to avoid such pitfalls, and instead either automatically select points to snapshot based on memory utilization [26], or require that the application developer specify where to snapshot in advance [8].

Though GEM's memory visualizer differs significantly from prior visualization tools, the primary novelty of GEM lies in its use of memory graphs to not only inspect memory but transform it. GEM uniquely structures memory mutations as graph transformation passes, and uses these transformation to impact system memory. While GEM's versatile framework for applying these transformations is unique, several individual transformation passes leverage past work.

In particular, GEM's techniques for compaction and reference shifting based on an address mapping closely resemble mark-compact garbage collection, which slides in-use objects towards one end of the heap by maintaining a "break table" which it uses to update references [11, 14, 27, 37]. Likewise, GEM's reference shifting based on an offset builds on existing techniques for portable migration. One such technique first converts all references to offsets relative to the beginning of the checkpoint, and then converts them back to absolute addresses once the checkpoint has been migrated [31]. GEM achieves the same result without this intermediate step, shifting references by the difference between the base addresses of the source and target heaps.

Similarly, the three transformative use cases built upon GEM adapt past work to the domain of embedded systems. Operating systems and storage systems commonly employ de-duplication at runtime [21, 24, 25, 35]. They eliminate duplicates at either the file level or the block level, since large-scale duplication results from storing multiple versions of the same file. Programs exhibit different patterns of duplication from storage systems. Large blocks are not redundant; duplication occurs at the granularity of individual objects. Instead, GEM's de-duplication is similar to runtime interning, which is supported by runtime systems such as the Oracle JVM and CPython [3, 19, 23]. However, runtime interning misses opportunities to consolidate objects within the code. GEM uniquely performs de-duplication at compile-time, eliminating the longest-lasting redundancies.

Likewise, snapshots and migration are well-studied. Within the domain of embedded systems, existing snapshot techniques were primarily designed for rollback and recovery, and feature design decisions which run contrary to GEM's dual goals of preserving memory and enabling migration. They either suffer from large memory overheads by storing a complete copy of the memory space on the device [15], or achieve space efficiency by generating partial snapshots [36, 41] which are insufficient for migration.

Alternative migration techniques have been developed for mobile agents which operate only at the moment of migration, as opposed to checkpointing continuously during execution [17, 20, 34]. These techniques instrument the source code, inflating code size. GEM's migration requires no changes to the application code, and only the addition of a single bytecode to the runtime system. Additionally, these techniques for mobile agents migrate one thread at a time, whereas GEM migrates the entire runtime state, including all threads and scheduling information.

Other work has similarly expanded the unit of migration, to an entire virtual machine [13, 40] or operating system [18]. Further, shadow drivers have been used to transparently migrate between platforms with equivalent, but not identical, hardware devices [22]. However, the midrange microcontrollers which GEM targets lack sufficient resources for this extra layer of abstraction. To enable migration between devices with different images in flash, GEM instead performs a series of off-line transformations, requiring no additional resources at runtime and capitalizing on the ease of manipulating a graph representation.

The final use case presented in this paper, compilation for heterogeneous memory architectures, accepts upper bounds on SRAM and flash that can be allocated to the Python library code. Other compilers for embedded systems similarly accept code-size parameters [29]. Rather than using this information to divide the code between different memory regions, as GEM does, they instead carefully craft code that will fit within a single memory space.

No other tool simultaneously supports all four use cases of GEM. At best, efforts have been made to combine two: prior work integrated de-duplication into migration to minimize latency [12, 33, 42]. Designed to hasten migration, the impact that these techniques have on memory is fundamentally different from that of GEM. One requires round-trip migration in order to see any space savings [42]; the others de-duplicate during a single migration, but at a page granularity rather than GEM's object granularity [12, 33].

7. Conclusions

Memory analysis and optimization in embedded systems is complicated by resource constraints and heterogeneity. By imposing structure on memory, managed runtime systems enable the development of tools to automate and simplify these tasks. This paper has presented one such tool, GEM, which leverages structured memory to refashion memory as a graph, facilitating its transformation. Designed for generality and synergy, GEM's flexible framework substantially eases the burden of memory optimization by allowing the same underlying graph transformation passes to be combined to implement a multitude of capabilities.

Four such capabilities have been implemented and evaluated in this paper: visualization, de-duplication, heterogeneous compilation, and transparent migration. Though the primary contribution of GEM is its versatile infrastructure and novel low-level transformations, the sample use cases built upon it exemplify the value that it brings to real challenges of managing embedded memory. GEM's interactive visualizer has facilitated the identification of system-level inefficiencies; its de-duplication has reclaimed up to 24% of the space consumed by the Python library code; its heterogeneous compilation has broadened the range of memory architectures within which the virtual machine can fit; and its transparent migration has enabled the migration of a running program, even amidst hardware and software incongruities between the source and destination.

GEM was implemented for an existing embedded runtime system, Owl. However, the concept of modeling memory as a graph, as well as the transformations that memory graphs facilitate, transcend any specific system. Thus, GEM was designed to be portable. In particular, the parser and unparser which translate between the system-specific object model and GEM's much more generic graph representation are auto-generated. With only minor changes to the parser generator, GEM could be ported to other managed runtime systems with well-defined type systems and memory organization.

8. Acknowledgements

This material is based upon work supported by the National Science Foundation Graduate Research Fellowship under Grant No. 1450681.

References

[1] Linux graphical disk usage analyser. https://wiki.gnome.org/Apps/Baobab.

[2] elua. http://www.eluaproject.net/.

[3] Java language and virtual machine specifications. http://docs.oracle.com/javase/specs/.

[4] owl. http://www.embeddedpython.org/.

[5] p14p. http://code.google.com/p/python-on-a-chip/.

[6] pycparser. http://pypi.python.org/pypi/pycparser/.

[7] Micro python. http://micropython.org/.

[8] E. E. Aftandilian, S. Kelley, C. Gramazio, N. Ricci, S. L. Su, and S. Z. Guyer. Heapviz: Interactive heap visualization for program understanding and debugging. In *ACM Symposium on Software Visualization*, 2010.

[9] T. W. Barr, R. Smith, and S. Rixner. Design and implementation of an embedded python run-time system. In *USENIX Annual Technical Conference*, 2012.

[10] S. M. Blackburn, R. Garner, C. Hoffmann, A. M. Khan, K. S. McKinley, R. Bentzur, A. Diwan, D. Feinberg, D. Frampton, S. Z. Guyer, M. Hirzel, A. Hosking, M. Jump, H. Lee,

J. E. B. Moss, A. Phansalkar, D. Stefanovic, T. VanDrunen, D. von Dincklage, and B. Weidermann. The dacapo benchmarks: Java benchmarking development and analysis. In *ACM Conference on Object-Oriented Programming Systems, Languages, and Applications*, 2006.

[11] C. J. Cheney. A non-recursive list compacting algorithm. In *Communications of the ACM*, volume 13, 1970.

[12] J.-H. Chiang, H.-L. Li, and T. cker Chiueh. Introspection-based memory de-duplication and migration. In *ACM SIGPLAN/SIGOPS International Conference on Virtual Execution Environments*, 2013.

[13] C. Clark, K. Fraser, S. Hand, J. G. Hansen, E. Jul, C. Limpach, I. Pratt, and A. Warfield. Live migration of virtual machines. In *Symposium on Networked Systems Design and Implementation*, 2005.

[14] J. Cohen and A. Nicolau. Comparison of compacting algorithms for garbage collection. In *ACM Transactions on Programming Languages and Systems*, volume 5, 1983.

[15] A. Cunei and J. Vitek. A new approach to real-time checkpointing. In *ACM SIGPLAN/SIGOPS International Conference on Virtual Execution Environments*, 2006.

[16] A. Erkan, T. VanSlyke, and T. M. Scaffadi. Data structure visualization with latex and prefuse. In *SIGCSE Conference on Innovation and Technology in Computer Science Education*, 2007.

[17] S. Fünfrocken. Transparent migration of java-based mobile agents. In *Personal Technologies*, volume 2, 1998.

[18] J. G. Hansen and E. Jul. Self-migration of operating systems. In *Workshop on ACM SIGOPS European Workshop*, 2004.

[19] M. Horie, K. Ogata, K. Kawachiya, and T. Onodera. String deduplication for java-based middleware in virtualized environments. In *ACM SIGPLAN/SIGOPS International Conference on Virutal Execution Environments*, 2014.

[20] T. Illman, T. K. F. Kargl, and M. Weber. Transparent migration of mobile agents using the java platform debugger architecture. In *Mobile Agents*, 2001.

[21] K. Jin and E. L. Miller. The effectiveness of deduplication on virtual machine disk images. In *Israeli Experimental Systems Conference*, 2009.

[22] A. Kadav and M. M. Swift. Live migration of direct-access devices. In *The First Workshop of I/O Virtualization*, 2008.

[23] K. Kawachiya, K. Ogata, and T. Onodera. Analysis and reduction of memory inefficiencies in java strings. In *ACM Conference on Object-Oriented Programming Systems, Languages, and Applications*, 2008.

[24] H. S. Koppula, K. P. Leela, and A. Agarwal. Learning url patterns for webage de-duplication. In *ACM International Conference on Web Search and Data Mining*, 2010.

[25] P. Kulkarni, F. Douglis, J. LaVoie, and J. M. Tracey. Redundancy elimination within large collections of files. In *USENIX Annual Technical Conference*, 2004.

[26] M. Marron, C. Sanchez, Z. Su, and M. Fahndrich. Abstracting runtime heaps for program understanding. In *IEEE Transactions on Software Engineering*, volume 39, 2013.

[27] P. McGachey and A. L. Hosking. Reducing generational copy reserve overhead with fallback compaction. In *International Symposium on Memory Management*, 2006.

[28] M. F. Mergen, V. Uhlig, O. Krieger, and J. Xenidis. Virtualization for high-performance computing. In *ACM SIGOPS Operating Systems Review*, volume 40, 2006.

[29] M. Naik and J. Palsberg. Compiling with code-size constraints. In *ACM SIGPLAN Conference on Languages, Compilers, and Tools for Embedded Systems*, 2002.

[30] S. Pheng and C. Verbrugge. Dynamic data structure analysis for java programs. In *IEEE International Conference on Program Comprehension*, 2006.

[31] B. Ramkumar and V. Strumpen. Portable checkpointing for heterogeneous architectures. In *International Symposium on Fault-Tolerant Computing*, 1997.

[32] S. P. Reiss. Visualizing the heap to detect memory problems. In *Visualizing Software for Understanding and Analysis*, 2009.

[33] C. P. Sapuntzakis, R. Chandra, B. Pfaff, and J. Chow. Optimizing the migration of virtual computers. In *USENIX Symposium on Operating Systems Design and Implementation*, 2002.

[34] T. Sekiguchi, H. Masuhara, and A. Yonezawa. A simple extension of java language for controllable transparent migration and its portable implementation. In *Coordination Languages and Models*, 1999.

[35] P. Sharma and P. Kulkarni. Singleton: System-wide page deduplication in virtual environments. In *International Symposium on High-Performance Parallel and Distributed Computing*, 2012.

[36] R. Smith and S. Rixner. Surviving peripheral failures in embedded systems. In *USENIX Annual Technical Conference*, 2015.

[37] S. Stanchina and M. Meyer. Mark-sweep or copying? a 'best of both worlds' algorithm and a hardware-supported real-time implementation. In *International Symposium on Memory Management*, 2007.

[38] *STM32F20xx / STM32F207xx*. STMicroelectronics, 2013.

[39] *STM32F373xx*. STMicroelectronics, 2014.

[40] T. Suezawa. Persistent execution state of a java virtual machine. In *ACM Conference on Java Grande*, 2000.

[41] H. Tabkhi, S. G. Miremadi, and A. Ejlali. An asymmetric checkpointing and rollback error recovery scheme for embedded processors. In *IEEE International Symposium on Defect and Fault Tolerance of VLSI Systems*, 2008.

[42] K. Takahashi, K. Sasada, and T. Hirofuchi. A fast virtual machine storage migration technique using data deduplication. In *International Conference on Cloud Computing, GRIDs, and Virtualization*, 2012.

[43] T. Zimmerman and A. Zeller. Visualizing memory graphs. In *Lecture Notes in Computer Science – Software Visualization*, 2002.

The nom Profit-Maximizing Operating System

Muli Ben-Yehuda

LightBits Labs
mulix@mulix.org

Orna Agmon Ben-Yehuda

Technion
ladypine@cs.technion.ac.il

Dan Tsafrir

Technion
dan@cs.technion.ac.il

Abstract

In the near future, cloud providers will sell their users virtual machines with CPU, memory, network, and storage resources whose prices constantly change according to market-driven supply and demand conditions. Running traditional operating systems in these virtual machines is a poor fit: traditional operating systems are not aware of changing resource prices and their sole aim is to maximize performance with no consideration of costs. Consequently, they yield low profits.

We present nom, a profit-maximizing operating system designed for cloud computing platforms with dynamic resource prices. Applications running on nom aim to maximize profits by optimizing simultaneously for performance and resource costs. The nom kernel provides them with direct access to the underlying hardware and full control over their private software stacks. Since nom applications know there is no single "best" software stack, they adapt their stacks' behavior on the fly according to the current price of available resources and their private utility from them, which differs between applications. We show that in addition to achieving up to 3.9x better throughput and up to 9.1x better latency, nom applications yield up to 11.1x higher profits when compared with the same applications running on Linux and OSv.

"And in this too profit begets profit." (Aeschylus)

1. Introduction

More and more of the world's computing workloads run in virtual machines on Infrastructure-as-a-Service (IaaS) clouds. Often these workloads are network-intensive applications, such as web servers or key-value stores, that serve their own third-party users. Each application owner charges the application's users for the service the application provides, thereby generating revenue. The application owner

also pays her cloud provider for the resources used by the virtual machine in which the application runs, thereby incurring expenses. The difference between the application owner's revenue and her expenses—and the focus of this work—is the application owner's profit, which she would naturally like to maximize. We depict this cloud economic model in Fig. 1.

The application owner's revenue depends on her application's performance. For example, the more simultaneous users the application can serve, the higher the revenue it generates. The application owner's expenses, on the other hand, depend on how much she pays the cloud provider. Today's IaaS cloud providers usually charge application owners a fixed sum per virtual machine that does not depend on market conditions. In previous work, we showed that the economic trends and market forces acting on today's IaaS clouds will cause them to evolve into Resource-as-a-Service (RaaS) clouds, where CPU, memory, network, and storage resources have constantly changing market-driven prices [7, 9, 10]. In RaaS clouds, the cloud providers will charge the application owners the current dynamic market prices of the resources they use.

IaaS clouds, and to a larger extent, RaaS clouds, represent a fundamentally new way of buying, selling, and using computing resources. Nevertheless, nearly all virtual machines running in today's clouds run the same legacy operating systems that previously ran on bare-metal servers. These op-

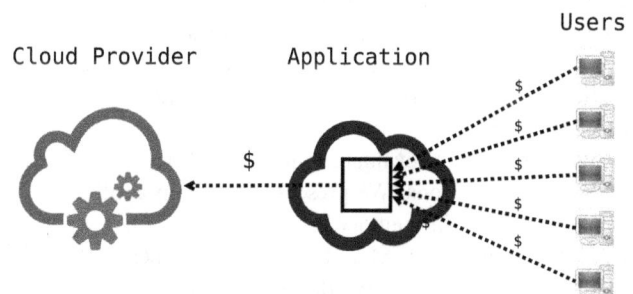

Figure 1: Cloud economic model: Applications run in the cloud. Users pay the application owner for the service the application provides. The application owner in turn pays the cloud provider for the cloud resources the application uses (e.g., network bandwidth).

erating systems were designed for the hardware available decades ago. They abstract away the underlying hardware from their applications and assume that every resource is at their disposal at no cost. Most importantly, they were designed solely for maximizing performance with no regard for costs. They neither know nor care that the resources they use in the cloud cost money, and that their prices might change, e.g., due to changes in supply and demand.

We argue that in clouds with dynamic pricing, where costs can be substantial and resource prices constantly change, running operating systems designed solely for maximal performance is counterproductive and may lead to lower profits and even net losses. Such clouds call instead for a *profit-maximizing* operating system, designed to yield maximal profit by optimizing for both performance and cost, by changing the amount of used resources and the way they are used. Maximal profit is reached not when revenue (performance) is highest but rather when the difference between revenue (performance) and expenses (cost) is highest. As such, profit-maximizing operating systems enable their applications to pick the right level of performance to operate at given current market conditions and resource prices. We show that applications running on a profit-maximizing operating system can yield an order of magnitude higher profit when compared with the same applications running on operating systems that optimize for performance exclusively.

We begin by presenting in greater depth the motivation for a profit-maximizing operating system. In Section 2, we present two ongoing trends that we believe will cause today's IaaS clouds to evolve into RaaS clouds with dynamic resource pricing. They are the increasingly finer spatial granularity and the increasingly finer temporal granularity of resources that can be allocated to guest virtual machines. We then present the changes that such clouds mandate in the system software stack.

In Section 3, we present nom, a profit-maximizing operating system we designed for clouds with dynamic pricing. Applications running on nom aim to maximize their profits from the resources available to them. We describe how nom's cost-aware design contributes to its flexibility, which allows each application to maximize its profit regardless of other applications' choices. Since applications know best about their SLA and valuation of the resources and configuration, nom applications are not forced to stick with good-for-all-but-optimal-for-none choices.

We showcase and evaluate nom's capabilities using network-intensive applications. We present three main applications, the memcached in-memory key-value store [26], the nhttpd web server, and the NetPIPE networking benchmark [66]. The performance of a network-intensive application is usually expressed through its throughput, latency, and jitter. The expenses the application incurs depend on the amount of bandwidth it uses (i.e., its throughput) and the current price of network bandwidth. Since the price of bandwidth is beyond the application's control, the application can only maximize its profits by controlling its throughput, which affects both revenue and expenses, and the latency and jitter its users experience, which affect its revenue.

In Section 4, we use utility functions to formalize the relationship between application throughput, latency, jitter, and the cost of network bandwidth. An application's utility function provides the application's expected profit from a certain mix of throughput, latency, and jitter, given the current price of network bandwidth and the load the application is under. For example, the simplified utility function below is a formalization of the scenario where the application owner benefits from increased throughput (T, measured for example in in Gigabits per second (Gbps)), but only as long as the application's users' average latency is below a certain latency service level objective (SLO) and the price the application owner pays her cloud provider per bandwidth unit (P, in $\frac{\$}{\text{Gbps}}$) is lower than her benefit from that bandwidth unit (α, also in $\frac{\$}{\text{Gbps}}$).

$$\text{profit} = \begin{cases} T \cdot (\alpha - P) & \text{latency} \leq \text{latency SLO} \\ 0 & \text{latency} > \text{latency SLO} \end{cases} \quad (1)$$

We consider three potential utility functions that differ in how the application's users pay for the service the application provides to them. We acknowledge that building utility functions is hard, but we believe it is worthwhile to do so in light of the substantially higher profits it yields.

Our profit-maximizing applications re-evaluate their utility functions at runtime whenever the price of bandwidth or the load they are under change, picking each time the mix of throughput, latency, and jitter that maximizes their utility function at that point in time. To enable each nom application to have fine-grained control over its throughput, latency, and jitter, nom provides each application with direct access to the virtual or physical NICs the application uses and with a private TCP/IP stack and network device drivers, linked into the application's address space. Each application can control its private stack's throughput, latency, and jitter, by modifying the stack's batching delay: the amount of time the stack delays incoming or outgoing packets in order to batch them together. Larger batching delays increase throughput (up to a limit) while also increasing latency and jitter. Smaller batching delays reduce latency and jitter but also reduce throughput. In nom, there is no "best" TCP/IP stack or "best" NIC device driver as in other operating systems, because there is no single stack or driver that will always provide the right mix of throughput, latency, and jitter, to every application at any given time.

We discuss the implementation of our nom prototype in Section 5 and evaluate it in Section 6. We show that nom's memcached, nhttpd, and NetPIPE outearn as well as outperform the same applications running on Linux and on the OSv cloud operating system [43]. When running on nom, our benchmark applications yield up to 11.1x higher profits from their resources while also achieving up to 3.9x better throughput and up to 9.1x better latency.

In Section 7 we discuss the pros and cons of writing a new profit-maximizing operating system from scratch vs. constructing it based on an existing operating system such as Linux. We survey related work in Section 8 and summarize the lessons we have learned building nom and the challenges that remain in Section 9.

2. Motivation

2.1 Dynamic resource pricing is coming

We have identified in previous work [7, 9] two important trends that we believe will lead to RaaS clouds, where different resources have constantly changing prices. These trends are already apparent in current IaaS clouds and their underlying hardware. They are the increasingly finer *spatial* granularity of resources that can be allocated to guest virtual machines and the increasingly finer *temporal* granularity in which resources can be allocated.

Both trends can be seen all the way down to the hardware. Intel Resource Director Technology, for example, enables cloud providers to monitor each virtual machine's CPU cache utilization and allocate specific cache ways to selected virtual machines [3]. Mellanox Connect-X2 and later NICs enable cloud providers to allocate adapter network bandwidth to up to 16 virtual machines and adapt the allocation in microsecond granularity.

Although most IaaS cloud providers today do not (yet) take advantage of such capabilities, they already provide limited dynamic pricing and are moving towards fully dynamic resource pricing. VMTurbo, for example, manufactures a private-cloud management layer that relies on resource pricing and an economic engine to control ongoing resource consumption. CloudSigma's pricing algorithm allows pay-as-you-go burst pricing that changes over time depending on how busy their cloud is; this algorithm prices CPU, RAM, and outgoing network bandwidth separately. Perhaps most notably, Amazon's EC2 spot instances have a dynamic market-driven price [6] that changes every few minutes.

Why are cloud providers going in this direction? Is it not simpler for everyone to just keep the price fixed? By frequently changing the price of different resources based on available supply and demand, cloud providers can communicate resource pressure to their clients (the applications/application owners) and influence their demand for these resources. By conveying resource pressure to clients, cloud providers incentivize their clients to economize when needed and consume less of the high-demand resources. By causing clients to economize, the cloud provider can improve machine density and run more client virtual machines on the same hardware and with the same power budget. Higher machine density means lower expenses, increased

profits, and better competitiveness. Improving profit margins by doing more work with the same hardware is especially important given the cloud price wars that have been ongoing since 2012 [9].

2.2 Dynamic pricing mandates change

A cloud with market-driven per-resource pricing differs from the traditional bare-metal platform in several important areas: resource ownership, economic model, and architectural support. These differences motivate changing the system software stack, and in particular, the operating systems and applications.

Resource ownership and control. On a traditional bare-metal server, the operating system is the sole owner of every resource. If the operating system does not use a resource, nobody else will. In a dynamic pricing cloud, the operating system (running in a virtual machine) unwittingly shares a physical server with other operating systems running in other virtual machines; it neither owns nor controls physical resources.

Economic model. In the cloud, each operating system owner (cloud user) and cloud provider constitute a separate, selfish economic entity. Every resource that the cloud provider makes available to users has an associated price. Each user may have a different incentive, different metrics she may want to optimize, and different valuations for available resources. The cloud provider may want to price its resources to maximize the provider's revenue or the users' aggregate satisfaction (social welfare) [10]; one cloud user may want to pay as little as possible for a given amount of work carried out by its virtual machines; another cloud user may want to maximize the work carried out, sparing no expense. But in all cases, in the cloud, the user pays the current going rate for the resources her operating system uses. On a traditional server, resources are there to be used at no cost.

Resource granularity. On a traditional server, the operating system manages entire resources: all cores, all of RAM, all available devices. In the cloud, the operating system will manage resources in an increasingly finer-grained granularity. This is a consequence of the economic model: once resources have prices attached to them, it is more efficient for both cloud provider and cloud users to be able to buy, sell, or rent resources on increasingly finer scales [7].

Architectural support. Operating systems running on traditional servers usually strive to support both the ancient and the modern. Linux, for example, only recently dropped support for the original Intel 386. Modern x86 cloud servers have extensive support for machine virtualization at the CPU, MMU, chipset, and I/O device level [67]. Modern I/O devices are natively sharable [58]. Furthermore, cloud servers usually present the operating systems running in virtual machines with a small subset of *virtual* devices. We contend that any new operating system designed for the cloud should eschew legacy support and take full advantage of the virtual and physical hardware available on modern servers.

In particular, the hypervisor can rely on hardware virtualization [67] and natively sharable I/O devices [58] for security, and give the guest operating system direct device assignment (in contrast with older exokernels, which had to protect their guests from one another).

3. nom Operating System Design

3.1 Requirements

Given the fundamental differences between the traditional bare-metal and the cloud run time platforms, we now ask: What requirements should be imposed on an operating system designed for running in virtual machines on cloud servers with dynamic pricing?

Maximize profit. The first requirement is to enable applications to maximize their profit. When resources are free, applications only have an incentive to optimize for performance. Performance is usually measured in some application specific metric, e.g., in cache hits per second for an in-memory cache or in transactions per second for a database. In the cloud, where any work carried out requires paying for resources and every resource has a price that changes over time, applications would still like to optimize for performance but now they are also incentivized to optimize for cost. Why pay the cloud provider more when you could pay less for the same performance? Thus the operating system should enable its applications to maximize their profits by enabling them to optimize for both performance and cost.

Expose resources. On a traditional server, the operating system's kernel serves multiple roles: it abstracts and multiplexes the underlying hardware, it serves as a library of useful functionality (e.g., file systems, network stacks), and it isolates applications from one another while letting them share resources. This comes at a price: applications must access their resources through the kernel, incurring run-time overhead; the kernel manages their resources in a one-size-fits-all manner; and the functionality the kernel provides, "good enough" for many applications, is far from optimal for any specific application.

In clouds with dynamic pricing, the kernel should get out of the way and let applications manage their resources directly. Moving the kernel out of the way has several important advantages: first, applications become elastic. They can decide when and how much of each resource to use depending on its current price, thereby trading off cost with performance, or trading off the use of a momentarily expensive resource with a momentarily cheap one. For example, when memory is expensive, one application might use less memory but more bandwidth while another might use less memory but more CPU cycles. Second, applications know best how to use the resources they have [24, 28, 35]. The kernel, which has to serve all applications equally, cannot be designed and optimized for any one application. Exposing physical resources directly to applications means that nearly all of the functionality of traditional kernels can be moved to

application level and tailored to each application's specific needs.

Isolate applications. When running in a virtual machine on a modern server, the operating system's kernel can rely on the underlying hardware and on the hypervisor for many aspects of safe sharing and isolation for which it was previously responsible. For example, using an IOMMU [36], the kernel can give each application direct and secure access to its own I/O device "instances" instead of multiplexing in software a few I/O devices between many applications. Those instances may be SRIOV Virtual Functions (VFs) [29, 58] or they may be paravirtual I/O devices [15, 30, 33, 62].

3.2 Principles

The primary distinguishing feature of nom is that it enables applications to maximize their profits by (1) optimizing their entire software stack's behavior for both performance and cost; and (2) changing their behavior on the fly according to the current price of resources. Traditional operating systems have a kernel that sits between applications and their I/O devices. The nom kernel, on the other hand, provides every application with safe direct access to its resources, including in particular its I/O devices. Recently proposed operating systems such as the cloud-targeted OSv [43] and Mirage [52, 53], or the bare-metal operating systems IX [18] and Arrakis [59], all of which can be considered to provide direct access of some sort, use it purely for performance. In nom, direct access enables each application to have its own private I/O stacks and private device drivers that are specialized for that application. In particular, IX's adaptive batching acts automatically for the whole operating system. It does not allow for individual optimization points, which are crucial for profit optimization.

The nom kernel itself is minimal. It performs three main functions: (1) it initializes the hardware and boots; (2) it enumerates available resources such as CPU cores, memory, network devices, and storage devices (and acts as a clearing house for available resources); and (3) it runs applications. Once an application is launched, it queries the kernel for available resources, acquires those resources, and from then on uses them directly with minimal kernel involvement.

3.3 CPU and scheduling

On startup, a nom application acquires one or more cores from the kernel. From then on until it relinquishes the core or cores, the application performs its own scheduling using user threads. The rationale behind user threading is that only the application knows what task will be profitable to run at any given moment on its CPU cores. Applications relinquish cores when they decide to do so, e.g., because CPU cycles have grown too expensive, in comparison with the benefit that the application draws from the core. This can happen because of resource pressure (CPU cycles become expensive because there is a shortage) or because the application's utility from CPU cycles momentarily dropped, for example because the application is waiting for I/O. Note that the application only hires a certain CPU cycle rate, it is still the responsibility of the nom scheduler to preempt applications if there are more applications than virtual CPUs.

The nom design minimizes the kernel's involvement in application data paths. Applications can make system calls for control-plane setup/teardown operations, e.g., to acquire and release resources, but high performance nom applications are unlikely to make any system calls in their data paths, since their software stacks and device drivers run entirely in user space.

3.4 Memory management

Each nom application runs in its own kernel-provided address space, unlike unikernel operating systems such as OSv [43] and Mirage [52, 53], where there is a single global address space. Each nom application manages its own page mappings, unlike applications in traditional operating systems. The kernel handles an application's page fault by calling the application's page fault handler from the kernel trampoline and passing it the fault for handling. The application would typically handle page faults by asking the kernel to allocate physical memory and map pages on its behalf. This userspace-centric page fault approach provides applications with full control over their page mappings, cache coloring [41], and the amount of memory they use at any given time. There is no kernel-based paging; applications that desire paging-like functionality implement it on their own [32]. The kernel itself is not pageable but its memory footprint is negligible.

3.5 I/O devices

The nom kernel enumerates all available physical devices on start-up and handles device hot-plug and hot-unplug. The kernel publishes resources such as I/O devices to applications using the *bulletin board*, an in-memory representation of currently available resources that is mapped into each application's address space. The bulletin board was inspired by MOSIX's [14] distributed bulletin board [11]. When an application acquires a device resource, the kernel maps the device's memory-mapped I/O (MMIO) regions in the application's address space and enables the application to perform programmed I/O (PIO) to the device. The application then initializes the device and uses it.

Most modern devices, whether virtual devices such as virtio [62] and Xen's frontend and backend devices [15], or natively-sharable SRIOV devices [58], expect to read and write memory directly via direct memory access (DMA). Since nom's model is that applications bypass the kernel and program their devices directly, devices driven by nom applications should be able to access the memory pages of the applications driving them. At the same time, these devices should not be able to access the memory pages of other applications and of the kernel.

The way nom handles DMA-capable devices depends on whether the virtual machine has an IOMMU for intra-guest protection [71]. Providing virtual machines with IOMMUs for intra-guest protection requires either an emulated IOMMU [12] or a two-level IOMMU such as ARM's sMMU or Intel's VT-d2. When an IOMMU is available for the virtual machine's use, the nom kernel maps the application's memory in the IOMMU address space of that device and subsequently keeps the MMU's page tables and the IOMMU's page tables in sync.

As far as we know, no cloud provider today exposes an IOMMU to virtual machines. To enable nom applications to drive DMA capable devices until such IOMMUs are present, the nom kernel can also run applications in trusted mode. In this mode the kernel exposes guest-virtual to guest-physical mappings to applications and applications program their devices with these mappings. This means that in trusted mode, each nom instance should only contain applications that are trusted not to take over the virtual machine by programming a device to write to memory they do not own. Untrusted applications should be sandboxed in separate nom instances.

When a device owned by a nom application raises an interrupt, the kernel receives it and the kernel trampoline calls a userspace device handler registered by the application driving that device. It is the application's responsibility to handle device interrupts correctly: acknowledge the interrupt at the device and interrupt controller level and mask/unmask device interrupts as needed.

Polling may lead to better performance than interrupts but interrupts can reduce CPU utilization [22, 37, 46, 54, 64]. Since nom applications have full control over their software stacks and their devices, they decide when to wait for interrupts and when to poll devices directly, thereby trading off CPU cycles for performance.

3.6 Networking

The nom operating system provides a default userspace network stack, based on the lwIP network stack [23], and default network device drivers, including a driver for the virtio [62] virtnet network device. They are provided as a convenience and as a basis for modifications. Applications that wish to yield even higher profits are encouraged to run with their own customized network stack and network device drivers.

The default network stack and virtnet device driver already enable applications which use them to adapt their behavior on the fly, by tuning the *batching delay*. The batching delay controls the stack's and driver's behavior when sending and receiving packets. Applications can use the batching delay to trade-off throughput, latency, and jitter. Setting the batching delay to 0μsec means no delay: each incoming and outgoing packet is *run to completion*. Each packet the application transmits (tx packet) traverses the entire TCP/IP stack and the device driver and is sent on the wire immediately. Each packet the application receives (rx packet) is passed from the wire to the driver, to the stack, and to the application, before the next packet is handled.

Setting the batching delay to Wμsec means delaying packets by batching them together at various stages in the stack and in the driver such that no packet is delayed for more than Wμsec. Tx packets are batched together by the stack and then passed on to the driver as a batch. The driver batches all of the small batches of packets passed to it by the stack together into one large batch. When either the transmit ring buffer is close to overflowing or the first packet in the large batch has waited Wμsec, the driver transmits the large batch to the device.

The timing of arrival of rx packets is not controlled by the stack or driver but rather by the device. When $W > 0$, the driver receives incoming packets from the wire but does not pass them on to the stack for processing. The batch is kept at the driver level until at least one of the following happens: (1) Wμsec have passed; (2) the batch grows beyond a predefined maximum and threatens to overflow the receive ring buffer; or (3) there are no additional packets to receive, e.g., because the connection has been closed. The driver then passes all of the incoming packets together to the TCP/IP stack for processing.

Network-intensive applications usually optimize for throughput, latency, and jitter. Throughput is defined as the number of bytes they can send or receive in a given time period or the number of operations they can carry out. Latency is broadly defined as how long it takes to transfer or receive a single packet or carry out a single operation. Applications are usually concerned with either average latency or with tail latency, defined as the latency of the 99th percentile of packets or operations. Jitter has many possible definitions. For simplicity, we define jitter as the standard deviation of the latency distribution.

A larger batching delay, up to a limit, usually provides better (higher) throughput but worse (higher) latency and jitter. A smaller batching delay usually provides better (lower) latency and jitter but worse (lower) throughput. In Section 4 we discuss how applications can use utility functions to pick the right mix of throughput, latency, and jitter, given the current price of network bandwidth. After picking the optimal mix for current conditions, applications that use the default network stack and virtnet device driver can modify the stack's batching delay to achieve the desired throughput, latency, and jitter.

3.7 Price-awareness

Optimizing for cost requires that applications be aware of the current price of resources. The `priced` daemon queries the cloud provider via provider-specific means (e.g., the provider's REST API) for the current price of resources. It then publishes those prices to all applications through the bulletin board. To avoid the need for applications to continuously poll the bulletin board, yet enable them to react quickly to price changes, `priced` also notifies applications

of any change in the price of their resources, using a generic high-performance IPC mechanism that uses shared memory for bulk data transfer and cross-core IPIs for notifications.

4. Economic model and utility of bandwidth

To maximize profit, nom applications attempt to extract the maximal benefit from the network resources they have available to them. This requires that the application be able to formulate and quantify its benefit from network resources given their current prices. The standard game-theoretic tool for doing this is a utility function: a function that is private to each application and assigns numerical values—"utilities", or in our case, profit—to different outcomes.

We consider an application acting as a server, e.g., a web server or a key-value store. The application generates revenue when it gets paid by its users for the service it provides. We assume that the amount it gets paid is a function of its throughput, latency, and jitter. The application benefits from increased throughput because higher throughput means serving more users or providing them with more content. We assume that the amount the application gets paid increases linearly with its throughput.

The application benefits from reduced latency and jitter because it can provide its users with better quality of service. Better quality of service means improved user satisfaction. To quantify user satisfaction, we adopt an existing cloud provider compensation model. Cloud providers such as GoGrid [2], NTT [4], and Verizon [5] assume that their users are satisfied as long as their service level objectives (SLOs) are met; when the provider fails to meet a user's SLO, most providers will offer their users compensation in proportion to the users' payment for periods in which the service did not meet the SLO. For example, Gogrid's Service Level Agreement (SLA) reads as follows: "A '10,000% Service Credit' is a credit equivalent to one hundred times Customer's fees for the impacted Service feature for the duration of the Failure. (For example, where applicable: a Failure lasting seven hours would result in credit of seven hundred hours of free service [. . .])."

We assume that an SLA using equivalent terms exists between the application and its users. Although cloud providers list minimal throughput, maximal latency, and maximal jitter as their SLA goals, we simplify the function by only considering latency.

We assume that the cloud provider charges the application in proportion to the outbound bandwidth it consumes. Charging by used bandwidth is reasonable for several reasons. First, it is easy for the cloud provider to monitor. Second, bandwidth consumption by one application can directly affect the quality of service for other applications running on the same cloud when there is resource pressure (limited outgoing bandwidth). Third and most important, this method of charging is commonly used in today's clouds. Amazon, for example, charges for outbound traffic per GB after the first

GB, which is free. CloudSigma charges for outbound traffic after the first 5TB/month.

The application does not necessarily know why the price of bandwidth rises or falls. The cloud provider may set prices to shape traffic, as CloudSigma started doing in 2010, or the price may be set according to supply and demand, as Amazon does for its spot instances [6]. The price may even be set randomly, as Amazon used to do [6]. In Kelly's [40] terms, the application is a price taker: it assumes it cannot affect the prices. It neither knows nor cares how the provider sets them. This assumption is reasonable when the application's bandwidth consumption is relatively small compared with the cloud's overall network bandwidth. The application does know that it will pay for the bandwidth it uses according to its current price.

The utility functions that we use in this work formalize the application's profit from different mixes of throughput, latency, and jitter, given the current price of bandwidth. Any such function must satisfy the *utility function axiom*: it must weakly monotonically increase as throughput increases and weakly monotonically decrease as bandwidth cost, latency, and jitter increase. In other words, the more throughput the application achieves for the same total cost, latency, and jitter, the more it profits. As latency and jitter increase, the application gets paid less or compensates its users more, so profit goes down. The higher the price of bandwidth, the higher the application's costs, so again profit goes down.

Putting all of the above together, we present three example utility functions which are consistent with the utility function axiom. We begin with the **penalty** utility function, a generalization of the simple utility function presented in the introduction (Eq. (1)). In the simple utility function, the application owner benefits from increased throughput (T), but only as long as the application's users' average latency is below a certain latency service level objective (SLO) and the price the application owner pays her cloud provider (P) per bandwidth unit is lower than her benefit from that bandwidth unit (α.) In other words, in the simple utility function, users either pay or they don't. In the penalty utility function, the application pays its users a penalty (i.e, the users pay less) if samples of the latency distribution violate the SLO. The size of the penalty depends on the probability of violating the SLO. We define the penalty utility function in Eq. (2) as follows:

$$U_{\text{penalty}} = T \cdot (\alpha \cdot (1 - \min(1, X \cdot \mathcal{N}(L_0, L, \sigma))) - P), \quad (2)$$

where T denotes throughput in $\frac{\text{Gbit}}{\text{s}}$ or application operations/second, α denotes the application owner's valuation of useful bandwidth in \$/Gbit or \$/operation, and X denotes the penalty factor from not meeting the user's SLO (e.g., 100 in the GoGrid SLA). L denotes the mean latency (in μsecs), L_0 denotes the maximal latency allowed by the SLA, and σ denotes the latency's standard deviation (jitter). $\mathcal{N}(L_0, L, \sigma)$

denotes the probability that a normally distributed variable with mean L and standard deviation σ will be higher than L_0. In other words, it is the probability that a latency sample will not meet the latency SLO, and thus trigger compensation to the application's user. P denotes the price that the cloud provider charges the application for outgoing network bandwidth. The provider's price is set in \$/Gbit, but the application may translate it internally to \$/operation.

In the case where the sampled latency is always within the SLO and thus $\mathcal{N} \to 0$, Eq. (2) is reduced to $T \cdot (\alpha - P)$, motivating the application to use as much bandwidth as possible, provided the value it gets from sending data (α) is higher than the price it pays for sending that data (P). Conversely, when every latency sample falls outside the SLO, Eq. (2) is reduced to $-T \cdot P$, giving negative utility, since the penalties for violating the SLA far outweigh any benefit. It is better in this case to send nothing at all, to at least avoid paying for bandwidth.

In addition to the penalty utility function, we also consider two additional, simpler, function forms that fit the axioms and represent other business models. These functions are inspired by Lee and Snavely [47], who showed that user valuation functions for delay are usually monotonically decreasing, with various shapes, which are not necessarily linear. Hence, we consider both a linear *refund* utility function (which is common in the literature because it is easy to represent) and a reciprocal *bonus* utility function, which captures the diminishing marginal return, characteristic of some of the functions that Lee and Snavely found.

In the **refund** utility function in Eq. (3), the application compensates its user by giving it a progressively larger refund as the mean latency rises, capped at a refund of 100% of the user's payment. As in the penalty utility function, α denotes the application owner's valuation of useful bandwidth. The β parameter is the extent of the refund.

$$U_{\text{refund}} = T \cdot (\max(0, \alpha - \beta \cdot L) - P), \quad (3)$$

In the **bonus** utility function in Eq. (4), the application gets a bonus from its users for small latency values. The bonus decays to zero as latency grows and cannot exceed some pre-negotiated threshold, δ. γ is the extent of the bonus.

$$U_{\text{bonus}} = T \cdot (\alpha + \min(\frac{\gamma}{L}, \delta) - P), \quad (4)$$

The parameters α, β, γ, δ, and X, are application-specific: they characterize its business arrangements with its users. Price (P) is dictated by the cloud provider and changes over time.

We note that the application does not "choose" any function or parameters that it desires: the utility function is simply a formalization of the application owner's business relations and agreements with its users and with its cloud provider. These relations and agreements include how much the application owner pays its cloud provider for bandwidth, how much the application's users pay the application owner, how the application owner compensates its users for violating their SLAs, etc. Having said that, by understanding the behavior of the utility function, the application owner may try to strike more beneficial deals with its cloud providers and its users. Furthermore, the application can adapt its behavior on the fly, trading off throughput, latency, and jitter so as to maximize its profit given current bandwidth price.

5. Implementation

We implemented a prototype of nom, including both ring 0 kernel and representative ring 3 applications. The prototype runs in x86-64 SMP virtual machines with multiple vCPUs on top of the KVM [42] hypervisor. It can run multiple applications with direct access to their I/O devices. It can also run on bare-metal x86-64 servers with SRIOV devices, without an underlying hypervisor, but that is not its primary use-case.

We implemented three representative applications that use the penalty, refund, and bonus utility functions to adapt their behavior on the fly: memcached, a popular key-value storage [26], nhttpd, a web server, and NetPIPE [66], a network ping-pong benchmark. All three applications run with private copies of the default nom lwIP-based network stack and the virtnet virtio NIC device driver. All three applications optimize for both performance and cost by adapting their stack and driver's behavior on the fly to achieve the throughput, latency, and jitter that maximize their current utility function given the current price of network bandwidth.

We implemented nhttpd from scratch and ported Net-PIPE and memcached from Linux. The ports were relatively straightforward, since nom supports—but does not mandate—most of the relevant POSIX APIs, including pthreads (via userspace threading), sockets, and libevent. The main missing pieces for application porting are limited support for floating point (SSE) in userspace and missing support for signals.

The nom kernel is approximately 8,000 lines of code. The network stack and NIC device drivers are approximately 45,000 lines code. Both are implemented mostly in C, with a little assembly.

6. Evaluation

6.1 Methodology

The evaluation aims to answer the following questions: (1) Does optimizing for cost preclude optimizing for performance? (2) Does optimizing for both cost and performance improve application profit? and (3) Is being able to change behavior at runtime important for maximizing profits?

We evaluate nom applications against the same applications running on Linux and on OSv [43]. The applications run in virtual machines on an x86-64 host with four Intel Core(TM) i7-3517U CPUs running at 1.90GHz and 4GB of

memory. The host runs Linux Mint 17 "Qiana" with kernel 3.13.0-24 and the associated KVM and QEMU versions. The host does not expose an IOMMU to virtual machines.

OSv and nom applications run in an x86-64 guest virtual machine with a single vCPU and 128MBs of memory. Linux applications run in a virtual machine running Linux Mint 17.1 "Rebecca", which did not boot with 128MB, so we gave it a single vCPU and 256MB of memory.

We focus on data transfer prices, because they are the most dominant factor. According to CloudSigma's pricing[55], one CPU core/hour costs about twice as much as one GB/hour of RAM, and about half as much as one GB of outbound data transfer. In network intensive applications (the benchmarks we use consume hundreds of GBs/hour), this makes the cost of cores and memory negligible compared with the cost of bandwidth. In particular, we neglect Linux's need for twice the amount of memory (compared with OSv and nom) and the fact that nom and Linux consume excess CPU cycles in comparison with OSv. Another reason for our focus on optimizing profit from network is that applications are usually inherently elastic when network availability changes drastically. Furthermore, to use CloudSigma's data again, the variability in the bandwidth price is much higher than in the price of RAM or CPU.

Our experimental setup approximates a cloud with dynamic bandwidth prices and assumes that the cloud provider either does not charge or charges a fixed sum for all other resources. Each application runs for two minutes. During the first 60 seconds, the price of bandwidth is \$1/Gb. After 60 seconds, the price rises to \$10/Gb. This situation can occur, for example, when the application starts running on a relatively idle cloud but then a noisy, network-intensive application joins it, driving up the price. The price changes are inspired by price changes made by real cloud providers: CloudSigma's burst prices for bandwidth may be tripled during the day. Within 15 minutes they may be doubled [56]. Amazon EC2's prices for full servers have jumped by several orders of magnitude in the past, and they still jump by an order of magnitude [57].

We run memcached, nhttpd, and NetPIPE, on Linux, OSv, and nom, and evaluate all three applications with all three utility functions described in Section 4. The utility functions take into account price, throughput, and latency, and the penalty utility function also takes into account jitter. Applications running on Linux and OSv use the default Linux and OSv stacks and device drivers and are not price-aware.

Applications running on nom use the default lwIP and virtnet device driver. They know the throughput, latency, and jitter they expect to achieve for different settings of the batching delay. The relationship between batching delay and throughput, latency, and jitter may be generated online and refined as the application runs or generated offline [10, 35]. We generated it offline. The applications use this information and the current price of network bandwidth as input to their utility functions, tuning their stacks at any given moment to the batching delay that maximizes their profits. When the price of network bandwidth or the load they are under changes, they may pick a different batching delay if they calculate that it will improve their profit.

We vary the load during the experiment. During the first 60 seconds, we generate a load that approximates serving **many** small users. During the second 60 seconds, we generate a load that approximates serving a **single** important user at a time. The `memcached` load is generated with the `memaslap` benchmark application running with a GET/SET ratio of 90/10 (the default). The `nhttpd` load is generated with the `wrk` benchmark application requesting a single static file of 175 bytes in a loop. The `NetPIPE` server runs on the operating system under test and the `NetPIPE` client runs on the Linux host. `memcached` and `nhttpd` run in multiple threads/multiple requests mode, approximating serving many small users, or in a single thread/single request mode, approximating serving a single user at a time. The `NetPIPE` client either runs in bi-directional streaming mode (many) or in single request mode (single) with message size set to 1024 bytes. In all cases, to minimize physical networking effects, the load generator runs on the host, communicating with the virtual machine under test through the hypervisor's virtual networking apparatus. All power saving features are disabled in the host's BIOS and the experiments run in single user mode.

We run each experiment five times and report the averages of measured values. The average standard deviation of throughput and latency values between runs with the same parameters is less than 1% of the mean for `memcached` and less than 3% of the mean for `NetPIPE`. In `nhttpd` experiments, the single user scenario exhibits average standard deviation of both throughput and latency that is less than 1% of the mean. The many users scenario, however, exhibits average standard deviation of 10% of the mean for throughput values and 73% of the mean for latency values.

6.2 Performance

We argued that cloud applications should be optimized for cost. Does this preclude also optimizing them for performance? To answer this question, we begin by comparing the throughput, latency, and jitter achieved by nom applications with those achieved by their OSv and Linux counterparts. Throughput and latency results are the average throughput and latency recorded during each part of each experiment.

We show in Fig. 2, Fig. 3, and Fig. 4 the throughput and latency achieved by `memcached`, `nhttpd`, and `NetPIPE`, respectively, during the first 60 seconds, when they serve as **many** users as possible, and during the second 60 seconds, when they only serve the most important users, a **single** user at a time. For all three applications and both scenarios, nom achieves better (higher) throughput and better (lower) latency than both OSv and Linux. Taking `memcached` as an

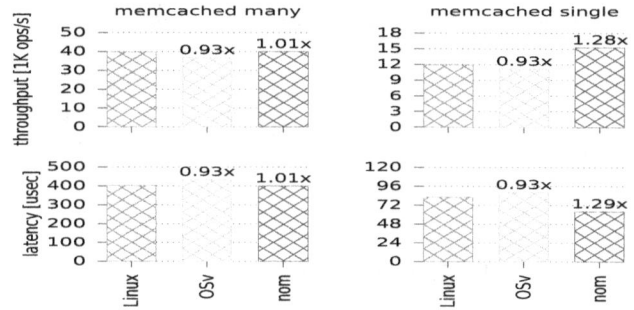

Figure 2: `memcached` throughput and latency

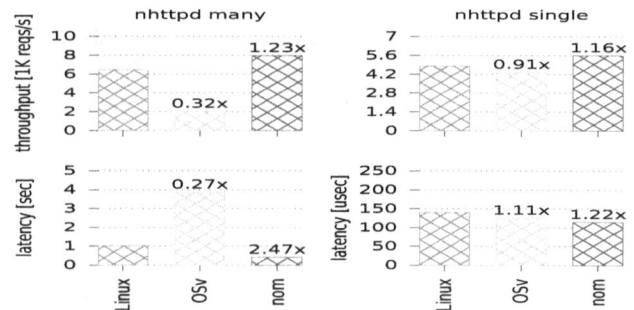

Figure 3: `nhttpd` throughput and latency

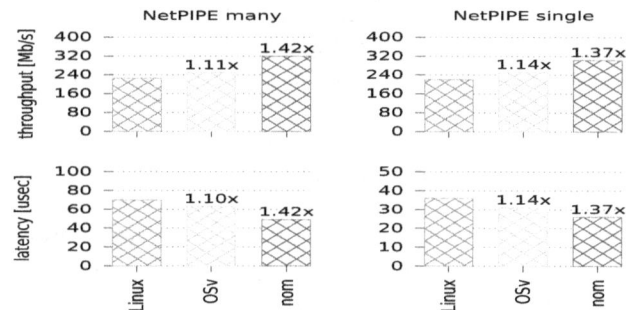

Figure 4: `NetPIPE` throughput and latency

example, we see that nom achieves 1.01x–1.28x the throughput of Linux, whereas OSv only achieves 0.93x. We also see that nom achieves average latency that is 1.01x–1.29x better than Linux (vs. 0.93x for OSv) with up to 4x better jitter when compared with Linux and up to 588x better jitter when compared with OSv. (Jitter is shown in Table 1.) `nhttpd` on nom achieves 1.2x–3.9x better throughput and up to 9.1x better latency than Linux and OSv, and `NetPIPE` achieves up to 1.42x better throughput and latency.

6.3 What makes nom fast?

Network applications running on nom achieve up to 3.9x better throughput and up to 9.1x better latency than their Linux and OSv counterparts (Fig. 2, Fig. 3, and Fig. 4).

Scenario	OS	Latency (μsec)	Jitter (μsec)
many	Linux	402	499
	OSv	434	24,148
	nom	399	121
single	Linux	82	14
	OSv	88	7,638
	nom	63	13

Table 1: memcached latency and jitter

Metric	OS	many	single
#exits/sec	Linux	43,146	90,166
	OSv	43,144	51,237
	nom	10,834	18,280
#irq injections/sec	Linux	20,245	12,194
	OSv	21,768	12,368
	nom	999	999
CPU utilization	Linux	75%	65%
	OSv	59%	63%
	nom	87%	98%

Table 2: Average exit rate, interrupt injection rate, and CPU utilization running memcached

This improvement is by virtue of nom's design and through careful application of several rules of thumb for writing high-performance virtualized systems. In particular, nom, as a cloud operating system, tries hard to keep the hypervisor out of the I/O path.

Table 2 shows the average number of exits per second for Linux, OSv, and nom when running memcached. We can see that nom causes 2.8x–4.9x fewer exits than Linux and OSv. One of the key causes of expensive hypervisor exits is injecting and acknowledging interrupts [29]. Since each nom application has its own device driver, it can decide when to wait for interrupts and when to poll the device directly. We can see in Table 2 that the hypervisor only injects approximately 1,000 interrupts to nom while memcached is running. These 1,000 interrupts are all timer interrupts, which can be avoided by implementing tickless mode in the nom kernel. There are no device interrupts because all three nom applications described previously switch to polling mode as soon as they come under heavy load. Linux and OSv, in contrast, take approximately 20K–22K interrupts in the many users scenario and approximately 12K interrupts in the single user scenario. We can also see that nom's CPU utilization is 87%–98%, higher than Linux and OSv's 59%–75%. Since in our evaluation scenario CPU cycles are "free", the nom applications make the right choice to trade off CPU cycles for better throughput and latency by polling the network device. Linux and OSv applications, which do not control their software stacks and device drivers, cannot make such a tradeoff.

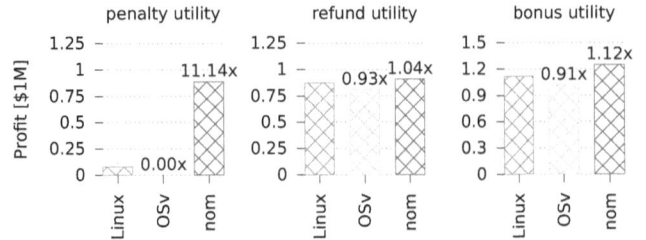

Figure 5: memcached profit

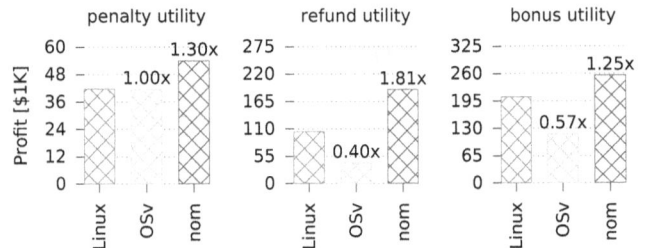

Figure 6: nhttpd profit

In addition to being "hypervisor friendly" by avoiding costly exits, nom's applications, default TCP/IP stack, and default virtnet device drivers are tuned to work well together. We eliminated expensive memory allocations on the I/O path in the applications, network stacks and device drivers, and avoided unnecessary copies in favor of zero-copy operations on the transmit and receive paths. We also used the time stamp counter (TSC) to track and reduce the frequency and cycle costs of data path operations.

Despite the 2.8x–4.9x difference in number of exits and 12x–22x difference in number of interrupts, nom's throughput and latency for memcached are only up to 1.3x better than Linux's. This disparity is caused by nom's default network stack and default virtnet device driver, which memcached uses, being not nearly as optimized as Linux's. We expect to achieve better performance and higher profits by optimizing and further customizing the stack and the driver to each application's needs. For example, instead of using the socket API, memcached's internal event handling logic could call into internal network stack APIs to bypass the relatively slow socket layer [31, 38, 61]. Further optimizations and customization remain as future work.

6.4 Profit

Next, we investigate whether optimizing for both performance and cost does indeed increase profit. Using the penalty, refund, and bonus utility functions presented in Section 4, we calculate how much money the applications running on Linux, OSv, and nom made. Bandwidth prices fluctuate as described in the methodology section. α is set to $20 \frac{\$}{\text{Gbit}}$, β is set to $10 \frac{\$ \cdot s}{\text{Gbit}}$, γ is set to $0.01 \frac{\$}{\text{Gbit} \cdot s}$ and δ is set to $+ \inf$ (i.e., there is no limit on the bonus). The penalty for violating the latency SLO in the penalty function (X) is 100,

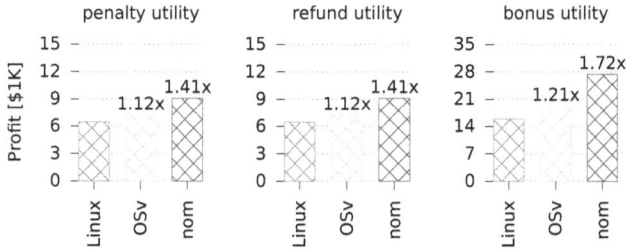

Figure 7: `NetPIPE` profit

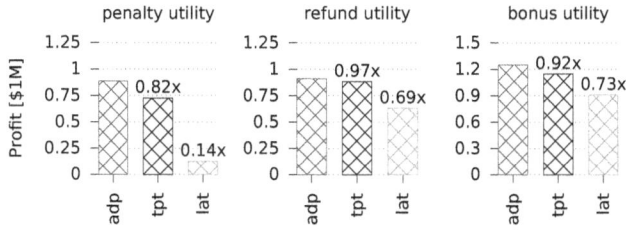

Figure 8: `memcached` profit: static vs. adaptive behavior

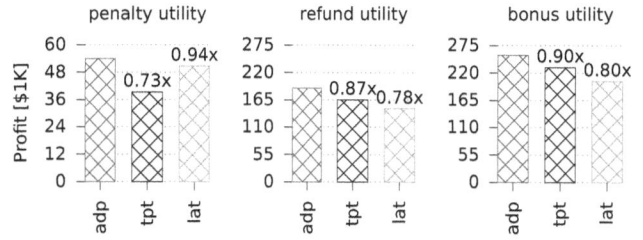

Figure 9: `nhttpd` profit: static vs. adaptive behavior

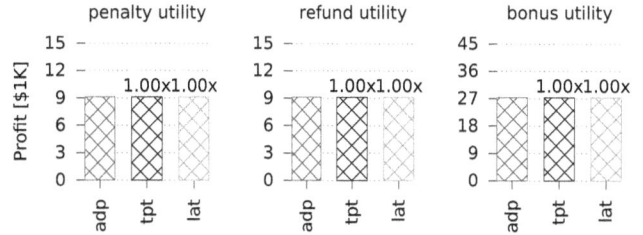

Figure 10: `NetPIPE` profit: static vs. adaptive behavior

and the maximal latency allowed by the SLA is 750µsec. We show in Fig. 5, Fig. 6, and Fig. 7 memcached's, nhttpd's, and NetPIPE's profits. We can see that nom makes more money than either Linux or OSv with every utility function and every application. To use the penalty utility function and memcached as an example, for every $1 of profit Linux makes, nom makes over 11x more profit, $11.14. OSv does not profit at all due to its average latency of 7,638µsec for the single case, more than ten times the latency SLO of 750µsec. For other applications and penalty functions the difference between operating systems is not as large, but nom always yields the highest profits.

6.5 What makes nom profitable?

The nom operating system has better performance and yields higher profits than Linux and OSv. Let us now focus on only nom (rather than Linux and OSv) and answer the question: To maximize profits, is it enough to run nom applications with the settings that provide the best performance, or must applications also change their behavior on the fly when conditions change? To answer this question, we repeated the profit experiments from the previous section. This time we compared nom applications with static behavior that lead to (1) the best throughput or (2) the best latency with applications that adapt their behavior. We ran each application for 120 seconds, with price and load changing after 60 seconds. Each 120 second run used a fixed batching delay in the range of 0–40µsec.

Fig. 8, Fig. 9, and Fig. 10 show the resulting profits. For the nom applications with static behavior and a fixed batching delay, each setting of the batching delay gave different throughput, latency, and jitter results. In the **tpt** column, we calculated the profit using the throughput and latency re-

sulting from the batching delay that gave the best absolute throughput. In the **lat** column, we used the throughput and latency resulting from running the nom application with the fixed batching delay that gave the best absolute latency. In the **adp** (adaptive) column, the nom application changed the batching delay when the price or load changed.

As can be seen in Fig. 8 and Fig. 9, for both memcached and nhttpd, varying the batching delay depending on the current price and load yields higher profit than running with any fixed batching delay. Taking the penalty utility function as an example, we see that running with the throughput-optimized batching delay would give memcached 82% of the profit, but running with this setting would only give nhttpd 73% of the profit. Likewise, running with the latency-optimized batching delay would give nhttpd 94% of the profit, but would give memcached only 14% of the profit. Hence we conclude that there is no single "one size fits all" batching delay that is optimal for all applications at all times. Furthermore, there can be no single "best" stack and single "best" device driver for all applications at all times. Each application's ability to change its stack's behavior, whether through tuning or more aggressive means, is crucial for maximizing profit.

Unlike memcached and nhttpd, NetPIPE (Fig. 10) shows no difference between columns. This is because NetPIPE is a synthetic ping-pong benchmark; its throughput is the inverse of its latency. When running on nom, NetPIPE tunes its stack to always run with batching delay 0, minimizing latency and maximizing throughput.

6.6 Effect of batching on throughput and latency

To understand the effect of the batching delay on application throughput and latency, we ran each application in both scenarios with a fixed batching delay between 0–40µsec.

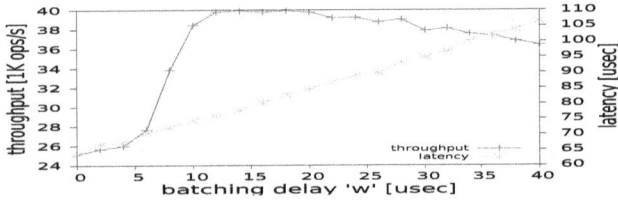

Figure 11: memcached throughput (in the many scenario) and latency (in the single scenario) as a function of batching delay

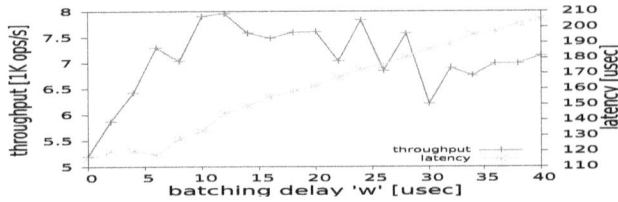

Figure 12: nhttpd throughput (in the many scenario) and latency (in the single scenario) as a function of batching delay

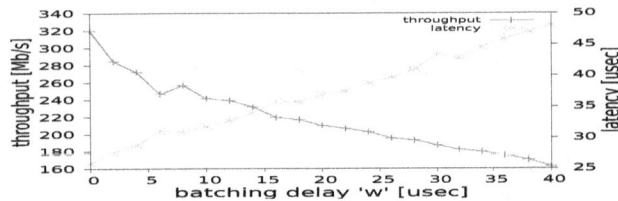

Figure 13: NetPIPE throughput (in the many scenario) and latency (in the single scenario) as a function of batching delay

Fig. 11, Fig. 12, and Fig. 13 show throughput and latency as a function of the batching delay for memcached, nhttpd, and NetPIPE, respectively. The throughput value shown is the throughput achieved in the "many" scenario, which is higher than the throughput achieved in the "single" scenario. The latency value shown is the latency achieved in the "single" scenario, which is lower (better) than the latency achieved in the "many" scenario.

We can see that for memcached throughput achieves a local optimum at 14μsec, for nhttpd the optimum is 12μsec, and for NetPIPE a delay of 0μsec (no delay) is best. Latency for all applications is best (lowest) with no batching delay, and each microsecond of batching delay adds approximately another microsecond of latency.

6.7 Throughput/latency Pareto frontier

Varying the batching delay affects both throughput and latency. Fig. 14, Fig. 15, and Fig. 16 show (throughput, latency) pairs with selected batching delays noted above the points representing them for memcached, nhttpd, and NetPIPE, respectively. For both memcached and nhttpd there is a clear *Pareto frontier*, shown in blue: a set of (throughput, latency) pairs that are not dominated by any other (throughput, latency) pair. Taking memcached as

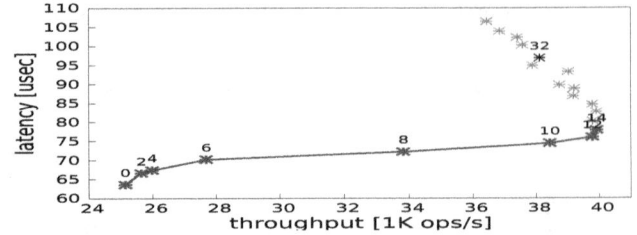

Figure 14: The memcached throughput and latency Pareto frontier

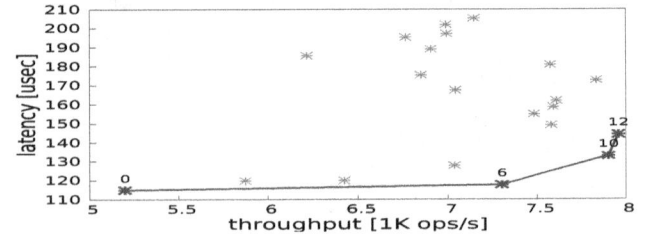

Figure 15: The nhttpd throughput and latency Pareto frontier

an example, we see that using a batching delay of 10μsec can yield throughput of approximately 38K ops/s with latency of 74μsec. Using a batching delay of 32μsec (shown as a black point with '32' above it), can also yield throughput of approximately 38K ops/s with latency of approximately 96μsec. Therefore, batching delay 10 dominates 32 because it provides the same throughput with lower latency. With a different batching delay, memcached can also achieve higher throughput: a batching delay of 14μsec provides approximately 40K ops/s, but not without also increasing latency to 77μsec. Therefore both point 10 (38K ops/s, 74μsec) and point 14 (40K ops/s, 77μsec) are on the memcached throughput/latency Pareto frontier, but point 32 is not. nhttpd's Pareto frontier includes batching delays 0 and 6–12. NetPIPE's Pareto frontier includes a single point, 0. The batching delay settings that are on the Pareto frontier produce better (throughput, latency) pairs than all other batching delays not on the Pareto frontier, but no one point on the Pareto frontier can be considered better than any other point on the frontier. Whereas a performance-optimized operating system is designed to find the "best" (throughput, latency) point for all cases, nom profit-maximizing applications pick the working point on the Pareto frontier that maximizes their profit at any given time *given current price and load*. When the price and/or load change, they may pick a different working point. Our experiments with nom show that there is no single "best" setting for all applications, scenarios and prices.

7. Discussion

There are two ways one could go about building a profit-maximizing operating system: based on an existing operat-

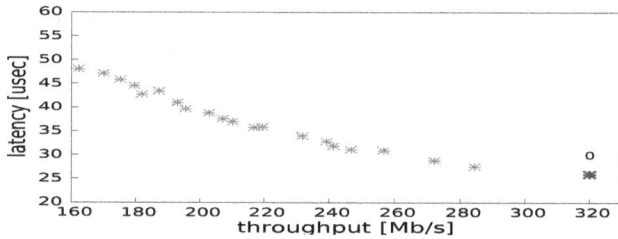

Figure 16: The `NetPIPE` throughput and latency Pareto frontier

ing system or from scratch. To turn Linux, for example, into a profit-maximizing operating system, one could have it run applications in virtual machines using a mechanism such as Dune [17] and provide applications with direct access using direct device assignment [72] or VFIO [69]. The applications themselves would need to be modified to adapt to the changing prices of resources and would still need userspace stacks and device drivers. The primary difference between building a profit-maximizing operating system from scratch and basing it on an existing operating system is how one constructs the kernel.

We felt that going the Linux route would have constrained the design space, so we decided to implement nom from scratch to allow a wider and deeper investigation of the design space. Additionally, at its core, the profit-maximizing kernel is a *nonkernel*: a kernel that does as little as possible. Basing it on Linux seemed wasteful.

In addition to maximizing profits and improving performance, the nom approach has several advantages when compared with traditional kernels and exokernels. These include reduced driver complexity, since drivers now run completely in userspace, each driver instance serving a single application; easier debugging, development and verification of drivers and I/O stacks, for the same reason; a simpler and easier to verify trusted-computing-base in the form of the nom kernel itself [44]; and a system that we hope is more secure overall, for the same reason. The nom approach can also be useful for systems where operating power is a concern, by letting applications tune their resource requirements to the current thermal envelope limits.

The main disadvantages of the nom approach are that it forsakes legacy architectures and applications. It is designed and implemented for the kind of modern hardware available on cloud servers and will not run on older bare-metal machines. Likewise, it is not at its best when running legacy applications; realizing its benefits to the fullest extent requires some level of cooperation and effort on the part of the application developer. We believe that in the cloud, breaking away from legacy is no longer unthinkable.

8. Related work

The nom design draws inspiration from several ideas in operating system and hypervisor construction. In addition to the original MIT exokernel [24, 25] and single address space op-

erating systems [34, 48], nom also borrows from past work on userspace I/O (e.g., [19, 20, 27, 65, 70]), virtual machine device assignment (e.g., [49, 50, 72]), multi-core aware and extensible operating systems (e.g., [16, 45]), and library operating systems (e.g., [13, 60, 68]). It shares the underlying philosophy of specializing applications for the cloud with Mirage [52, 53] and the underlying philosophy of a minimal kernel/hypervisor with NoHype [39]. OSv [43] is a single application operating system designed for running in cloud environments. Arrakis [59] and IX [18] both provide applications with direct access to their I/O devices on bare-metal servers. All of these operating systems, however, optimize for performance. IX uses adaptive batching like nom, but it batches packets automatically at the operating system level, unaware of specific application needs that might arise in light of SLAs. Furthermore, it does not support different working points for different application: it only regards congestion as its input. As far as we are aware, nom is the first and only operating system that maximizes profit by optimizing for both performance and cost.

The case for clouds with dynamic resource pricing (RaaS clouds) was first made by Agmon Ben-Yehuda et al. [7, 9]. On the basis of existing trends in the current IaaS industry, they deduced that the cloud business model must change: resources must be allocated on an economic basis, using economic mechanisms inside each physical machine. Ginseng [10] was the first implementation of a RaaS cloud for allocating memory. It showed that running elastic memory applications inside a traditional operating system such as Linux can be problematic due to the kernel abstracting away the hardware.

A common theme in cloud research is optimizing for cost. ExPERT [8] and Cloudyn [1] schedule workloads on clouds by taking into account both performance and cost. Optimizing for multiple goals was also previously explored in the context of power consumption. Lo et al. [51] balanced power consumption and latency. Ding et al. [21] optimized the energy-delay product.

9. Conclusions and future work

Clouds with dynamic pricing pose new challenges but also provide an opportunity to rethink how we build system software. We propose the nom profit-maximizing operating system, a new kind of operating system that is designed and optimized for both performance and cost. The current nom prototype shows that there is no single "best" network stack or driver. Instead, nom applications maximize their profits by having private application-specific software stacks and changing their behavior on the fly in response to changing resource prices and load conditions.

The current nom prototype focuses specifically on network-intensive applications in clouds with dynamic bandwidth pricing. We are continuing to investigate profit-maximizing operating systems along several dimensions. First, we are investigating how to extract maximal value from every resource: CPU, memory, network, storage, and power. Second, we are investigating software and hardware mechanisms that can help applications change their behavior on the fly, while also achieving high performance. And third, we are investigating how to construct application-specific profit-maximizing I/O stacks and device drivers—preferably through automatic code synthesis [63].

10. Acknowledgments

This research was funded in part by the Prof. A. Pazi Foundation and by the Israeli Ministry of Science and Technology (grant #3-9779).

References

[1] Cloudyn Use Cases (Online). https://www.cloudyn.com/use-cases/.

[2] GoGrid Service Level Agreement (Online). http://www.gogrid.com/legal/service-level-agreement-sla.

[3] Intel Xeon processor E5 v3 family. http://www.intel.com/content/dam/www/public/us/en/documents/manuals/64-ia-32-architectures-software-developer-manual-325462.pdf.

[4] NTT Service Level Agreement (Online). http://www.us.ntt.net/support/sla/network.cfm.

[5] Verizon Service Level Agreement (Online). http://www.verizonenterprise.com/about/network/latency/.

[6] O. Agmon Ben-Yehuda, M. Ben-Yehuda, A. Schuster, and D. Tsafrir. Deconstructing Amazon EC2 spot instance pricing. In *IEEE International Conference on Cloud Computing Technology and Science (CloudCom)*, 2011.

[7] O. Agmon Ben-Yehuda, M. Ben-Yehuda, A. Schuster, and D. Tsafrir. The Resource-as-a-Service (RaaS) cloud. In *USENIX Conference on Hot Topics in Cloud Computing (HotCloud)*, 2012.

[8] O. Agmon Ben-Yehuda, A. Schuster, A. Sharov, M. Silberstein, and A. Iosup. Expert: Pareto-efficient task replication on grids and clouds. In *IEEE International Parallel & Distributed Processing Symposium (IPDPS)*, 2012.

[9] O. Agmon Ben-Yehuda, M. Ben-Yehuda, A. Schuster, and D. Tsafrir. The rise of RaaS: The Resource-as-a-Service cloud. *Communications of the ACM (CACM)*, 57(7):76–84, July 2014. ISSN 0001-0782. doi: 10.1145/2627422. URL http://doi.acm.org/10.1145/2627422.

[10] O. Agmon Ben-Yehuda, E. Posener, M. Ben-Yehuda, A. Schuster, and A. Mu'alem. Ginseng: Market-driven memory allocation. In *Proceedings of the 10th ACM SIGPLAN/SIGOPS International Conference on Virtual Execution Environments*, VEE '14, 2014.

[11] L. Amar, A. Barak, Z. Drezner, and M. Okun. Randomized gossip algorithms for maintaining a distributed bulletin board with guaranteed age properties. *Concurrency and Computation: Practice and Experience*, 21(15):1907–1927, 2009. ISSN 1532-0634. doi: 10.1002/cpe.1418. URL http://dx.doi.org/10.1002/cpe.1418.

[12] N. Amit, M. Ben-Yehuda, D. Tsafrir, and A. Schuster. vIOMMU: efficient IOMMU emulation. In *USENIX Annual Technical Conference (ATC)*, 2011.

[13] G. Ammons, D. D. Silva, O. Krieger, D. Grove, B. Rosenburg, R. W. Wisniewski, M. Butrico, K. Kawachiya, and E. V. Hensbergen. Libra: A library operating system for a JVM in a virtualized execution environment. In *ACM/USENIX International Conference on Virtual Execution Environments (VEE)*, 2007.

[14] A. Barak, S. Guday, and R. G. Wheeler. *The MOSIX Distributed Operating System: Load Balancing for UNIX*. Springer-Verlag New York, Inc., Secaucus, NJ, USA, 1993. ISBN 0387566635.

[15] P. Barham, B. Dragovic, K. Fraser, S. Hand, T. Harris, A. Ho, R. Neugebauer, I. Pratt, and A. Warfield. Xen and the art of virtualization. In *ACM Symposium on Operating Systems Principles (SOSP)*, 2003.

[16] A. Baumann, P. Barham, P.-E. Dagand, T. Harris, R. Isaacs, S. Peter, T. Roscoe, A. Schüpbach, and A. Singhania. The multikernel: a new OS architecture for scalable multicore systems. In *ACM Symposium on Operating Systems Principles (SOSP)*, 2009. doi: http://dx.doi.org/10.1145/1629575.1629579.

[17] A. Belay, A. Bittau, A. Mashtizadeh, D. Terei, D. Mazieres, and C. Kozyrakis. Dune: Safe user-level access to privileged cpu features. In *Symposium on Operating Systems Design & Implementation (OSDI)*, 2012.

[18] A. Belay, G. Prekas, A. Klimovic, S. Grossman, C. Kozyrakis, and E. Bugnion. Ix: A protected dataplane operating system for high throughput and low latency. In *Symposium on Operating Systems Design & Implementation (OSDI)*, 2014.

[19] A. M. Caulfield, T. I. Mollov, L. A. Eisner, A. De, J. Coburn, and S. Swanson. Providing safe, user space access to fast, solid state disks. In *ACM Architectural Support for Programming Languages & Operating Systems (ASPLOS)*, 2012.

[20] Y. Chen, A. Bilas, S. N. Damianakis, C. Dubnicki, and K. Li. UTLB: a mechanism for address translation on network interfaces. *SIGPLAN Not.*, 33:193–204, October 1998. ISSN 0362-1340. doi: 10.1145/291006.291046. URL http://dx.doi.org/10.1145/291006.291046.

[21] Y. Ding, M. Kandemir, P. Raghavan, and M. J. Irwin. A helper thread based EDP reduction scheme for adapting application execution in cmps. In *IEEE International Parallel & Distributed Processing Symposium (IPDPS)*, 2008.

[22] C. Dovrolis, B. Thayer, and P. Ramanathan. HIP: hybrid interrupt-polling for the network interface. *ACM SIGOPS Operating Systems Review (OSR)*, 35:50–60, 2001. ISSN 0163-5980. doi: http://doi.acm.org/10.1145/506084.506089. URL http://doi.acm.org/10.1145/506084.506089.

[23] A. Dunkels. Design and implementation of the lwIP TCP/IP stack. In *Swedish Institute of Computer Science*, volume 2, page 77, 2001.

[24] D. R. Engler and M. F. Kaashoek. Exterminate all operating system abstractions. In *USENIX Workshop on Hot Topics in Operating Systems (HOTOS)*, pages 78–83. IEEE Computer Society, 1995.

[25] D. R. Engler, M. F. Kaashoek, and J. O'Toole Jr. Exokernel: an operating system architecture for application-level resource management. In *ACM Symposium on Operating Systems Principles (SOSP)*, 1995.

[26] B. Fitzpatrick. Distributed caching with memcached. *Linux J.*, 2004(124):5–, Aug. 2004. ISSN 1075-3583. URL http://dl.acm.org/citation.cfm?id=1012889.1012894.

[27] G. R. Ganger, D. R. Engler, M. F. Kaashoek, H. M. Briceno, R. Hunt, and T. Pinckney. Fast and flexible application-level networking on exokernel systems. *ACM Transactions on Computer Systems (TOCS)*, 20(1):49–83, February 2002.

[28] A. Gordon, M. Hines, D. Da Silva, M. Ben-Yehuda, M. Silva, and G. Lizarraga. Ginkgo: Automated, application-driven memory overcommitment for cloud computing. In *Runtime Environments/Systems, Layering, & Virtualized Environments workshop (ASPLOS RESOLVE)*, 2011.

[29] A. Gordon, N. Amit, N. Har'El, M. Ben-Yehuda, A. Landau, D. Tsafrir, and A. Schuster. ELI: Bare-metal performance for I/O virtualization. In *ACM Architectural Support for Programming Languages & Operating Systems (ASPLOS)*, 2012.

[30] A. Gordon, N. Har'El, A. Landau, M. Ben-Yehuda, and A. Traeger. Towards exitless and efficient paravirtual I/O. In *The 5th Annual International Systems and Storage Conference (SYSTOR)*, 2012.

[31] S. Han, S. Marshall, B.-G. Chun, and S. Ratnasamy. Megapipe: A new programming interface for scalable network i/o. In *Symposium on Operating Systems Design & Implementation (OSDI)*, pages 135–148, Hollywood, CA, 2012. USENIX. ISBN 978-1-931971-96-6. URL https://www.usenix.org/conference/osdi12/technical-sessions/presentation/han.

[32] S. M. Hand. Self-paging in the Nemesis operating system. In *Symposium on Operating Systems Design & Implementation (OSDI)*, pages 73–86, Berkeley, CA, USA, 1999. USENIX Association. ISBN 1-880446-39-1. URL http://portal.acm.org/citation.cfm?id=296812.

[33] N. Har'El, A. Gordon, A. Landau, M. Ben-Yehuda, A. Traeger, and R. Ladelsky. Efficient and scalable paravirtual I/O system. In *USENIX Annual Technical Conference (ATC)*, 2013.

[34] G. Heiser, K. Elphinstone, J. Vochteloo, S. Russell, and J. Liedtke. The mungi single-address-space operating system. *Software: Practice and Experience*, 28(9):901–928, 1998. ISSN 1097-024X. doi: 10.1002/(SICI)1097-024X(19980725)28:9⟨901::AID-SPE181⟩3.0.CO;2-7. URL http://dx.doi.org/10.1002/(SICI)1097-024X(19980725)28:9⟨901::AID-SPE181⟩3.0.CO;2-7.

[35] M. Hines, A. Gordon, M. Silva, D. D. Silva, K. D. Ryu, and M. Ben-Yehuda. Applications know best: Performance-driven memory overcommit with ginkgo. In *IEEE International Conference on Cloud Computing Technology and Science (CloudCom)*, 2011.

[36] Intel. Intel virtualization technology for directed I/O, architecture specification. ftp://download.intel.com/technology/computing/vptech/Intel(r)_VT_for_Direct_IO.pdf, Feb 2011. Revision 1.3. Intel Corporation. (Accessed Apr 2011).

[37] A. Itzkovitz and A. Schuster. MultiView and MilliPage—fine-grain sharing in page-based DSMs. In *Symposium on Operating Systems Design & Implementation (OSDI)*, 1999.

[38] E. Jeong, S. Wood, M. Jamshed, H. Jeong, S. Ihm, D. Han, and K. Park. mtcp: a highly scalable user-level tcp stack for multicore systems. pages 489–502, Seattle, WA, Apr. 2014. USENIX Association. ISBN 978-1-931971-09-6. URL https://www.usenix.org/conference/nsdi14/technical-sessions/presentation/jeong.

[39] E. Keller, J. Szefer, J. Rexford, and R. B. Lee. No-hype: virtualized cloud infrastructure without the virtualization. In *ACM/IEEE International Symposium on Computer Architecture (ISCA)*, New York, NY, USA, 2010. ACM. ISBN 978-1-4503-0053-7. doi: http://doi.acm.org/10.1145/1815961.1816010.

[40] F. Kelly. Charging and rate control for elastic traffic. *European Transactions on Telecommunications*, 8, 1997.

[41] R. E. Kessler and M. D. Hill. Page placement algorithms for large real-indexed caches. *ACM Transactions on Computer Systems (TOCS)*, 10(4):338–359, Nov. 1992. ISSN 0734-2071. doi: 10.1145/138873.138876. URL http://doi.acm.org/10.1145/138873.138876.

[42] A. Kivity, Y. Kamay, D. Laor, U. Lublin, and A. Liguori. KVM: the Linux virtual machine monitor. In *Ottawa Linux Symposium (OLS)*, 2007. http://www.kernel.org/doc/ols/2007/ols2007v1-pages-225-230.pdf. (Accessed Apr, 2011).

[43] A. Kivity, D. Laor, G. Costa, P. Enberg, N. Har'El, D. Marti, and V. Zolotarov. Osv—optimizing the operating system for virtual machines. In *USENIX Annual Technical Conference (ATC)*, 2014.

[44] G. Klein, K. Elphinstone, G. Heiser, J. Andronick, D. Cock, P. Derrin, D. Elkaduwe, K. Engelhardt, R. Kolanski, M. Norrish, T. Sewell, H. Tuch, and S. Winwood. seL4: formal verification of an os kernel. In *ACM Symposium on Operating Systems Principles (SOSP)*, 2009.

[45] O. Krieger, M. Auslander, B. Rosenburg, R. W. Wisniewski, J. Xenidis, D. Da Silva, M. Ostrowski, J. Appavoo, M. Butrico, M. Mergen, A. Waterland, and V. Uhlig. K42: building a complete operating system. In *ACM SIGOPS European Conference on Computer Systems (EuroSys)*, 2006.

[46] A. Landau, M. Ben-Yehuda, and A. Gordon. SplitX: Split guest/hypervisor execution on multi-core. In *USENIX Workshop on I/O Virtualization (WIOV)*, 2011.

[47] C. B. Lee and A. E. Snavely. Precise and realistic utility functions for user-centric performance analysis of schedulers. In *International Symposium on High Performance Distributed Computer (HPDC)*, 2007.

[48] I. Leslie, D. McAuley, R. Black, T. Roscoe, P. Barham, D. Evers, R. Fairbairns, and E. Hyden. The design and implementation of an operating system to support distributed multimedia applications. *Selected Areas in Communications, IEEE Journal on*, 14(7):1280–1297, Sep 1996. ISSN 0733-8716. doi: 10.1109/49.536480.

[49] J. LeVasseur, V. Uhlig, J. Stoess, and S. Götz. Unmodified device driver reuse and improved system dependability via virtual machines. In *Symposium on Operating Systems Design & Implementation (OSDI)*, 2004.

[50] J. Liu, W. Huang, B. Abali, and D. K. Panda. High performance VMM-bypass I/O in virtual machines. In *USENIX Annual Technical Conference (ATC)*, pages 29–42, 2006.

[51] D. Lo, L. Cheng, R. Govindaraju, L. A. Barroso, and C. Kozyrakis. Towards energy proportionality for large-scale latency-critical workloads. In *Proceeding of the 41st Annual International Symposium on Computer Architecuture*, ACM/IEEE International Symposium on Computer Architecture (ISCA), pages 301–312, Piscataway, NJ, USA, 2014. IEEE Press. ISBN 978-1-4799-4394-4. URL http://dl.acm.org/citation.cfm?id=2665671.2665718.

[52] A. Madhavapeddy, R. Mortier, R. Sohan, T. Gazagnaire, S. Hand, T. Deegan, D. McAuley, and J. Crowcroft. Turning down the lamp: software specialisation for the cloud. In *USENIX Conference on Hot Topics in Cloud Computing (HotCloud)*, 2010.

[53] A. Madhavapeddy, R. Mortier, C. Rotsos, D. Scott, B. Singh, T. Gazagnaire, S. Smith, S. Hand, and J. Crowcroft. Unikernels: Library operating systems for the cloud. In *ACM Architectural Support for Programming Languages & Operating Systems (ASPLOS)*, 2013.

[54] J. C. Mogul and K. K. Ramakrishnan. Eliminating receive livelock in an interrupt-driven kernel. *ACM Transactions on Computer Systems (TOCS)*, 15:217–252, 1997. ISSN 0734-2071. doi: http://doi.acm.org/10.1145/263326.263335. URL http://doi.acm.org/10.1145/263326.263335.

[55] Note1. https://www.cloudsigma.com/pricing/ accessed in October 2015.

[56] Note2. Kovacs, Kristof, "Charting CloudSigma Burst Prices", http://kkovacs.eu/cloudsigma-burst-price-chart, July 2012, accessed October 2015.

[57] Note3. Paavolainen Santeri, http://santtu.iki.fi/2014/03/20/ec2-spot-market/, March 2014, accessed October 2015.

[58] PCI SIG. Single root I/O virtualization and sharing 1.0 specification, 2007.

[59] S. Peter, J. Li, I. Zhang, D. R. K. Ports, D. Woos, A. Krishnamurthy, T. Anderson, and T. Roscoe. Arrakis: The operating system is the control plane. In *Symposium on Operating Systems Design & Implementation (OSDI)*, 2014.

[60] D. E. Porter, S. Boyd-Wickizer, J. Howell, R. Olinsky, and G. C. Hunt. Rethinking the library OS from the top down. In *ACM Architectural Support for Programming Languages & Operating Systems (ASPLOS)*, 2011.

[61] L. Rizzo. Netmap: a novel framework for fast packet I/O. In *USENIX Annual Technical Conference (ATC)*, 2012.

[62] R. Russell. virtio: towards a de-facto standard for virtual I/O devices. *ACM SIGOPS Operating Systems Review (OSR)*, 42 (5):95–103, 2008.

[63] L. Ryzhyk, A. Walker, J. Keys, A. Legg, A. Raghunath, M. Stumm, and M. Vij. User-guided device driver synthesis. In *Symposium on Operating Systems Design & Implementation (OSDI)*, pages 661–676, Broomfield, CO, Oct. 2014. USENIX Association. ISBN 978-1-931971-16-4. URL https://www.usenix.org/conference/osdi14/technical-sessions/presentation/ryzhyk.

[64] J. H. Salim, R. Olsson, and A. Kuznetsov. Beyond Softnet. In *Anual Linux Showcase & Conference*, 2001. URL http://portal.acm.org/citation.cfm?id=1268488.1268506.

[65] L. Schaelicke and A. L. Davis. Design Trade-Offs for User-Level I/O Architectures. *IEEE Trans. Comput.*, 55:962–973, August 2006. ISSN 0018-9340. URL http://portal.acm.org/citation.cfm?id=1159194.

[66] Q. O. Snell, A. R. Mikler, and J. L. Gustafson. Netpipe: A network protocol independent performance evaluator. *IASTED International Conference on Intelligent Information Management and Systems*, 6, 1996.

[67] R. Uhlig, G. Neiger, D. Rodgers, A. L. Santoni, F. C. M. Martins, A. V. Anderson, S. M. Bennett, A. Kagi, F. H. Leung, and L. Smith. Intel virtualization technology. *Computer*, 38(5): 48–56, 2005. ISSN 0018-9162. doi: 10.1109/MC.2005.163. URL http://dx.doi.org/10.1109/MC.2005.163.

[68] E. Van Hensbergen. P.R.O.S.E.: partitioned reliable operating system environment. *SIGOPS Oper. Syst. Rev.*, 40(2):12–15, Apr. 2006. ISSN 0163-5980. doi: 10.1145/1131322.1131329. URL http://doi.acm.org/10.1145/1131322.1131329.

[69] vfio. VFIO driver: non-privileged user level PCI drivers. http://lwn.net/Articles/391459/, Jun 2010. (Accessed Feb., 2015).

[70] T. von Eicken, A. Basu, V. Buch, and W. Vogels. U-Net: a user-level network interface for parallel and distributed computing. In *ACM Symposium on Operating Systems Principles (SOSP)*, New York, NY, USA, 1995.

[71] P. Willmann, S. Rixner, and A. L. Cox. Protection strategies for direct access to virtualized I/O devices. In *USENIX Annual Technical Conference (ATC)*, 2008.

[72] B.-A. Yassour, M. Ben-Yehuda, and O. Wasserman. Direct device assignment for untrusted fully-virtualized virtual machines. Technical Report H-0263, IBM Research, 2008.

Enabling Hybrid Parallel Runtimes
Through Kernel and Virtualization Support

Kyle C. Hale   Peter A. Dinda

Department of Electrical Engineering and Computer Science
Northwestern University
{k-hale, pdinda}@northwestern.edu

Abstract

In our hybrid runtime (HRT) model, a parallel runtime system and the application are together transformed into a specialized OS kernel that operates entirely in kernel mode and can thus implement exactly its desired abstractions on top of fully privileged hardware access. We describe the design and implementation of two new tools that support the HRT model. The first, the Nautilus Aerokernel, is a kernel framework specifically designed to enable HRTs for x64 and Xeon Phi hardware. Aerokernel primitives are specialized for HRT creation and thus can operate much faster, up to two orders of magnitude faster, than related primitives in Linux. Aerokernel primitives also exhibit much lower variance in their performance, an important consideration for some forms of parallelism. We have realized several prototype HRTs, including one based on the Legion runtime, and we provide application macrobenchmark numbers for our Legion HRT. The second tool, the hybrid virtual machine (HVM), is an extension to the Palacios virtual machine monitor that allows a single virtual machine to simultaneously support a traditional OS and software stack alongside an HRT with specialized hardware access. The HRT can be booted in a time comparable to a Linux user process startup, and functions in the HRT, which operate over the user process's memory, can be invoked by the process with latencies not much higher than those of a function call.

This project is made possible by support from the United States National Science Foundation through grant CCF-1533560 and from Sandia National Laboratories through the Hobbes Project, which is funded by the 2013 Exascale Operating and Runtime Systems Program under the Office of Advanced Scientific Computing Research in the United States Department of Energy's Office of Science. We also thank Madhav Suresh and Conor Hetland for their help with NESL and NDPC.

VEE '16, April 02 - 03, 2016, Atlanta, GA, USA
Copyright is held by the owner/author(s). Publication rights licensed to ACM.
ACM 978-1-4503-3947-6/16/04...$15.00
DOI: http://dx.doi.org/10.1145/2892242.2892255

1. Introduction

Considerable innovation in parallelism is occurring today, targeting a wide range of scales from mobile devices to exascale computing. How to execute parallel languages with high performance and efficiency is a question of wide interest. Our focus is on parallel runtime systems, the medium through which these languages interact with the operating system and the hardware. Many interaction models are possible, and the innovation and change driven by parallelism itself makes feasible the adoption of other models. We are studying one such model in depth.

A hybrid runtime (HRT) is a parallel runtime system, along with its application, that runs entirely in *kernel mode* on the target hardware. That is, an HRT is a parallel runtime stack that has either been developed as an operating system kernel or has been ported to become an OS kernel—it is a hybrid of a kernel and a parallel runtime. Because an HRT has fully privileged access to the machine, it can use all hardware features available on the machine, it can create whatever OS level abstractions are suitable to it, and it can use those abstractions without any system call overheads. In contrast, in today's common model of a parallel runtime running in user mode on top of a general purpose or even lightweight kernel, the parallel runtime cannot use privileged features of the hardware, it is limited to the abstractions exposed through the system call interface, and even those abstractions come at the cost of a system call.

We previously argued the *case* for HRTs [37], and we now describe the design, implementation, and evaluation of two *tools* we have developed to support the creation and execution of HRTs, and evaluate the HRT model. The first tool, the Nautilus Aerokernel (we usually just write "Aerokernel"), is a kernel framework specifically designed to support the creation of HRTs. It provides a basic kernel that can be booted within milliseconds after boot loader execution on a multicore, multisocket machine, accelerator, or virtual machine. Aerokernel includes basic building blocks such as simple memory management, threads, synchronization, IPIs and other in-kernel abstractions that a parallel runtime can be ported to or be built on top of to become an HRT. While

Aerokernel provides functionality, it does not require the HRT to use it, nor does it proscribe the implementation of other functionality. Aerokernel was developed for 64-bit x86 machines (x64) and then ported to the Intel Xeon Phi.

Our evaluation of Aerokernel includes three aspects. First, we give detailed microbenchmark evaluations, comparing its functionality and performance to that of analogous facilities available at user-level on Linux that are typically used within parallel runtimes. Aerokernel functionality such as thread creation and events operate up to two orders of magnitude faster than Linux due to their implementation and by virtue of the fact that there is no kernel/user boundary to cross. They also operate with much less variation in performance, an important consideration for many models of parallelism, particularly with scale. The second aspect of our evaluation is to consider the challenges of porting parallel runtimes to Aerokernel. We describe ports of three runtimes, the Legion runtime [4], the NESL VCODE engine [12], and a home-grown nested data parallel language. Even the most complex of these, Legion, was feasible to port to Aerokernel to become an HRT. Finally, we do application benchmarking using Sandia National Lab's HPCG, comparing Legion on Linux and the Legion/Aerokernel HRT on x64 and Xeon Phi.

While running an HRT on bare metal is suitable for some contexts (e.g., an accelerator or a node of a supercomputer), we may also want to use an HRT in shared contexts or ease the porting of runtimes that have significant dependencies on an existing kernel. Our second tool, the hybrid virtual machine (HVM), facilitates these use cases. HVM is an extension to the open source Palacios virtual machine monitor (VMM) [48] that makes it possible to create a VM that is internally partitioned between virtual cores that run a "regular" operating system (ROS), and virtual cores that run an HRT. The ROS cores see a subset of the VM's memory and other hardware, while HRT cores see all of it and may be granted specialized physical hardware access by the VMM. The ROS application can invoke functions in the HRT that operate over data in the ROS application. Finally, the HRT cores can be booted independently of the ROS cores using a model that allows an HRT to begin executing in 10s of microseconds, and with which an Aerokernel-based HRT can be brought up in 10s of milliseconds. This makes HRT startup in the HVM comparable in cost to `fork()/exec()` functionality in the ROS. In effect, the HVM allows a portion of an x64 machine to act as an accelerator.

Our contributions are as follows.

- We describe in detail the design of the Nautilus Aerokernel kernel framework and how it differs from other kernels.

- We describe the implementation of Aerokernel on x64 and Phi. As far as we are aware, Aerokernel is only the second non-Intel kernel on the Phi.

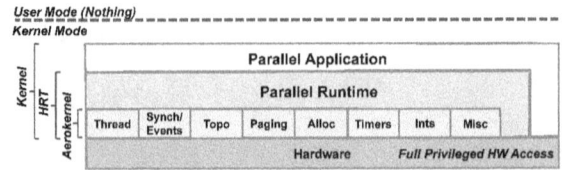

Figure 1: Structure of Aerokernel.

- We microbenchmark Aerokernel on x64 and Phi, particularly focusing on threads and events.

- We describe our experiences with porting three runtimes, including Legion, to become Aerokernel-based HRTs.

- We give application benchmark results for HPCG on Legion, comparing Aerokernel with Linux, on x64 and Phi.

- We describe the design, implementation, and performance evaluation of the HVM concept.

The Nautilus Aerokernel and the HVM extensions to Palacios are open-source and publicly available at `v3vee.org`.

2. Nautilus Aerokernel

Aerokernel design and implementation has been driven by studying parallel runtimes, including the three (Legion, NESL, NPDC) described in Section 4, the SWARM data flow runtime [49], ParalleX [43], Charm++ [44], the futures and places parallelism extensions to the Racket runtime [64, 65, 63], and nested data parallelism in Manticore [34, 33] and Haskell [20, 21]. We have studied these codebases and in the case of Legion, NPDC, SWARM, and Racket, we also interviewed their developers to understand their views of the limitations of existing kernel support.

Aerokernel is *not* a general purpose kernel. In fact, there is not even a user space. Instead, its design focuses specifically on helping parallel runtimes to achieve high performance as HRTs. The non-critical path functionality of the runtime is assumed to be delegated, for example to the host in the case of an accelerator or to the ROS portion of an HVM. The abstractions Aerokernel provides are based on our analysis of the needs of the runtimes we examined. Our abstractions are optional. Because an HRT runs entirely at kernel level, the developer can also directly leverage all hardware functionality to create new abstractions.

Our choice of abstractions was driven in part to make it feasible to port existing parallel runtimes to become Aerokernel-based HRTs. A more open-ended motivator was to facilitate the design and implementation of new parallel runtimes that do not have a built-in assumption of being user space processes.

2.1 Design

Aerokernel is designed to boot the machine, discover its capabilities, devices, and topology, and immediately hand control over to the runtime. Figure 1 shows the basic structure, showing the functionality provided by Aerokernel in the context of the runtime and application. Note that Aerokernel is a thin layer in the HRT model, and that in this model there is no user space. The runtime and the application have full access to hardware and can pick and choose which Aerokernel functionality to use. The entire assemblage of the figure is compiled into a multiboot2-compliant kernel.

We focus the following discussion on functionality where Aerokernel differs most from other kernels. In general, the defaults for Aerokernel functionality strive to be simple and easy to reason about from the HRT developer's viewpoint.

Threads   In designing a threading model for Aerokernel, we considered the experiences of others, including work on high-performance user-level threading techniques like scheduler activations [2] and Qthreads [67]. Ultimately, we designed our threads to be lightweight in order to provide an efficient starting point for HRTs. Aerokernel threads are *kernel* threads. A context switch between Aerokernel threads *never* involves a change of address spaces. Aerokernel threads can be configured to operate either preemptively or cooperatively, the latter allowing for the elimination of timer interrupts and scheduling of threads exactly as determined by the runtime.

The nature of the threads in Aerokernel is determined by how the runtime uses them. This means that we can directly map the logical view of the machine from a runtime's point of view (see Section 4.1) to the physical machine. This is not typically possible to do with any kind of guarantees when running in userspace. In fact, this is one of the concerns that the Legion runtime developers expressed with running Legion on Linux. The default scheduler and mapper binds a thread to a specific hardware thread as selected by thread creator, and schedules round-robin. The runtime developer can easily change these policies.

Another distinctive aspect of Aerokernel threads is that a thread fork (and join) mechanism is provided in addition to the common interface of starting a new thread with a clean new stack in a function. A forked thread has a limited lifetime and will terminate when it returns from the current function. It is incumbent upon the runtime to manage the parent and child stacks correctly. This capability is leveraged in our ports of NESL and NDPC.

Thread creation, context switching, and wakeup are designed to be fast and to leverage runtime knowledge. For example, maximum stack sizes and context beyond the GPRs can be selected at creation time. Because interrupt context uses the current thread's stack, it is even possible to create a single large-stacked idle thread per hardware thread and then drive computation entirely by inter-processor interrupts (IPIs), one possible mapping of an event-driven parallel runtime such as SWARM.

Synchronization and events   Aerokernel provides several variants of low-level spinlocks, including MCS locks and bakery locks. These are similar to those available in other kernels, and comparable in performance.

Aerokernel focuses to a large extent on asynchronous events, which are a common abstraction that runtime systems often use to distribute work to execution units, or workers. For example, the Legion runtime makes heavy use of them to notify logical processors (Legion threads) when there are Legion tasks that are ready to be executed. Userspace events require costly user/kernel interactions, which we *eliminate* in Aerokernel.

Aerokernel provides two implementations of condition variables that are compatible with those in pthreads. These implementations are tightly coupled with the scheduler, eliminating unnecessary software interactions. When a condition is signaled, the default Aerokernel condition variable implementation will simply put the target thread on its respective hardware thread's ready queue. This, of course, is not possible from a user-mode thread.

When a thread is signaled in Aerokernel it will not run until the scheduler starts it. For preemptive threads, this means waiting until the next timer tick, or an explicit yield from the currently running thread. Our second implementation of condition variables mitigates this delay by having the signaling thread "kick" the appropriate core with an IPI after it has woken up the waiting thread. The scheduler recognizes this condition on returning from the interrupt and switches to the awakened thread.

The runtime can also make direct use of IPIs, giving it the ability to force immediate execution of a function of its choosing on a remote destination core. Note that the IPI mechanism is unavailable when running in user-space.

Topology and memory allocation   Modern NUMA machines organize memory into separate domains according to physical distance from a physical CPU socket, core, or hardware thread. This results in variable latency when accessing memory in the different domains and also means achieving high memory bandwidth requires leveraging multiple domains simultaneously. Platform firmware typically enumerates these NUMA domains and exposes their sizes and topology to the operating system in a way that supports both modern and legacy OSes.

Aerokernel captures this topology information on boot and exposes it to the runtime. The page and heap allocators in Aerokernel allow the runtime to select which domains to allocate from, with the default being that allocations are satisfied from the domain closest to the current location of the thread requesting the allocation. All allocations are done immediately. This is in contrast to the policy of deferred allocations whose domains are determined on first touch, the typical default policy for general purpose kernels. A consequence is that a runtime that implements a specific execution policy, for example the owner-computes rule (e.g., as in HPF [39]) or inspector-executor [26], can more easily reason about how to efficiently map a parallel operation to the memory hardware.

A thread's stack is allocated using identity-mapped addresses based on the initial binding of the thread to a hardware thread, again to the closest domain. Since threads do not by default migrate, stack accesses are low latency, even across a large stack. If the runtime is designed so that it does not allow or can fix pointers into the stack, even the stack can be moved to the most friendly domain if the runtime decides to move the thread to a different hardware thread.

We saw NUMA effects that would double the execution time of a long-running parallel application on the Legion runtime. While user-space processes do typically have access to NUMA information and policies, runtimes executing in the Aerokernel framework have *full* control over the placement of threads and memory and can thus enjoy guarantees about what can affect runtime performance.

Paging Aerokernel has a simple, yet high-performance paging model aimed at high-performance parallel applications. When the machine boots up, each hardware thread identity-maps the entire physical address space using large pages (2MB and 1 GB pages currently, 512 GB pages when available in hardware) to create a single *unified* address space. Optionally, the identity map can be offset into the "higher half" of the x64 address space (Section 5.3). An Aerokernel-based kernel can also be linked to load anywhere in the physical address space.

The static identity map eliminates expensive page faults and TLB shootdowns, and reduces TLB misses. These events not only reduce performance, but also introduce unpredictable OS noise [31] from the perspective of the runtime developer. OS noise is well known to introduce timing variance that becomes a serious obstacle in large-scale distributed machines running parallel applications. The same will hold true for single nodes as core counts continue to scale up. The introduction of variance by OS noise (not just by asynchronous paging events) not only limits the performance and predictability of existing runtimes, but also limits the *kinds* of runtimes that can take advantage of the machine. For example, runtimes that need tasks to execute in synchrony (e.g., in order to support a bulk-synchronous parallel [35] application or a runtime that uses an abstract vector model) will experience serious degradation if OS noise comes into play.

The use of a single unified address space also allows fast communication between threads, and eliminates much of the overhead of context switches. The only context switches are between kernel threads, so no page table switch or kernel-triggered TLB flush ever occurs. This is especially useful when Aerokernel runs virtualized, as a large portion of VM exits come from paging related faults and dynamic mappings initiated by the OS, particularly using shadow paging. A shadow-paged Aerokernel exhibits the minimum possible shadow page faults, and shadow paging can be more efficient

that nested paging, except when shadow page faults are common [3].

Timers Aerokernel optionally enables a per-hardware thread scheduler tick mechanism based on the Advanced Programmable Interrupt Controller (APIC) timer. This is only needed when preemption is configured.

For high resolution time measurement across hardware threads, Aerokernel provides a driver for the high-precision event timer (HPET) available on most modern x64 machines. This is a good mapping for real-time measurement in the runtimes we examined. Within per-hardware thread timing, the cycle counter is typically used.

Interrupts External interrupts in Aerokernel work just like any other operating system, with the exception that by default only the APIC timer interrupt is enabled at bootup (and only when preemption is configured). The runtime has complete control over interrupts, including their mapping, assignment, and priority ordering.

2.2 Implementation

The process of building Aerokernel as a minimal kernel layer with support for modern x64 NUMA machines took six person-months of effort on the part of seasoned OS/VMM kernel developers. Aerokernel, which was developed from scratch, comprises about 25,000 lines of code: about 23,000 lines of C, 1000 lines of assembly, 200 lines of C++, and the rest in various scripting languages. Building a kernel, however, was not our main goal. Our main focus was supporting the porting and construction of runtimes for the HRT model.

The Legion runtime was the most challenging and complex of the three runtimes to bring up in Aerokernel. Legion is almost twice the size of Aerokernel, consisting of about 43,000 lines of C++. Porting Legion and the other runtimes took a total of about four person-months of effort—three person-months as described in Section 4, and one person-month in extensions to Aerokernel. In the end a modest 800 lines of additional code (650 C, 150 C++) needed to be added to Aerokernel, primarily to support C++.

This suggests that exploring the HRT model for existing or new parallel runtimes, especially with a small kernel like Aerokernel designed with this in mind, is a perfectly manageable task for an experienced systems developer.

2.3 Xeon Phi

We have ported Aerokernel to the Intel Xeon Phi. Although the Phi is technically an x64 machine, it has differences that make porting a kernel to it challenging. These include the lack of much PC legacy hardware, a distinctive APIC addressing model, a distinctive frequency/power/thermal model, and a bootstrap and I/O model that is closely tied to Intel's MPSS stack. Our port consists of two elements.

Philix is a set of tools to support booting and communicating with a third-party kernel on the Phi in compliance with Intel's stack, while at the same time not requiring the kernel to itself support the full functionality demanded of MPSS. Philix also includes basic driver support for the Phi that can be incorporated into the third-party kernel. This includes console support on both the host and Phi sides to make debugging a new Phi kernel easier. Philix comprises 1150 lines of C.

Our changes to add Phi support to Aerokernel comprised about 1350 lines of C. This required about 1.5 person months of kernel developer effort, mostly spent in ferreting out the idiosyncrasies of the Phi.

3. Microbenchmarks

We now evaluate the performance of the basic primitives in Aerokernel that are particularly salient to HRT creation, comparing them to Linux user-level and kernel-level primitives. The performance of basic primitives is important because runtimes build on these mechanisms. Although they can use the mechanisms cleverly (Legion's task model is effectively a thread pool model, for example), making the underlying primitives and environment faster can make runtimes faster, as we shall see.

Experimental setup We measure performance on an x64 NUMA machine and on an Intel Xeon Phi. The x64 configuration is a 2.1GHz AMD Opteron 6272 (Interlagos) server machine with 64 cores and 128 GB of memory. The cores are spread across 4 sockets, and each socket comprises two NUMA domains. All CPUs within one of these NUMA domains share an L3 cache. Within the domain, CPUs are organized into 4 groups of 2 hardware threads. The hardware threads share an L1 instruction cache and a unified L2 cache. Hardware threads have their own L1 data cache. We configured the BIOS for this machine to "Maximum performance" to eliminate the effects of power management. This machine also has a "freerunning' TSC, which means that the TSC will tick at a constant rate regardless of the operating frequency of the processor core. For Linux tests, it runs Red Hat 6.5 (1.5 years old at the time of this writing) with the stock Linux kernel binary version 2.6.32. It is important to note that this kernel has been highly optimized by Red Hat. For example, it uses the transparent huge page mechanism.

For the Xeon Phi tests, we use a Xeon Phi 3120A PCI accelerator along with the Intel MPSS 3.4.2 toolchain, which uses a modified 2.6.38 Linux kernel. It is important to point out that this is the current kernel binary shipped by Intel for use with Intel Xeon Phi hardware.

We use the `rdtscp` instruction to enforce proper serialization of instructions when timing using the cycle counter. Measurements are taken over at least 1000 runs with results shown as box plots or CDFs.

Threads Figure 2 compares thread creation latency between Linux userspace (pthreads), Linux kernel threads, and Aerokernel threads. We compare with pthreads because runtimes (such as Legion) build on these mechanisms. While

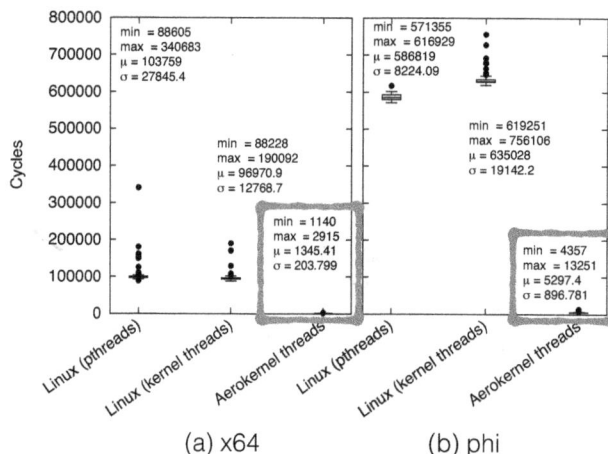

(a) x64   (b) phi

Figure 2: Thread creation latency. Aerokernel thread creations are on average two orders of magnitude faster that Linux userspace (pthreads) or kernel thread creations and have at least an order of magnitude lower variance.

thread creation may or may not be on the performance critical path for a particular runtime the comparison demonstrates the lightweight capabilities of Aerokernel. The cost measured is the time for the thread creation function to return to the creator thread. For Aerokernel, this includes placing the new thread in the run queue of its hardware thread. A thread fork in Aerokernel has similar latency since the primary difference compared to ordinary thread creation has to do with the content of the initial stack for the new thread. The time for the new thread to begin executing is bounded by the context switch time, which we measure below.

On both platforms, thread creation in Aerokernel has two orders of magnitude lower latency on average than both Linux options, and, equally important, the latency has little variance. Thread creation in Aerokernel also scales well, as, like the others, it involves constant work. From an HRT developer's point of view, these performance characteristics potentially makes the creation of smaller units of work feasible, allows for tighter synchronization of their execution, and allows for large numbers of threads.

Figure 3 illustrates the latencies of context switches between threads on the two platforms, comparing Linux and Aerokernel. In both cases, no floating point or vector state is involved—the cost of handling such state is identical across Linux and Aerokernel. The average cost of an Aerokernel context switch on the x64 is about 10% lower than that of Linux, but Aerokernel exhibits a variance that's lower by a factor of two. On the Phi, Aerokernel exhibits two orders of magnitude lower variance in latency and more than factor of two lower average latency. The instruction count for a thread context switch in Aerokernel is much lower than that for Linux. On the x64, this does not have much effect because the hardware thread is superscalar. On the other hand, the hardware thread on the Phi is not only not su-

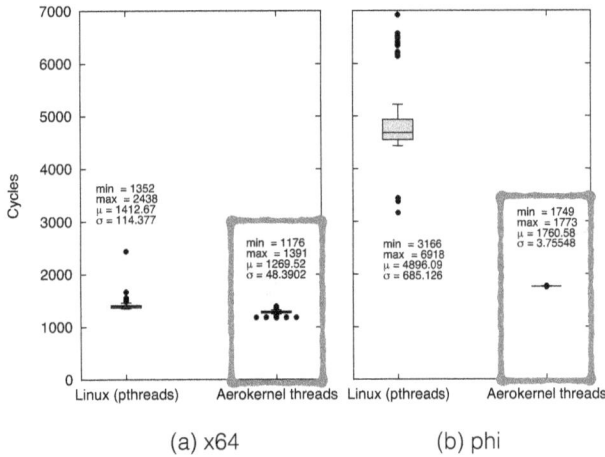

(a) x64   (b) phi

Figure 3: Thread context switch latency. Aerokernel thread context switches similar in average performance to Linux on x64 and over two times faster on Phi. In both cases, the variance is considerably lower.

perscalar, but four hardware threads round-robin instruction-by-instruction for the execution core. As a consequence, the lower instruction count translates into a much lower average latency on the Phi.

The lower average context switch costs on the Phi translate directly into benefits for an HRT developer because it makes it feasible to more finely partition work. On both platforms, the lower variance makes more fine grain cooperation feasible. The default policies described in Section 2.1, combined with the performance characteristics shown here are intended to provide a predictable substrate for HRT development. The HRT developer can also readily override the default scheduling and binding model while still leveraging the fast thread creation/fork and context switch capabilities.

Events   Figure 4 compares the event wakeup performance for the mechanisms discussed in Section 2.1 on the two platforms. We measure the latency from when an event is signaled to when the waiting thread executes. We compare the cost of condition variable wakeup in user mode in Linux with our two implementations of them (with and without IPI) in Aerokernel. We also show the performance of the Linux fast user space mutex ("futex") primitive, and of a oneway IPI, which is the hardware limit for an event wakeup.

For condition variables, the latency measured is from the call to `pthread_cond_signal` (or equivalent) and the subsequent wakeup from `pthread_cond_wait` (or equivalent). The IPI measurement is the time from when the IPI is initiated until when its interrupt handler on the destination hardware thread has written a memory location being monitored by the source hardware thread.

The average latency for Aerokernel's condition variables (with IPI) is five times lower than that of Linux user level on both platforms. It is also three to five times lower than the futex. Equally important, the variance in this latency is much

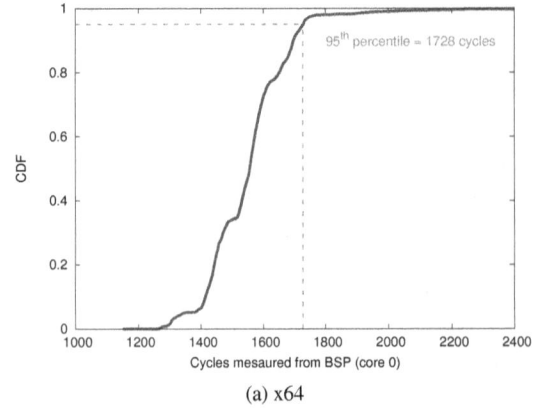

(a) x64

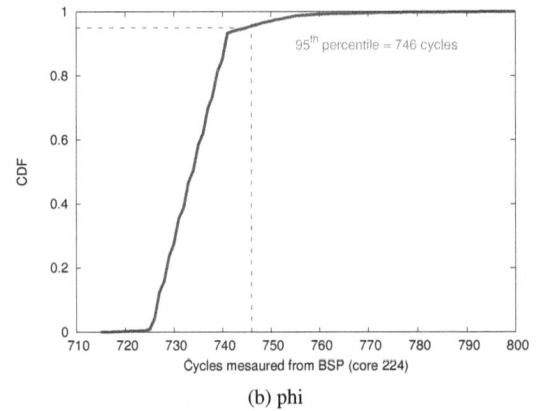

(b) phi

Figure 5: CDF of IPI one-way latencies, the hardware limit of asynchronous signaling that is available to HRTs.

lower on both platforms, by a factor of three to ten. From an HRT developer's perspective, these performance results mean that much "smaller" events or smaller units of work can feasibly be managed, and that these events and work can be more tightly synchronized in time.

Because they operate in kernel mode, HRTs can make direct use of IPIs and thus operate at the hardware limit of asynchronous event notification, which is one to three thousand cycles on our hardware. Figure 5 illustrates the latency of IPIs, as described earlier, on our two platforms. The specific latency depends on which two cores are involved and the machine topology. This is reflected in the notches in the CDF curve. Note however that there is little variation overall—the 5th and 95th percentile are within hundreds of cycles.

4. Experiences in creating HRTs

We now describe our experience in using Aerokernel to transform parallel runtime systems into HRTs—to convert these user-level systems and their applications into kernels.

4.1 Legion

The Legion runtime system is designed to provide applications with a parallel programming model that maps well to

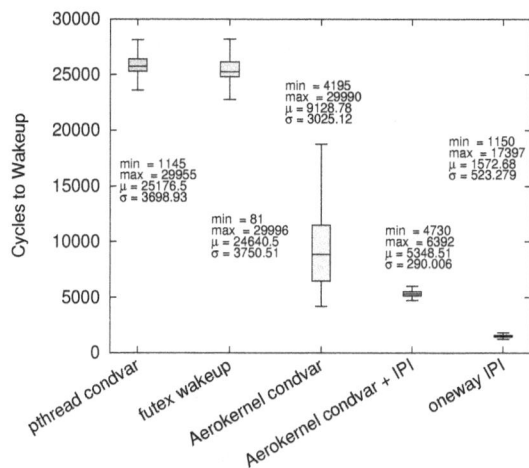

(a) x64

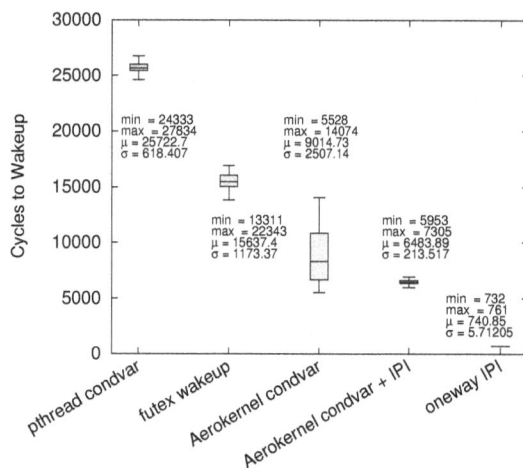

(b) phi

Figure 4: Event wakeup latency. Aerokernel conditional variable wakeup latency is on average five times faster than Linux (pthreads), and has 3–10 times less variation.

heterogeneous architectures [4, 66]. Whether the application runs on a single node or across nodes—even with GPUs—the Legion runtime can manage the underlying resources so that the application does not have to. Legion is of particular interest as an HRT because the primary focus of the Legion developers is on the design of the runtime system. This not only allows us to leverage their experience in designing runtimes, but also gives us access to a system designed with experimentation in mind. Further, the codebase has reached the point where the developers' ability to rapidly prototype new ideas is hindered by abstractions imposed by the OS.

Under the covers, Legion bears similarities to an operating system and concerns itself with issues that an OS must deal with, including task scheduling, isolation, multiplexing of hardware resources, and synchronization. The way that a complex runtime like Legion attempts to manage the machine to suit its own needs can often conflict with the services and abstractions provided by the OS.

As Legion is intended for heterogeneous hardware it is designed with a multi-layer architecture. It is split up into the *high-level* runtime and the *low-level* runtime. The high-level runtime is portable across machines, and the low-level runtime contains all of the machine-specific code. There is a separate low-level implementation called the *shared low-level runtime*. This is the low-level layer implemented for shared memory machines. All of our modifications to Legion when porting it to Aerokernel were made to this component. Outside of optimizations using hardware access, and understanding the needs of the runtime, the port was straight-forward.

Legion, in its default user-level implementation, uses pthreads as representations of logical processors, so the low-level runtime makes heavy use of the pthreads interface. We

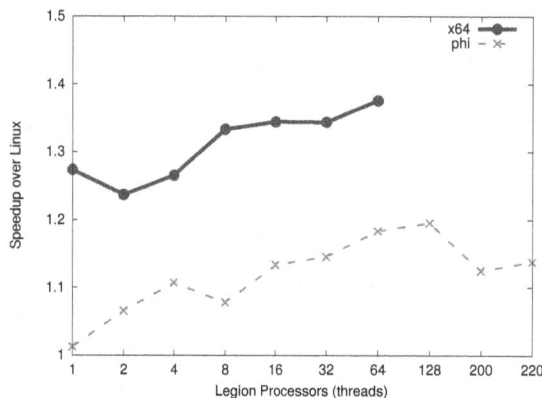

Figure 6: Aerokernel speedup of Legion HPCG (x64+phi).

created a variant that made use of the Aerokernel interface, particularly for threads and events. Our port is based on Legion as of October 2014 (commit e22962d), which can be found on legion.stanford.edu. The port to Aerokernel involved 1.5 person-months of effort, and approximately 200 lines of C/C++ code were added to Legion to support it. Probably the most complex part of the effort involved enhancing the building and linking logic so that the result was compatible with the Aerokernel model. The Legion distribution includes numerous test codes which we used to evaluate the correctness of our work.

To evaluate the performance benefits of applying the HRT model to Legion using Aerokernel, we used the HPCG (High Performance Conjugate Gradients) macrobenchmark. HPCG is an application benchmark effort from Sandia National Labs that is designed to help rank top-500 supercomputers for suitability to scalable applications of national interest [27, 38]. Los Alamos National Laboratory has ported

167

HPCG to Legion, and we used this port to further evaluate our Aerokernel variant of Legion. HPCG is a complex benchmark (∼5100 lines of C++) that exercises many Legion features. Recall that Legion itself comprises another ∼43,000 lines of C++.

Figure 6 shows the speedup of the HPCG/Legion in Aerokernel over HPCG/Legion on Linux as a function of the number of Legion processors being used. Each Legion processor is bound to a distinct hardware thread. On the Phi, Aerokernel is able to speed up HPCG by up to 20%. On x64, Aerokernel increases its performance by almost 40%. We configured HPCG for a medium problem size which, on a standard Linux setup, runs for roughly 2 seconds. We see similar results for other HPCG configurations.

There are many contributors to the increased performance of HPCG in Aerokernel, particularly fast condition variables. An interesting one is simply due to the simplified paging model. On x64 the Linux version exhibited almost 1.6 million TLB misses during execution. In comparison, the Aerokernel version exhibited about 100.

4.2 NESL

NESL [12] is a highly influential implementation of nested data parallelism developed at CMU in the '90s. Recently, it has influenced the design of parallelism in Manticore [34, 33], Data Parallel Haskell [20, 21], and arguably the nested call extensions to CUDA [56]. NESL is a functional programming language that allows the implementation of complex parallel algorithms in a compact and high-level way. NESL programs are compiled into abstract vector operations known as VCODE through a process known as flattening. An abstract VCODE interpreter then executes these programs on physical hardware. Flattening transformations and their ability to transform nested (recursive) data parallelism into "flat" vector operations while preserving the asymptotic complexity of programs is a key contribution of NESL [13] and recent work on using NESL-like nested data parallelism for GPUs [9] and multicore [8] has focused on extending flattening approaches to better match such hardware.

As a proof of concept, we ported NESL's existing VCODE interpreter to Aerokernel, allowing us to run any program compiled by the out-of-the-box NESL compiler. We also ported NESL's sequential implementation of the vector operation library CVL, which we have started parallelizing. Currently, vector operations with the exception of scans execute in parallel. The combination of the core VCODE interpreter and a CVL library form the VCODE interpreter for a system in the NESL model.

While this effort is a work in progress, it gives some insights into the challenges of porting this kind of parallel runtime to become an HRT. In summary, such a port is quite tractable. Our modifications to the NESL source code release[1] currently comprise about 100 lines of Make-

file changes and 360 lines of C source code changes. About 220 lines of the C changes are in CVL macros that implement the point-wise vector operations we have parallelized using Aerokernel's thread fork/join facilities. The remainder (100 Makefile lines, 140 C lines) reflect the amount of glue logic that was needed to bring the VCODE interpreter and the serial CVL implementation into Aerokernel. The hardest part of this glue logic is assuring that the compilation and linking model match that of Aerokernel, which is reflected in the Makefile changes. The effort took about one person-month to bring to this point.

4.3 NDPC

We are creating a different implementation of a subset of the NESL language which we refer to as "Nested Data Parallelism in C/C++" (NDPC). This is implemented as a source-to-source translator whose input is the NESL subset and whose output is C++ code (with C bindings) that uses recursive fork/join parallelism instead of NESL's flattened vector parallelism. The C++ code is compiled directly to object code and executes without any interpreter or JIT. Because C/C++ is the target language, the resulting compiled NDPC program can easily be directly linked into and called from C/C++ codebases. NDPC's collection type is defined as an abstract C++ class, which makes it feasible for the generated code to execute over any C/C++ data structure provided it exposes or is wrapped with the suitable interface. We made this design decision to further facilitate "dropping into NDPC" from C/C++ when parallelism is needed. In the context of Figure 7, our intent is that the runtime processing of a call to an NDPC function will include crossing the boundary between the general purpose and specialized portions of the hybrid virtual machine.

The generated code uses a runtime that is written in C, C++, and assembly that provides preemptive threads and simple work stealing. Code generation is greatly simplified because the runtime supports a thread fork primitive. The runtime guarantees that a forked thread will terminate at the point it attempts to return from the current function. The NDPC compiler in turn guarantees the code it generates for the current function will only use the current caller and callee stack frames, that it will not place pointers to the stack *on* the stack, and that the parent will join with any forked children before it returns from the current function. The runtime's implementation of the thread fork primitive can thus avoid complex stack management. Furthermore, it can potentially provide fast thread creation, despite the fork semantics, because it can avoid most stack copying as only data on the caller and callee stack frames may be referenced by the child. In some cases, the compiler can determine the maximum stack size (e.g., for a leaf function), and supply this to the runtime, further speeding up thread creation.

The runtime supports being compiled to operate in user level, using pthreads or an internal fibers implementation, or to operate in kernel level using Aerokernel. The Aerokernel

---

[1] Available from www.cs.cmu.edu/~scandal/nesl/nesl3.1.html

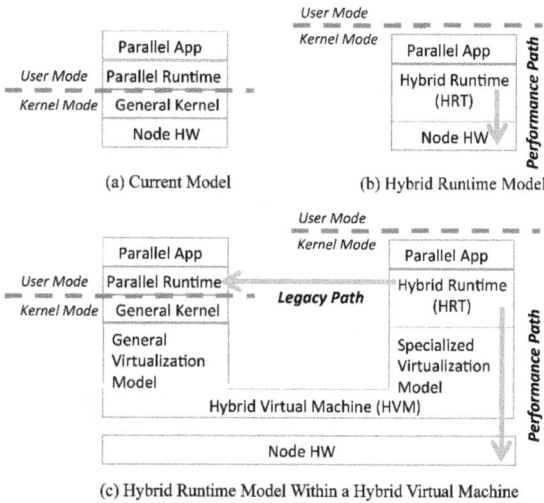

Figure 7: Overview of the HVM and the HRT.

support consists of only 150 lines of code. As with the NESL VCODE port (Section 4.2) the primary challenges in making NDPC operate at kernel-level within Aerokernel have to do with assuring that the compilation and linking models match those of Aerokernel. Currently, we are able to compile simple benchmarks such as nested data parallel quicksort into Aerokernel kernels and run them. NDPC is a work in progress, but the effort to bring it up in Aerokernel in its present state required about a person-week of effort.

5. Hybrid virtual machine

We currently envision four deployment models for an HRT:

- *Dedicated*: the machine is dedicated to the HRT, for example on a machine is an accelerator or a node of a supercomputer. This is the model used in the previous section.

- *Partitioned*: the machine is a supercomputer node that is physically partitioned [57], with a partition of cores dedicated to the HRT.

- *VM*: The machine's hypervisor creates a VM that runs the HRT.

- *HVM*: The machine's hypervisor creates a VM that is internally partitioned and runs both the HRT and a general purpose OS we call the "regular" OS (ROS).

For the *VM* and *HVM* deployment models, the hypervisor partitions/controls resources, and provides multiprogramming and access control. In the *HVM* model, the HRT can leverage both kernels, as we describe in detail here. Note that in an HVM, the ROS memory is vulnerable to modification by the HRT, but we think of the two as a unit; an unrelated process would be run in a separate VM (or on the host).

The purpose of the hybrid virtual machine (HVM) environment, illustrated in Figure 7, is to enable the execution of an HRT in a virtual environment simultaneously with the ROS. That is, a single VM is shared between a ROS and an

HRT. The virtual environment exposed to the HRT may be different from and indeed much lower-level than the environment exposed to the ROS. It can also be rebooted independently of the ROS. At the same time, the HRT has access to the memory of the ROS and can interrupt it. In some ways, the HRT can be viewed as providing an "accelerator" for the ROS and its applications, and the HVM provides the functionality of bridging the two. Using the HVM, the performance critical elements of the parallel runtime can be moved into the HRT, while runtime functionality that requires the full stack remains in the ROS.

We have developed a prototype HVM environment in the context of the Palacios open source VMM. The concepts and prerequisites of our prototype are not specific to Palacios and could be readily implemented in other VMMs. Our prototype comprises about 3,500 lines of C and assembly.

5.1 Model

The user creates a virtual machine configuration, noting cores, memory, NUMA topology, devices, and their initial mappings to the underlying hardware. An additional configuration block specifies that this VM is to act as an HVM. The configuration contains three elements: (1) a partition of the cores of the VM into two groups: the HRT cores and the ROS cores, which will run their respective kernels; (2) a limit on how much of the VM's physical memory will be visible and accessible from a ROS core; and (3) a multiboot2-compliant kernel, such as an HRT built on top of Aerokernel. We extend the multiboot2 specification to support HRTs. The existence of a special header in the multiboot section of the ELF file indicates that the HRT boot model described here is to be followed instead of the standard multiboot2 model.

The remainder of the model can be explained by considering the view of a ROS core versus that of an HRT core. The VMM maintains the following invariants for a ROS core: (1) Only the portion of the VM's physical memory designated for ROS use is visible and accessible. (2) Inter-processor interrupts (IPIs) can be sent only to another ROS core. (3) Broadcast, group, lowest-priority, and similar IPI destinations consider only the ROS cores. An HRT core, on the other hand, has no such constraints. All of the VM's physical memory is visible and accessible. IPIs can be sent to any core, and broadcast, group, lowest-priority and similar IPI destinations can consider either all cores or only HRT cores. This is set by the HRT. Generally speaking, interrupts from interrupt controllers such as IOAPICs and physical interrupts can be delivered to both ROS and HRT cores. The default is that they are delivered only to ROS cores, but an HRT core can request them. Broadcast, group, lowest priority, and similar destinations are computed over the ROS cores and any requesting HRT cores.

5.2 Protection

The invariants described above are implemented through two techniques. The memory invariants leverage the fact that

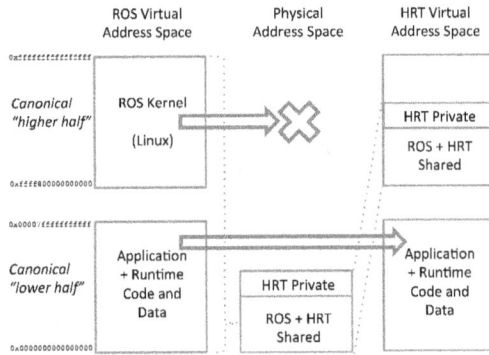

Figure 8: Merged address space.

each core in the VMM we use, similar to other VMMs, maintains its own paging state, for example shadow or nested page tables. This state is incrementally updated due to exits on the core, most importantly due to page faults or nested page faults. For example, a write to a previously unmapped address causes an exit during which we validate the access and add the relevant page table entries in the shadow or nested age tables if it is an appropriate access. A similar validation occurs for memory-mapped I/O devices. We have extended this model so that validation simply takes into account the type of core (ROS or HRT) on which the exit occurred. This allows us to catch and reject attempts by a ROS core to access illegal guest physical memory addresses.

The interrupt invariants are implemented by extensions to the VMM's APIC device. At the most basic level, IPI delivery from any APIC, IOAPIC, or MSI takes into account the type of core from which the IPI originates (if any) and the type of core that it targets. IPIs from a ROS core to an HRT core are simply dropped. External interrupts targeting an HRT core are delivered only if previously requested. Additionally, the computations involved with broadcast and group destinations for IPIs and external interrupts are modified so that only cores that are prospective targets are included. Similarly, the determination of the appropriate core or cores for a lowest priority destination includes only those cores to which the interrupt could be delivered under the previous restrictions. These mechanisms allow us to reject any attempt to send an HRT core an unwanted interrupt.

5.3 Merged address space

The HRT can access the entire guest physical address space, and thus can operate directly on any data within the ROS. However, to simplify the creation of the legacy path shown in Figure 7, we provide the option to merge an address space within the ROS with the address space of the HRT, as is shown in Figure 8. When a merged address space is in effect, the HRT can use the same user-mode virtual addresses that are used in the ROS. For example, the parallel runtime in the ROS might load files and construct a pointer-based data structure in memory. It could then invoke a function within its counterpart in the HRT to operate on that data.

Item	Cycles	Time
Address Space Merger	$\sim$33 K	15 μs
Asynchronous Call	$\sim$25 K	11 μs
Synchronous Call (different socket)	$\sim$1060	482 ns
Synchronous Call (same socket)	$\sim$790	359 ns

Figure 9: Round-trip latencies of ROS$\leftrightarrow$HRT interactions (x64).

To achieve this we leverage the canonical 64-bit address space model of x64 processors, and its wide use within existing kernels, such as Linux. In this model, the virtual address space is split into a "lower half" and a "higher half" with a gap in between, the size of which is implementation dependent. In a typical process model, e.g., Linux, the lower half is used for user addresses and the higher half is used for the kernel.

For an HRT that supports it, the HVM arranges so that the physical address space is identity-mapped into the higher half of the HRT address space. That is, within the HRT, the physical address space mapping (including the portion of the physical address space only the HRT can access) occupies the same portion of the virtual address space that is occupied by the ROS kernel, the higher half. Without a merger, the lower half is unmapped and the HRT runs purely out of the higher half. When a merger is requested, we map the lower half of the ROS's current process's address space into the lower half of the HRT address space. For a Aerokernel-based HRT, this is done by copying the first 256 entries of the PML4 from the PML4 pointed to by the ROS's CR3 to the HRT's PML4 and then broadcasting a TLB shootdown to all HRT cores.

Because the parallel runtime in the ROS and the HRT are co-developed, the responsibility of assuring that page table mappings exist for lower half addresses used by the HRT in a merged address space is the parallel runtime's. For example, the parallel runtime can pin memory before merging the address spaces, or introduce a protocol to send page faults back to the ROS. The former is not an unreasonable expectation in a high performance environment as we would never expect to be swapping.

5.4 Communication

The HVM model makes it possible for essentially any communication mechanism between the ROS and HRT to be built, and most of these require no specific support in the HVM. As a consequence, we minimally defined the *basic* communication between the ROS, HRT, and the VMM using shared physical memory, hypercalls, and interrupts.

The user-level code in the ROS can use hypercalls to sequentially request HRT reboots, address space mergers, and asynchronous sequential or parallel function calls. The VMM handles reboots internally, and forwards the other two requests to the HRT as interrupts. Because additional information may need to be conveyed, a data page is shared between the VMM and the HRT. For a function call request, the page essentially contains a pointer to the function and its arguments at the start and the return code at completion. For an address space merger, the page contains the CR3 of the calling process. The HRT indicates to the VMM when it is finished with the current request via a hypercall.

After an address space merger, the user-level code in the ROS can also use a single hypercall to initiate synchronous operation with the HRT. This hypercall ultimately indicates to the HRT a virtual address which will be used for future synchronization between the HRT and ROS. A simple memory-based protocol can then be used between the two to communicate, for example for the ROS to invoke functions in the HRT, without VMM intervention.

Figure 9 shows the measured latency of each of these operations, using Aerokernel as the HRT.

5.5 Boot and reboot

The ROS cores follow the traditional PC bootstrap model with the exception that the ACPI and MP tables built in memory show only the hardware deemed visible to the ROS by the HVM configuration.

Boot on an HRT core differs from both the ROS boot sequence and from the multiboot2 specification [58], which we leverage. Multiboot2 for x86 allows for bootstrap of a kernel into 32-bit protected mode on the first core (the BSP) of a machine. Our extension allows for bootstrap of a kernel in full 64-bit mode. There are two elements to HRT boot—memory setup and core bootstrap. These elements combine to allow us to *simultaneously* start all HRT cores immediately at the entry point of the HRT. At the time of this startup, each core is running in long mode (64-bit mode) with paging and interrupt control enabled. The HRT thus does not have much bootstrap to do itself. A special multiboot tag within the kernel indicates compatibility with this mode of operation and includes requests for how the VMM should set up the kernel environment.

In memory setup, which is done only once in the lifetime of the HRT portion of the VM, we select an HRT-only portion of the guest physical address space and lay out the basic machine data structures needed: an interrupt descriptor table (IDT) along with dummy interrupt and exception handlers, a global descriptor table (GDT), a task state segment (TSS), and a page table hierarchy that identity-maps physical addresses (including the higher-half offset as shown in Figure 8, if desired) using the largest feasible page table entries. We also select an initial stack location for each HRT core. A simple ELF loader then copies the HRT ELF into memory at its desired target location. Finally, we build a multiboot2 information structure in memory. This structure is augmented with headers that indicate our variant of multiboot2 is in use, and provide fundamental information about the VM, such as the number of cores, the APIC IDs, interrupt vectoring, and the memory map, including the areas containing the memory

Item	Cycles (and exits)	Time
HRT core boot of	~135 K	
Aerokernel to `main()`	(7 exits)	61 μs
Linux `fork()`	~320 K	145 μs
Linux `exec()`	~1 M	476 μs
Linux `fork()` + `exec()`	~1.5 M	714 μs
HRT core boot of	~37 M	
Aerokernel to idle thread	(~2300 exits)	17 ms

Figure 10: HRT reboot latencies in context (x64).

setup. Because bootstrap occurs on virtual hardware this information can be much simpler than that supplied via ACPI.

In core bootstrap, which may be done repeatedly over the lifetime of the HRT portion of the HVM, the registers of the core are set. The registers that must be set include the control registers (IDTR, GDTR, LDTR, TR, CR0, CR3, CR4, EFER), the six segment registers including their descriptor components, and the general purpose registers RSP, RBP, RDI, and RAX. The point is that core bootstrap simply involves setting about 20 register values. The instruction pointer (RIP) is set to the entry point of the HRT, while RSP and RBP are set to the initial stack for the core, and RDI points to the multiboot2 header information and RAX contains the multiboot2 cookie.

Unlike a ROS boot, all HRT cores are booted together simultaneously. The HRT is expected to synchronize these internally. In practice this is easy as a core can quickly find its rank by consulting its APIC ID and looking at the APIC ID list given in the extended multiboot2 information.

Fast HRT Reboot Because core bootstrap involves changing a small set of registers and then reentering the guest, the set of HRT cores can be rebooted very quickly. An HRT reboot is also independent of the execution of the ROS, and an HRT can be therefore be rebooted many times over the lifetime of the HVM. We allow an HRT reboot to be initiated from the HRT itself, from a userspace utility running on the host operating system, and via a hypercall from the ROS, as described above.

Figure 10 illustrates the costs of rebooting an HRT core, and compares it with the cost of typical process operations on a Linux 2.6.32 kernel running on the same hardware. An HRT core can be booted and execute to the first instruction of Aerokernel's `main()` in ~50% of the time it takes to do a Linux process `fork()`, ~13% of the time to do a Linux process `exec()` and ~8% of the time to do a combined `fork()` and `exec()`. The latter is the closest analog in Linux to what the HRT reboot accomplishes. Note also that timings on Linux were done "hot"—executables were already memory resident.

A complete reboot of Aerokernel on the HRT core to the point where the idle thread is executing takes 17 ms. This time is also blindingly fast compared to the familiar norm of booting a physical or virtual machine. We anticipate that this time will further improve for two reasons. First, we can in principle skip much of the general purpose startup code in Aerokernel, which is currently executed, given that we know exactly what the virtual hardware looks like. Second, by starting the core from a memory and register snapshot, specifically at the point of execution we desire to start from, we should be able to even further short-circuit startup code.

It is important to note that even at 17 ms, a complete Aerokernel reboot is 60 to 300 times faster than a typical 1-5 minute node or server boot time. It should be thought of in those terms, similar to the MicroReboot concept [18] for cheap recovery from software failures. We can use HRT reboots to address many issues and, in the limit, treat them as being on par with process creation in a traditional OS.

6. Related work

The design of Aerokernel was influenced by early research on microkernels [51, 11, 10] and even more by Engler and others' work on exokernels [29, 30]. Using exokernel terminology, Aerokernel can be thought of as a kind of library OS for a parallel runtime, but we shed the notion of privilege levels for the sake of functionality and performance. Other important OS projects in the vain of thin kernel layers include KeyKOS [14], ADEOS [69], and the Stanford Cache Kernel [25]. More recently there has been a resurgence of ideas from exokernel in the context of virtualization. Dune uses hardware virtualization support to allow applications to have access to a certain protected hardware features [7]. Arrakis leverages virtualized I/O devices in a similar vain in order to allow hardware access [59]. OSv [45], Unikernels [53], and the Drawbridge and Bascule libOSes [60, 6] are other examples. OSv, for example, does not eliminate the user/kernel distinction. Aerokernel is unique in that it is designed to support the hybrid runtime model, giving parallel runtimes unfettered access to the full feature set of the machine. Aerokernel is conceptually similar to Libra [1], but Libra does not provide a notion of a large shared address space between Libra/J9 and the Linux support VM. Furthermore, Aerokernel does not require HVM capability in order to run. That is, it does not rely on Palacios as an exokernel layer. For example, we can quickly boot a hybrid runtime instance on raw Xeon Phi hardware. Aerokernel's fast bootstrap capability exists independent of the HVM environment. Linux containers [54] provide fast-launching virtual instances as well, but they still maintain a user/kernel distinction and do not allow the use of a specialized kernel.

Aerokernel bears some similarity to other single address space OSes (SASOSes), including Opal [24], Singularity [42], Scout [55], and Nemesis [61]. Aerokernel targets single-node performance, particularly for many-core machines. We therefore drew inspiration from some notable projects with similar goals, including Barrelfish [5], Tessellation OS [52], Corey [15], K42 [47], and, of course, work on scaling Linux [16]. PTask [62] provides kernel-level abstrac-tions for GPUs, including a data flow abstraction that can be used by the kernel itself. None of this work explicitly shapes an OS around the needs of parallel runtime systems. As far as we are aware, this is a unique property of Aerokernel.

The HPC community has long felt that OSes "get in the way". Ferreira and Hoefler both explored the performance impact of OS noise on large-scale parallel applications [31, 32, 40]. Lightweight kernels such as Kitten [48] and mOS [68] attempt to mitigate the problem, but granting runtimes fully privileged access is not one of the solutions explored. There has been a decades-long interest in bridging the gap between complex hardware and the programmer through languages and runtime systems which is now seeing a resurgence in the exascale space. Languages and language implementations coming from the HPC community, such as OpenARC [50], Chapel [22], UPC [19], CoArray Fortran [28], and X10 [23] could be users of the hybrid runtime concept. Swift [46]'s model of many tiny tasks is of particular resonance. Another common thread in bridging the gap between complex hardware and the programmer is to enhance program and runtime execution by manipulating the system from user level. COSMIC [17] targets the Intel Phi, while Juggle [41] targets NUMA machines. The HRT model allows direct control of decisions that such systems can only encourage.

Other approaches to realizing the split-machine model shown in Figure 7 exist. Dune, described above, provides one alternative. Guarded modules [36] could be used to give portions of a general-purpose virtualization model selective privileged access to hardware, including I/O devices. Pisces [57] would enable an approach that could eschew virtualization altogether by partitioning the hardware and booting multiple kernels simultaneously without virtualization.

7. Conclusion

We introduced the hybrid runtime (HRT) model, in which a parallel runtime system and its application are transformed into a specialized OS kernel that can take direct advantage of all hardware features. Two core tools, the Nautilus Aerokernel and HVM, enable the model. Aerokernel provides a suite of functionality specialized to HRT development that can perform up to two orders of magnitude faster than the general purpose functionality in the Linux kernel while also providing much less variation in performance. Aerokernel functionality leads to 20-40% performance gains in an application benchmark for the Legion runtime system on x64 and Xeon Phi. HVM is VMM functionality that allows us to simultaneously run two kernels, an HRT and a traditional kernel, within the same VM, allowing a runtime to benefit from the performance and capabilities provided by the HRT model while not losing the performance non-critical functionality of the traditional kernel.

References

[1] AMMONS, G., APPAVOO, J., BUTRICO, M., DA SILVA, D., GROVE, D., KAWACHIYA, K., KRIEGER, O., ROSENBURG, B., HENSBERGEN, E. V., AND WISNIEWSKI, R. W. Libra: A library operating system for a jvm in a virtualized execution environment. In *Proceedings of the 3rd International Conference on Virtual Execution Environments (VEE 2007)* (June 2007), pp. 44–54.

[2] ANDERSON, T. E., BERSHAD, B. N., LAZOWSKA, E. D., AND LEVY, H. M. Scheduler activations: Effective kernel support for the user-level management of parallelism. In *Proceedings of the 13th ACM Symposium on Operating Systems Principles (SOSP 1991)* (Oct. 1991), pp. 95–109.

[3] BAE, C., LANGE, J., AND DINDA, P. Enhancing virtualized application performance through dynamic adaptive paging mode selection. In *Proceedings of the 8th International Conference on Autonomic Computing (ICAC 2011)* (June 2011).

[4] BAUER, M., TREICHLER, S., SLAUGHTER, E., AND AIKEN, A. Legion: Expressing locality and independence with logical regions. In *Proceedings of Supercomputing (SC 2012)* (Nov. 2012).

[5] BAUMANN, A., BARHAM, P., DAGAND, P. E., HARRIS, T., ISAACS, R., PETER, S., ROSCOE, T., SCHÜPBACH, A., AND SINGHANIA, A. The Multikernel: A new OS architecture for scalable multicore systems. In *Proceedings of the 22nd ACM Symposium on Operating Systems Principles (SOSP 2009)* (Oct. 2009), pp. 29–44.

[6] BAUMANN, A., LEE, D., FONSECA, P., GLENDENNING, L., LORCH, J. R., BOND, B., OLINSKY, R., AND HUNT, G. C. Composing OS extensions safely and efficiently with Bascule. In *Proceedings of the 8th ACM European Conference on Computer Systems (EuroSys 2013)* (Apr. 2013), pp. 239–252.

[7] BELAY, A., BITTAU, A., MASHTIZADEH, A., TEREI, D., MAZIÈRES, D., AND KOZYRAKIS, C. Dune: Safe user-level access to privileged CPU features. In *Proceedings of the 10th USENIX Conference on Operating Systems Design and Implementation (OSDI 2012)* (Oct. 2012), pp. 335–348.

[8] BERGSTROM, L., FLUET, M., RAINEY, M., REPPY, J., ROSEN, S., AND SHAW, A. Data-only flattening for nested data parallelism. In *Proceedings of the 18th ACM SIGPLAN Symposium on Principles and Practice of Parallel Programming (PPoPP 2013)* (Feb. 2013), pp. 81–92.

[9] BERGSTROM, L., AND REPPY, J. Nested data-parallelism on the GPU. In *Proceedings of the 17th ACM SIGPLAN International Conference on Functional Programming (ICFP 2012)* (Sept. 2012), pp. 247–258.

[10] BERSHAD, B. N., SAVAGE, S., PARDYAK, P., SIRER, E. G., FIUCZYNSKI, M. E., BECKER, D., CHAMBERS, C., AND EGGERS, S. Extensibility, safety and performance in the SPIN operating system. In *Proceedings of the 15th ACM Symposium on Operating Systems Principles (SOSP 1995)* (Dec. 1995), pp. 267–283.

[11] BLACK, D. L., GOLUB, D. B., JULIN, D. P., RASHID, R. F., DRAVES, R. P., DEAN, R. W., FORIN, A., BARRERA, J., TOKUDA, H., MALAN, G., AND BOHMAN, D. Microkernel operating system architecture and Mach. In *Proceedings of the USENIX Workshop on Micro-Kernels and Other Kernel Architectures* (Apr. 1992), pp. 11–30.

[12] BLELLOCH, G. E., CHATTERJEE, S., HARDWICK, J., SIPELSTEIN, J., AND ZAGHA, M. Implementation of a portable nested data-parallel language. *Journal of Parallel and Distributed Computing 21*, 1 (Apr. 1994), 4–14.

[13] BLELLOCH, G. E., AND GREINER, J. A provable time and space efficient implementation of NESL. In *Proceedings of the 1st ACM SIGPLAN International Conference on Functional Programming (ICFP 1996)* (May 1996), pp. 213–225.

[14] BOMBERGER, A. C., FRANTZ, W. S., HARDY, A. C., HARDY, N., LANDAU, C. R., AND SHAPIRO, J. S. The KeyKOS nanokernel architecture. In *Proceedings of the USENIX Workshop on Micro-kernels and Other Kernel Architectures* (Apr. 1992), pp. 95–112.

[15] BOYD-WICKIZER, S., CHEN, H., CHEN, R., MAO, Y., KAASHOEK, F., MORRIS, R., PESTEREV, A., STEIN, L., WU, M., DAI, Y., ZHANG, Y., AND ZHANG, Z. Corey: An operating system for many cores. In *Proceedings of the 8th USENIX Conference on Operating Systems Design and Implementation (OSDI 2008)* (Dec. 2008), pp. 43–57.

[16] BOYD-WICKIZER, S., CLEMENTS, A. T., MAO, Y., PESTEREV, A., KAASHOEK, M. F., MORRIS, R., AND ZELDOVICH, N. An analysis of Linux scalability to many cores. In *Proceedings of the 9th USENIX Symposium on Operating Systems Design and Implementation (OSDI 2010)* (Oct. 2010).

[17] CADAMB, S., COVIELLO, G., LI, C.-H., PHULL, R., RAO, K., SANKARADASS, M., AND CHAKRADHAR, S. COSMIC: Middleware for high performance and reliable multiprocessing on xeon phi coprocessors. In *Proceedings of the 22nd ACM Symposium on High-performance Parallel and Distributed Computing (HPDC 2013)* (June 2013), pp. 215–226.

[18] CANDEA, G., KAWAMOTO, S., FUJIKI, Y., FRIEDMAN, G., AND FOX, A. Microreboot: A technique for cheap recovery. In *Proceedings of the 6th USENIX Symposium on Operating Systems Design and Implementation (OSDI 2004)* (Dec. 2004), pp. 31–44.

[19] CARLSON, W., DRAPER, J., CULLER, D., YELICK, K., BROOKS, E., AND WARREN, K. Introduction to upc and language specification. Tech. Rep. CCS-TR-99-157, IDA Center for Computing Sciences, May 1999.

[20] CHAKRAVARTY, M., KELLER, G., LESHCHINSKIY, R., AND PFANNENSTIEL, W. Nepal—nested data-parallelism in haskell. In *Proceedings of the 7th International Euro-Par Conference (EUROPAR 2001)* (Aug. 2001).

[21] CHAKRAVARTY, M., LESHCHINSKIY, R., JONES, S. P., KELLER, G., AND MARLOW, S. Data parallel haskell: A status report. In *Proceedings of the Workshop on Declarative Aspects of Multicore Programming* (Jan. 2007).

[22] CHAMBERLAIN, B., CALLAHAN, D., AND ZIMA, H. Parallel programmability and the chapel langauge. *International Journal of High Performance Computing Applications 21*, 3 (Aug. 2007), 291–312.

[23] CHARLES, P., DONAWA, C., EBICIOGLU, K., GROTHOFF, C., KIELSTRA, A., VON PRAUN, C., SARASWAT, V., AND SARKAR, V. X10: An object-oriented approach to non-uniform cluster computing. In *Proceedings of the 20th ACM SIGPLAN Conference on Object-oriented Programming, Systems, Languages, and Applications (OOPSLA 2005)* (Oct. 2005), pp. 519–538.

[24] CHASE, J. S., LEVY, H. M., LEVY, H. M., FEELEY, M. J., FEELEY, M. J., LAZOWSKA, E. D., AND LAZOWSKA, E. D. Sharing and protection in a single address space operating system. *ACM Transactions on Computer Systems 12*, 4 (Nov. 1994), 271–307.

[25] CHERITON, D. R., AND DUDA, K. J. A caching model of operating system kernel functionality. In *Proceedings of the 1st USENIX Symposium on Operating Systems Design and Implementation (OSDI 2004)* (Nov. 1994).

[26] DAS, R., UYSAL, M., SALTZ, J., AND HWANG, Y.-S. Communication optimizations for irregular scientific computations on distributed memory architectures. *Journal of Parallel and Distributed Computing 22*, 3 (September 1994), 462–478.

[27] DONGARRA, J., AND HEROUX, M. A. Toward a new metric for ranking high performance computing systems. Tech. Rep. SAND2013-4744, Sandia National Laboratories, June 2013.

[28] DOTSENKO, Y., COARFA, C., AND MELLOR-CRUMMEY, J. A multi-platform co-array fortran compiler. In *Proceedings of the 13th International Conference on Parallel Architectures and Compilation Techniques (PACT 2004)* (Sept. 2004), pp. 29–40.

[29] ENGLER, D. R., AND KAASHOEK, M. F. Exterminate all operating system abstractions. In *Proceedings of the 5th Workshop on Hot Topics in Operating Systems (HotOS 1995)* (May 1995), pp. 78–83.

[30] ENGLER, D. R., KAASHOEK, M. F., AND O'TOOLE, JR., J. Exokernel: An operating system architecture for application-level resource management. In *Proceedings of the 15th ACM Symposium on Operating Systems Principles (SOSP 1995)* (Dec. 1995), pp. 251–266.

[31] FERREIRA, K. B., BRIDGES, P., AND BRIGHTWELL, R. Characterizing application sensitivity to OS interference using kernel-level noise injection. In *Proceedings of Supercomputing (SC 2008)* (Nov. 2008).

[32] FERREIRA, K. B., BRIDGES, P. G., BRIGHTWELL, R., AND PEDRETTI, K. T. Impact of system design parameters on application noise sensitivity. *Journal of Cluster Computing 16*, 1 (Mar. 2013).

[33] FLUET, M., RAINEY, M., REPPY, J., AND SHAW, A. Implicitly threaded parallelism in manticore. In *Proceedings of the 13th ACM SIGPLAN International Conference on Functional Programming (ICFP 2008)* (Sept. 2008), pp. 119–130.

[34] FLUET, M., RAINEY, M., REPPY, J., SHAW, A., AND XIAO, Y. Manticore: A heterogeneous parallel language. In *Proceedings of the Workshop on Declarative Aspects of Multi-core Programming (DAMP 2007)* (Jan. 2007), pp. 37–44.

[35] GOERBESSIOTIS, A. V., AND VALIANT, L. G. Direct bulk-synchronous parallel algorithms. *Journal of Parallel and Distributed Computing 22*, 2 (1994), 251–267.

[36] HALE, K. C., AND DINDA, P. A. Guarded modules: Adaptively extending the VMM's privilege into the guest. In *Proceedings of the 11th International Conference on Autonomic Computing (ICAC 2014)* (June 2014), pp. 85–96.

[37] HALE, K. C., AND DINDA, P. A. A case for transforming parallel runtimes into operating system kernels. In *Proceedings of the 24th International Symposium on High-performance Parallel and Distributed Computing (HPDC 2015)* (June 2015), pp. 27–32.

[38] HEROUX, M. A., DONGARRA, J., AND LUSZCZEK, P. HPCG technical specification. Tech. Rep. SAND2013-8752, Sandia National Laboratories, October 2013.

[39] HIGH PERFORMANCE FORTRAN FORUM. High Performance Fortran language specification, version 2.0. Tech. rep., Center for Research on Parallel Computation, Rice University, January 1996.

[40] HOEFLER, T., SCHNEIDER, T., AND LUMSDAINE, A. Characterizing the influence of system noise on large-scale applications by simulation. In *Proceedings of Supercomputing (SC 2010)* (Nov. 2010).

[41] HOFMEYR, S., COLMENARES, J. A., IANCU, C., AND KUBIATOWICZ, J. Juggle: Proactive load balancing on multicore computers. In *Proceedings of the 20th ACM Symposium on High-performance Parallel and Distributed Computing (HPDC 2011)* (June 2011), pp. 3–14.

[42] HUNT, G. C., AND LARUS, J. R. Singularity: Rethinking the software stack. *SIGOPS Operating Systems Review 41*, 2 (Apr. 2007), 37–49.

[43] KAISER, H., BRODOWICZ, M., AND STERLING, T. ParalleX: An advanced parallel execution model for scaling-impaired applications. In *Proceedings of the 38th International Conference on Parallel Processing Workshops (ICPPW 2009)* (Sept. 2009), pp. 394–401.

[44] KALÉ, L. V., RAMKUMAR, B., SINHA, A., AND GURSOY, A. The Charm parallel programming language and system: Part II–the runtime system. Tech. Rep. 95-03, Parallel Programming Laboratory, University of Illinois at Urbana-Champaign, 1994.

[45] KIVITY, A., LAOR, D., COSTA, G., ENBERG, P., HAR'EL, N., MARTI, D., AND ZOLOTAROV, V. OSv—optimizing the operating system for virtual machines. In *Proceedings of the 2014 USENIX Annual Technical Conference (USENIX ATC 2014)* (June 2014).

[46] KRIEDER, S., WOZNIAK, J., ARMSTRONG, T., WILDE, M., KATZ, D., GRIMMER, B., FOSTER, I., AND RAICU, I. Design and evaluation of the GeMTC framework for gpu-enabled many-task computing. In *Proceedings of the 23rd ACM Symposium on High-performance Parallel and Distributed Computing (HPDC 2014)* (June 2014), pp. 153–164.

[47] KRIEGER, O., AUSLANDER, M., ROSENBURG, B., WISNIEWSKI, R. W., XENIDIS, J., DA SILVA, D., OSTROWSKI, M., APPAVOO, J., BUTRICO, M., MERGEN, M., WATER-

LAND, A., AND UHLIG, V. K42: Building a complete operating system. In *Proceedings of the 1st ACM European Conference on Computer Systems (EuroSys 2006)* (Apr. 2006), pp. 133–145.

[48] LANGE, J., PEDRETTI, K., HUDSON, T., DINDA, P., CUI, Z., XIA, L., BRIDGES, P., GOCKE, A., JACONETTE, S., LEVENHAGEN, M., AND BRIGHTWELL, R. Palacios and kitten: New high performance operating systems for scalable virtualized and native supercomputing. In *Proceedings of the 24th IEEE International Parallel and Distributed Processing Symposium (IPDPS 2010)* (Apr. 2010).

[49] LAUDERDALE, C., AND KHAN, R. Towards a codelet-based runtime for exascale computing. In *Proceedings of the 2nd International Workshop on Adaptive Self-Tuning Computing Systems for the Exaflop Era (EXADAPT 2012)* (Mar. 2012), pp. 21–26.

[50] LEE, S., AND VETTER, J. OpenARC: Open accelerator research compiler for directive-based, efficient heterogeneous computing. In *Proceedings of the 23rd ACM Symposium on High-performance Parallel and Distributed Computing (HPDC 2014)* (June 2014), pp. 115–120.

[51] LIEDTKE, J. On micro-kernel construction. In *Proceedings of the 15th ACM Symposium on Operating Systems Principles (SOSP 1995)* (Dec. 1995), pp. 237–250.

[52] LIU, R., KLUES, K., BIRD, S., HOFMEYR, S., ASANOVIĆ, K., AND KUBIATOWICZ, J. Tessellation: Space-time partitioning in a manycore client OS. In *Proceedings of the 1st USENIX Conference on Hot Topics in Parallelism (HotPar 2009)* (Mar. 2009).

[53] MADHAVAPEDDY, A., MORTIER, R., ROTSOS, C., SCOTT, D., SINGH, B., GAZAGNAIRE, T., SMITH, S., HAND, S., AND CROWCROFT, J. Unikernels: Library operating systems for the cloud. In *Proceedings of the 18th International Conference on Architectural Support for Programming Languages and Operating Systems (ASPLOS 2013)* (Mar. 2013), pp. 461–472.

[54] MENAGE, P. B. Adding generic process containers to the Linux kernel. In *Proceedings of the Linux Symposium* (June 2007), pp. 45–58.

[55] MONTZ, A. B., MOSBERGER, D., O'MALLEY, S. W., PETERSON, L. L., AND PROEBSTING, T. A. Scout: A communications-oriented operating system. In *Proceedings of the 5th Workshop on Hot Topics in Operating Systems (HotOS 1995)* (May 1995), pp. 58–61.

[56] NVIDIA CORPORATION. Dynamic parallelism in CUDA, Dec. 2012.

[57] OAYANG, J., KOCOLOSKI, B., LANGE, J., AND PEDRETTI, K. Achieving performance isolation with lightweight co-kernels. In *Proceedings of the 24th International ACM Symposium on High Performance Parallel and Distributed Computing (HPDC 2015)* (June 2015), pp. 149–160.

[58] OKUJI, Y. K., FORD, B., BOLEYN, E. S., AND ISHIGURO,

K. The multiboot specification—version 1.6. Tech. rep., Free Software Foundation, Inc., 2010.

[59] PETER, S., AND ANDERSON, T. Arrakis: A case for the end of the empire. In *Proceedings of the 14th Workshop on Hot Topics in Operating Systems (HotOS 2013)* (May 2013).

[60] PORTER, D. E., BOYD-WICKIZER, S., HOWELL, J., OLINSKY, R., AND HUNT, G. C. Rethinking the library OS from the top down. In *Proceedings of the 16th International Conference on Architectural Support for Programming Languages and Operating Systems (ASPLOS 2011)* (Mar. 2011), pp. 291–304.

[61] ROSCOE, T. Linkage in the Nemesis single address space operating system. *ACM SIGOPS Operating Systems Review 28*, 4 (Oct. 1994), 48–55.

[62] ROSSBACH, C. J., CURREY, J., SILBERSTEIN, M., RAY, B., AND WITCHEL, E. Ptask: Operating system abstractions to manage gpus as compute devices. In *Proceedings of the Twenty-Third ACM Symposium on Operating Systems Principles (SOSP 2011)* (2011).

[63] SWAINE, J., FETSCHER, B., ST-AMOUR, V., FINDLER, R. B., AND FLATT, M. Seeing the futures: Profiling shared-memory parallel Racket. In *Proceedings of the 1st ACM SIGPLAN Workshop on Functional High-performance Computing (FHPC 2012)* (Sept. 2012).

[64] SWAINE, J., TEW, K., DINDA, P., FINDLER, R., AND FLATT, M. Back to the futures: Incremental parallelization of existing sequential runtime systems. In *Proceedings of the ACM SIGPLAN International Conference on Object-Oriented Programming, Systems, Languages, and Applications (OOPSLA 2010)* (October 2010).

[65] TEW, K., SWAINE, J., FLATT, M., FINDLER, R., AND DINDA, P. Places: Adding message passing parallelism to racket. In *Proceedings of the 7th Dynamic Languages Symposium (DLS 2011)* (Oct. 2011), pp. 85–96.

[66] TREICHLER, S., BAUER, M., AND AIKEN, A. Language support for dynamic, hierarchical data partitioning. In *Proceedings of the 2013 ACM SIGPLAN International Conference on Object-oriented Programming, Systems, Languages, and Applications (OOPSLA 2013)* (Oct. 2013), pp. 495–514.

[67] WHEELER, K. B., MURPHY, R. C., AND THAIN, D. Qthreads: An API for programming with millions of lightweight threads. In *Proceedings of the 22nd International Symposium on Parallel and Distributed Processing (IPDPS 2008)* (Apr. 2008).

[68] WISNIEWSKI, R. W., INGLETT, T., KEPPEL, P., MURTY, R., AND RIESEN, R. mOS: An architecture for extreme-scale operating systems. In *Proceedings of the 4th International Workshop on Runtime and Operating Systems for Supercomputers (ROSS 2014)* (June 2014).

[69] YAGHMOUR, K. Adaptive domain environment for operating systems. `http://www.opersys.com/ftp/pub/Adeos/adeos.pdf`.

Sweet Spots and Limits for Virtualization

Carl Waldspurger
(Moderator)
Independent Consultant

Emery Berger
(Panelist)
University of Massachusetts Amherst

Abhishek Bhattacharjee
(Panelist)
Rutgers University

Kevin Pedretti
(Panelist)
Sandia National Laboratories

Simon Peter
(Panelist)
University of Texas at Austin

Chris Rossbach
(Panelist)
VMWare Resaerch Group
& University of Texas at Austin

Abstract

This year at VEE, we added a panel to discuss the state of virtualization: what problems are solved? what problems are important? and what problems may not be worth solving? The panelist are experts in areas ranging from hardware virtualization up to language-level virtualization.

Moderator: Carl Waldspurger

Carl Waldspurger has a long record of innovation in systems software and virtualization. As a consultant and technical advisor, he works closely with engineering and research teams on a range of topics including virtualized datacenter analytics, storage caching, security, resource management, and hardware support for processor-level QoS. Carl is active in the research community, and is currently serving as the program co-chair for FAST '17.

While at VMware, Carl led the design and implementation of processor scheduling and memory management for the ESX hypervisor, and was the architect for VMware's Distributed Resource Scheduler (DRS). Prior to VMware, he was a researcher at the DEC Systems Research Center. Carl holds a Ph.D. in computer science from MIT, for which he received the ACM Doctoral Dissertation Award.

Panelists

Emery Berger. Emery Berger is a Professor in the Collegeof Information and Computer Sciences at the University of Massachusetts Amherst, where he co-directs the PLASMA lab (Programming Languages and Systems at Massachusetts) and is a regular visiting researcher at Microsoft Research. He is the creator of a number of influential software systems including Hoard, a fast and scalable memory manager that accelerates multithreaded applications (used by companies including British Telecom, Cisco, Credit Suisse, Reuters, Royal Bank of Canada, SAP, and Tata, and on which the Mac OS X memory manager is based); DieHard, an error-avoiding memory manager that directly influenced the design of theWindows 7 Fault-Tolerant Heap; and DieHarder, a secure memory manager that was an inspiration for hardening changes made to the Windows 8 heap. He is currently serving / surviving as Program Chair for PLDI 2016, and maintains his blood-caffeine level at roughly 0.94.

Abhishek Bhattacharjee. Abhishek Bhattacharjee is an

VEE '16, April 2-3, 2016, Atlanta, GA, USA.
ACM 978-1-4503-3947-6/16/04
DOI: http://dx.doi.org/10.1145/2892242.2892249

assistant professor in the department of Computer Science at Rutgers University. His research interests like at the intersection of architectures and systems software. He received his PhD from Princeton University in 2010. His research is partly funded by an NSF Career award, and in the past, his work has been selected for IEEE Micro's Top Picks in Computer Architecture journal.

Kevin Pedretti. Kevin Pedretti is a Principal Member of the Technical Staff at Sandia National Laboratories in the Center for Computing Research. His research is centered on scalable system software for extreme-scale parallel computing platforms, with specific focus on lightweight operating systems, networking, and power management. He is the lead of the Kitten Lightweight Kernel project and is a collaborator on the Palacios Virtual Machine Monitor, which together are seeking to leverage virtualization to increase the functionality and flexibility of HPC system software stacks. Recent work has explored the use of lightweight virtualization to enable application composition, allowing discrete simulation, analysis, and tool components to be composed with one another across virtual machine boundaries.

Simon Peter. Simon is an assistant professor at the University of Texas at Austin, where he leads research in operating systems and networks. He received a Ph.D. in Computer Science from ETH Zurich in 2012 and an MSc in Computer Science from the Carl-von-Ossietzky University Oldenburg, Germany in 2006. Before joining UT Austin in 2016, he was a research associate at the University of Washington from 2012-2016. For his work on the Arrakis high I/O performance operating system, he received the Jay Lepreau best paper award (2014) and the Madrona prize (2014). He has conducted further award-winning systems research at various locations, including MSR SVC and Cambridge, Intel Labs, and UC Riverside.

Chris Rossbach. Chris Rossbach is a Senior Researcher at VMware Research Group, an Assistant Professor at the University of Texas at Austin, and an alumnus of Microsoft Research's Silicon Valley Lab. He received his PhD in computer science from The University of Texas at Austin in 2009. Chris' research focuses on operating system and architectural support for emerging hardware, particularly those that leverage concurrency. He is interested in concurrency in the broadest sense, but has a particular affinity for exploring abstractions that enable systems to take advantage of concurrency to improve performance and mechanisms that simplify the development of parallel programs.

Author Index

www.ingramcontent.com/pod-product-compliance
Lightning Source LLC
Chambersburg PA
CBHW080428230326
R18018900001B/R180189PG41598CBX00010B/1